Sharing Peace

Andy:

With deep gratitude
for an unexpected
friendship.

Grace & peace,

[signature]
Aug
2013

Sharing Peace

Mennonites and Catholics in Conversation

Edited by

Gerald W. Schlabach
and
Margaret Pfeil

Foreword by

Msgr. John A. Radano

A Michael Glazier Book

Collegeville, Minnesota

www.litpress.org

A Michael Glazier Book published by Liturgical Press

Cover design by David Manahan, OSB. Cover illustration by Mary Pat Collins.

Unless otherwise noted, references to papal documents are from the Vatican's digital archives, accessible at http://www.vatican.va/holy_father/index.htm.

Scripture texts in this work are taken from the *New Revised Standard Version Bible* © 1989, Division of Christian Education of the National Council of the Churches of Christ in the United States of America. Used by permission. All rights reserved.

1   2   3   4   5   6   7   8   9

Library of Congress Cataloging-in-Publication Data

Sharing peace : Mennonites and Catholics in conversation / edited by
Margaret R. Pfeil and Gerald W. Schlabach.
     pages   cm
   "A Michael Glazier book."
   ISBN 978-0-8146-8017-9 — ISBN 978-0-8146-8019-3 (e-book)
   1. Interdenominational cooperation.   2. Catholic Church.   3. Mennonite
 Church USA.   4. Peace—Religious aspects—Christianity.   I. Pfeil, Margaret R.
 BV625.S54   2013
 280'.042—dc23   2012048202

Contents

Foreword

This volume brings to a wider public a set of essays, presented by notable scholars at a conference held at Notre Dame University in 2007, that analyze *Called Together to be Peacemakers*, the report of the International Mennonite-Catholic Dialogue (1998–2003). The essays give a critical appreciation of *Called Together*, showing its ecumenical significance, illustrating its strong points, suggesting its weaknesses, and, in many ways, pointing to issues that could be taken up in a continuing international dialogue or in Mennonite and Catholic cooperation at the grassroots level.

Called Together touches on a number of neuralgic points in the Mennonite-Catholic relationship, including certain episodes in history, commitment and approaches to peace, the healing of memories, and respective views on the nature of the church, sacraments, and ordinances. The report's findings both enable Catholics and Mennonites to see these issues in a new perspective (and with more agreement than previously) and help them move beyond previous hostilities, while recognizing that the dialogue must continue. This book reflects further on these new perspectives. It thus demonstrates that *Called Together* represents another important example of the way in which, through dialogue in the modern ecumenical movement, the bitter conflicts of the sixteenth century are now giving way to concerted mutual efforts of reconciliation, as churches respond to Jesus' prayer for the unity of his disciples (cf. John 17:21).

Among international dialogues in which the Roman Catholic Church has participated, *Called Together*'s concentration on a theology of peace is the most intense, bringing into constructive conversation the rich experience of Mennonites, one of the historic peace churches, with the vast literature and practice of Catholic social teaching. Its reflection on the healing of memories made a substantial contribution to this important ecumenical need, addressed also in other bilateral relationships. Christian communions that have been separated for centuries need to study, seek, and especially experience together the grace of healing memories and relationships as they look toward a future characterized by continuing reconciliation and the hope of Christian unity.

Two appendices in this volume include, first, the report *Called Together to Be Peacemakers* and, second, an illustration of the reception and significant application of the report, namely, the "Mennonite and Catholic Contribution to the World Council of Churches' *Decade to Overcome Violence*" (2007). This was a common effort by representatives of the Pontifical Council for Promoting Christian Unity, the Mennonite World Conference, and the WCC. Building on *Called Together*, they together made another contribution to the wider ecumenical movement.

The many reports of international dialogues conducted by separated churches, especially since Vatican II, are important in fostering the church unity. These reports should be studied seriously. We are indebted to the editors, Margaret Pfeil and Gerald Schlabach, for this fine volume, which studies intensely one important dialogue report. Both are deeply committed to fostering Mennonite and Catholic relationships, as are many of the contributing authors. The stimulating essays in this volume help open the ecumenical achievements of *Called Together* to the public. It is a significant contribution to ecumenical literature from which readers will greatly benefit.

John A. Radano
Seton Hall University
January 1, 2013

Preface

The day: January 24, 2002. The place: Assisi. In the wake of the 9/11 attacks on the World Trade Center in New York and on the Pentagon in Washington, DC, as well as war in Afghanistan and the sense of many that the world was living through a "clash of civilizations," Pope John Paul II convened leaders from the world's most prominent religions, and from across Christian traditions in particular, to converge, pray, and rededicate themselves to peace in the hometown of one of Christianity's most beloved and peaceable saints: Saint Francis. The leaders of differing religious communities had gone to respective sites in order to pray for peace simultaneously, if not quite together. Afterwards, they returned for a closing ceremony to solemnly renounce any use of violence in the name of religion and urge humanity to embrace the work of peace. One by one, leaders from Catholic, Eastern Orthodox, Protestant, Sikh, Islamic, Confucian, Buddhist, and Jewish communities rose to so pledge, all according to their own spiritual idiom. In a moment the pope himself would bring the litany and the day to its climax as he mustered all the force that his Parkinson's disease–ravaged voice would allow, in order to call out:

> Violence never again! War never again! Terrorism never again!
> In the name of God, may every religion bring upon the earth
> Justice and Peace, Forgiveness and Life, Love![1]

But first, one last Christian leader spoke up for the global community he represented and, indeed, for all of the religious traditions who had just then preceded him. That leader was a Mennonite—Dr. Mesach Krisetya of Indonesia, president of the Mennonite World Conference.

---

[1] "Reading by Some of the Representatives of a Common Text of Commitment to Peace," Day of Prayer for Peace in the World (conference, Assisi, January 24, 2002), http://www.vatican.va/special/assisi_20020124_en.html.

We, as persons of different religious traditions, will tirelessly proclaim that peace and justice are inseparable, and that peace in justice is the only path which humanity can take towards a future of hope. In a world with ever more open borders, shrinking distances and better relations as a result of a broad network of communications, we are convinced that security, freedom and peace will never be guaranteed by force but by mutual trust. May God bless these our resolutions and grant justice and peace to the world.[2]

That Vatican choreographers chose the smallest of all the religious bodies represented on stage to finalize the solemn promises of all representatives is remarkable enough. But that is not all. At its highest levels of leadership, the Roman Catholic Church was attending with utmost seriousness to the centuries-long witness of peace and nonviolence by Mennonites. And behind the scenes there was even more to this staging, with signals to follow in the years to come.

The Mennonites, of All People!

The Mennonite family of faith now includes more than 1.6 million believers, 60 percent of whom are African, Asian, or Latin American. The Mennonite faith traces its roots back to the Anabaptist or Radical Reformation movement in sixteenth-century Europe. In 1525, only a few years after Martin Luther sparked the Protestant Reformation in 1517, Anabaptist groups began breaking away both from Luther's movement and from the Reformed movement in Switzerland that would soon find its leader in John Calvin. The Anabaptists believed that by tying the pace and direction of their reform to the sponsorship of town councils and princes, the "magisterial" (i.e., princely) Reformers were compromising their commitment to biblical authority and distancing themselves from the nonviolent path by which Christians were to follow their crucified Lord as disciples. To reject infant baptism and baptize adults upon confession of faith instead was not just a matter of biblical precedent or sacramental propriety for Anabaptists. It was a necessity if Christians are to align their allegiance to Christ through a church distinct from the civil community or nation-state. Even though Anabaptist/Mennonite theology has arguably remained closer to Catholicism in key ways than that of mainline Reformers, it has been easy to see

[2] Ibid.

the Mennonite tradition as a double distancing—a break first from Roman Catholicism and then from newly established Protestant churches.

Changing Seating Arrangements in the World Church

The January 2002 event was the second time that John Paul II convened such a gathering in Assisi. Compared to the treatment of the Mennonite World Conference (MWC) president at the first World Day of Prayer for Peace in Assisi in 1986, the Holy See's treatment of Krisetya in 2002 could not be more different. At the first Assisi gathering in 1986, the seating arrangement had seemed to assume exactly the double departure that Mennonites presumably made from Roman Catholicism. The distance between MWC President Paul Kraybill and Pope John Paul II—and the symbolic distance between the Christian communions they represented—could not have been greater. Seated in a line extending from one side of the papal chair had been leaders of non-Christian religions. Seated in another line extending from the other side of the papal chair had been leaders of Christian communions, with a final seat reserved for a leading Jewish rabbi, in light of the special relationship between Judaism and Christianity.[3] Seated next to the rabbi—as far from the pope as a Christian tradition apparently could be—was then-president of MWC, Paul Kraybill.

Something had dramatically changed in just sixteen years. Likely impelled by John Paul II's passionate commitment to peacemaking and his own experience with the power of active nonviolence,[4] the Vatican took an interest in interchurch dialogue with Mennonites despite their small numbers. For although Mennonites are not the only church family that traces its ancestry back to sixteenth-century Anabaptists, and although they often stand with the Society of Friends (Quakers) and Church of the Brethren as the three most commonly listed "historic peace churches," the Anabaptist/Mennonite tradition regularly serves in both scholarly and ecumenical circles as paradigmatic for both the Radical Reformation tradition and historic peace

[3] That special relationship of what Christians see as continuity with the ancient faith and people of Israel has led one theologian to call Judaism a "non-non-Christian religion," and has led the Vatican itself to house its Commission for Religious Relations with the Jews not within its Pontifical Council for Interreligious Dialogue, but as a special unit within the Pontifical Council for Promoting Christian Unity.

[4] Pope John Paul II, *Centesimus Annus: . . . On the Hundredth Anniversary of Rerum Novarum* (1991), §§ 22–23, 51–52, accessible http://www.vatican.va/holy_father /john_paul_ii/encyclicals/documents/hf_jp-ii_enc_01051991_centesimus-annus_en.html.

church theology. One explanation for why Mennonites, above all, have played this role may be that in North America and Europe they have acculturated more than their Amish, Hutterite, and other "Old Order" cousins, yet not so much as Quakers or the Church of the Brethren (at least until recently). The result in the twentieth century was Mennonite intellectual leaders emerging as leading historians and theologians. Their historians have sought to recover the record and wisdom of their tradition using modern tools of scholarship, and their leading theologians have both engaged the larger culture and dialogued with ecumenical partners, while retaining a distinct collective identity.[5] Meanwhile, the much-respected work of the relief, development, and peacebuilding organization Mennonite Central Committee has placed Mennonites into collaborative relationships with other Christian peacemakers and justice advocates in countless on-the-ground situations of conflict and human need around the world, beginning in 1920 and with increasing urgency throughout the latter half of the twentieth century and current. A papacy impassioned to strengthen the work and witness of the church on behalf of world peace (in the face of what John Paul II called a modern "culture of death") turned to Mennonites as a dialogue partner and teacher, of sorts.

Historic Dialogue, New Relationships

In 1998, therefore, the Pontifical Council for Promoting Christian Unity had joined with Mennonite World Conference to launch a five-year international dialogue. Since the Second Vatican Council sealed its commitment to ecumenical dialogue, the Catholic Church had engaged in approximately fifteen such sessions, none of which included a worldwide communion as small as the Mennonites. From 1998 to 2003, delegations of roughly seven people from the two communions met once a year for a full week. They prayed, studied, discussed, debated, and visited one another's local congregations, parishes, and religious communities. "The general purpose of the dialogue was to learn to know one another better, to promote better understanding of the positions on Christian faith held by Catholics and Mennonites, and to contribute to the overcoming of prejudices that have long existed between

[5] Among twentieth-century Mennonite historians, Harold S. Bender is especially influential, while among twentieth-century Mennonite theologians, John Howard Yoder is especially prominent.

them."[6] Participants later reported that "The atmosphere in the meetings was most cordial. Each side presented its views on the theological issues as clearly and forcefully as possible, seeking to foster an honest and fruitful dialogue." As usual in such ecumenical dialogues, the task was for conversation partners to clearly state their views, so that it would be "possible to begin to see which parts of the Christian heritage are held in common by both Mennonites and Catholics, and where they have strong differences."[7] Indeed, discussions were often frank and probing:

> In presenting their respective views on history, dialogue members did not refrain from allowing one another to see clearly the criticism each communion has traditionally raised against the other. At the same time, dialogue participants did this with the kind of self-criticism that is needed if an authentic search for truth is to take place. The constant hope was that clarifications in both areas of study, historical and theological, might contribute to a healing of memories between Catholics and Mennonites.[8]

The most obvious result of the international dialogue was its groundbreaking final report, *Called Together to Be Peacemakers*, with sustained attention not only to peacemaking theology but also to key historical watersheds in the fourth and sixteenth centuries, to ecclesiology (theology of the church), to understandings of the sacraments and church ordinances, and to repentance for past persecutions and recriminations. Published in 2004, it is this document that occasioned the July 2007 conference at the University of Notre Dame three years later, which, in turn, has produced the papers in the present book. But that lineage is hardly what is most important about the dialogue.

If the international dialogue between Mennonites and Catholics is significant because of its mere existence, its final report set in motion at least two other historic processes. First, the Notre Dame conference reflected in the following pages was only one of a number of regional meetings held to

---

[6] Mennonite World Conference and Pontifical Council for Promoting Church Unity, *Called Together to Be Peacemakers: Report of the International Dialogue Between the Catholic Church and Mennonite World Conference, 1998–2003.* Included as an appendix to the present book, the document is also available on various websites including http://bridgefolk.net/theology/dialogue, and was officially published in the Vatican publication *Information Service* 2003-II/III, no. 113 (2004). Quotation is from § 15.

[7] *Called Together to Be Peacemakers*, § 20.

[8] Ibid.

study and discuss the document. Catholics and Mennonites met in various formats in Canada, Colombia, Germany, and elsewhere. In addition, abridged versions of the dialogue with study questions were published in both English and German.[9] Those involved in high-level ecumenical dialogues between churches sometimes voice regret that their labors do not always receive attention or have an impact in "the pews"; the code word for this challenge is the need for a broader "reception" in the churches. But at least on the Mennonite side—where theologians identify their church as part of the "Believers Church tradition" and aspire to churchwide participation in discernment and decision-making—Mennonite World Conference insisted that before launching a new round of Catholic and Mennonite dialogue, church bodies throughout the Mennonite world should have the opportunity to study and comment upon the report. Of course this does not mean that every faithful Mennonite, or even every Mennonite pastor, knows about the dialogue or its final report. Yet compared to many other ecumenical reports and interchurch documents, the fruit of the Mennonite-Catholic dialogue between 1998 and 2003 has been remarkably well "received" among Mennonites. Even on the Catholic side, where the church's immensely larger size means that developments such as these are easily missed, various commentators have held up Mennonite-Catholic dialogue with its grassroots dimensions as a model for the ecumenical movement.[10]

New Relationships, Shared Witness

Second, the sense of being "called together" to be peacemakers has already issued in a most unprecedented, shared witness. Even while Mennonite-Catholic dialogue had been unfolding, Mennonites and other historic peace

---

[9] Mennonite World Conference and Pontifical Council for Promoting Church Unity, *Called Together to Be Peacemakers: Report of the International Dialogue Between the Catholic Church and Mennonite World Conference, 1998–2003*, abr. ed. with discussion questions, eds. Willard Roth and Gerald W. Schlabach, Bridgefolk Series, no. 3 (Kitchener, ON: Pandora Press, 2004); Fernando Enns and Hans-Jochen Jaschke, eds., *Gemeinsam berufen, Friedensstifter zu sein: Zum Dialog zwischen Katholiken und Mennoniten*, im Auftrag der Arbeitsgemeinschaft Mennonitischer Gemeinden in Deutschland (Schwarzenfeld; Paderborn: Neufeld Verlag; Bonifatius Verlag, 2008).

[10] Margaret O'Gara, "Ecumenical Dialogue: The Next Generation," (presidential address, CTSA convention, June 5–8, 2008) *Catholic Theological Society of America Proceedings* 63 (2008): 87; Christopher Ruddy, "Our Ecumenical Future: How the Bishops Can Advance Christian Unity," *America* 203, no. 13 (November 8, 2010): 15.

church leaders were also having an impact on more Protestant ecumenical conversations. Among other things, they had convinced the World Council of Churches to launch a *Decade to Overcome Violence* project (2001–2010) to find a fresh consensus about truly Christian ways to work for human security that transcends the centuries-old debate between just-war and pacifism. As it prepared to draft an "Ecumenical Call to Just Peace" for a final international peace convocation scheduled to take place in Jamaica in May 2011, the WCC's general secretary invited input from church bodies around the world. Although a number of academic institutions, Christian peace groups, and congregations responded, only two wider confessional bodies did so— Mennonite and Catholic. Together.

As one way to follow up on their international dialogue, the Vatican's Pontifical Council for Promoting Christian Unity invited a delegation of Mennonite World Conference representatives to Rome in October 2007. Participants took the opportunity to finalize a joint "contribution" to the WCC's *Decade to Overcome Violence* that offered a biblical/theological foundation for peace and peacemaking, a spirituality of Christian discipleship following the Prince of Peace, and suggestions for action and continued discussion.[11] Building on *Called Together to Be Peacemakers*, the theology of the joint contribution to the WCC project was even more seamless, with differing Catholic or Mennonite emphases hard to discern. "The Church is called to be a peace church," Catholics and Mennonites affirmed together. "This calling is based on the conviction we hold in common as Catholics and Mennonites, that the Church, founded by Christ, is to be a living sign and an effective instrument of peace." Few people and fewer Christians would say that they oppose peace, of course; debates are always centered on how to get there. The document is honest about continuing differences concerning the means to peace, noting, for example, that "for both Catholics and Mennonites the ultimate personal and ecclesial challenge is to spell out the consequences of the cross for our teaching on peace and war, and for our response in the face of injustice and violence." But simply to center ongoing debates around the cross already marks out a new consensus. For Catholics, after all, joining a cross-centered consensus represents movement

---

[11] Mennonite World Conference and Pontifical Council for Promoting Church Unity, "A Mennonite and Catholic Contribution to the World Council of Churches' *Decade to Overcome Violence*," (report from Mennonite–Catholic Conference, Rome, October 23–25, 2007), http://www.overcomingviolence.org/fileadmin/dov/files/iepc/Mennonite_and_Catholic_contribution_to_DOV.pdf.

away from their traditional tendency to use "natural law" approaches to think about war and violence. But Mennonites, too, have had to move historically in order to affirm that "in the absence of justice and human rights, peace is a mirage," and "the Gospel's vision includes active nonviolence for defense of human life and human rights, economic justice for the poor, and solidarity among peoples."

The bottom line: "Reconciliation, nonviolence, and active peacemaking belong to the heart of the Gospel." Not an add-on. Not just an option for particularly heroic saints or particularly dedicated activists. Not simply a this-worldly concern but at "the heart of the Gospel." When Mennonites and Catholics can say that together, to the world, and to all who claim the name of Christ, then something is happening that deserves far greater attention. The choreography of Assisi 2002 was hardly a fluke.

◻ ◻ ◻

Frankly, then, a driving motivation first for the 2007 conference at the University of Notre Dame and secondly for the present book has been to call attention to the significance and already-emerging fruit of Mennonite-Catholic dialogue. If critics occasionally remark that Catholic social teaching is Catholicism's "best kept secret," then, unfortunately, Mennonite-Catholic dialogue and its implications for Catholic peace teaching are an even better kept secret. Nowhere else in the corpus of its authoritative teaching[12] has the Catholic magisterium so definitively endorsed active nonviolence as normative.[13] And when the Catholic Church has gone on to address the wider Christian community on matters of war and peace, standing shoulder-

---

[12] Different kinds of pronouncements by popes, bishops, and Vatican offices enjoy different levels of authority, and the subtleties of infallible versus definitive versus authoritative but noninfallible Catholic teachings inevitably invite controversy and disputation. But when the Pontifical Council for Promoting Christian Unity participates in an ecumenical dialogue and issues a final report, those parts of such a document that not only report on deliberations but offer shared theological affirmations carry at least as much authority as pronouncements by other pontifical councils. Furthermore, in the case of *Called Together to Be Peacemakers*, delegates to the Mennonite-Catholic dialogue of 1998–2003 report that the Catholic bishop who cochaired the dialogue insisted that the Congregation for the Doctrine of the Faith (CDF) vet the document before its publication. Heading the CDF at the time was Cardinal Joseph Ratzinger, soon to become Pope Benedict XVI.

[13] To be sure, for the Catholic Church to embrace normative nonviolence does not entirely distance the church from the possibility of justifiable war as a legitimate exception when it truly is a last resort. But it does strengthen the stringency of just-war thinking.

to-shoulder with Mennonites as it did when it issued the historically un-precedented and theologically seamless joint statement to the WCC, then Mennonites have clearly found their voice within global Christianity, while Catholic officialdom is clearly speaking with a different accent. Theologians, ethicists, prelates, and social activists alike need to know this!

At the same time, and despite its title, *Called Together to Be Peacemakers* is about much more than peace theology or peacemaking—at least if we understand these terms in a narrow sense that collapses them into peace activism alone. Everything in *Called Together*, the 2007 conference, and the present book is indeed about the work of reconciliation. For as Scott Appleby points out in chapter 1, in an almost sacramental way, *Called Together* embodies the very work of Christian reconciliation that it calls for. But in order to truly engage Mennonites or other historic peace churches in a reconciliatory way, Catholics must also be ready to discuss all the Christian practices and theological commitments that these communions consider to be "the things that make for peace." And in order to engage Catholics in a truly reconciliatory way, Mennonites must be ready to discuss all that the Roman church believes to be signs and offices that are necessary to mark the unity—and thus the peace—of the church itself. As a result, no document, conference, or book on how Mennonites and Catholics are "called together to be peacemakers" could pursue peace without also engaging in sustained conversation concerning ecclesiology, practices of worship and sacrament, honest assessment of the history that has divided these communities, past persecution and martyrdom—all hopefully opening toward mutual confes-sion of past wrongs and a "healing of memories."

The structure of the 2007 conference and of this book have therefore followed the essential structure of *Called Together to Be Peacemakers*. By way of overview and introduction, an opening panel including three participants in the international dialogue began by surveying the significance of the document. The conference then took up the document's major themes— "Considering History Together," "The Nature of the Church," "Sacraments and Ordinances," and "Our Commitment to Peace"—with paired presenta-tions from both Catholic and Mennonite thinkers. Finally, similar to the way that *Called Together* had concluded by looking forward "Toward a Healing of Memories," a final presentation and respondents explored the possibilities for a shared Mennonite and Catholic future.

Along with hopes that the conference would provide a setting for reflec-tion and reception of the *Called Together* dialogue (particularly in North America), promoting awareness among both Mennonites and Catholics as to how the international dialogue between their churches is already bearing fruit was a major objective. Namely, the conference sought not only to review *Called Together* but to seed ideas for continuing scholarship and dialogue in both churches. As we now share an edited version of the conference, that hope continues.

Indeed, to conclude by acknowledging conference sponsors and hosts is to recognize a few of the many places where collaboration and dialogue between Mennonites and Catholics continues to go forward. The conference was organized by the Mennonite-Catholic Theological Colloquium, which is in turn a project of Bridgefolk, a movement of sacramentally-minded Mennonites and peace-minded Roman Catholics who come together to celebrate each other's traditions, explore each other's practices, and honor each other's contributions to the mission of Christ's church. The Associated Mennonite Biblical Seminary in Elkhart, Indiana, with its Institute of Mennonite Studies, is home to a number of scholars who have given leadership to dialogue with Catholics and other Christian traditions. The Kroc Institute for International Peace Studies at the University of Notre Dame graciously hosted the conference; other programs at Notre Dame provided various forms of sponsorship—the Theology Department, the Kellogg Institute for International Studies, the Cushwa Center for the Study of American Catholicism, and The Catholic Social Tradition Program. Finally, special thanks go to Shalom Communications, a foundation administered by the family of the late Mennonite theologian, Notre Dame professor, and longtime ecumenist, John Howard Yoder. By God's grace, Mennonites and Catholics could surely have begun to collaborate and converse in various ways and places around the world in the latter half of the twentieth century. But as Dr. Yoder's former students, now privileged to follow the development of Mennonite-Catholic dialogue closely through their work in Bridgefolk, the editors can hardly imagine how it would have proceeded without his legacy.

Margaret Pfeil   Gerald W. Schlabach
University of Notre Dame   University of Saint Thomas
Notre Dame, Indiana   Saint Paul, Minnesota

PART 1

The Significance of
Called Together to Be Peacemakers

This was a new process of reconciliation. The two dialogue partners had had no official dialogue previous to this, and therefore started afresh. Our purpose was to assist Mennonites and Catholics to overcome the consequences of almost five centuries of mutual isolation and hostility. We wanted to explore whether it is now possible to create a new atmosphere in which to meet each other. After all, despite all that may still divide us, the ultimate identity of both is rooted in Jesus Christ.

Called Together to Be Peacemakers, paragraph 2

Since the beginning of the twentieth century, separated Christian communions have come into closer contact, seeking reconciliation with each other. Despite ongoing divisions, they have started to cooperate with one another to their mutual benefit and often to the benefit of the societies in which they give witness to the Gospel. . . . Many factors have contributed to this contemporary movement. Among them are conditions and changes in the modern world. For example, the destructive power of modern weapons in a nuclear age has challenged Christians everywhere to reflect on the question of peace in a totally new way—and even to do so together. But the basic inspiration for dialogue between separated Christians has been the realization that conflict between them impedes the preaching of the Gospel and damages their credibility. Indeed, conflict between Christians is a major obstacle to the mission given by Jesus Christ to his disciples. It is difficult to announce the good news of salvation "so that the world may believe" (*Jn* 17:21) if those bearing the good news have basic disagreements among themselves.

Called Together to Be Peacemakers, paragraphs 8–9

Chapter 1

Christian Peacebuilding

The Growing Edge
of the Catholic-Mennonite Conversation

Scott Appleby

After five years of groundbreaking dialogue between Mennonite and Roman Catholic leaders, *Called Together to be Peacemakers* is an eloquent and historic document. We can measure the significance of the document in three ways.

First, *Called Together* represents the first dialogue of its kind between these churches. Indeed, this is the first time Mennonites and Catholics have formally recognized each other at all, in any constructive or positive sense, after nearly five centuries marred by behavior and attitudes that are precisely the opposite of what the Gospel of Jesus Christ enjoins—namely love of enemy, not to mention love of neighbor. They'll know we are Christians by our love? Hardly! Roman Catholics who wish to invite into their consciences an attitude of repentance for the historical sins of their coreligionists should spend some time perusing *Martyrs Mirror*, the book of final testaments from thousands of Anabaptists who were executed between 1524 and 1660. Roman Catholics, wielding the sword of the state, were their chief persecutors, with Lutherans and some Calvinists also sharing in the ignominy. Ironically, one of the justifications Catholics gave for their hostility was the Anabaptist endorsement of religious freedom, which post–Vatican II Catholics now take for granted. The Mennonites and other religious descendants of the martyrs hardly deserve blame for the stony silence, punctuated by mutual denunciations that characterized much of the post-Reformation relations (or lack of thereof) between Catholics and Mennonites: "Peace Church? Mennonites are not a Church." "Catholicism, the Grand Inquisitor, a Disturber of the Peace." Away, thankfully, with five centuries of polemics! No more. *Called*

Together to be Peacemakers marks a new era and initiates us into the practice of peacebuilding for the world and, not incidentally, within the Body of Christ.

Called Together formally recognizes and thereby significantly advances an emerging convergence between the historic peace churches and the Roman Catholic Church, precisely on the question of what it means to be a follower of the Prince of Peace. This is a second mark of its historic significance. Over the past forty-five years in particular and sparked by the Second Vatican Council, Catholics have rediscovered and reacquainted themselves with the New Testament notion of discipleship and *imitatio Christi*. To be sure, Catholics had been practicing the imitation of Christ for centuries, in ways that included a witness against violence, an embrace of nonviolence, and an intuitive wariness of that cooperation with evil that accompanies alliances with the state. But ever since the Constantinian era (fourth century CE), the practice of nonviolence had been the province of a minority of Catholics; the Catholic Church itself has been a just-war, state-centered ethical tradition. Beginning in the 1930s, however, when Dorothy Day founded the Catholic Worker movement, American Catholics have had increasing access to an alternative to the statist, just-war tradition. A growing minority has discovered (!) that nonviolence is a biblical and apostolic tradition and, thus, a precious legacy for every Christian. Catholic theologians, including members of the hierarchy, have begun to develop their own articulation of what it means to be a "peace church" on the basis of Catholic theologies and ecclesiologies.

Learning from the example of the historic peace churches is now possible for Catholics. *Called Together* gives eloquent testimony to what we Catholics are learning. Among the classes I teach here at Notre Dame is "Introduction to Peace Studies." Eighty-five percent of undergraduates at Notre Dame are Roman Catholic. As I develop various aspects of peace studies and we come to the subject of religion and the role of churches, typically a student will ask, "Are we a peace church?" And I have to say, "Not quite yet. But we're getting there." No doubt *Called Together* also contains implications for Mennonites—what they have and will continue to learn from the experiences and strengths of Catholicism, including hard-won lessons from the almost inevitable struggle of engaging with and trying to influence the "earthly powers," including the state.

A third significance of *Called Together* is the very process that produced it. The document is a model not only of ecumenical dialogue but also of that to which it points. (In that regard, Catholics might even call it a "small 's' sacrament.") In other words, *Called Together* is a guide to—and an exemplar of—the healing of memory, truth-telling, reconciliation, and conflict transformation about which it speaks. As the document unfolds, it provides examples, lessons, guidelines, and a model of what it would mean to rethink history together. There is no such thing as a neutral point of view, but *Called Together* offers a noncontested, nonpolemical point of view, in which we recover the past and heal memory together through a new method that begins with collaboration, partnership, and the first steps toward reconciliation. This makes the document an exemplar that points to, demonstrates, and models what it teaches.

In sum, *Called Together to Be Peacemakers* serves as a platform for further progress in ecumenical dialogue and interchurch collaboration. As such, it deserves to be celebrated, publicized, and extended. The rest of this essay will focus on possible paths forward – strategies for extending the dialogue and collaboration. These comments are premised on the assumption that Mennonites and Catholics are pivotal to the development of a broader theology, ethics, and practice of Christian peacebuilding.

Incorporating the Experiences and Insights of Peacebuilders[1]

Called Together is a document produced by church officials, academics, and a sprinkling of pastors. With regard to the latter, however, a question arises: How fully did discussions, deliberations, and final documents incorporate the experiences and insights of grassroots actors? The dialogue process and resulting document had many goals, and these required historians, theologians, and ecclesiologists. Were there also meaningful contributions from those Mennonites and Catholics who have actually been building peace "on the ground" for years? After all, the real action—the action that is as real and important as that of the church leaders who produced *Called Together*—has been occurring in fields of violent conflict including hot and cold wars, revolutions, and civil strife. It has been occurring wherever Catholic and Mennonite peacebuilders have been collaborating, interacting, and learning from one another. Significant skills, concepts, techniques, and methods of preventing violence have been taking place as Mennonites and Catholics partner to mediate conflict and pursue transitional justice amid societies that are moving away from war, attempting to rebuild their

---

[1] In peace studies and peace research, the preferred term is now "peacebuilding," a term that incorporates the full conflict cycle and conveys the sense that peace in this world is never fully *made* but is a process in constant flux and evolution. See John Paul Lederach and R. Scott Appleby, "Strategic Peacebuilding: An Overview," in Daniel Philpott and Gerard F. Powers, eds., *Strategies of Peace: Transforming Conflict in a Violent World* (Oxford University Press, 2010), 19–44.

court systems and political institutions, and seeking to reintegrate former belligerents into society through truth-telling, apology, forgiveness, and, where possible, reconciliation.

Indeed, Mennonite-Catholic collaboration for peace has been developing in an especially intense way since the late nineties, in the very period when *Called Together* was being formulated. The document does not systematically draw upon the local wisdom of on-the-ground Mennonite-Catholic collaboration, however. Paragraph 213, near the end of the document, does refer to local initiatives that "we hear of," "in several parts of the world":

> Locally as well, in several parts of the world, some Catholics and Mennonites [are] already engaged with each other in theological dialogue and in practical cooperation. In various places collaboration between the Mennonite Central Committee and Caritas or Catholic Relief Services is taking place in humanitarian causes. We hear of Mennonites working with Catholics in the USA, in the Middle East, and in India, to name but a few examples. And even though numerous local Catholic-Mennonite initiatives are unofficial and personal, they serve the wider church by helping to overcome false caricatures about and mutual prejudices of each other.

But as a description of what is actually unfolding, this is woefully understated. To me, the truly exciting advances taking place are in this arena of what we might call "ecumenical and strategic peacebuilding." The next phase of Mennonite-Catholic dialogue might usefully focus on this "growing edge" of the collaboration.

Allow me briefly to expand on this point. *Called Together* stands as an overdue acknowledgement of areas of complementarity and continuing tension between Catholics and Mennonites, and a review of the journey of the two Christian communions, up until the end of the Cold War. One can certainly trace the convergences back to the publication of "The Challenge of Peace: God's Promise and Our Response," the US Catholic bishops' groundbreaking pastoral letter on war and peace in 1983. The historic peace churches had a significant influence on *The Challenge of Peace*. Some of the most exciting developments in Mennonite-Catholic collaboration and dialogue around peacemaking, however, have occurred since then.[2] Now that

---

[2] A curious error or typo in the document may be inadvertently revealing. Paragraph 13 of *Called Together to Be Peacemakers* notes how the US Conference of Catholic Bishops drew upon expertise from outside the Catholic Church, especially Mennonite theologian John Howard Yoder, "in the course of writing its pastoral statement on peace in 1993

we have more than a decade of direct and extensive Mennonite-Catholic collaboration, we need to draw upon this on-the-ground collaboration as raw material for further joint theological reflection and the next stage of institutional and ecclesial partnership. We are at the threshold of a most exciting period, and *Called Together* points—but only points—toward the areas in which real collaboration and ecumenical dialogue are taking place, such as in Bogotá, Colombia; Mindanao, Philippines; around the Great Lakes of Africa; and elsewhere.

I have recently returned from the fourth annual meeting of the Catholic Peacebuilding Network (CPN), held in Bogotá. The CPN could be renamed the Catholic-Mennonite Peacebuilding Network. Consider just some of the core faculty from our own Kroc Institute for International Peace Studies at Notre Dame, which is one of the founding institutions of the CPN. Among our distinguished faculty are Robert Johansen, Church of the Brethren; Larissa Fast, Mennonite; John Paul Lederach, Mennonite; George Lopez, a "Quaker-ized" Catholic who cut his teeth in peace studies at Earlham College; Jerry Powers, Catholic; Dan Philpott, Catholic; and Scott Appleby, Catholic. Our faculty thus represents the convocation of a kind of small-scale Mennonite-Catholic dialogue. It may be dangerous to claim that we constitute a microcosm in any regard, but if we are, I can say from a Catholic perspective that our department would not be an effective peace institute without our "peace church" colleagues, not only because of what they bring our department's teaching, research, and outreach, but also because of what we Catholics learn daily from them.

John Paul Lederach, in particular, is a remarkable gift to our faculty and to the world of peacebuilding, and I appreciate John Paul more deeply every year. For example, although I have read John Paul's writings, I understood his ideas and his presence, so to speak, much better when I saw him in the Colombian context. A master of "the elicitive method" of situating conflict resolution and mediation approaches in their deep cultural contexts, he has learned much from Colombia, which is a setting of sustained violence extending back over fifty years. Building peace or making peace in Colombia almost seems oxymoronic. "What are you talking about?" one is tempted to ask. Lederach's conception of peacebuilding makes sense everywhere in the world. Yet when one reads *The Moral Imagination* or some of Lederach's

---

[sic]." *The Challenge of Peace* was, of course, published ten years earlier in 1983. Even as a typo that went unnoticed, this misstatement seems to reflect the short shrift that *Called Together* gives to this monumental development.

earlier works—where he writes of building platforms, relationships, and networks, creating webs, and sustaining peace through times of endemic violence—and then accompanies him in Colombia itself, the impact of his concept of the "moral imagination" of the people caught in conflict is impossible to miss. It is *the* natural resource of indigenous as well as visiting peacebuilders. Hundreds of people who have been influenced by his writings, translated or written in Spanish, turned out to see him in this 90 percent Catholic country. John Paul has worked closely with Catholics not only in Colombia but also in Mindanao, West Africa, and elsewhere—the Catholics he has met have a deep understanding of the church as *koinonia* (communion), a concept that they share with Mennonites. Lederach is helping them live out their sense of *koinonia* and apply it to peacebuilding.

Lederach thus is an embodiment of Catholic-Mennonite dialogue. The ideas he has developed as the core of his peacebuilding approach are world renowned. And I would argue that they are also profoundly Catholic or at least resonant with the depth of Catholicism. For example, his understanding of elicitive learning and the elicited method for understanding culture resonates deeply with the Second Vatican Council's vision of inculturation. Likewise, when John Paul speaks about accompaniment, it is a nuanced and practical outworking of what Catholic social teaching has come to celebrate as "solidarity." What does it mean to accompany? Christians and their churches accompany the victims of violence, as well as those working for justice. In a Catholic setting, John Paul plumbs the meaning of "accompaniment" and "presence" by tapping their deep theological roots in Eucharist and communion. There are other affinities in his own work between a Catholic religious imagination and a Mennonite religious imagination, and we could devote an entire seminar to the way that this very influential scholar/practitioner blends what, in the final analysis, is nothing less than profound Christianity. We can call it "Mennonite" or "Roman Catholic," but the practices of accompaniment, real presence, healing of memory, and solidarity with victims constitute a living bridge between the two traditions.

Each of our traditions offer strengths the other does not possess, or has not yet fully developed in its plumbing of the Christian mystery. The hierarchical structure of the Roman Catholic Church, for example, has been a source of division in the past, but it is also being recognized as a potentially profound resource for strategic peacebuilding. Peacebuilding requires the integration of vertical and horizontal actors and institutions across international, national, and local levels. The Catholic Church is often present in conflict settings at all of these various levels—certainly locally in the parish but also regionally with the bishops and globally with the Vatican. The multifaceted social analysis of conflict transformation, adopted by peacebuilders both Catholic and Mennonite, finds a slumbering ally in the universal presence of Catholicism.

The challenge, of course, is to wake up Catholic bishops and other religious leaders to their inherent capacity to exercise "a peacebuilding presence"—not as an add-on to their pastoral duties but as a constituent element of them. Bishops, too, are called to be peacemakers! And many in Africa and Asia and the Americas are now coming alive to the possibility. Catholic partners, in short, are already active at the grassroots and middle social levels, but now they must become ever more active at the top of the social pyramid, so that the hierarchical, transnational configuration of the Roman Catholic Church becomes a vital resource for local peacebuilders as well as elite actors.

One of the architects of *Called Together to be Peacemakers* is Father Drew Christianson, SJ, an expert on the history of the Catholic Church's diplomatic and peacemaking successes (and failures) from the twentieth century to the present. Much official Roman Catholic diplomacy and conflict mediation has occurred at the elite and interstate level. Strengthening the bonds between this essential work "at the top," and the myriad grassroots presences and programs of local Catholic peacebuilders, is a particularly important challenge for the Catholic Church nowadays. The apostolic work of building and making peace is most likely to succeed when top-level and on-the-ground efforts are integrated.

If Mennonites might be able to draw on Catholic networks and experience in statecraft, Catholics are learning from Mennonites about the local dynamics of peacebuilding and, especially, about the challenges of mobilizing people for nonviolent social action. The peace churches are old hands at grassroots relationship building, conflict resolution, and mediation. Meanwhile, the Roman Church has more recently been gravitating toward civil society as an agent of change through Catholic social teaching.

All of us are taking advantage of globalization, of ecumenical dialogue and collaboration, and of "new facts in the field." Catholics have tended to focus on the hierarchy's role in Catholic peacemaking. Today, the Catholic Church in parts of Africa continues to play a key role in regional and international peacemaking by making use of its diplomatic resources and connections. Yet the international diplomacy of African bishops is increasingly and deliberately coordinated with the church's grassroots peacebuilding. This resonates powerfully with theologies in the Catholic Church that emphasize inculturation and "constructing local theologies."[3]

The Growing Edge for Catholics

Insofar as Catholic social teaching has only recently come to recognize local and civil society as key resources for social transformation, Catholic theologies have yet to fully process the lessons. It is necessary now to begin to identify theological and ethical resources for peacebuilding.[4] Catholic sacramentality and Christian theologies of grace, for example, shape and are being reshaped by the experiences of local, regional, and national churches active in peacebuilding. Do we need to revise theological categories to fully recognize and name their work? And are we not called, by texts from the *Martyrs Mirror* to Vatican II's *Dignitatis Humanae* (Declaration on Religious Liberty), to revisit yet again the church-state understandings that Reformation and early modern Catholics in Europe developed with such traumatic consequences for other Christians? The need for a revised and renewed approach to "Christian statecraft" and "Christian public responsibility" becomes urgent when bishops and archbishops living amid failed states in Africa tell us, as they did at a CPN conference last year in Burundi, that the church has become the only viable alternative to the state.

Implied in *Called Together* (at least as I read it), is an important challenge to Catholics as they develop a deeper and more resonant peace tradition. The Mennonite challenge to Catholicism is the sober, shrewd, and historically rooted Anabaptist witness against the state and warnings about Christian entanglements with the state. This has been the Mennonite witness, the Anabaptist witness. And there is a deep irony in the recognition that the seasoned, experienced, and alternately world-embracing and world-judging Roman Catholic Church has often failed to learn the right Christian lessons from that experience; at times, the church has remained (willfully?) naïve about, or not fully repentant of, the consequences of compromising Gospel purity in the name of political stewardship. Mennonites and others remind

---

[3] See, for example, the writings of Robert Schreiter, CSSP, including *Constructing Local Theologies* (Maryknoll, NY: Orbis Books, 1985); *The New Catholicity: Theology between the Global and the Local* (Maryknoll, NY: Orbis Books, 1997); and *Global Catholicism: Contested Claims* (Maryknoll, NY: Orbis Books, 2002).

[4] For an initial attempt, see Robert J. Schreiter, R. Scott Appleby and Gerard Powers, eds. *Peacebuilding: Catholic Theology, Ethics and Praxis* (Orbis, 2010).

Catholics of the more dubious consequences of their way of witnessing to the state through positive engagement.

I say this not to reject the Catholic approach but to urge its reform. Taking responsibility for the world, including its dirty old politics, is a genuine Christian response to the doctrines of original sin and redemptive grace. (Of course it is not the only possible, authentic response, and this plurality is the great strength and mystery of Christianity.) Catholicism is responsible to and for the world in a way that the Anabaptist tradition would probably not feel comfortable with. Catholics are a sacramental people and therefore a people fully immersed in the created world, which, perhaps regrettably, includes diplomats, politicians, kings, and knaves. Attending to these souls is part of the one Christian witness. But it comes with a danger of corruption and violence through the accouterments of earthly power. In the modern period, it is all too easy for the nation-state to usurp the living God. We thus need the Anabaptist witness to recognize the extent to which Constantinian arrangements can produce unintended and dire results, tarnishing the apostolic work of the church.

If Catholics are increasingly open to the Anabaptist peace witness and their emphasis on biblical discipleship, it is partly because the Second Vatican Council had already signaled that the New Testament teachings we had traditionally called "counsels of perfection" should be extended beyond the clergy and religious to all baptized. This development has in turn reflected a larger retrieval of scriptural models for apostolic life that Catholics have embraced and celebrated in the latter half of the twentieth century. A historical perspective helps to explain these developments. We might begin with the gross failures of Catholic diplomacy and statecraft during the first half of the twentieth century. Alignment with fascism and fascist regimes—most notably, Franco's Spain—proved morally disastrous for Catholics. Fear of atheistic communism drove some members of the church to fail to strenuously oppose the horrors committed by Franco and (some would argue, more controversially) Hitler. Catholic self-criticism at the highest levels of the church concerning state entanglements followed this disgraceful period. Duly chastened, the popes of Vatican II turned away from concordats with states to an engagement with culture through the institutions and networks of civil society. *Gaudium et Spes*, Vatican II's pastoral constitution on the church in the modern world, ushered in a new era of biblical theology for Catholics even as it urged critical engagement with the world and the transformation of unjust political systems. And not the least, the person, vision, and example of Pope John Paul II provided a tremendous embodiment of these themes.

Mennonites challenge Catholics above all by insisting that nonviolence is integral to the Gospel of Jesus Christ and thus morally obligatory. Clearly there is a trajectory within Catholicism toward increasing levels of support for nonviolence, even to the point where it has arguably become the preferred option in the context of modern warfare. Scrutiny of just-war teaching is ongoing in many circles, including within the hierarchy, with various sides raising radical questions. On the one hand, politically neoconservative Catholic polemicist George Weigel has recently questioned whether the "mainstream" Christian tradition has ever really insisted on a "presumption against the use of force." Yet it is not clear that the criteria for justifiable war, even on their own terms, can be fulfilled in today's United States or Europe, given that the formation of political authorities and warriors in the Christian virtues is itself a condition for the invocation of the just-war tradition. Thus, despite conservative arguments, I believe the mainstream direction after John Paul II is toward placing the burden of proof on just-war criteria. If that is true, the tables have turned.

So can we truly speak of a Catholic theology of peace? A robust and influential social doctrine, yes. Relevant papal encyclicals and statements, yes. But a *systematic* theological statement that requires Catholics to rethink parts of their theological heritage and ecclesiology—to say nothing of a theology emergent from the prayerful experiences and testimony of grassroots and civil society peacebuilders, from Bogotá to Mindanao? Not yet! And so, without underestimating the long-standing contribution that Catholic diplomats, policymakers, and other elite-level actors have made as peace-*makers*, we must conclude that a Catholic theology of peacebuilding "from the ground up" has yet to transform the sensibilities of most Catholics. We very much need to continue learning from Mennonites and the work that has made them leaders in conflict transformation and reconciliation.

The Growing Edge for Mennonites

Even as Roman Catholicism evolved in its war and peace teachings and practices during the twentieth century, so too have the peace churches. Most notably, Mennonites have shifted away from absolute nonresistance to engagement with the world. While there are various ways to narrate the shift, it has meant recognition that faithfulness to Christ may require active and deliberate resistance to evil and to warfare. Catholics can help make an effective argument in favor of this shift. The Catholic experience of engagement with the world offers lessons, both positive and negative, for

Mennonites as you continue to struggle through questions such as: *What level of engagement with the world is proper? When must engagement take the form of resistance, and when collaboration? How does one give witness?*

Catholic social teaching is a terrific resource for Catholics—and why not for Mennonites?—in pondering such questions. It offers a sophisticated though still-developing map for responsible Christian engagement with the state and other political powers that claim sovereignty over individuals as well as nations. The continuing reluctance of some Mennonites to engage—not merely shun or protest—the powers-that-be hinders the collective work of Christian peacebuilding. Work for justice must confront governments, political leaders, and the institutions of the state, including the military. But "confront" is only one step toward the goal of reform and transformation, which is the full responsibility of the church. Can Catholics and Mennonites together construct an ethic of engagement with a corrupt, post-Christian secular order—an ethic that would protect the church from betraying its transcendent, divine mission of peace while enabling it to exercise positive influence in the course of world affairs?

Active, nonviolent resistance to evil must eventually move beyond critique; it requires the positive construction of a just social order. Peacebuilding has to engage the state; it has to engage political powers with sophistication. Grassroots relationship-building and ground-level conflict transformation is essential, but unless one learns how to interact effectively with states and governments, budgets and military, peacebuilding will not fulfill its potential or live up to its calling. Peacebuilding must be vertical as well as horizontal; it must engage higher levels of society *in order to* build sustainable peace and justice at the local level. Mennonites are still learning how to extend their peacebuilding witness into these arenas. But though we come at the question from different angles, we share a common challenge: how to engage political power in a way that preserves Christian witness yet makes acceptable compromises with the state. Mennonites as well as Catholics might reject the word "compromise" out of some well-intentioned but ultimately misplaced preference for "purity"—a version of the heresy of the Donatists, who insisted on a kind of moral rigor that left no room for human failing, repentance, or the possibility of actual moral transformation. Politics *is* the art of compromise and political theology the art of incremental, gradual transformation. If we expect to build the kingdom in a day, or to win every political battle, we might as well retreat into the caves of Qumran.

A faithful answer will not just be politically mature, however; it will also be ecclesiastically grounded. Mennonite ecclesiology is biblically rooted, congregational, horizontal. Can Mennonites develop it more systematically into a resource for peacebuilding? An outsider looks at the Mennonite world and is puzzled. What, for example, is the relationship between Mennonite Central Committee as a relief, development, and peacebuilding agency, and the Mennonite churches? What are the accountability structures to ensure that MCC is guided by the churches' ecclesiological wisdom? And are the churches sufficiently informed of, and sympathetic to, the exigencies of delivering relief and mediating conflict in the real world? Catholics know both the frustrations and the advantages of working through a global institution that has a long history of diplomacy, statecraft, and what we now call "humanitarian intervention." Despite its reputation and self-understanding as a centralized hierarchical organization, however, the Roman Catholic Church is, in its own way, a supremely local and uncoordinated church, with a thousand flowers (and a few weeds) blooming everywhere. As the Mennonite peace witness expresses itself through an increasingly global church, might the experience of Catholics offer instruction?

Conclusion

Called Together to be Peacemakers is a remarkable achievement, not only because it traces and advances Mennonite-Catholic convergences, but also because it honestly articulates some of our continuing theological tensions. Catholic sacramentalism, for example, stands in tension with a theology of the cross. Discipleship, in the Anabaptist/Mennonite understanding, may stand in tension with Catholicism's commitment to statecraft, citizenship, and even membership in the institutional, visible church. Discipleship may require Catholics to be prophetic against their own institutions. Catholic understandings of the Mystical Body of Christ—Catholic mystagogy, which can overemphasize the interior journey and the immanent Spirit to the exclusion of the mundane—stands in tension, at times, with a prophetic, liberationist Christian activism.

In the field of peace and conflict studies we "preach" that conflicts and tensions are not merely problems but opportunities for transformation. And so it is with these tensions within and between Catholic and Mennonite expressions of Christianity. Working to resolve or ease tensions such as these, therefore, could indicate a way forward not only for ecumenical dialogue but also for both Catholic and Mennonite theological self-understandings. In this respect, the theological and ecclesial contexts within which both of our communions think about peace are an understudied resource for peacemaking.

As noted, part of the significance of *Called Together* is the striking way in which it embodies the very practices of reconciliation and healing toward which it points. Thus we need not fear to name the ongoing challenges that one tradition puts to the other, for this too is necessary both for the healing of memories and for mutual transformation. Reconciliation depends on truth-telling, a complicated and far-from-straightforward process. *Called Together* opens the path in this direction, however, by offering us new lenses by which to view our respective histories and, thus, a way to work together for a common future dedicated to the ushering in of the practices and realities of mercy, peace, and justice.

Chapter 2

Response to Scott Appleby's

"Christian Peacebuilding

The Growing Edge
of the Catholic-Mennonite Conversation"

Helmut Harder

I want to thank the sponsoring institutions and the planners of this conference for their initiative in making the conversation of these two days
possible. It is timely that we take a scrutinizing look at the International Catholic-Mennonite Dialogue Report through theological glasses. It
has been four years since the report was issued. While the report has had
wide circulation in the Mennonite World Conference family and some in
the Roman Catholic Church, we've had nothing like what this conference
promises us. I look forward to these days together.

A second similar conference is scheduled to be held at Hamburg University at the end of September. I am certain that the results of this conference
here and the one in Hamburg will figure prominently as some of us gather
in Rome in mid-October to take account of the gamut of responses that the
dialogue report has evoked.

My assignment here is to offer a response to Scott Appleby's talk. Obviously
I will need to be selective and brief. I plan to respond against the backdrop
of my own experience as someone involved in the dialogue between 1998
and 2003.

Scott begins provocatively, as he says, by calling *Called Together to Be Peacemakers* a "marvelous document," but then registering some criticisms of the
report—and thus of the Mennonite-Catholic dialogue as such. He observes
correctly that *Called Together* is dated, since it only brings us up to the end
of the Cold War, while the real action of peacebuilding that has occurred
since the early 1990s is hardly taken into account. This is unfortunate, Scott

goes on to say, since developments on the ground constitute raw material for joint theological reflection and for the next stage of institutional/ecclesial partnership. Thus while the document may be useful in itself, it is not "a fully prophetic reading of the 'signs of the times.'"

In this light, the subtitle of his presentation, "A First 'Official' Step on the Path to Ecumenical Peacebuilding," issues something of a critique of the dialogue and of the title, *Called Together to Be Peacemakers*. First, the Mennonite-Catholic dialogue was, at best and perhaps all too much, an initial "step," a beginning, a "clearing of the throat." Second, it presents the "official" line; in other words, it is a product of the church's elite. Third, its focus should be on peacebuilding, not on peacemaking.

I can certainly affirm the first point: this was only a first step. But somewhat defensively I must say this: Given that our communities had not engaged in global Catholic-Mennonite church-to-church dialogue since things came to an abrupt halt in the mid-sixteenth century, that first step was formidable and huge. Regarding his second point that the dialogue was official and elitist, I can only object on behalf of the humble nonelitist Mennonite delegation and let the Catholics deal with their own claims and perceptions in this respect. Thirdly, concerning the implication that we should be speaking of peacebuilding rather than peacemaking, I will admit to some reservations about the title of our report at the time we chose it, even though I was partial to the decision. Scott's provocation makes me think I should have voiced my concerns more loudly at the time, for two reasons provided below.

First, in our deliberations at the third annual Week of Dialogue, held at the Thomashof Retreat Centre near Karlsruhe, Germany, Mennonite dialogue member Andrea Lange made a case for the Mennonite Church as a confessional "peace" church while Catholic member Drew Christiansen named the Roman Catholic Church a "peacemaking" church. In the end—and it was near the end—we chose Drew's Catholic characterization for the title of our report. Our intention was to highlight action-oriented peacemaking rather than a more confessional-oriented identity. I would have preferred that we entitle the document "Called Together to Be Peace Churches," and then let initiatives flow from that foundational confession. Now Scott has suggested "peacebuilding" in place of "peacemaking," and with that he has given us something further to think about.

My second reservation about the title is that it gives the impression that our entire five-year dialogue was about peace theology. This was not the case, formally speaking. The explicit discussion on peace comprises 45 of the 215 paragraphs. As the report outline indicates, we divided our time more or less equally between historical eras and issues, theological themes, and a quest for the healing of memories. Peace theology constituted one of three major themes in the theological sector of that three-part division; the other two theological themes were the church and sacraments (particularly the rites of baptism and the Eucharist / Lord's Supper). We dedicated about one-ninth of our time together to dialogue on themes and issues related to "our commitment to peace." That leads me to say that the overall title can be somewhat misleading. The title came about because we wanted to speak a word of hope and direction for our future collaboration and we wanted to say a word in favor of "ethical ecumenism." In that sense, I welcome Scott's contribution to what we had envisioned for the future. But I anticipate that we will be dealing with a broader spectrum of themes and issues in these days than the title implies.

In the second section of his paper, Scott offers three architectonic principles: First, the evolution of Catholic and Mennonite pathways with respect to church-state relations have paved the way for Catholic-Mennonite convergence; this path is well worth treading, maintaining, and developing. Second, the theological / ecclesial context of the two churches is an understudied resource for peacebuilding. Third, the genius (my word) of *Called Together to Be Peacemakers* lies in this: that it models the virtues it enjoins and its medium and message are in accord. The dialogue's focus on the healing of memories, on the art of reconciliation, and on truth-telling provide gestures for a new hermeneutic whereby to discern the past and envision the future.

Scott implies that the first of these three—the growing convergence of Catholics and Mennonites with respect to church-state relations—is an area where Mennonites have taken the lead in challenging Roman Catholicism. For the second principle—that the theological and ecclesiological promptings signify an understudied resource for peacebuilding—Mennonites have some things to learn from Catholics. He leans in the same direction regarding the third principle—that *Called Together* offers resources for a new hermeneutic for peacebuilding. Catholics have much to offer from their vantage point as a global institution with a long history of diplomacy, statecraft, and "humanitarian intervention."

I see these as solid architectonic principles. They fortify the basis for our pursuit of "ethical ecumenism" through expressions of "full communion" in accordance with two first-century apostolic words—one from a letter initially addressed to the church at Rome and the other from a Roman prison initially addressed to the church at Ephesus:

For the kingdom of God is not food and drink but righteousness and peace and joy in the Holy Spirit. The one who thus serves Christ is acceptable to God and has human approval. Let us then pursue what makes for peace and for mutual upbuilding." (Rom 14:17-19)

[Make] every effort to maintain the unity of the Spirit in the bond of peace. There is one body and one Spirit just as you were called to the one hope of your calling, one Lord, one faith, one baptism, one God and Father of all, who is above all and through all and in all. But each of us was given grace according to the measure of Christ's gift." (Eph 4:3-7)

Chapter 3

The Significance of the
Mennonite-Catholic Dialogue

A Mennonite Perspective

Alan Kreider

T he international dialogue between Mennonites and Catholics was an improbable event. In annual dialogues scattered across five years, seven representatives of the Roman Catholic Church met together with seven representatives from the Mennonite Church. After five centuries in which the two traditions had not officially spoken with each other, and in which there was "mutual isolation and hostility,"[1] the delegates came together to know each other better and to seek a healing of memories. They worshipped together, ate together, and laughed together. They engaged in careful thought and candid speech. They became friends who wanted to understand each other. And by 2003 they had produced *Called Together to be Peacemakers*, the document that we will be reflecting upon in this conference. The event was improbable not least because of the disparity of size between the two bodies. Why was the Roman Catholic billion talking to the Mennonite million? In the long journeys of the two traditions, why is it *now* that this elephant and this mouse are "called together to be peacemakers?"

Why Now?

The document does not answer this question systematically, but I find four reasons embedded in it. First, the "destructive power of modern weapons in a nuclear age" challenges Catholics and Mennonites to reflect on peace.[2]

---

[1] *Called Together to be Peacemakers: Report of the International Dialogue between the Catholic Church and Mennonite World Conference, 1998–2003*, par. 2.

[2] Ibid., par. 9.

Second, Mennonites and Catholics are now able to participate in ecumenical conversation because Mennonites, after centuries of isolation, are integrating into wider society, while Catholics, responding to the Second Vatican Council, are entering into multilateral ecumenical conversations. Third, throughout the West—in Europe and North America—Catholics are now for the first time experiencing "disestablishment," life "as a minority church."[3]

Finally and decisively, both traditions, Catholic and Mennonite, share a concern for mission in the West. Both traditions are facing the challenge of "how to communicate the faith in an increasingly secular world."[4] In the document I sense a leitmotiv rooted in John 17:21-23: "Mission requires that Christians seek to become 'one' for the sake of their witness to Jesus Christ and the Father."[5] Conflict between Christians, the document observes, "impedes the preaching of the Gospel and damages their credibility."[6] And the notion, implicit but eloquent throughout, is that the two traditions can assist each other as they engage in mission together. This mission—God's mission—advocates and enacts the Gospel of peace before "the watching world"[7] so that people may believe and come to salvation. God's mission is not only to save individuals but also to reconcile "all peoples in the peace of Christ"[8]—and not only all peoples but all of creation (Col 1:20). Catholics and Mennonites are "called together to be peacemakers" for the sake of God's mission.

So What?

So what is the significance of *Called Together to be Peacemakers* and the dialogue that produced it? I shall look at five areas. I shall concentrate on the West because the situation of Christians in many parts of the global South is often unlike our situation here, and, as a result, Christians there will read the document very differently than we do.

The first element of significance in *Called Together* is *encounter*: the dialogue enabled the two traditions to meet each other in a new way. Mennonites

---

[3] Ibid., par. 49.

[4] Ibid., par. 209.

[5] Ibid., par. 96.

[6] Ibid., par. 9.

[7] John Howard Yoder, *Body Politics: Five Practices of the Christian Church before the Watching World* (Nashville: Discipleship Resources, 1992).

[8] *Called Together*, par. 175.

and Catholics did not simply talk to each other; rather, by visiting churches, they encountered each other's realities as well as ideals.

The dialogue opened Mennonites to the richness of the Catholic tradition. Mennonite delegates were theologically literate; some of them already had extensive engagement with the Catholic intellectual and spiritual traditions. The dialogue intensified the acquaintance of the Mennonites with the sanctity of many Catholics across the centuries and today, with the vitality of contemporary ecclesial movements, such as Focolare, and with the depth and sophistication of the Catholic conciliar documents. The dialogue enabled the Mennonite participants to take these riches seriously.

The dialogue also opened Catholics to the witness of the Mennonite tradition. Several of the Catholic participants already knew something of the Mennonite tradition. The dialogue invited Catholics to listen to the pain still present in a tradition that originated amidst persecution; it invited Catholics to face the downside of Christendom. But Catholic participants also discovered that we Mennonites who have lived on the margins of the Christian world have perspectives—on Christocentric peacemaking, discipleship, and congregational process, for example—that are worth sharing with other Christians. In the severe repression of sixteenth-century Europe, in which both Catholics and magisterial Protestants harried and killed Anabaptists, our movement could have died out. But we Mennonites believe that God protected us so that we could embody and articulate a vision that over the centuries has developed treasures to share with other Christians. The Mennonite participants recognize that we do not possess the whole truth; but we persist in believing that we are a voice in the choir of God's church. Our style of being Christian and our way of reading both the Bible and early church documents can be helpful to all Christians. Mennonites offered these perspectives to Roman Catholics.

This encounter enabled each tradition to deepen its self-understanding. Seeing the Christian faith from the perspective of another strand of Christian experience also deepened each tradition's respect for the other tradition and heightened its call to Christian solidarity. In the civilization called Christendom, in which Christianity was the default religion of the people of a political area, Christians were most conscious of ways in which their truth differed from the errors of other Christians. Their attempts to communicate their faith were directed towards other Christians—erroneous Christians. Post-Christendom is a different world. In it, Christianity is a minority religion; in it, in the words of an Austrian archbishop, Christians are "faced with a cold wind of resistance."[9] In this cold but bracing world Christians (including both Catholics and Mennonites) become aware not primarily of our differences but of what we hold in common in Jesus Christ. In a world of diverse worldviews and faiths—paganism, secularism, and the great world religions—our truthful encounter with each other thus strengthens our witness.

The second element of significance is *unity*. For over four hundred fifty years, unity has been problematic for Mennonites. Mennonites, the document reports, now see unity "an urgent imperative to be obeyed,"[10] but this is a relatively recent insight for most of us. We Mennonites have not been sufficiently sensitive to the agony of a divided church. Our tradition originated in fragmentation, and we have become a movement that has continued to split. We have not, I believe, often registered how deeply this offends Christians in other traditions, including Catholics. And we have not appreciated how severely this impedes God's mission. The Mennonite participants in the dialogue appear to have registered this. They state: "We regret Anabaptist words and deeds that contributed to fracturing the body of Christ."[11]

Catholics, on the other hand, have always emphasized unity. However, now—in a post-Christendom situation—Catholics seem to realize that unity brought about by the coerced Christianization of Europe was not sustainable. And so the Catholic participants "acknowledge the Church's failure when she justified the use of force in evangelism, sought to create and maintain a unitary Christian society by coercive means, and persecuted religious minorities."[12]

The journey towards unity will be a long one. The international dialogue led Mennonites and Catholics to recognize that they share "the substantial amount of the Apostolic faith" and "see each other as brothers and sisters in Christ."[13] The document also suggests ways forward on the road to unity, even as it recognizes the realities: Catholics cannot offer the Eucharist to

[9] Franz Cardinal König, "The Pull of God in a Godless Age," *The Tablet* (September 18, 1999), 1251.

[10] *Called Together*, par. 197.

[11] Ibid., par. 203.

[12] Ibid., par. 55. The document does not address the question of whether official ecclesial unity makes sense when its members, as during World War II, are busy killing each other.

[13] Ibid., par. 210.

Mennonites, and Mennonites, even after this conversation, cannot say that they accept Roman Catholic infant baptism.[14]

The third element of significance is *history*. The participants in the dialogue recognized that Catholics and Mennonites have had "negative images and narrow stereotypes"[15] of each other. They therefore spent considerable time engaged in a common rereading of the history of the church in late antiquity, the late Middle Ages, and the sixteenth century. In the spirit of the Vatican document *Memory and Reconciliation*, they attempted to engage in rigorous historical analysis, "using all of the information available" in order to reconstruct the events and *mentalités* of the past and, thus, to move towards a "purification of memory."[16]

How successful was this process? Did it purify the memory of the two traditions? To some extent, I believe it did. The process reminded participants of the vitality of church life and piety in the late Middle Ages, of the monastic renewal movements and mystical currents which influenced the early Anabaptists, of the Catholic martyrs of the Reformation era. It pointed out how the Anabaptist practice of baptizing those who had been baptized as infants "had an extremely provocative effect" and "could only be considered heretical."[17]

But the process had limits. One was the document's failure to engage in rigorous historical analysis, using "all of the information available," for example, on the contentious issue of the origin of infant baptism; responsible historical research by scholars of many Christian traditions will simply no longer allow a retrojection of medieval Catholic practice back into the early Christian centuries.[18] More serious, the document underplayed the struc-

---

[14] Ibid., pars. 140, 137. No doubt many Mennonite congregations receive as members Christians baptized as Catholics without requiring them to be baptized as believers and hence implicitly accept validity of Catholic infant baptisms.

[15] Ibid., par. 23.

[16] International Theological Commission, "Memory and Reconciliation: The Church and Faults of the Past," 4.1 (Vatican City: The Holy See, December 1999), http://www.vatican.va/roman_curia/congregations/cfaith/cti_documents/rc_con_cfaith_doc_20000307_memory-reconc-itc_en.html.

[17] *Called Together*, par. 40.

[18] The dialogue's treatment of this issue was, in my view, inadequate. In section 62 Catholics state their understanding of the baptism of children as a tradition that goes back to the apostles; they root their position in texts—the *Apostolic Tradition*, Origen and Cyprian. Mennonites, on the other hand, consider infant baptism to be a later development which was generalized in the fourth century; Mennonites cite no texts, although they could have done so. So, in section 62, Catholic evidence confronts Mennonite

tural effects of Christendom, whose apparent unity had been brought about by coercion, in which people whom the church considered to be heretics could be given over to the secular powers to be, as Thomas Aquinas put it, "exterminated."[19] This was not simply a matter in which the "weaknesses of so many of [the Church's] sons and daughters" gave into intolerance.[20] This was a system built upon coercion, which the Christians of the early centuries had specifically repudiated,[21] but which popes and theologians joined Aquinas in justifying, and which canon 3 of the fourth Lateran Council of 1215 "admonished and induced and if necessary compelled by ecclesiastical

---

opinion. In section 116 Catholics again state that the baptism of infants is a practice of ancient tradition; and again they cite texts, both in the document and in footnote 109, in which a list of sources culminates in Notre Dame liturgy professor Maxwell E. Johnson's "comprehensive study of the question" in his *The Rites of Christian Initiation: Their Evolution and Interpretation* (Collegeville, MN: The Liturgical Press, 1999). But Johnson does not say what the Catholic contributions to the document say. Whereas the Catholic contributors retroject classic Catholic baptismal practice back into the early centuries, Johnson has been reading the sources with fresh eyes. He writes, on p. 157 (his italics): "from Augustine on, infant baptism will become seen as *necessary* and *expected*, rather than permitted, in the life of the Church." Johnson here says pretty much what I said in my contribution to the third dialogue, based on recent studies of texts and epigraphy. See Alan Kreider, "Conversion and Christendom: An Anabaptist Perspective" (2003). I contended that prior to the fourth century some infants were baptized soon after birth and so were some children; the majority of infants and children were not baptized (though it depended on local custom); the dominant model of early baptism was that of carefully catechized believers. In the early fifth century, Augustine in his debates with the Pelagians came to make the baptism theologically necessary for the salvation of the infant, as soon as possible after birth. In the sixth century the Roman state proceeded to make baptism of infants legally necessary, and backed this up with severe penalties. The entire society became Christian, and a sign of membership in society was baptism. If one neglected or opposed baptism, one was suspected of heresy, and the churchmen handed unrepentant heretics over to the secular arm for execution. So the Anabaptists, who opposed this system, were indeed provocative and "heretical" (40), and they were killed for their provocative heresy; they were early participants in the deconstruction of coercive Christendom. Mercifully, our document (62 and 143) says that Catholic and Mennonite scholars need to give further study to the question of infant baptism. To some extent this has happened: see the exchanges between Alan Kreider and Frederick C. Bauerschmidt in Gerald W. Schlabach, ed., *On Baptism: Mennonite-Catholic Theological Colloquium, 2001–2002* (Kitchener, ON: Pandora Press, 2004).

[19] *Summa Theologiae*, II–II, q. 11, a. 3. See http://www.newadvent.org/summa/3011.htm#article3.

[20] *Called Together*, pars. 201–2.

[21] Alan Kreider, "Violence and Mission in the Fourth and Fifth Centuries," *International Bulletin of Missionary Research* 31, no. 3 (2007): 125–33.

censure." *Dignitatis Humanae*, which the Catholics cited, states: "the doctrine of the Church that no one is to be coerced into faith has always stood firm."[22] Our document reports, "Mennonite readings of medieval history doubt such a claim." What a limp response! This was the place for Mennonites to plead for what *Memory and Reconciliation* promises: "all of the information available." The Mennonites' sixteenth-century Anabaptist predecessors would have listened to the Catholic claims about coercion with utter disbelief. The Anabaptists perceived that the religious unity of Christendom, articulated by leading theologians and churchmen, was a false unity because it was a forced unity, and hence it could not be a sustainable unity. The process of dialogue made it clear that Mennonites and Catholics, for the sake of the purification of memory, have further historical work to do.

But in history there are seeds of renewal. Our document points to the process called *ressourcement*: "self-renewal of a people from the original sources of its own life."[23] It was the Catholics, of course, who invented the term *ressourcement*. Scholars deeply immersed in patristics did much to shape the thought of Vatican II. Mennonites in the same period were engaged in a parallel process of *ressourcement*. In the 1940s, church historian Harold S. Bender inspired a generation of Mennonites with "the recovery of the Anabaptist Vision,"[24] and this did much to shape the perspectives of many theologians including the late John Howard Yoder. *Ressourcement* is an ongoing process, in which Christians are continually renewed by a deeper reading of the sources, which may lead them to reexamine their earlier historical understandings. For example, historical research has enabled current Mennonites to understand Anabaptism less romantically than Harold Bender did.[25] In post-Christendom, *ressourcement* points back to "the original sources of the church's own life"—back to the Bible, read by scholars and in a disciplined way in congregations and small groups; back also to the documents of the pre-Christendom church. This period, prior to the coerced christianization of the West, I believe, offers us

[22] *Dignitatis Humanae* (Declaration on Religious Freedom), section 12, in *The Documents of Vatican II: The Message and Meaning of the Ecumenical Council*, ed. Walter M. Abbott (New York: America Press, 1966).

[23] Avery Dulles, SJ, "Tradition and Creativity in Theology," *First Things*, no. 27 (November 1992): 23.

[24] Harold S. Bender, "The Anabaptist Vision," *Church History* 13, no.1 (1944): 3–24; and widely reprinted, not least in Guy F. Hershberger, ed. *The Recovery of the Anabaptist Vision* (Scottdale, PA: Herald Press, 1957).

[25] E.g., see C. Arnold Snyder, "The Birth and Evolution of Swiss Anabaptism, 1520–1530," *Mennonite Quarterly Review* 80, no.4 (2006): 501–646.

models of church life and mission that are particularly helpful to Christians who cannot control the world (implied by section 58).

Purification of memory and *ressourcement*: these approaches to history are hopeful. In our missional situation, we can only offer the watching world a view of ourselves—and of our past—that is true. We Mennonites, for example, must confess that during World War II in Europe it was the Catholics and not the Mennonites that produced a Franz Jägerstätter, who chose to resist the Nazi Germany's war of aggression in following his Catholic Christian conscience and was executed for it. I rejoice in his beatification. For the sake of mission before the watching world, we are called to be one, but we must also be penitent and undefensive, inviting people to join churches that preach forgiveness to the world because we ourselves are continually being renewed in God's forgiveness.

The fourth element of significance is the *sacraments*. In the dialogue, the Mennonite participants encountered a Catholic sacramental theology that is confident and compendious. The Catholics spoke especially of the Eucharist, which for them is "the source and summit of the whole life of the church."[26] When the Eucharist is celebrated, Christ is there, "made really present under the species of bread and wine,"[27] but Christ is also, according to *Sacrosanctum Concilium* (Constitution on the Sacred Liturgy), section 7, present in the celebrant, in the word that is proclaimed, and in the assembly of worshippers, the people of God.[28] Mennonites in contrast spoke more guardedly about the presence of Christ. The Lord's Supper, for Mennonites, is a memorial and sign, but in it there is "effectual power" to bring change in the participants and the community of faith, making them "one loaf together"; Christ is present, "not in the elements as such, but in the context as a whole, including the communion of the gathered congregation."[29] In baptism, Mennonites emphasized that the new believers act: they give witness to the work of God and the Holy Spirit in their lives, they signify their commitment to follow Christ as his disciples, they commit themselves to give and receive counsel in the congregation and to participate in God's mission. In the baptismal event God also acts and "something happens." Evidence of God's action is the life of the baptized and the baptizing community.[30]

[26] *Called Together*, par. 117.
[27] Ibid., par. 138.
[28] Ibid., par. 118.
[29] Ibid., par. 126.
[30] Ibid., par. 123.

In these presentations of the two traditions' approaches to sacraments and ordinances, I sense room for gift-sharing. Mennonites today are not of one mind, but many experience a deep longing for the presence and action of God in the sacraments; these Mennonites would like to have communion more intensely and frequently. Catholics can help Mennonites reflect more deeply on what many of us already know but lack words to describe: that at the table God is present and active. And Mennonites can bear testimony, out of long experience in mutual accountability and community building, that Christ is present in the assembled people. Thereby Mennonites can be a resource to Catholics, who believe in Christ's presence in the elements, that they may also learn the joy of "becoming what they receive."[31] Missionally, before the watching world, this is vital because people today are hungry not just for words or ideas, but for the reality of God, and they are astonished and attracted when they see Christ embodied in people who follow him with transformed lives.

The fifth element of significance is *peace*. In the dialogues, Mennonites were astonished to discover the extent to which their views and Catholic views converged. A special moment in the third dialogue occurred when Drew Christiansen presented his paper "What is a Peace Church? A Roman Catholic Perspective." Drew opened Mennonite eyes to the rapid developments since Vatican II in which the church has sought to view war "with a whole new perspective." This presentation filled me with joy, and also with intrigue at the sight of what appeared to be a church in motion. So our document records, in a way that is quite astonishing to those who did not take part in the process, the language of convergence. It reads: "The peace witness of both Mennonites and Catholics is rooted in Jesus Christ 'who is our peace, who has made us both one.'"[32] Mennonites and Catholics agree that "the Church is called to be a peace church, a peacemaking church."[33]

This convergence is encouraging, but only time will tell how significant it is. As the document makes clear, both traditions are on journeys in the area of peacemaking. Many Mennonites, for example, are moving from nonresistance to active nonviolence,[34] and Catholics must be on a multitude of journeys of which that sketched in our document is only one. The document helpfully

[31] Ibid., par. 119.

[32] Ibid., par. 174.

[33] Ibid., par. 175. Six consecutive footnotes (174–79) root points of convergence in both Roman Catholic conciliar documents and Mennonite confessions.

[34] Ibid., par. 170.

clarifies differences between Catholic and Mennonite approaches. One of these has to do with the role of the pope, backed by the Vatican diplomatic corps, as peacemaker.[35] Mennonite leaders may establish contacts with Iranian president Ahmadinejad, as they did in 2006 and 2007,[36] but the Mennonite approach is lower key—working primarily through the long-standing presence of peaceworkers on the ground. A second difference, indicated by the telltale phrase "a culture of peace," has to do with the scope of peacemaking. The Catholic approach, in the Christendom tradition, is to work so that the entire civil society will become a culture of peace; the church functions as an instrument that fosters institutions practicing nonviolence in public life.[37] The Mennonite approach, as indicated in a recent book that I coauthored, *A Culture of Peace: God's Vision for the Church*,[38] attempts to envision and equip congregations and parishes so that they will be cultures of peace. From there the practices of peacemaking—learned in the congregations—can radiate outwards into every area of the society's life. Scattered through our document are many of these practices: giving and receiving counsel;[39] participating in mutual accountability, reproof, guidance, binding and loosing in ethical decisions;[40] engaging in good conflict and mediation.[41] It is arguably these practices learned in congregations that have enabled Mennonites, according to Scott Appleby, to be "the 'elder statesmen' in the rapidly growing but still inchoate field of religiously motivated conflict transformation."[42] My sense is that the Catholic and Mennonite ways of creating cultures of peace are complementary. Catholics can help Mennonites by broadening our vision about the possibility of peaceable institutions in the wider society and also by reminding us that it is justice that enables peace,[43] and Mennonites can

[35] Ibid., par. 155. For an assessment see Drew Christiansen, SJ, "Benedict XVI: Peacemaker," in *America* 197, no. 2 (July 16, 2007).

[36] Mark Beach, "U.S. Religious Leaders Meet President Mahmoud Ahmadinejad," *MCC News and Events* (September 22, 2006), http://acommonplace.mcc.org/news/news/2006/2006-09-22_sponsorsmeeting.html.

[37] *Called Together*, par. 152.

[38] Alan Kreider, Eleanor Kreider, and Paulus Widjaja, *A Culture of Peace: God's Vision for the Church* (Intercourse, PA: Good Books, 2005).

[39] *Called Together*, par. 122.

[40] Ibid., par. 168.

[41] Ibid., par. 169.

[42] R. Scott Appleby, *The Ambivalence of the Sacred: Religion, Violence, and Reconciliation* (Lanham, MD: Rowman & Littlefield, 2000), 144.

[43] *Called Together*, par. 151.

remind Catholics that the truth of the Gospel of peace will be tested and the virtues of Christian peacemakers will be formed among those who share life in parishes and congregations.

Difficulties

There are, of course, areas of difficulty as well as difference. We Mennonites are pleased when Catholics affirm "the superiority of nonviolent means." But we remain suspicious of the doctrine of the just war, even if it is "applicable only to exceptional cases."[44] We Mennonites would like to know how Catholics believe the doctrine of the just war originated; to what extent did it come from the teaching and way of Jesus, and to what extent from ancient pagan thinkers? We Mennonites would like to know what it would take for the church to declare a war unjust; if—as the *Catechism of the Catholic Church*, article 2309, puts it—it is up to "those who have responsibility for the public good" to determine whether a war has moral legitimacy, we wonder whether there ever will be an unjust war. Will a Catholic bishop, we wonder, ever deny communion to a Catholic politician who votes appropriations for an unjust war? In our document,[45] the Catholics reiterate the concept, dominant since the fourth century, that "nonresistance is a 'counsel of perfection'" for exceptional Christians who seek the way of Christ more deeply, and we Mennonites sigh. But then on February 18, 2007, Pope Benedict XVI, in his Angelus message, states that Jesus' Sermon on the Mount was "a 'manifesto' presented to everyone," and we smile. The pope goes on: "Loving the enemy is the nucleus of the 'Christian revolution.'"[46] We beam and say, "Yes!"

Many Mennonites are watching these developments with keen interest. We imagine the debates that go on in the Vatican and among bishops and moral philosophers, we read reports of the Catholic Peace Fellowship delegates' visit to the Vatican, and we pray for our Catholic brothers and sisters. We pray with concern, for we know how vital the Catholic approach to this issue is to the entire Christian church in mission today. There is, in the watch-

[44] Ibid., par. 159.

[45] Ibid., par. 188.

[46] "Benedict XVI Calls for a 'Christian Revolution:' Invites Faithful to Respond to Evil with Good," Zenit.Org (February 18, 2007), http://www.zenit.org/article -18941?l=english; also available at http://www.catholicpeacefellowship.org/nextpage .asp?m=2308.

ing world, no objection more widely held about Christians than this—that Christianity, like other monotheistic faiths, is fundamentally a violent religion. This Enlightenment truism has become a part of secular orthodoxy, and we Christians can only disprove this when we are "called together to be peacemakers" and express this peacemaking in every area of our lives.

Hope

I conclude with hope. I believe that what Jesus prayed for in John 17 is precious: that Christian unity is necessary for Christian mission. I believe also that Christian unity cannot be achieved cheaply or by force. And I believe that, in the fullness of time, God will answer Jesus' prayer. So when Mennonites and Catholics meet to engage in truthful, disciplined dialogue and find God calling us together to be peacemakers, I believe that the missional God is at work. Much remains to be done, not only among church leaders, missiologists, peace activists, and theologians, but also in every parish and congregation. As friendships grow and projects of cooperative witness and service emerge, Catholics and Mennonites—the billion and the million—will drink from each other's wells. Then a fund of memories will build up that will not need to be healed, for the memories will be whole.

Chapter 4

The Significance
of the Mennonite-Catholic Dialogue

A Catholic Perspective

Drew Christiansen, SJ

Allow me to begin with a word of thanks to Margie Pfeil for inviting me to participate in this forum and, in particular, for assigning me to respond to Alan Kreider. Alan contributed to the third dialogue session at Karlsruhe, Germany, where I became an admirer of his work. I contributed a paper at the same meeting. I am delighted to be reunited with Alan here today.

It is also appropriate today that I note the deep debt that the dialogue owes to the University of Notre Dame for laying the groundwork for theological understanding between Catholics and Mennonites. I refer especially to the university's appointment of John Howard Yoder to the faculty of theology here in the 1970s. For my part, my role as a consultant to the Catholic team drew heavily on what I learned over five years as John Howard's colleague under the Golden Dome.

Significance of the Dialogue: An Exchange of Gifts

Finally, it is important to take note of the role Saint John's Abbey has played as home for the North American dialogue known as "Bridegefolk." Mennonites have long esteemed monasticism for its fidelity to the ideals of early Christianity. In some ways, it seems to me, the Mennonite-Catholic dialogue shares in the spirit of monastic ecumenism, as found at Taize and Bose, as well as that of intermonastic dialogue, where boundaries between traditions are less rigid than we often find in purely theological encounters, and where both sides savor deeply the exchange of gifts between their two communities.

This dialogue is significant for another reason as well. The title of our report, *Called Together to Be Peacemakers*, points to a special pastoral convergence that distinguishes it from reports of dialogues that focus on resolution of theological differences. The practice of peacemaking unites us where history and doctrine still have a potential to divide. Ecumenically, as Richard Gaillardetz has argued, building on the work of Francis Sullivan and Walter Kasper, this dialogue demonstrates how the Catholic Church finds non-Catholic "ecclesial communions," "at the level of their concrete pastoral life, [may] be fostering a form of Christian community that more effectively brings its members into communion with God and Christ" than occurs in some Catholic communities.[1] While the heart of our collaboration, in this case, is our common peace witness, that common witness represents a recognition on the Catholic side that in the church of Christ, "orthopraxis," as much as orthodoxy, has a vital role to play in promoting church unity. It is for this reason I have proposed that when the formal dialogue resumes, the natural place to begin will be with the doctrine of sanctification, a teaching in which our two traditions hold much in common.

In the brief time that remains to me, I would like to respond to three specific issues Alan has raised in his remarks: reading history, confessing religious coercion, and promoting many styles of peacemaking.

Confronting History

One feature of the dialogue process, which seemed small and even otiose at first, was that at each session, the summary reports of the previous sessions were reworked. As a result, we had the benefit of that clarity that comes only with time and repeated discussion, as well as of added insight that arises from the study of other issues. The common reading of history, since it was the work of the first session, drew the most benefit from this process of revision. The talent of our church historians aside, it is one reason this portion of the report reads so well.

With respect to history, I think the evolution of historiography will continue to produce new perspectives on the historical paradigms that, in the past, helped define our two traditions. No doubt for Catholics of the pre–Vatican II era, like those of a certain subset of Catholics today, their view of church history

---

[1] Richard R. Gaillardetz, *The Church in the Making:* Lumen Gentium, Christus Dominus, Orientalium Ecclesiarum, Rediscovering Vatican II Series (New York: Paulist Press, 2006), 168.

was much informed by the hierarchical/institutional model of the church that prevailed from the seventeenth through the early twentieth century. In the mid-twentieth century *ressourcement*, the return to the sources, especially the fathers of the church, made possible the retrieval of alternative perspectives on ecclesiology, like those of Yves Congar. This *ressourcement* informed the Second Vatican Council's decrees on the church (*Lumen Gentium*), ecumenism (*Unitatis Redintegratio*), and the laity (*Apostolicam Acuositatem*).[2] Likewise, the council itself allowed greater attention to the conciliar and other reform movements prior to the Reformation. Subsequent historical studies, especially of pastoral life as John O'Malley has shown, have illuminated a quite different church history than provided by the institutional model.[3]

For Mennonites, the notion of "Constantinian Fall" of the church has, I think, played the kind of imaginative role that the notion of the monarchical papacy did for Catholics of my youth and still does for the restorationist party today. In each case, the notion has encapsulated an idealized account of the past that has served to forge the community's identity and organize its theological worldview. The place of Constantine and more generally the role that structures of empire played in the organization of the medieval church needs to be opened up to the fresh air of history. Of particular importance, I think, is the so-called "Germanization" of Christianity in the West, which did far more than Constantine to militarize Christianity.[4]

---

[2] For a brief sketch of Yves Congar's life and work, see Peter J. Bernardi, SJ, "Passion for Unity," *America*, April 2005, 8–11. On *Lumen Gentium*, see Richard R. Gaillardetz, *The Church in the Making: Lumen Gentium, Christus Dominus, Orientalium Ecclesiarum* (Mahwah: Paulist Press, 2006). Also, Edward Idris Cassidy, *Ecumenism and Interreligious Dialogue: Unitatis Redintegratio, Nostra Aetate* (Mahwah: Paulist Press, 2005). Both Gaillardetz and Cassidy's books are part of the publisher's Rediscovering Vatican II series. The council's *Apostolicam Actuositatem* (Decree on the Apostolic Life of the Laity) may be found in *The Documents of Vatican II*, ed. Walter M. Abbott, SJ (New York: America Press, 1966), 489–521.

[3] Examples of such studies influencing more complex views of church histories in advance of the Second Vatican Council are Gerhard B. Ladner, *The Idea of Reform: Its Impact on Thought and Action in the Age of the Fathers* (Cambridge: Harvard University Press, 1959) and Brian Tierney, *Foundations of the Conciliar Theory: The Contribution of Canonists from Gratian to the Great Schism* (Cambridge: Cambridge University Press, 1955). In *Trent and All That: Renewing Catholicism in the Early Modern Era* (Cambridge: Harvard University Press, 2001), John W. O'Malley surveys the development of modern church historiography, especially the impact of the social history of religious practice on historians' models of the Catholic Church reform.

[4] See James C. Russell, *The Germanization of Early Medieval Christianity: A Sociohistorical Approach to Religious Transformation* (New York: Oxford University Press, 1994). Russell

Another complexifying factor, as Peter Brown has shown, is the recognition that there were many mini-Christendoms across Europe in the late antique and early medieval periods, among various language groups and cultures.[5] With these two factors we should also weigh the influence of the pastoral strategies that church leaders such as Gregory the Great followed as the Roman Empire collapsed in the West.[6]

The anti-Constantinian critique, it seems to me, suffers from two drawbacks. First, it shares in the "Great Man" theory of history, attributing too much to one influential, and therefore overly symbolic, ruler. The influence of imperial Christianity, moreover, was arguably far greater in the East than in the West. Second, it puts too little weight on other social and intellectual factors shaping Christianity in late antiquity and too much on political factors, which weighed less in the West following the barbarian invasions. I would argue, in short, for a social reading of Christian history that takes into account the encounter between Christianity and Germanic and other tribal groups and thus complements a political reading focused on Constantine and the ecclesial institutions and practices he either created or for which he laid the foundations.

Confessing Religious Coercion

I agree with Alan that the Catholic Church has to face honestly its role in shaping rationales for religious coercion and for developing and applying the machinery of religious repression.[7] While *Dignitatis Humanae* (Declaration on Religious Freedom) of Vatican II set out a standard for religious freedom, including freedom from coercion, in this day and age it is no longer intellectually acceptable to say, as the decree did, that religious freedom has always been

---

was not the first to identify this phenomenon. Ernst Troeltsch in his classic *The Social Teaching of the Christians Churches*, vol. 1 (Louisville: Westminster/Knox Press, 1992), commented on these influences nearly a century ago.

[5] See Peter Brown, *The Rise of Western Christendom: Triumph and Diversity, 200–1000* (Cambridge: Blackwell, 1996). Also, Richard Fletcher, *The Barbarian Conversion: From Paganism to Christianity* (Berkeley: University of California Press, 1999) and Judith Herrin, *The Formation of Christendom* (Princeton: Princeton University Press, 1989).

[6] On Gregory's pastoral strategy, see Brown, 133–47. Brown also reviews the strategies of other pastors in the Western church, including Caesarius of Arles, Gregory of Tours, and Columba.

[7] For a brief sketch of changing Catholic attitudes towards religious coercion, see Drew Christiansen, SJ, "From *Disciplina* to the Day of Pardon," *America* 195, no. 9 (October 2006): 17–29.

the teaching or the practice of the church. If such contrary-to-fact assertions ever lent support to the church's authority, it no longer does so.

On this point, the first prayer for forgiveness at the Day of Pardon led by the late Pope John Paul II on the first Sunday of Lent in the year 2000 should be our standard. It asks God's pardon for "sins committed in the service of the Truth." These include:

- sins of intolerance and violence against dissidents,
- wars of religion,
- acts of violence and oppression during the Crusades, and
- methods of coercion employed by the Inquisition.[8]

That is a pretty complete list, what we used to call an "integral confession" of sins. But the whole Catholic world still needs to appropriate our need for pardon, and likewise we need to repudiate our collective self-deception in portraying religious freedom as the constant teaching of the church.

Styles of Peacemaking

Alan also rightly calls attention to the on-the-ground peacemaking that Mennonites have practiced in recent decades. We must remember, however, that even among Mennonites, active nonviolence and peacemaking in its various forms are late twentieth-century developments, following the historic peace churches' efforts after two world wars to throw off the legacy of non-resistant pacifism.[9] There is also, as Ronald Musto has shown, a long history of a multifarious Catholic peacemaking in the pre-Reformation church; and even in the modern period of the nation-state. Even when peacemaking and especially pacifism were eclipsed in Catholicism, there have been witnesses like Bartolomeo de las Casas, Dorothy Day, Gordon Zahn, and the recently beatified Franz Jaegerstatter.[10] In Catholic practice, moreover, the axiom of Paul VI, "If you want peace, work for justice," has shaped postconciliar

[8] For texts from the Day of Pardon, see "Service of Pardon," *Origins* 29, no. 40 (2000): 645, 667–68.

[9] See Donald F. Durnbaugh and Charles W. Brockwell, Jr., "The Historic Peace Churches: From Sectarian Origins to Ecumenical Witness," in *The Church's Peace Witness*, ed. Marvin E. Miller and Barbara Nelson Gingerich (Grand Rapids: Eerdmans Publishing Company, 1994), 182–95.

[10] On peacemaking in the Catholic Church, see Ronald Musto, *The Catholic Peace Tradition* (Maryknoll: Orbis Books, 1986). An extraordinary scholarly achievement,

Catholic peace work and still holds in significant ways.[11] The relation of justice to peace, I believe, stands as one of the principal areas in need of clarification as we build a common peace witness.

I would assert that no single model for peacemaking exists. Even in its recent Mennonite history, as John Paul Lederach and Cynthia Sampson have shown, there have been a variety of approaches to building peace, and they need not be restricted to on-the-ground approaches, though the grassroots efforts are often key.[12] The world is not made up solely of small, intentional communities. If that were true, the Catholic Peacebuilding Network, with its cooperation between Catholics and Mennonites, would never have gotten off the ground. So, it is appropriate for the church to work for peace in a variety of ways in a multiplicity of social settings, from mediation by lay movements like Sant'Egidio and Focolare, to human rights advocacy by diocesan justice and peace commissions, to social teaching and lobbying by episcopal conferences and, yes, to Vatican diplomacy.[13] A large well-established religious institution is bound to have complex, differentiated ways of working for peace. While our traditional ecclesiologies as well as the sociology of our churches may take us in somewhat different directions, practical collaboration in peacemaking has already led to a mutual appreciation of the historic gifts of our traditions in peacemaking at various levels of society.

Finally, one related issue needing clarification as we undertake a common witness to peace is our respective views of society. The view of the world as a complex society does not belong to Catholics alone. John Howard Yoder himself rejected "the little Christendom" view of Mennonite existence put forth by Harold S. Bender as the "Anabaptist Vision." More recently, a range

---

Musto's book is, in my opinion, one of the unheralded, great works of Catholic social history in the twentieth century.

[11] Paul VI, *Populorum Progressio* (On the Development of Peoples), in *Catholic Social Thought: The Documentary Tradition*, ed. David J. O'Brien and Thomas A. Shannon (Maryknoll: Orbis Books, 1992), esp. nos. 76–80. Also, see Allan Figueroa Deck, SJ, "Commentary on *Populorum progressio* (On the Development of Peoples)," in *Modern Catholic Social Teaching: Commentaries and Interpretations*, ed. Kenneth R. Himes, OFM, et al. (Georgetown: Georgetown University Press, 2004), 292–314.

[12] See *From the Ground Up: Mennonite Contributions to International Peacemaking*, ed. Cynthia Sampson and John Paul Lederach (New York: Oxford University Press, 2000) for personal accounts of a rich variety of Mennonite efforts at peacemaking.

[13] See David Smock, "Catholic Contributions to International Peace," (special report, United States Institute of Peace, April 9, 2001). The first part, pp. 3–8, is a summary of my own presentation, "Catholic Peacemaking: *Pacem in terris* to *Centesimus annus*."

of Mennonite theologians concerned with the encounter with the secular world have developed a number of theological approaches to the church's engagement with the world.[14] As together we take up the practice of peace, I hope we will resist the temptation to canonize just one type or one family of peacemaking activities based on a preferred social unit and make use of all the gifts God has given us for the common good, or, as Mennonites would say, "for the peace of the city."

[14] Harold S. Bender's "The Anabaptist Vision" was first published in *Church History* 13 (March 1944), 3–24. Though critical of Bender's thesis, John Howard Yoder remained skeptical of the ability of Christians to engage positively with the secular world. See, e.g., *For the Nations: Essays Public and Evangelical* (Grand Rapids: Eerdmans Publishing Company, 1997) and his "How H. Richard Niebuhur Reasoned," in *Authentic Transformation: A New Vision of Christ and Culture*, Glen H. Stassen, D. M. Yeager and John Howard Yoder (Nashville: Abingdon Press, 1996), 31–90.

For other Mennonite, world-engaging approaches to witnessing in the world, see Thomas N. Finger, *Christian Theology: An Eschatological Approach*, vol. 2 (Scottdale: Herald Press, 1989), 271–96; Ted Grimsrud, "Anabaptist Faith and American Democracy," *Mennonite Quarterly Review* 78, no. 3 (July 2004): 341–62, and Duane K. Friesen, *Artists, Citizens, Philosophers: Seeking the Peace of the City: An Anabaptist Theology of Culture* (Scottdale: Herald Press, 2000).

On the reciprocal challenges Catholics and Mennonites face in relationship to the world, see Drew Christiansen, SJ, "The Wider Horizon," in *Just Policing, Not War: An Alternative Response to World Violence*, ed. Gerald W. Schlabach (Collegeville: Liturgical Press, 2007), 191–214.

PART 2

Considering History Together

Our common re-reading of the history of the church will hopefully contribute to the development of a common interpretation of the past. . . . Christians can take responsibility for the past. They can name the errors in their history, repent of them, and work to correct them. Mennonite theologian John Howard Yoder has written: "It is a specific element in the Christian message that there is a remedy for a bad record. If the element of repentance is not acted out in interfaith contact, we are not sharing the whole gospel witness." . . . Such acts of repentance contribute to the purification of memory, which was one of the goals enunciated by Pope John Paul II during the Great Jubilee of the Year 2000. The purification of memory aims at liberating our personal and communal consciences from all forms of resentment and violence that are the legacy of past faults.

Called Together to Be Peacemakers, paragraphs 27–28

When conflict occurs within an institution and separation ensues, discourse easily takes on the nature of self-justification. As Mennonites and Catholics begin discussion after centuries of separate institutional existence, we need to be aware that we have developed significant aspects of our self-understandings and theologies in contexts where we have often tried to prove that we are right and they are wrong. We need tools of historical research that help us to see both what we have in common as well as to responsibly address the differences that separate us. Mennonites now have almost five centuries of accumulated history to deal with, along with a growing experience of integration into the established society. Catholics, on the other hand, increasingly find themselves in situations of disestablishment where they are faced with the same questions as Mennonites were facing as a minority church in an earlier era. These facts could help both traditions to be more open to the concerns of the other, and to look more carefully at the fifteen centuries of commonly shared history as well as the different paths each has taken since the sixteenth century.

Called Together to Be Peacemakers, paragraph 49

Chapter 5

Rightly Remembering
as Re-Membering

John D. Roth

In the spring of 1525 the Swiss reformer Ulrich Zwingli angrily denounced a group of former students who were pushing the Reformation in Zurich in a radical direction. The Anabaptists might appear to be earnest reformers, he fulminated, but the real goal of their program was merely a return to "a new monasticism."[1] In the centuries since the Reformation, heirs of the Anabaptists (groups like the Mennonites, Hutterites, and Amish) have almost always identified themselves more closely with the Protestant tradition than with the spirituality and practices of late medieval Catholicism. Yet Zwingli's identification of the Anabaptists with monasticism—an association noted negatively by nearly all of the Reformers—was not completely misplaced. As a growing number of historians have amply demonstrated, Anabaptist piety drew heavily on currents of late medieval spirituality; and the socially-embodied practices that emerged out of that piety—a disciplined, voluntary community characterized by mutual aid, a commitment to nonviolence, and a pattern of life visibly different from the society around them—did indeed bear striking parallels to medieval monasticism.[2] If we recall that the first generation of Anabaptists were all nurtured in the rituals and doctrine and

---

[1] *The Sources of Swiss Anabaptism: The Grebel Letters and Related Documents*, ed. Leland Harder (Scottdale, PA: Herald Press, 1985), 354. Only shortly thereafter, Wolfgang Capito repeated the charges (ibid., 82).

[2] Among the first to note this connection were Arnold Snyder, *The Life and Teaching of Michael Sattler* (Scottdale, PA: Herald Press, 1984) and Dennis D. Martin, "Catholic Spirituality and Anabaptist and Mennonite Discipleship," *Mennonite Quarterly Review* 62 (January 1988): 5–25. For a helpful overview of the specific connections between Anabaptism and monasticism see Abraham Friesen, "Anabaptism and Monasticism: A Study in Parallel Developments of Historical Patterns," *Journal of Mennonite Studies* 6 (1988): 174–97.

worldview of late medieval Catholicism, and that they continued to describe their faith in the language of the Apostles' Creed, the practices of the early church, and a theological vocabulary deeply formed by Catholic tradition, then it is correct to say that we share a "common Christian history."

The recovered memory of those spiritual debts is now bearing fruit among Mennonites in a remarkable variety of ways: a keen interest in the disciplines of prayer, a new openness to liturgical forms of worship, the conversations and friendships fostered by the Bridgefolk gatherings, and, now, the published report of the International Dialogue between the Catholic Church and the Mennonite World Conference. At the same time, however, the very fact that these memories needed to be recovered at all is a reminder that "remembering history together" is always a *human* undertaking—one vulnerable to the limitations of human finitude and sin.

Although we sometimes frame this problem as one of historical amnesia, the deeper challenge is not so much forgetfulness, as it is a distorted, incomplete or selective memory—a dis-membering—that is often pressed into the service of legitimating our distinct traditions. Few moments in the history of the Christian church better illustrate the temptation to "dis-membering" than the opening decades of the sixteenth century. The Reformers grounded their emerging understanding of the church not only in new theological arguments but also in a new reading of church history—one mapped to claims about the continuity of the biblically-based doctrine of justification over Catholic claims of continuity in canon law, tradition, or the institutional authority of the magisterium. Defenders of the church responded in kind by narrating the Reformers' theological arguments as little more than a recrudescence of earlier heresies that had long since been refuted.[3]

Not surprisingly, encounters between Catholics and radical reformers of the sixteenth century further reinforced these habits of dis-membering.[4] For the Catholics, it began with something as basic as a name. In this setting, it is worth recalling that participants in the radical reform movement that began

---

[3] See, for example, Johannes Eck's *Enchiridion locorum communium adversus Lutherum*, which ran through 46 editions between 1525 and 1576, or his *Confutatio pontificia*, which listed 404 heresies embedded within the Lutheran Augsburg Confession of 1530. The text is reprinted in: *The Augsburg Confession, A Collection of Sources*, ed. J. M. Reu (Ft. Wayne, IN: Concordia Theological Seminary Press), 349–83.

[4] The *Catholic Encyclopedia* of 1917 defines Anabaptism as "A violent and extremely radical body of ecclesiastico-civil reformers which first made its appearance in 1521 at Zwickau . . . and still exists in milder forms."

in Zurich in the early 1520s never regarded themselves as "Anabaptists" (or re-baptizers). They generally identified themselves simply as "brethren," or by the name of local leaders. Although they shared the conviction that a believer's baptism, rather than an infant's baptism, marked the entrance of the new Christian into the church, they would have never reduced their theological identity to this solitary concern. Moreover, they insisted that the term "Anabaptist" was simply empirically wrong. If, as they taught, the water sprinkled on a baby soon after the moment of birth was merely water, then they were emphatically not "re-baptizing" but baptizing correctly for the first time. The act of remembering that introduced the term "Anabaptist" was a conscious move on the part of ecclesial and secular authorities to associate the reformers with the ancient Donatist and Manichean heresies whose views on baptism, according to canon law, were worthy of capital punishment.[5]

The radical reformers, for their part, did not hesitate to denounce the church of Rome in equally imprecise and intemperate language: Thielman van Braght, for example, could make an almost casual reference to the "Romish priests . . . and their self-invented idolatry;" and Menno Simons warned of a coming judgment for the "abominations" of the papal system that he summarized as "pride and pomp, excess, gluttony, tyranny, bloodthirstiness, adultery, and fornication," the likes of which "no heart can conceive, no tongue express, no pen describe."[6] The theological divide that eventually opened between radical reformers and the Catholic Church—nurtured by memories of persecution and faithful endurance in the face of suffering— made it possible for generations of Mennonite historians to virtually erase the Catholic Church from their collective memory, writing Anabaptist history by jumping straight from Constantine to the sixteenth century, as if the intervening thousand years of church history never happened. It comes

---

[5] That twentieth-century Mennonite historians and theologians in North America rehabilitated the term "Anabaptist" as a heroic badge of identity and even pride—an anchor against the blandishments of individualistic, nationalistic Protestantism to which Mennonites had become increasingly enamored—is yet another instance of the powerful role of memory in shaping contemporary identity. For the quintessential expression of this rehabilitation, see Harold S. Bender, *The Anabaptist Vision* (Scottdale, PA: Herald Press, 1944).

[6] *The Bloody Theater or Martyrs Mirror of the Defenseless Christians*, ed. Thieleman J. van Braght (Amsterdam, 1660; Scottdale, PA: Herald Press, 1950), 740; Menno Simons, *The Complete Works of Menno Simons*, ed. John C. Wenger (Scottdale, PA: Herald Press, 1956), 114.

as no great surprise, then, that the *Mennonite Encyclopedia* article on "Catholicism and Anabaptism" concludes its overview of relations between the two groups with the laconic summary: "There are unbridgeable differences between Catholicism and Anabaptism."[7] It is against this background that members of the International Dialogue embarked on the daunting challenge of "reconsidering history together."

In this brief essay I will offer a few critical reflections on that effort, focusing especially on the concept of a "purification of memories" and the historical summaries of the "Constantinian Era" and the "rupture" between Catholics and Anabaptists in the sixteenth century. On a more constructive note, I will close with a description of a later chapter of church history that both traditions share, and suggest that a fruitful agenda for ecumenical conversations in the future would explore how resources in the Catholic tradition might help Mennonites to respond more faithfully to the challenges that these developments pose.

Even though much of what follows may sound critical of *Called Together to Be Peacemakers*, I am keenly aware of the historical significance of this moment. My intention is not to merely rehearse or reinstate our points of differences, but to recognize—I hope in a spirit of charity—that the path to genuine reconciliation must often pass through difficult terrain.

Purification of Memories

Although the concluding section of the report is titled "Toward a *Healing* of Memories" (emphasis added) the primary rubric for historical reflection in the document is something called a "*purification* of memories" (emphasis added). The language of "purification of memories" seems to have emerged in Catholic circles in the flurry of theological conversations surrounding the Jubilee celebrations of 2000, specifically in the context of Pope John Paul II's various statements of penitence on behalf of the church for its historical wrongdoings. There is a richness in this phrase whose meaning is developed with great nuance and sensitivity in the report of the International Theological Commission on "Memory and Reconciliation."[8]

---

[7] Cornelius J. Dyck, ed., *The Mennonite Encyclopedia: A Comprehensive Reference Work on the Anabaptist-Mennonite Movement*, vol. 5 (Scottdale, PA: Herald Press, 1990), s.v. "Catholicism and Anabaptism."

[8] Cf. the Bull of Indiction of the Great Jubilee of the Year 2000, *Incarnationis Mysterium* (Nov. 29, 1998), and a subsequent theological memorandum issued by an Interna-

Still, many Mennonite readers are likely to find the phrase "purification of memories" somewhat alien. The ritual images associated with the word "purification" helpfully remind us that the church is the primary context for our collective remembering; but those same associations may suggest to Mennonite ears that this "purification" is primarily the vocationally task of the high priests of history—something that is performed on behalf of the people and is then completed. Once we purify our respective texts of their errors, in a spirit of proper penitence, the logic goes, we can then get on with life as usual.[9]

For others, however, negative associations with the phrase, "purification of memory," are likely to be more visceral: sixteenth-century authorities, drawing on rhetorical traditions stretching back for nearly a millennium, frequently used the language of "purification" as an argument against the toleration of so-called heretics in their midst. Eliminating these contaminants served to "purify" not only the body politic but also the Body of Christ. When authorities explicitly joined "purification" to "memory"—by identifying the radical reformers as "Anabaptists" and, hence, heretics subject to the death penalty—the result was a sort of "purification of memories" that none of us wants to repeat.

The phrase "right remembering" suggests a slightly different way of framing our task in language that may be more readily understood by Mennonite lay people. In the context of Christian ecumenism, "right remembering" implies at least three things: first, a mutual commitment to honesty and accuracy in recounting the historical details as accurately as possible, and in such a way that each of us could recognize ourselves in the story that emerges.

Second, "right remembering" includes a theological commitment to allow our stories to be judged by the larger drama of God's movement in history, always alert to the ways in which God's gift of grace that we rightfully celebrate within our traditions cannot be separated from judgment. Thus, memory is always the occasion for confession as well as celebration.

Finally, "right remembering" should transform us. If nothing changes in our attitudes, convictions, or practices as a result of our encounter with each other's version of the past—if ecumenical dialogue is little more than

---

tional Theological Commission called "Memory and Reconciliation: The Church and the Faults of the Past," Congregation for the Doctrine of the Faith (Dec. 1999).

[9] A paragraph explicating the phrase (par. 198 of *Called Together to be Peacemakers*), for example, calls on both groups to seek forgiveness from God and each other in a "penitential spirit," but then quickly assures readers that in so doing "they do not modify their convictions about the Christian faith."

church theologians hammering out the contractual language of doctrine so as to reach some minimal linguistic agreement—then we probably have not remembered "rightly." "Right remembering" should make all of us better Christians, drawing us into closer communion with God and with each other.

I suspect that much of what I have suggested here, albeit in a very sketchy fashion, is not at odds with the "purification of memories." But from a Mennonite perspective it may be worth asking whether other ways of framing our task might be more helpful.

"Considering History Together"

Of the four distinct historical eras addressed in the document, I found myself in near complete agreement with the first section ("A Profile of the Religious Situation in Western Europe on the Eve of the Reformation") and the last section ("Toward a Shared Understanding of the Middle Ages"). These are complex themes, of course, encompassing an enormous body of literature, which the authors have summarized in a succinct and balanced fashion.

Most of my reservations focus on the middle two sections—"The Rupture Between Catholics and Anabaptists" and "The Constantinian Era." It probably would be unhelpful to list all of the questions of emphasis or interpretation that surfaced in these sections, but I will note three specific points, and then address a larger theme that, from my perspective as a Mennonite historian, merits closer attention.

Baptism

Given the significance of baptism in the rupture of the sixteenth century, it is odd that the topic receives relatively little attention as a matter of historical—rather than merely theological—debate. Where the topic arises in the historical context, the text seems to beg for a more careful treatment. According to paragraph 62, for example, Catholic arguments in defense of pedobaptism are grounded in specific patristic texts and "long-held tradition . . . going back to the first centuries of Christianity." Mennonites, by contrast, "*consider* the introduction of the practice of infant baptism as a later development."[10] The implication of such wording is that Catholics are arguing from real historical sources and out of a deep tradition, whereas Mennonites merely hold an opinion. This is not the place to rehearse the

---

[10] *Called Together*, emphasis added.

well-known twentieth-century debate between Joachim Jeremias and Kurt Aland, or to review the complex history of the practice of baptism in the early church.[11] But I find it unfortunate that the joint reading of history did not engage this foundational historical question in a more substantive way.[12]

It is equally striking that the document makes almost no mention of the profound *political* significance of pedobaptism in the sixteenth century.[13] It is impossible to understand the vehemence of the sixteenth-century debates— or the frequent association of believers' baptism with criminal charges of treason or sedition—without an understanding of the stake that temporal authorities had in the baptism of infants. Within the logic of Christendom, baptism marked the entrance of the child into feudal society. Baptism conferred a legal, political, and economic identity seemingly inseparable from its sacramental significance. A shared rereading of history, therefore, will need to be more attentive to the historical and political—as well as theological—dimensions of baptism in the Christian tradition.

Anabaptist Divisiveness and the Question of Church Unity

A second question relates to the issue of fragmentation within the Anabaptist movement and the larger theme of ecclesial unity. At several points, the document highlights "the diverse and sometimes conflicting currents within the Anabaptist movement."[14] Although it is a fact that the Anabaptist

[11] Everett Ferguson, "Inscriptions and the Origin of Infant Baptism," *Journal of Theological Studies* 30, no. 1 (1979): 37–46. Ferguson demonstrates that among the earliest references to child baptisms are those of children a considerable time after their births but just prior to their deaths—a kind of "child clinical baptism." See also David F. Wright, "Augustine and the Transformation of Baptism," in Alan Kreider, ed. *The Origins of Christendom in the West* (New York: T & T Clark, 2001), 287–310.

[12] For another perspective, for example, formulated by Christians outside of Mennonite circles, see the Lima Report on Baptism, Eucharist, and Ministry: "While the possibility that infant baptism was practiced in the apostolic age cannot be excluded, baptism upon personal profession of faith is the most clearly attested pattern in the New Testament documents." Faith and Order Paper, no. 111 (Geneva, 1982), p. 4, par. 11. According to church historian David Wright, "The Jeremias-Aland debate issued in no consensus, although among New Testament scholars the view is increasingly widespread that infant baptism was not practiced in the New Testament churches." David F. Wright, "The Origins of Infant Baptism—Child Believers' Baptism?" *Scottish Journal of Theology* 40 (1987): 1–23, here p. 3.

[13] Cf. par. 40 of *Called Together.*

[14] *Called Together.* Paragraphs 38 and 50 both make this point. In paragraph 50, the diversity within the Radical Reformation serves the purpose of underscoring the "complicated

movement did not emerge fully formed, within a generation re-baptizing groups had coalesced into three closely-related streams—the Swiss Brethren, the Mennonites, and the Hutterites—who recognized their shared history and regarded themselves as part of a coherent tradition even while maintaining distinctive identities. I make this point not to deny the confusion of the first decade of the movement; clearly, the radical reformers were not of one mind in the 1520s. But a note of caution is merited here, simply because an emphasis on the diversity of Anabaptist groups has a deep historical pedigree that has rarely had a purely descriptive intent. From the very beginning, critics of the Anabaptists highlighted the fragmentation of the movement, often to exaggerated extremes, in order to make the theological point that any rupture with the universal church was bound to replicate itself *ad infinitum*. Thus, Johannes Gast listed seven Anabaptist groups in 1544, but by 1573, Georg Eder claimed to identify thirty-eight different sects, a listing that the Catholic priest Christoph Erhard expanded to forty-three in his anti-Anabaptist polemic of 1589.

Equally significant are several related questions that the document does not seem to problematize. First, for example, to what degree did the execution of the movement's most gifted leaders within its first five years exacerbate the diversity among Anabaptists, and what role did persecution play in disrupting communication? Second, was the variety found within the Anabaptist movement of a fundamentally different character than the differences in emphasis and practice that separated a lay Catholic in Spain from the Templars of northern Europe, the Benedictines in Normandy, the Brethren of the Common Life in the Netherlands, or the Jesuits in Vienna? Third, and even more to the point, does the implicit critique of Anabaptist

---

situation of the sixteenth century rupture within Christianity," an observation immediately followed by the conclusion: "The oppression and persecution of Anabaptists and Mennonites need to be perceived and evaluated within the framework of a society that resorted to violent 'solutions' rather than to dialogue." True enough, but what conclusions are readers to make from this observation: if the Anabaptist movement had been less "diverse" would Catholic authorities have been more inclined to show leniency? The same question emerges in statements like the following: "They [Catholics] saw Anabaptists as restoring old heresies that had been condemned long ago. All this was complicated by the fact that during the sixteenth century, Catholic theologians were writing against people whom the state, at the request of both Catholic and Protestant princes, had already condemned to death at the Diet of Speyer, and who therefore lived outside the protection of the law" (par. 42). Again, the statement is factually correct. But what, exactly, is implied by this description of the historical context: that because the state had condemned a class of people to live outside the protection of the law, the theological judgments of Catholic theologians against them are somehow justified?

diversity really imply a question-begging normative assumption about ecclesial structures—specifically, a sacerdotal hierarchy, anchored in the magisterial office and the claims of the pope to speak as the Vicar of Christ on behalf of all true Christians? Alternately, might the local, embodied, particularity of Mennonite ecclesiology, even amidst its apparent diversity, represent a different, yet theologically coherent, way of thinking about the Body of Christ ("where two or three are gathered in my name")? In my judgment, "right remembering" will require us to address more explicitly our different ecclesiological assumptions and how those differences might also shape our theological worldviews and our interpretations of the past.

The Use of Violence in Religious Matters: What Is the Price of Unity?

Both of these themes—baptism and ecclesiology—are tributaries that feed into another, even more central, cluster of questions: namely, the way the historical sections of *Called Together to Be Peacemakers* treat the difficult question of coercion and violence, particularly in relation to religious beliefs. Here again, my concerns can only be suggestive, and will almost certainly lack the appropriate nuance. So I look forward to continuing dialogue.

One reason Mennonites have forgotten their deep debts to the Catholic piety of the late Middle Ages is that their forbearers experienced the church in the sixteenth century less as a spiritual parent than as a sovereign judge. Clearly, the issues surrounding the Catholic Church's response to Anabaptism are complex, but for the moment I would call attention to one particular historical instance in order to illustrate the larger concern that I have with this section on history. On April 23, 1529, the Holy Roman Emperor—drawing explicitly on the counsel of canon lawyers and with the overwhelming affirmation of the Catholic estates—issued an edict that required every political authority in the Holy Roman Empire to execute "without an ecclesiastical trial" anyone in their jurisdiction who had undergone baptism as an adult, and to do so on the charges of *heresy*. Moreover, the Edict of Speyer demanded that the same penalty—execution without trial—apply to all parents who refused to allow their newborn child to be baptized, and to all those who gave material support to the Anabaptists, even if they should later recant.[15]

[15] "One vorgend der geistlichen richter inquisicion," Rainer Wohlfiel and Hans-Jürgen Goertz, *Gewissensfreiheit als Bedingung der Neuzeit: Fragen an die Speyerer Protestation von 1529* (Göttingen: Vandenhoeck & Ruprecht, 1980). Though stark in the clarity of their conditions, the terms of the Edict of Speyer simply summarized a series of territorial

As a social historian by training, I readily acknowledge the many contextual considerations behind this edict: anxiety about the advance of the Turks, a genuine concern for social and political order, the righteous zeal of a Christian prince eager to maintain the unity of the church, a fear that heretical ideas would infect innocent souls, and, not least, a well-established legal tradition of executing heretics. But unlike the Protestant Reformers who frequently took great pains to insist that the Anabaptists should be killed for the *political* crimes of sedition or treason, Catholic authorities almost never made such a distinction—certainly not in the Edict of Speyer.[16] Anabaptists were to be killed for bad faith, as heretics and as blasphemers against God. The emperor framed the edict in his role as "protector of our holy Christian faith;" the law was to be promulgated "through the pulpit by means of learned, Christian preachers." It long preceded the debacle at the Münster in 1535, and I know of no evidence—at least in the German-speaking territories—of a Catholic theologian in the sixteenth century raising a voice of protest against the law, although there are numerous examples of princes and imperial cities that refused to carry out the order.[17]

The language of "Considering History Together" suggests that the Constantinian alignment of the church with the state was a kind of historical accident—certainly not constitutive to the church's identity. Paragraph 54, for example, notes a historical shift in the Catholic tradition moving from a "suppressed church" to a "tolerated church" to a "triumphant church."

---

mandates against the Anabaptists that had been in force since 1526, now in systematic form and applicable to all of the territories within the Holy Roman Empire. The edict defended these terms by appealing explicitly to the Justinian Code, and the established practice of exercising the death penalty against the Manicheans and the Donatists who had also been accused of the crime of rebaptism. The mandate of 1529 was renewed in 1544 and 1551. At one point, the Catholic Elector of the Palatinate, on the basis of a memorandum of the Kanzler Florenz von Venningen, did refuse to execute an Anabaptist in Alzey without an ecclesiastical inquisition, arguing that the Anabaptist was guilty of a spiritual offense rather than a temporal or ecclesiastical. The inquisitional court, however, ended up sentencing him to death.

[16] *Schriften von Evangelischer Seite gegen die Täufer*, ed. Robert Stupperich (Münster: Aschendorffsche Verlagsbuchhandlung, 1983).

[17] The church as the mediator of God's grace has a moral obligation to denounce sin, to exercise discipline, to spare the weak from infection of heresy, and to help the state in the preservation of civic order. Johann Fabri, "Etliche Sermone wider die gottlosen Wiedertäufer," (2:671–700) and Gregor Brietkopf, "Dass die Wiedertaufe irrig sei," in *Flugschriften gegen die Reformation (1525–1530)*, ed. Adolf Laube (Berlin: Akademie Verlag, 2000), 2:701–16.

It then goes on to acknowledge "that the power of the state was used to enforce Christian doctrines," that "to some extent Christians even accepted the use of violence . . . to enforce orthodoxy," and that "this arrangement led in some cases to forced conversion of large numbers of people, to coercion in matters of faith, and to the application of the death penalty against 'heretics.'" Most strikingly, the document "repudiates those aspects of the Constantinian era that were departures from some characteristic Christian practices and deviations from the Gospel ethic." Mennonites will certainly affirm this repudiation. We do not take such statements for granted!

Yet it nonetheless remains unclear what larger conclusions the reader is to draw from this 1400 year marriage of church and state, especially when only a few paragraphs later the document quotes this much more ambivalent concession from the *Declaration on Religious Freedom*: "there has *at times appeared* a *way of acting* that was hardly in accord with the spirit of the Gospel"—suggesting that the problem was more one of *perception* than actual fact—which is then followed by the astonishing assertion that "the doctrine of the Church that no one is to be coerced into faith has always stood firm."[18]

From the perspective of the sixteenth-century Anabaptists and most Mennonite historians of the period, the experience of church-supported violence was not a matter of a few overzealous clerics or a momentary deviation in practice from an otherwise clearly-stated doctrinal conviction. Instead, the readiness of the church to defend its interests with coercive violence—to turn the sword of the empire against those whom it had identified as heretics—appears to be a deep and persistent historical motif, symbolized by the emergence of a "triumphant church" in the centuries following Constantine and valorized in the writings of a long list of august fathers of Catholic doctrine.[19]

I raise these concerns fully aware of the steadfast testimony to the gospel of peace that has been kept alive in some parts of the Catholic Church throughout its long and rich tradition. And I am deeply grateful for the significant, often courageous, initiatives of the contemporary church in support of peace and reconciliation efforts around the world. But in my judgment the document does not sufficiently engage the larger historical

[18] *Called Together*, par. 61. Emphasis added.
[19] In "The Revelation of the Babylonian Whore," a polemical narration of church history probably penned by the civil engineer and lay theologian Pilgram Marpeck, a willingness to use lethal violence to defend the Body of Christ against its enemies marked the crucial distinction between the true church and its evil simulacrum.

issues related to coercion and conscience that seem to be inherent to the very logic of "Christendom."

Competing Liturgies and the Challenge of Christian Formation

In a more constructive vein, I wish to conclude with a few thoughts on how "right remembering" in the context of the Mennonite-Catholic dialogue might help Mennonites be more faithful Christians in the future. The chronological focus of "Considering History Together" ends in the sixteenth century. Yet our shared historical experience in the intervening centuries since also bears attention in our conversations together. And it is to that experience that I now briefly turn.

In his landmark book, *Theopolitical Imagination*, Catholic theologian William Cavanaugh traces the rise of the modern nation state and the emergence of global capitalism within the framework of "liturgical practices."[20] On the surface, the religious language of liturgy might sound completely foreign to the disciplines of political science and economics. Yet, as Cavanaugh compellingly argues, neither the modern state nor the logic of consumer capitalism are morally neutral structures. Both are grounded in deep narratives about human nature and human destiny, both offer an "alternative soteriology to that of the church," and both are firmly rooted in ritual practices that mimic those of the *ekklesia*.

No story is more central to the mythology of the modern state than its claim to have rescued society from the chaos of religious conflict emerging out of the sixteenth century—a fiction, Cavanaugh argues, that masks the way in which the so-called "wars of religion" were themselves generated by the formation of nation-states.[21] But the myth of the state as the neutral adjudicator saving civil society from religious passions has endured. And the result has been a sharp separation of the sacred and secular that has consigned "religion" to the private world of the individual and situated the church as merely one more interest group within civil society.

Cavanaugh's political narrative finds an equally insightful economic counterpart in the work of Catholic political scientist Michael Budde. In

---

[20] William Cavanaugh, *Theopolitical Imagination: Discovering Liturgy as a Political Act in an Age of Global Consumerism* (New York: T & T Clark, 2002).

[21] Moreover, as the last four centuries have made abundantly clear, the state has turned out to be a false soteriology, breeding more violence than ever before as a "habitual discipline for binding us one to another" (ibid., 46).

The (Magic) Kingdom of God, Budde moves beyond the standard critiques of globalization to trace the way in which modern economies in the West can be sustained only by a steady increase in consumption—consumer desires that must somehow be steadily renewed and expanded. Thus, the bellwether of the American economy today is no longer General Motors, but instead the Disney Group and a host of other "culture industries" that wield enormous influence over what we value and how we spend our time and our money. Because these enormous telecommunication, media, and marketing conglomerates focus so resolutely on human desire, Budde argues, and because they are so pervasive in their influence, they pose a direct challenge to Christian formation—all the more so when the church itself increasingly imitates the marketing techniques and consumer-oriented assumptions of the culture industries. The only solution, Budde concludes, is a "radically reformed and revitalized vision of the church and its role in Jesus' mission," that more seriously takes up the challenge of Christian catechesis.[22]

Although Cavanaugh and Budde are writing out of a Catholic context, I must confess that their analysis—greatly abbreviated here—describes the condition of Mennonites in North America with disturbing accuracy. We are a rapidly acculturating church that is deeply confused about the nature of conversion and Christian formation.[23] For many of us, the political freedoms of modern democracy and the benefits of carrying a US passport count for more than our allegiance to the Body of Christ. We are overwhelmed by the economic tsunami of consumerism, shaped more deeply by the steady barrage of media appeals than by the vows we made at our baptisms. Despite a great deal of theological language to the contrary, the actual practices in our congregations are moving increasingly in the direction of individualistic, privatized, and experiential forms of faith. Far too often our congregations reflect the social and economic divisions of the culture around us; our commitment to service is increasingly disconnected from the worship of God; and our public witness to the world has been deeply shaped by the tired political categories of the liberal left and the conservative right.

If these concerns are real—and a recent study of the Mennonite Church USA suggests that they are—what sorts of insights might the Catholic tradition have to offer that would help Mennonites resist the blandishments

---

[22] Budde, *The (Magic) Kingdom of God: Christianity and Global Culture Industries* (Boulder, CO: Westview Press, 1997), 96.

[23] Conrad Kanagy, *Signposts for the Journey* (Scottdale, PA: Herald Press, 2007).

of false gods and to "remember rightly" our deeper identity as members of the Body of Christ? I am sure there are many such resources, some of them celebrated explicitly, no doubt, in the ongoing conversations that Bridgefolk has sponsored.

For the moment I want to highlight two themes that have stirred my imagination during the past year as I have tried to sense the movement of God in our midst. The first is a renewal of Mennonite worship rooted more centrally in the celebration of the Lord's Supper. Traditionally, Mennonites have had a fairly thin theology of worship and are somewhat unreflective in their approach to the sacraments (what we often call "ordinances") in our liturgical life. As a consequence, a growing segment of the "peace and justice" oriented activists in our circles sees little organic connection between their public actions and congregational life and some have jettisoned worship altogether. At the same time, many local Mennonite congregations, sensing a deficit in their worship life, are borrowing new worship practices willy-nilly from all across the Christian spectrum—the good, the bad, and all too frequently, the ugly.

I am very aware of the danger of instrumentalizing Christian liturgy. Yet I am increasingly convinced that if Mennonites are going to resist the false soteriologies of the state and the marketplace, it will start with a deeper understanding of liturgical worship in general, and of the Lord's Supper in particular. "Right remembering" at the Lord's Supper means that the gathered church reorients itself in time and space, and in so doing, it renarrates the world of the nation and economy from the deeper and truer story of Christ's life, death, resurrection, and ascension.[24] In the Lord's Supper we participate once again in the cruciform nature of Christ's body, and, in so doing, we are caught up in the resurrection as well—the real presence of Christ—by our participation in the living body of Christ. Through God's grace, we are truly re-membered as participants with God in the task of making creation whole—of restoring broken relationships and rightly "re-membering" a church that is so often dis-membered. The celebration of communion is a *political* act because it calls forth a fundamentally different way of being in relationship with each other—as brothers and sisters who wash each other's

---

[24] There is, of course, a rich literature on the themes of "right remembering" and the Lord's Supper as an act of re-membering. I have especially appreciated the work of William Cavanaugh, *Torture and Eucharist* (Malden, MA: Blackwell Publishing, 1998), esp. 229–52 as well as Miroslav Volf, *The End of Memory: Remembering Rightly in a Violent World* (Grand Rapids, MI: William B. Eerdmans, 2006).

feet, rather than as citizens or consumers. A deeper attentiveness to worship is essential for the future health and well-being of the Mennonite Church; and I think that it can happen only if Mennonites are willing to be instructed out of the rich theological insights of the Catholic tradition, particularly in regards to the Eucharist.

At the same time, "right remembering" calls us to transformation not only in our worship but also in the daily practices of our life together and our witness to the world. We will not have remembered Christ's body and blood rightly—indeed, we eat and drink Christ's body "unto our own damnation" (1 Cor 11:34)—if our liturgical practices do not also transform the life and body of believers during the six-and-a-half days of the week when we are not gathered in formal worship.

In October of 2006, the Amish community at Nickel Mines, Pennsylvania, stunned the watching world, confounding, if only for a moment, even the culture industries and the national logic of the "war on terror." It was not merely the fact of their forgiveness in the face a horrific crime but also the sense that this response was so immediate, so reflexive, so concrete, so unequivocal. Of all the Anabaptist groups today, the Amish have been the most successful in forming Christians capable of resisting the liturgies of the nation-state and the assumptions of consumer capitalism. They are also the group that has maintained the greatest continuity with the monastic tradition. They embody the characteristics that Zwingli found so repugnant when he accused the Anabaptists of being a "new monasticism."

This suggests a second gift that Mennonites might receive from the Catholic tradition if we can remember history "rightly." For nearly 1500 years, Catholic monasteries have cultivated the practices of Christian formation. More than any other Christian body, they have consciously integrated worship and work, piety and practice, faith and discipleship. Today, as allegiance to the nation-state is the most powerful unifying force in our fear-ridden society, as the world is flattened by the global economy and the marketing interests of the culture industries, and as identity itself becomes increasingly abstract, portable, and diffuse, the concrete and disciplined practices of the monastic rule offer clues into Christian formation that Mennonites should take very seriously. Only if we nurture thick, local, relations of mutual dependence, accountability, and vulnerability—drawing heavily on the insights of monastic communities—will we be able to resist the idolatries of the nation-state and the marketplace.

As we continue to deepen our understandings of each other in the years ahead, I hope that we can engage in vigorous debate about our various perspectives on history, with a view toward a more empathetic and truthful version of our shared past. But I also hope that our conversations can help Mennonites to "rightly remember" who they are (and whose they are) through a fuller experience of corporate worship, anchored in the Lord's Supper. And I hope that "right remembering" will point us in the direction of a life-long catechesis in which the Spirit's presence elicited in the liturgy will be made manifest in concrete practices of Christian discipleship, so that our worship might draw us not only into deeper communion with God but also into "a common life worthy of the gospel" (Phil 1:27).[25]

[25] This translation is that of Stephen E. Fowl and appears throughout his commentary, *Philippians*, Two Horizons New Testament Commentary (Grand Rapids, MI: W.B. Eerdmans, 2005).

Chapter 6

Called Together to *Ressourcement*

John C. Cavadini

I begin this paper by offering my thanks to John Roth for his beautiful paper. In response, I would like to take my cue from the title of our session today, "Considering History Together," which itself comes from the title of the first major division of *Called Together to Be Peacemakers*. The introduction of this section of *Called Together*, as John has already reminded us, speaks of studying the history of the church together and calls us to a common rereading of the history of the church. Taking my cue from these texts, I would like to offer two things: first, a suggestion for a specific *kind* of consideration of history together; and second, an example or demonstration of it. Of course, since I have written this example or demonstration myself, it cannot actually be a demonstration of how to do it together—nonetheless it is an idea and an illustration of the idea. So, a suggestion and an illustration:

Suggestion: Joint *Ressourcement*

To begin with the suggestion, I want to take a further cue from paragraph 58 of *Called Together to be Peacemakers*, under the heading, "Areas of Future Study," in Section D on the Constantinian era (a section that John Roth and I both seem to have taken up). Up until this section, "Considering History Together," or rereading history together, seems mainly to have had the character of reconsidering *church history proper*, in the sense of the history of customs and institutions. As the document moves on from the Constantinian era to the Middle Ages, that emphasis continues, until we arrive at the second main division of the document, "Considering Theology Together." By contrast, this section focuses mainly on ecclesiology and sacramentology from a *systematic* rather than a historical point of view. In other words, the document moves fairly abruptly from history of the church, institutional history, to systematic theology. I believe the drafters of the document made the right decision in setting things up this way, in order to embrace, first of all, the purification of memories or the right remembering that can only be the fruit of re-viewing church history together—as John has just so persuasively reminded us—and offering, in the second place, a summary of our starting points in terms of theological convergences and divergences.

I would propose that a second step would be to look more closely together at the history of *theology*, in order to link more closely the historical concern of the first major division with the theological concern of the second major division. The document, of course, does not exclude the history of theology from consideration, especially from future consideration, but the sections that speak of this tend to represent a relatively minor key in the document as a whole, sounded mainly in connection with very specific issues. For example, at paragraph 143, we read that "it is necessary to study together the history of the origin and development of the theology and practice of baptism, the development of the doctrine of original sin, and other mat-ters." Paragraph 58 is also one of the passages of the document sounding this minor key, though for me in a particularly suggestive way. Paragraph 58, after all, brings up the *ressourcement* of theology in the Catholic Church:

> We can agree that through a reading together of the sources of the early church, we are discovering ways of overcoming the stereotypes that we have had of each other. The *ressourcement* [return to the sources] that the Catholic church engaged in when preparing for the Second Vatican Council enriched Catholicism, and a parallel movement is beginning in contemporary Anabaptism. With the use of early Christian sources, we can affirm new ways of understanding the question of continuity and of renewal in history.

I would add that with the use of early Christian sources, we can affirm new ways of understanding the question of "continuity and renewal" in theology, not just in history. Catholic theology did not merely intend the *ressourcement* that the document mentions to renew our sense of history, or even for that matter of the history of theology itself, but of theology as a whole— period. Would it not be fruitful—and here is my suggestion—to have Catholics and Mennonites reading texts together, from the history of theology, in order to engage in what we might call a joint *ressourcement*? These texts would not have to be limited to sources from the early church era. Nor would the texts have to be limited to those issues of obvious concern that are identified as "theological divergences," though such could be emphasized. Our memories, as sorely as they need purification or "righting," also need renewal and expansion, and our theological imagination is always in need of the infusion of vision proper to our discipline (that is, theology). This can come from texts that are not overtly related to the "theological divergences" that the document identifies, but that one side or the other treasures, or both.

To return to the sources treasured by each side or both sides can certainly generate renewal if the Second Vatican Council is any indication, since the Council was, in part, the fruit of the *nouvelle theologie* that came through *ressourcement*. For one thing, if we engage in theology proper, we can never simply return to the past or reread the texts of the past as though they are in any simple way purely in the past. Whether we acknowledge it or not, these texts are like theological genes that continue to find expression in the ways that we think in the present. Returning to the texts together is a little like widening the pool of genes that could very well find expression today. We ourselves, as we talk together, increase the possibilities for the expression of the genes in this widened pool. For we are rereading these texts now with some—perhaps many—common concerns. We may find that texts that had been divisive when read only from the perspective of the concerns that divide us may take on a new light when we re-discover them as resources we can hold in common for developing shared concerns, some of which surely transcend the concerns both of the Constantinian era and of the Reformation era itself. The divisive element or elements in the texts might then look different.

Also, there is nothing like reading texts in their literary and historical contexts in order to gain a better feel for theological positions that, when stated as part of a later systematic theology, may seem almost abstract. It is true, for example, that the Catholic Church regards the church as both the Body and the Spouse or Bride of Christ—to select one image that the document itself selects (Body) and one image it does not take up (Spouse). However, do we really know what these images meant when Origen, Cyprian, Augustine, or others used them? Do we know how the images were connected to each other in ways crucial for understanding them on their own? Do we know how, when so connected, they function in their particular literary and ecclesial contexts? What if a theology of the church that is less agreeable in the abstract to one party is seen to function in a particular writer or context in a way that is agreeable to a different theological concern of the same party? This discovery might provide access to the theological position hitherto regarded as disagreeable, since its meaning would have shifted somewhat. The possibility might then open for imagining how the disagreeable doctrine could function in the present in a way that is analogous to the past but that neither party had hitherto imagined, or that they had both in a way forgotten.

Our memories always need expanding. Over the course of study, think of what could happen: texts are discussed around common ideals and hopes, around new issues, and in our own new contexts, with the kinds of pressures that are being brought to bear on Christianity across the board. (John mentioned some of these at the end of his talk.) Eventually it may appear that the common theological tradition we both can claim is wider than either of us had imagined. This expanded tradition might even include some of the texts critical of the other tradition! Perhaps we would want to keep working out of this common deposit of texts, once discovered.

Example: Augustine on Church and Eucharist

So far I have been concentrating on my suggestion—namely, that we consider rereading some texts together—in order to see how our distinctive perspectives might bring out elements in the texts that we might not have seen apart from our dialogue. Not all of these texts seem problematic but many are. Now I would like to move on to my example.

It comes from Augustine. I am suspecting that Augustine is not, perhaps, the first theologian who leaps to mind as a resource in the Mennonite tradition. Handily, though to a lesser extent, he is not the first to leap to mind for Catholics either! To read Augustine is always to engage in a liminal activity in some way, since his legacy is so diverse and controverted.

I propose a text from book 10 of the *City of God* in which Augustine offers a theology of the church and of the Eucharist. Judging from the theological considerations in *Called Together to Be Peacemakers*, perhaps it will be less accessible, though hopefully not too disagreeable, to those formed in Mennonite sensibilities, since it focuses so emphatically on the theology of the church and of the Eucharist. Yet I would like to show that this very theology of the church and of the Eucharist functions in a way that may correspond to a Mennonite sensibility much more than might have been expected from a theologian such as Augustine writing in the post-Constantinian era. For my part, perhaps if I had not been alert to the way a Mennonite reader might be reading Augustine—and I confess that this alertness goes back to conversations that predate my reading of *Called Together to Be Peacemakers*—I might not have seen as fully the possibilities and valences in this text. So, I offer it as an example or illustration of the rereading of texts that I had suggested above. It is an example from a position that I occupy, of course. I offer it as something that might be helpful; it might not be, in which case, you can just press the delete key should it ever appear on your computer!

In book 10, sections 1–6 of Augustine's *City of God*, the question that he takes up is: What constitutes true worship of God? Augustine is here engaged in larger polemic against Platonists, which began in book 8 and extends to the end of book 10, with reprises in later books. Augustine is critical especially of Platonist endorsement or toleration of the worship of gods less than the one true and transcendent God—that is, their toleration of idolatry. Augustine had established, as early as the opening of book 8 in the *City of God* (8.1) that Plato and his philosophical descendants knew the one true God. For Augustine, the problem with Platonism, however, was always summed up by Romans 1:21-23: "for though they knew God, they did not honor him as God or give thanks to him. . . . Claiming to be wise, they became fools; and they exchanged the glory of the [incorruptible] God for images resembling [that which is corruptible]." Those verses from Romans almost presented his own complete analysis of Platonist philosophy. He applied them directly to the Neoplatonist philosophers such as Porphyry, beginning at *City of God* 8.10–12.[1] Augustine yields the concession that they knew the true God, and yet, although they did recognize the true God, they refused to worship him properly and continued to tolerate or endorse polytheistic worship. For Augustine, this was always the fatal flaw of Platonist philosophy as he knew it, a kind of "bad faith," to use an anachronistic twentieth-century expression.

It is the recognition of this inconsistency, and the desire to analyze it and repudiate it, that brings Augustine in book 10 to ask precisely what does constitute true worship of God, the worship that will make the worshippers happy. It is, he says, to be designated by the Greek term *latreia*. And after examining the matter further, he concludes that the essence of *latreia* is sacrifice, for no one would argue that sacrifice is to be rendered to any being not divine (10.4). True worship of God is a matter of the heart, and the external sacrifices are signs or sacraments of the true sacrifice of the heart, which, Augustine says, is mercy or compassion when done for the sake of God. Acts of compassion, or the works of mercy—depending on how you translate *opera misericordiae*—are meant to help us lose the form of worldly desire and to be reformed by submission to God (drawing upon Rom 12:1-2, *City of God* 10.6).

This is not as easy as it may seem. Augustine points out at the very beginning of the *City of God* that the earthly city—that is, the fellowship of human

---

[1] Translations from the *City of God* are taken from Saint Augustine, *City of God*, trans. Henry Bettenson (London: Penguin Classics, 1984).

beings and angels defined by worldly desire and most visibly represented in the worldly empire—boasts precisely of mercy as its greatest accomplishment!

> The king and founder of this city [God] has revealed in the Scriptures of his people that God *resists the proud but gives grace to the humble* (James 4.6). This is God's prerogative. But the arrogant human spirit in its swelling pride has claimed it as its own, and delights in hearing this verse quoted in its own praise: "to spare the conquered and beat down the proud." (*City of God* 1, preface)

Augustine matches the citation from James with a citation from the *Aeneid* (6.853). He is saying that the Roman Empire takes mercy—"sparing the conquered"—as its most prized accomplishment.

The form of worldly desire is pride (*superbia*), and it reveals itself in the desire for praise at any cost, in place of the praise of God, and eclipsing praise of God. Perversion of the works of mercy into imperial self-glorification is, in fact, the special work of empire, so that what is the very best act a human being can perform, revealing the human being at his or her most generous, free, and loving, fails to achieve its true end in glorifying God, the Creator of this human being, and instead is turned toward the glorification of the empire that "spares the conquered" in dramatic acts of mercy only to solidify its grasp on the imaginations of oppressed and oppressor both.

This perversion of compassion is the primal blight of the imagination. That which would reflect in human beings the beauty of God's form and so offer praise to God—that is, mercy or compassion—is reduced to a moment in a project of self-glorification, of self-worship, the quest for cultural prestige, until there seems to be nothing left *other* than the quest for praise and prestige, and no greater purpose for human beings than to contribute their personal prestige to the glory of the empire and to receive personal prestige in turn.

The empire comes to define the scope of human excellence (*virtus*) by co-opting the very worship of God (compassion) for itself. Under this regime, an actual pure work of compassion done for the sake of God—that is, for no ulterior motive—is unimaginable, because it would seem to be done for absolutely nothing, an unimaginably profound *sacrifice* done without hope of any benefit whatsoever. That, of course, is a precise description of the sacrifice of Christ in his incarnation and passion. It *is* an unimaginable act of mercy or compassion in which the Word of God, through whom all things were made, became flesh and dwelt among us.

The church comes into being by this sacrifice. It is a fellowship, or *societas*, defined by God's compassion, conformed to it, and in that way undergoing purification from the form of worldly love. In other words, the sacrifice of Christ creates a community whose very existence is formed by nonworldly love, by the humility of God the Word in assuming human nature and suffering in solidarity with us, and ultimately by the continuing presence of Christ's sacrifice in the bonds of mutual love formed among the members of the Church, his Body.

The Body of Christ *is* the compassion of Christ, present as a fellowship in transformation, in renovation, in reformation. This solidarity and transformation is sacramentally represented and enacted in the Eucharist. Thus Christ is both the priest, himself making the offering, and the oblation. This is the reality, the *res*, of which the daily sacrifice of the church is the *sacramentum*. For the church, being the Body of which he is the head, learns to offer itself through him. Again, beginning with a citation from Romans 12:

> "For just as we have many members in one body, and all the members have not the same functions, so we are many but we make up one body in Christ, and individually we are members of one another, possessing gifts according to the grace which has been given us." This is the sacrifice of Christians, who are many, making up one body in Christ. This is the sacrifice that the church continuously celebrates in the sacrament of the altar, a sacrament well known to the faithful, where it is shown to the church that she herself is offered in the offering which she presents to God. (*City of God* 10.6)

The church is a *congregatio societasque*, a congregation and fellowship or society, offered to God as a universal sacrifice through the great priest in order that we might be his Body. In other words, we are not purified by our own power or excellence (*virtus*) but by the mercy or compassion of God, which defines us as a *societas*, and which conforms our works, our poor little allotment of virtue, to that mercy. We do not have to fall back on the narrow mercy of our own hearts. We do not have to fall back on whatever speck of excellence or virtue we might muster up, hoping all the while to put it on our personal CVs to ensure it will go down in history in the archives of magnificently praiseworthy compassion.

The perfect worship of God is the eucharistic life, the continual offering of Christ to us and for us, the continual formation of that *societas* whose loves and works are being transformed in Christ's compassion and configured to it. Here is a solidarity that is a clear alternative to the empire—not as a political entity, not as a worldly city, but as a fellowship of love available to people of *any* nation or city. And it provides immediate perspective on the imperial project, shows it up for the limited enterprise it truly is, for the shocking limitation of vision and imagination that it has always been and, if only we can see it properly, still is. The fact that this solidarity is not an alternative state or earthly city is what is captured in the metaphor Augustine uses frequently in the text, especially in the latter books: that of pilgrimage. If there is anything that has a claim to being the just society on earth, it is this pilgrim people—precisely not as a worldly entity or power, as yet another settled perfection claiming praise for itself, but a fellowship founded in the humility of Christ, aware of its own imperfection and its continual need for re-formation. It is a justice that breeds longing and not complacency.[2]

Conclusion

There it is—my example. It is Augustine's image of the eucharistic community, the body of Christ, formed by the sacrifice presented and re-presented at the altar, as a community of loving resistance, re-visioning in love. I present it thinking, or perhaps presuming to think, it offers a vision of a eucharistically-defined community that might provide access for Mennonites to what Catholics mean when they talk about the Body of Christ in the world. I offer it also to us Catholics, who are probably, mostly, not true to this vision if we were to be honest about it, as we let the transforming power of the sacrament be wasted in the comfort of mediocrity or worse. And yet to my mind, the beauty of this theology is that it argues that the love of Christ present in the sacrament and forming the community can never be gainsaid, and is always present to critique the very community that claims it as its own. Paradoxically, this is a critique that perhaps we can hear better when it comes from brothers and sisters in Christ who may not have preserved, from the Catholic point of view, the fullness of the doctrine itself.

I am convinced that the separation of the churches is an evil (not a good), but that God can, without changing the evil into a good, bring good out of the evil. That is the characteristic work of God, and only of God, according to Augustine (see, for example, *City of God* 13.4, on death). And that good which God brings will be the path back to unity.

---

[2] For a more extensive discussion of these points, see John C. Cavadini, "Ideology and Solidarity in Augustine's *City of God*," in *Augustine's City of God: A Critical Guide*, ed. James Wetzel, Cambridge Critical Guides (New York: Cambridge University Press, 2012), 93–110.

PART 3

The Nature of the Church

Mennonites and Catholics agree that mission is essential to the nature of the Church. Empowered and equipped by the Holy Spirit, whose coming was promised by Jesus Christ, it is the mission of the Church to bring the Good News of salvation to all nations by proclaiming the Gospel in word and in deed to the ends of the earth. . . . We also agree that the Church's mission is carried out in the world through every follower of Jesus Christ, both leadership and laity. A dimension of the mission of the Church is realized when the Church is present among people of all nations. Thereby the divinely destined unity of humanity as one people of faith is called into being from peoples of many tongues and nations. Mission requires that Christians seek to become "one" for the sake of their witness to Jesus Christ and to the Father, and that they make "every effort to maintain the unity of the Spirit in the bond of peace." It belongs to the mission of the Church to present Jesus Christ to the world and to extend the work of Christ on earth.

Called Together to Be Peacemakers, paragraph 96

Catholics and Mennonites agree that the Church is a chosen sign of God's presence and promise of salvation for all creation. Catholics speak of this by affirming that the Church is "the universal sacrament of salvation at once manifesting and actualizing the mystery of God's love for humanity." Mennonites express the promissory character of the Church by proclaiming that "in God's people the world's renewal has begun," and that "the church is the new community of disciples sent into the world to proclaim the reign of God and to provide a foretaste of the church's glorious hope." We agree that the Church is still underway toward its heavenly goal, and we believe that God will sustain the faithful Church unto the realization of its glorious hope. Here and now the Church manifests signs of its eschatological character and thus provides a foretaste of the glory yet to come.

Called Together to Be Peacemakers, paragraph 99

Chapter 7

The Vine That Nourishes
the Peace Church

C. Arnold Snyder

As Mennonites and Catholics read the section of *Called Together to be Peacemakers* on ecclesiology or the nature of the church—primarily paragraphs 84 to 92—they should ask themselves two crucial questions. First: "At what points does this ring true to my knowledge and experience of my church tradition?" And further, "At what points would I like to amend or nuance the description of my tradition?" Asking and answering questions such as these help prepare us to engage the other tradition.

The answers to such questions will vary from person to person. Coloring my own reflections is my vocation as an historian. I can't help but read contemporary ecclesiological statements in light of my own study of my tradition, particularly its sixteenth-century origins. Fortunately, not everyone is cursed with this particular perceptual ailment, but it is my own angle of vision and I need to own it and report on how it has skewed my reading of section II.A. of *Called Together*, on "The Nature of the Church."

First of all, I am happy to be able to say that virtually all that I read in the document concerning the Mennonite understanding about the nature of the church does "ring true" to what I know as an historian. It also rings true to what I have experienced as a member of the Mennonite Church. Thus I can add my own "amen" to the work of the framers of this document. What I found intriguing, however, were the small points of dissonance that, taken together, seemed to point us Mennonites to some further reflection. These points will be my focus.

Images of the Church—Concurrence and Shift

The three images of the church that open the section on "The Nature of the Church—namely the image of the church as the people of God, the Body of Christ, and the community of the Holy Spirit (pars. 84, 85, 86)—are all centrally important biblical ecclesial images that have shaped and continue to shape our Mennonite understanding of the church.

For our sixteenth-century forebears, the church as the new Israel, *the people of God* under the new covenant, was an extremely important concept that colored their reading of the Old Testament and the New. With their baptism, which they understood as the sign of the new covenant, they had become part of the covenanted people of God, under Christ—the covenanted people of which the Old Testament had spoken only figuratively. This understanding of a "progressive" continuation of the people of God in the newly-covenanted church, and the hermeneutic it called forth, is no longer in vogue among us. Indeed, the biblical references in our document are all New Testament references. But the image of the church as God's people continues to shape our tradition.

The church as *the Body of Christ* was an especially central biblical image in our faith tradition. In fact, the best way to dramatize the importance of this image is to remember that in the sixteenth century, the Body of Christ, the *corpus christi*, was in fact the phrase that designated the sacrament of the altar. Our faith parents maintained that the real presence of Christ was present to the world not in the sacrament of the altar, but rather was embodied in living members in the form of the church itself. So, calling the church the Body of Christ evoked a sacramental resonance in the sixteenth century. To call the church by this name suggested that it was in this way that God's grace would be made present in the world, as well as divine purity, holiness, and Christ-likeness.

Finally, the church as *the community of the Holy Spirit* was absolutely crucial to the ecclesial understanding of our tradition, for the church was the direct outgrowth and manifestation of the work of the Spirit. I will expand on these last two points presently.

The one biblical image I did not find in the opening part of the ecclesiology section of *Called Together*, but which nevertheless was prominent in sixteenth-century Anabaptist descriptions of the church, was the image of the church as the *Bride of Christ* (Rev 19:7). In the sixteenth century, the description of the church as the Bride of Christ appeared again and again, sometimes in martyr testimonies and often providing the subject of extended reflection. The Bride of Christ image pointed to a lively apocalyptic expectation that is absent today. But more than this, it also suggested an intimate union between the church and its members as the bride, and Christ the bridegroom, until his imminent coming. Finally, the true and faithful Bride of the Lamb in the book of Revelation contrasted with the philandering Whore of Babylon—and I will leave unmentioned who the Anabaptists identified as the fallen harlot.

The ecclesial image of the Bride of Christ underlined an expectation that the church would remain wholly committed to the vows it had made to the bridegroom. The Bride of Christ would live in corresponding chastity, obedience, faithfulness, purity, and all other "bride-like" virtues. The fact that the Bride of Christ ecclesial image was so central to our faith parents, but is so absent in a contemporary Mennonite description of ecclesiology, points to some shifts in our self-understanding as a church, about which I will comment shortly.

Paragraph 87 contains, in very concise form, some ecclesiological elements that have been extremely important in shaping our tradition. This is a paragraph that is worth unpacking and examining more closely. In quick succession the text mentions the baptism of believers, mutual admonition, and refusal to participate in warfare. Paragraph 88 then follows with the Mennonite emphasis on the church as a community of disciples.

The *baptism of believers* contains seminal understandings and provides all the crucial keys to understanding Mennonite ecclesiology, particularly in contrast to the Christian traditions that practice the baptism of infants. Balthasar Hubmaier identified the contrast with the Roman Catholic understanding extremely well. As a former Roman Catholic priest, doctor of theology and, for a time, vice rector of the University of Ingolstadt, he knew very well what he was supporting and what he was opposing. In a provocative and densely packed statement, Hubmaier said that

> the church is built upon our own faith and commitment . . . not the reverse. *A living faith is the foundation, and the church is the structure.* For if I did not believe the Gospel I would never believe the church, since the church is built upon the Gospel and not the Gospel upon the church. Thus St. Paul states: "For no one can lay any foundation other than the one already laid, which is Jesus Christ" 1 Cor 3[:11]. Christ says the same thing to Peter: "And I tell you that you are Peter, and on this rock (that is, upon [the rock which is] the faith you have just confessed) I will build my congregation or church, and the gates of Hades will not overcome it.[1]

In this ecclesiological affirmation, Hubmaier first opposed Augustine directly by placing the church in a penultimate location: the faith of believers in

---

[1] *Simple Confession*, 243–244; emphasis added.

Christ is the foundation, he wrote, and the church is the resulting structure. Hubmaier simply denied the truth of Augustine's famous statement that "For my part, I should not believe the gospel except as moved by the authority of the Catholic Church" (*Against the Letter of Mani, 5, 6, 397 AD*).[2] Augustine had it backwards, said Hubmaier, raising the Reformation call to reform of the church on the basis of faith in Christ.

Furthermore, Hubmaier also reinterpreted Matthew 16:18 in a radical Reformation manner. Against the traditional Catholic interpretation of this biblical text, which had provided explicit support for the apostolic succession of the bishops of Rome through Peter, Hubmaier asserted, instead, that the "rock" on which Jesus said he would build the church was the *faith* that Peter confessed, not Peter himself. Hubmaier thus pointed to 1 Corinthians 3:11 to say that the only foundation for the church is the one which has already been laid, which is Jesus Christ. For Hubmaier, the implication was that the church is constructed on this one foundation by believers who have faith in the Christ. A decade later Menno Simons would take 1 Corinthians 3:11 as his motto, and inscribe it on the title pages of all his writings. The point of all this, to repeat it again, is to affirm that "the church is built upon our own faith and commitment . . . not the reverse. *A living faith is the foundation, and the church is the structure*" (emphasis added).

The fact that in our Anabaptist and subsequent Mennonite tradition the church is made up only of those who have appropriated faith for themselves has enormous ecclesiological consequences. I would amend slightly the first italicized descriptive phrase in paragraph 87, which describes the church as a "fellowship of believers." That is correct, but even more precisely, Mennonites have understood the church to be a "fellowship of *covenanted* believers." When believers are baptized in water, Mennonites still hold, they are making a dual covenant—with God as well as with other believers in

---

[2] Philip Schaff, ed., *Nicene and Post-Nicene Fathers* (NPNF), series 1, vol. 4. Likewise, in "The Profit of Believing," section 35 (in NPNF series 1, vol. 3), Augustine argued that the great virtue evident among Christians should lead to acceptance of church authority: "This hath been brought to pass by the Divine Providence, through the prophecies of the Prophets, through the manhood and teaching of Christ, through the journeys of the Apostles, through the insults, crosses, blood, of the Martyrs, through the praiseworthy life of the Saints, and, in all these, according as times were seasonable, through miracles worthy of so great matters and virtues. When therefore we see so great help of God, so great progress and fruit, shall we doubt to hide ourselves in the bosom of that Church, which even unto the confession of the human race from [the] apostolic chair through successions of Bishops, hath held the summit of authority."

the fellowship. The covenant with God testifies to what is in the heart and soul of those requesting baptism: the "covenant of a good conscience before God" spoken of in 1 Peter 3:21. Some Anabaptists also spoke of an inner "spiritual marriage" to Christ which the water confirms, explicitly linking water baptism to the image of the church as the Bride of Christ.

The covenant with the fellowship of believers, on the other hand, is a covenant that Christians make with the living and breathing members of an actual congregation. In the original understanding of our tradition, one of the most important features of this congregational covenant was the commitment to "mutual accountability," as paragraph 87 notes in passing. Another was the promise of highest allegiance to Christ, over any other earthly or heavenly power. Still another was the promise to walk as disciples of Jesus, living as he commanded and as he himself lived (par. 88).

Strengths and Weaknesses

The ecclesiology resulting from this covenantal understanding of baptism has real strengths, but also some potential weaknesses:

First, the initial covenant made in baptism, the one made with God, not only implies but also demands a living spiritual relationship and divine visitation of grace. Water baptism stands as a signal of a spiritual awakening and renewal that the water simply confirms outwardly. Likewise, water baptism indicates the desire to continue in an intimate relationship with the living Bridegroom. Therefore the earthly church, formed visibly by water baptism, presupposes the continuing spiritual presence of God within each member and, thus, the spiritual presence of God is present in the church as a whole. This is the church as the "community of the Holy Spirit." But notice: this presence is only there *insofar as it is made present through the mediation of the church's members*. The church is Christ made present by faith, obedience, and action.

This ecclesial understanding requires a high degree of spiritual commitment and motivation on the part of all church members. The living connection of all branches to the vine—a favorite biblical image for the Anabaptists—must be maintained if the plant as a whole is going to remain alive and bear fruit.

If I may be self-critical at this point, it seems to me that this ecclesial understanding has both strengths and weaknesses. A weakness in our believers' church tradition surfaces not so much from the premise of the church being formed by believers engrafted onto the vine, as it does from the relative absence of spiritual practices and disciplines needed to maintain the engrafting.

Given that the spiritual "sap" must give life to the collective church, and that this sap must flow through all the individual member branches, one would think that spiritual practices and disciplines would feature prominently in our catechisms and "continuing education" programs. In the Mennonite churches with which I have been involved this is usually not the case.

In years past, when Mennonite communities were more insular and tightly-knit, this kind of spiritual teaching took place through the mentoring of family members, relatives, neighbors, and elders, in unstructured but very effective ways. With the rapid and growing disappearance of these communities, we Mennonites are looking for other models. Many among us look increasingly to the Catholic orders in particular, to learn from your traditions of spiritual teaching and mentoring.

To repeat, when the church is the result, the product, and the structure—built and made visible upon the faith of its members—divine grace must be mediated through individual members, or it is not mediated at all. Our ecclesial tradition does not share your Augustinian image of the "mother" church, in a certain sense standing apart from and nurturing its children. We do not have a strong clergy/laity distinction, as a rule, but rather value the ideal of a priesthood of all believers. In our tradition the church itself is the visible child of the faith of its members.

The ecclesial strength of the Mennonite understanding comes from the serious commitment that the Gospel demands of each member; there is no "cheap grace" in this ecclesial tradition! The result is a strong emphasis on discipleship, service, acting in the name of Christ, and so on. Appropriately enough, careful readers will note the many "doing and acting" words and phrases that are peppered throughout the descriptive paragraphs in the document we are studying. It seems to be a particular charism of the Mennonite Church to witness to the world in these practical, tangible and visible ways. And this is by no means a bad thing.

If the strength of this ecclesial understanding is its concrete manifestation of acts of discipleship, a further weakness (it seems to me) lies in the difficulty this constructed and "derived" church has in seeing itself as the vehicle by which divine grace, love, and forgiveness may be communicated to other believers in the faith community. This is evident, I believe, in the difficulties we have experienced historically with pastoring to those who have failed and the difficulty we have had in extending and granting forgiveness.

This brings me to my second major point and takes us back to the purity of the Bride of Christ. When believers in our tradition undertook the covenant sign of baptism, they promised mutual accountability and discipline as well. Anabaptists took this pledge with utmost seriousness in the sixteenth century; less conservative Mennonite churches today, such as those taking part in this Mennonite-Catholic dialogue, no longer practice mutual discipline with any intensity or consistency. Publicly embarrassing cases seem to be the primary instances in which fraternal admonition goes into motion. Sixteenth-century Anabaptists, by contrast, practiced "the ban" with a fervor that many of us find unnerving and distasteful today. The spiritual walk of members appears to have been under constant scrutiny. The purity of the Bride of Christ was to be guarded with zeal. Those under discipline were barred from participating in the Lord's Supper. They were welcomed back into the Body of Christ only after appropriate repentance – the church as a whole granting the "absolution" formerly granted by the priesthood of the Roman Catholic Church.

A strength of this ecclesiological understanding was the responsibility it placed on individual members and the church as a whole to be faithful and actually to care for the spiritual wellbeing of one another. This is no small thing. The church *had* to be a community of priests, mentors, brothers, and sisters, caring for the welfare of each other's souls. Walking in obedience was a corporate matter; the "community of saints" had a literal, not simply a symbolic meaning. But all the same, a weakness in this understanding was that, while it turned out to be a marvelous vehicle for the identification and punishment of sin and failure, for some reason it proved to be far less well equipped to extend forgiveness and grace.

The "binding and loosing" function of Matthew 18 has always been done "in the name of Christ," never in the name of church members. In the Catholic tradition from which the Anabaptists came, the priesthood carried out binding and loosing under the apostolic authority of the bishop of Rome. The church, thus understood, identified sin, defined penance, and also granted grace, forgiveness, and absolution in the name of Christ. The "mother church," acting in the name of Christ, could extend the grace and forgiveness of God to her sick and ailing children.

How does this work when the church is also the child, not the mother, and those making up the church also are in need of grace, forgiveness and absolution? Who presumes to stand in the place of Christ in a believers' church? In practice it has proven difficult—although not altogether impossible—to communicate a transcendent sense of God's grace and forgiveness. Ours is an ecclesial structure in which all believers, collectively, stand in the place of Christ. Sometimes we collectively shirk that responsibility—especially since we have been individualized, democratized, and liberalized. Perhaps the difficulty posed by having to "stand in the place of Christ" lies behind the phenomenon of contemporary Mennonites being attracted to popular evangelical theologies that stress grace and forgiveness through the atoning death of Christ, and that downplay mutual accountability and discipleship.

It seems to me that there are other paths that we Mennonites ought to explore. In what ways can the "otherness" of God, who extends grace and forgiveness to us all through the instrument of the church, be incorporated in more real ways into Mennonite ecclesiology? How can the "mothering" functions of the church find fuller expression in a believers' church ecclesiology? It seems to me that a stronger appreciation of the spiritual power of symbolism, worship, and liturgy would take us a long way toward a stronger church for the present day.

My third major point concerns the church in relation to the "powers of this world." The baptismal vow was one of highest allegiance to Christ, over all other powers. This meant that the church was necessarily standing in an "over-against" posture, vis-à-vis any competing political claims to ultimate allegiance. In the sixteenth century this stance automatically meant persecution. In twenty-first-century North America, in a culture of religious indifference, this principle simply means that Mennonites can believe as they wish—for the most part. Radical actions can quickly strain the limits, however—actions such as principled war tax resistance and other such challenges to political and economic authority. Most Mennonites today do not find it necessary to test the boundaries of their highest allegiance to Christ with radical actions. Civil society provides a broad acceptance of most religious convictions, and it is relatively easy to affirm convictions—to say simply, this we believe.

The radical "otherness" of the church, which sixteenth-century Anabaptists saw as an absolutely crucial identifying marker of the Body of Christ in the world, has been largely abandoned by Mennonites in the twenty-first century. The exceptions are our more radically conservative brethren who do maintain a visible distance and a minority of radical Mennonite activists among the "change-minded" Mennonites. Even our conviction that the church and the state must stand in separate spheres—which was such a radical proclamation in the sixteenth century—today registers a "so what?" in most citizens of liberal democratic societies since it carries constitutional guarantees.

Conclusions

A challenge for our present ecclesial understanding as Mennonites is the recovery of the sense that "living in Christ, through the church" is our *pri-*

mary religious, cultural, and political location and place of allegiance. While for some, heightened atonement theologies are what offer a form of cheap grace, the broader temptation for Mennonites, given our ecclesiology, is the attractive form of cheap grace that comes through blending into the cultural and political landscape, rendering us no longer "different" or marginalized. The point our parents in the faith made was that marginalization will indeed happen—if the church is truly being church. This conviction deserves to be revisited and pondered by Mennonites today.

Here is where the question of the nonresistant stance of our church tradition requires attention. First of all, it seems to me that the maintenance of a "peace witness" throughout five centuries testifies to the strength and value of an ecclesiology that places discipleship and following after Christ at the heart and center of church practice in the world. It is the Mennonite peace witness, I believe, that leads other denominations to want to dialogue with us; the document we are studying, after all, is entitled *Called Together to Be Peacemakers*. That a long-standing peace witness grew out of an ecclesiology such as ours, and that it failed to manifest itself as an integral part of other ecclesiologies, is something that is worth examination, analysis, and reflection.

As usual, however, I make a poor Mennonite cheerleader. I feel the need to enter two caveats. The first arises from a sentence in paragraph 90: "Peace is essential to the meaning and message of the Gospel and thus to the Church's self-understanding." This is a statement with which I agree, as far as it goes. The question for Mennonites in dialogue with other Christian traditions is, however, this: Are Christians who do *not* hold an understanding of peace to be an essential ecclesial practice also to be considered genuine Christians? There are some Mennonite voices who suggest that the answer should be "no." The definition of "gospel" is, in fact, peace, they would say. For some contemporary Mennonites, upholding a "peace position" becomes *the* litmus test of faithfulness to Christ. This is an issue on which I would like to see much more open discussion among Mennonites.

The second caveat I would enter with regard to the Mennonite peace position is one that I make with tiresome regularity, at every given opportunity. In brief, the Mennonite "peace position" as our document outlined it and as Mennonites generally present it for public consumption, is in fact an *ethic* of peace. It foregrounds obedience to Christ, discipleship, action in the world, refusal to participate in war, etc. These are very good and worthy things. But what is usually absent from such discussions of the "peace position" qua ethic are the spiritual underpinnings of that position, without which there would be no "peace position" at all. The biblical demands that followers of Jesus "love enemies" and "turn the other cheek" are clear and evident enough, but the supernatural ability to actually love enemies is another matter entirely. And it is a matter that we rarely address. Here we return to the question that arose earlier: when the church is expected to be the visible manifestation of a living faith, the spiritual connection to the vine is of utmost importance.

Sixteenth-century witnesses make it clear: They understood very well that loving enemies was "unnatural" and would happen only by God's intervening grace and power. Of course, "holding a peace position" is a good thing, very much preferable to its alternative. Nevertheless, it follows from our spiritual and ecclesiological understanding that what Jesus asked us to do was to become profoundly transformed, in the depths of our beings, into peaceful persons, in all our doings—not simply to avoid military service when a war happens to break out.

I would dearly like to see a conscious and energetic recovery of the more profound spiritual underpinnings of discipleship—peace witness included—in our ecclesial tradition. A church in which spiritual renewal and the continuing spiritual growth of its members is what forms and defines its essence, needs to nurture the continual engrafting of all branches to the vine, if there is to be any expectation of fruit.

A church that is the child of the faith of its members is an ecclesiological tradition that possesses unique strengths, but also poses unique challenges. It is a tradition that I own and claim, even though I am not an uncritical cheerleader. My hope for the Mennonite Church is that it continues to be open to growing more fully into the likeness of Christ. On my reading of our history and the challenges of the present post-Christian reality, I believe the strengths of our ecclesial tradition need further strengthening in three particular areas: First, we need to explore how we can better offer the grace and love of Christ, as priests, to one another and the world. Second, we need to better cultivate our spiritual engrafting to the true vine by the active teaching and practice of spiritual disciplines. And third, we need to expand and deepen the liturgical practices that open windows and doors onto the divine reality, which, after all, is the only source of our life. In all these things, our friendship and conversation with Roman Catholics has been, and will be, invaluable.

Chapter 8

A People Set Apart

Mary Doak

A Timely Document

This may well be an especially fruitful time for the reception by Catholics of the results of the recent five-year dialogue between representatives of the Mennonite and Catholic Churches.[1]

To be sure, the hopeful energy that attended Catholic involvement in ecumenical dialogues in the early postconciliar period has abated significantly. Within the Catholic community, there is more interest today in reclaiming the distinctness of our Catholic "identity" and less openness to rethinking long-standing, but potentially reformable, beliefs that separate us from other Christians.[2] If we are hoping for theological advances that overcome our community-dividing differences, this does not at all seem an auspicious time.

Nevertheless, the Catholic Church has now had nearly a half century to become accustomed to an official emphasis on peacemaking as a constitutive aspect of the Christian life, and many Catholics are ready to think more deeply about how we ought to be formed in and through the church for this

---

[1] The Mennonite-Catholic document, *Called Together to Be Peacemakers*, appropriately (in my judgment) allows each community to use the term "church" in that community's accustomed manner and without requiring a common theological judgment on what properly constitutes the Church of Jesus Christ. In referring to the Mennonite Church, I too do not intend to assert a theological position on the essence of "church," and I would caution that much misunderstanding and a little absurdity are likely to result from attempts to limit the range of meaning of common words (such as "church") to a specific theological denotation.

[2] Though a discussion of the problematic use of the term "identity" is beyond the scope of this essay, I am uncomfortable with the current focus on identity (especially as something established and static) in Catholicism and in Catholic institutions today. At least for institutions, the term "Catholic mission" rather than "Catholic identity" might be more productive.

vocation of peacemaking. Where better to look for help in thinking through the challenge to be people of peace than to those in the Anabaptist tradition who have consistently upheld a witness of peacemaking?

In fact, the Mennonite experience of church provides much of the energy behind current developments in ecclesiology within both Catholic and Protestant theology today. The Mennonite practice of being a community "in but not of the world" received powerful contemporary theological expression by John Howard Yoder; this theology profoundly influenced Stanley Hauerwas and has had considerable impact on contemporary Anglo-American Catholic and Protestant theology (including especially the Radical Orthodoxy movement). With so many hungering for a more countercultural church experience, it is not surprising that Catholics and Protestants seeking new ways of being church in the world are frequently turning to the Mennonite tradition. The document *Called Together to Be Peacemakers* is an especially helpful and challenging guide at this point because it invites us to study our traditions in their similarities and their differences, and to be open to the challenge of the other without falling into a too-easy harmonizing that fails to do justice to the specific insights of each side.

My focus here, as a Catholic theologian, will be on the discussion of the nature of the church, the topic that begins the comparison of Mennonite and Catholic theologies in *Called Together to Be Peacemakers*. Before attending to the details of the conversation on church, however, it is worth noting that the whole of the document witnesses to peacemaking. After all, it seeks reconciliation through the very practice of learning to know one another and our history with each other better. The theological discussion sets forth differences of belief and practice honestly, resisting the rhetorical temptations to downplay our differences or to focus our energy on persuading the other. Perhaps more importantly, this discussion of theological commonalities and differences is set within a larger review of our painful years of division that in turn calls both parties to a penitential repentance of wrongs done to the other. Hence, this document does not merely talk about peacemaking. Instead, the document itself witnesses to two faith communities engaged in building peace within the Christian community, as a necessary step toward the peacemaking Christians are called to embody in the world.[3]

---

[3] I here follow the terminology used by the document *Called Together to Be Peacemakers*, without intending to favor any particular form of increasing peace in the world. Earlier in this book, Scott Appleby argues for a different nomenclature, preferring "peacebuilding" over "peacemaking."

In appreciation of the work and the spirit of mutual engagement that is evident in *Called Together to Be Peacemakers*, my analysis of the document's ecclesiology section does not aim to defend a particular side in debate, but rather to explore the insights gained from bringing together these two quite different, yet sometimes surprisingly similar, perspectives. By discussing first the common points and then the differences in ecclesiology between Mennonites and Catholics, I hope to clarify that these differing perspectives are especially valuable for their complementary contributions to a theology of the church as servant of peace in the world.

A Common Ecclesiology

The specifically theological section of *Called Together to Be Peacemakers* begins with the nature of the church because, as the document explains, this is a good way for each side to introduce itself to the other. And, fortunately, both Mennonites and Catholics have well-developed theologies of the church. We learn that these two communities' ecclesiologies are rooted in the same trinitarian foundational images: the church as the people of God, as the Body of Christ, and as the temple (for Catholics) or community (for Mennonites) of the Holy Spirit. In brief, both sides agree that Christians should primarily understand the church to be a new people who, filled with the Holy Spirit, are united to continue the saving presence and work of Christ in the world.

This new people is founded by and nourished in the life of the triune God, so that a deeper "communion with God is at the heart of our new relationship to the world" (as the Catholic section especially emphasizes). Yet this church must be a *visible* people to witness to God in the world, a people united by the Holy Spirit not only in praise of God but also in love and in common mission to the world (as the Mennonite discussion emphasizes). Both Mennonites and Catholics further agree that the church's members need ongoing formation and that the church should be one in Christ, not only because Jesus prayed that all would be one, but also because disunity impedes our witness to the ultimate goal of union in God.

The uncovering of this profound common ground between Catholic and Mennonite ecclesiologies not only advances our conversation with each other but also increases our awareness of the theological depth of the convictions we share concerning what God calls us to be as church. Most Catholics will not be surprised that the Catholic side of the dialogue has selected these three focal images of the church; they are not only highlighted by the Second Vatican Council but also related to the Catholic celebration of the

Eucharist. However, I suspect that many Catholics might well be surprised to learn that the Mennonite tradition also shares these images of the church, notwithstanding the quite different Mennonite experiences of church and sacrament. This similarity-in-difference directs our attention to the very deep roots, in Scripture and in church tradition, of the understanding of the church as a people united by God to be the Body of Christ in the world.

Notably, both the Mennonite and the Catholic sides present these three foundational images of the church in such a manner that the images cohere together and inform each other. An ecclesiology focused on understanding the church to be a new people of God is not in conflict with an ecclesiology that emphasizes the church being the Body of Christ or a community unified in the Holy Spirit. Nor are we dealing with a low ecclesiology in which the image of the people of God emphasizes the merely human and sociological aspects of the church, in contrast to a high ecclesiology in which the image of the Body of Christ or the community of the Holy Spirit focuses on the presence and action of God in the church. Rather, as this document makes clear in discussing the three images together, for both Catholics and Mennonites, the church as people of God (when properly understood) is predicated on God's gracious act in calling us to communion together with God, forming us into the Body of Christ, and sending the Spirit to unite and strengthen us in our mission to the world. The church cannot be the new people of God with a saving presence in the world if it is merely a sociological phenomenon, a human gathering.

In addition to these shared, foundational images of the church, we find that both theologies affirm the importance of the personal holiness of the members of the church along with the indispensability of the ecclesial community in which faith is lived together with others. Again, these are not conflicting emphases or in tension with each other, but rather are mutually implicated. The Mennonite demand for personal commitment involves mutual accountability in the church, and the Catholic celebration of the holiness of the church is not an excuse for personal laxity but rather is upheld as a gift that enables its members to grow in holiness. Both Mennonites and Catholics thus understand Christianity to be a thoroughly ecclesial faith in which we are called to form a new community (or better, *communion*) and to be a new people that individually and collectively grows in holiness.

This presentation of the central ecclesiological beliefs of the Mennonite and Catholic communities in *Called Together to Be Peacemakers* serves to remind us that both traditions' theologies of the church unite what many (perhaps especially today) are inclined to separate: the individual *and* the community, the human *and* the divine. Rather than being alternatives in tension or even in competition with each other, this document properly presents these as integrally related aspects in which the human and the divine, the personal and the communal, necessarily increase together. This point further suggests that gift and challenge go together: we must strive to be the church that God's grace enables us to be.

One could say much more about the beautiful and inspiring vision of the church that this document presents as common ground for Catholics and for Mennonites. Nevertheless, what struck me was not the need for further theory on the nature of the church, but rather the need for some extended and detailed discussion of how we might better live what both sides agree we are called to live.

In the Catholic Church, especially with the current priest shortage, many Catholic parishes are so large that they function merely as sacramental and sometimes catechetical dispensaries. In such parishes, the laity come to get a booster shot of grace and maybe a theological update before returning to separate lives where they must struggle to witness alone against the sinful structures and practices in our world. Many are dissatisfied, finding themselves unformed and unprepared for the collective witness that is so needed today. This Mennonite-Catholic dialogue reminds us that both traditions value the ongoing formation of members of the church; surely both could be enriched by further sharing their different approaches to and experiences of the challenges of Christian formation in our times.

It is worth attending also to the fact that both Mennonites and Catholics find themselves in a context quite removed from the one in which they came of age: Catholicism is not the faith of a united Christendom and Mennonites are not legally excluded from civic and social participation. Both communities must continue to think anew about how, in our current circumstances, we can *be* the church we *proclaim* ourselves, especially with the consumer culture that permeates our world, endangering peace, justice, and the wellbeing of our planet. Is it not time to move beyond theoretical dialogue and to begin to share our successes and failures in being the church and in forming members for radical, collective discipleship? Both communities have long histories and rich traditions to draw upon; surely they could learn much from a practical dialogue about what has worked and what has failed in our various efforts to develop ecclesial structures that foster Christian freedom within communities united in visible witness and mutual accountability.

Differences: Christological and Eschatological Theologies of Peace

In addition to this depth of common ecclesiological ground, we must attend to what we might learn from the differences here, even as we draw upon our commonalities. A fairly subtle but significant difference between the Mennonite and Catholic approaches to the theology of the church as peacemaker emerges here, and I want to draw attention to this difference because both sides make an important contribution to Christian theology.

In explaining the centrality of peace to the witness of the church, the Mennonite position as we find it here is primarily Christological: called to be a community of disciples, the church must imitate its crucified Lord, whose nonviolent acceptance of unjust suffering transformed the world. This argument challenges Catholics (and all Christians) to reflect more deeply on what is entailed in proclaiming a God who redeems through suffering, and what this belief demands of us not only individually but also structurally in our ecclesial actions. On the other hand, the Catholic perspective as presented here invokes the eschatological goal of a united humanity in union with God, the goal that the church serves on earth. This Catholic perspective also relates peace integrally to the life of the church (as does the Mennonite focus on discipleship), since contemporary Catholic documents most essentially define the church by its call to be a sign and instrument on earth of that union with God and unity among humanity that is the fulfillment of all peace.

Both Christology and eschatology are, of course, important aspects of Christian theology and any full theology of the church's call to peacemaking must develop them. The Mennonite approach, with its call for a deepening of our understanding of God's redemptive act in Jesus Christ, is the perspective that theologies of peace more commonly invoke; for this reason, the Catholic eschatological approach deserves special attention, for it requires that we Christians broaden our perspective so that all that we are and do is understood in relation to our ultimate hope for human harmony.

This is a point that the Catholic side of this dialogue should have developed more fully. At least since the Second Vatican Council promulgated *Lumen Gentium* in 1964, the Catholic understanding of the church's role and function in the world has been defined in relation to our eschatological goal of a united humanity in union with God. In *Called Together to Be Peacemakers*, the Catholic discussion of the nature of the church appropriately begins with just this concept of the church: "For Catholics, the Church in Christ is like a sacrament or as a sign and instrument both of a very closely knit union with God and of the unity of the whole human race" (par. 71). Seventy-six paragraphs later, in the section focusing on "Our Commitment to Peace," the Catholic discussion refers back to this emphasis on unity, and correctly notes that, since this desired unity encompasses peace, peacemaking is integral to the church. Yet the lengthy presentation of the Catholic theology of the church itself does not develop or even mention the integral connection between the church's mission to be sign and instrument of human unity and the task of seeking peace with justice. Had the document's discussion of the Catholic perspective on the church underscored the peaceable implications of the church's mission, I believe it would have presented a more adequate Catholic perspective on the centrality of peacemaking to the task and gift of being the church. As it is, one can miss the full significance of peacemaking in Catholic ecclesiology, thus misunderstanding the witness for peace as though it were a derivative concern at some remove from the central thrust of the Gospel.

Those familiar with Catholic ecclesiology will further note that this longed for and partially present unity is not uniformity but rather a unity-in-diversity. The church is one and united, even while there is a distinction of gifts and roles among the baptized. Further, Catholicism maintains an eschatological hope that all of humanity will finally be united in its diversity. Indeed, the Catholic authors of our document noted, the Catholic Church seeks to encompass all legitimate diversity in its Catholic unity. I believe that this commitment to unity-in-diversity is an especially important contribution because it addresses the source of so much of our conflict today. In a world of increasing contact between peoples, we must learn to celebrate diversity as a gift (at least in principle) rather than as a threat.

More attention to the implications of this commitment to unity in diversity would also enrich our ecumenical dialogues, including this Mennonite-Catholic one. If we are serious about the commitment to unity-in-diversity that features so prominently in the hope for redemption that the church serves, then we ought not presume or suggest (as this document occasionally does) that differences necessarily entail disunity, separation, or conflict. Instead, we need to question our own Catholic presuppositions about the extent to which church unity requires uniformity of theology and practice.

The issue is not whether differences distinguish us (they certainly do) or whether differences can be joined in harmony (they certainly can), but rather how much difference can be allowed without threatening unity, and how much disagreement before disharmony? Perhaps more of our denominational differences should be celebrated as gifts rather than lamented as barriers to unity, especially when we have so much to learn from each other. If we are truly to be signs and instruments in this world of a harmonious unity-in-diversity, our ecumenical dialogues cannot continue to presume to have definitive, settled answers to the questions of how much theological uniformity is necessary for unity and how much theological difference can be accepted as legitimate diversity.

Differences: Magisterium and Mission

Yet another difference emerges from this document's discussion of Mennonite and Catholic ecclesiologies, and begs for further attention. Even a casual reader of *Called Together to Be Peacemakers* is likely to notice that the Catholic discussion of the church spends considerable time reflecting on the importance of the magisterium's role in interpreting revelation, whereas the Mennonites' presentation expands on the call of the church to a radical witness in the world—a witness that separates the church from the state, calls Christians to be a communion of saints now, and requires a peace church in service to the world. Of course, these topics are where we find some of the most obvious disagreements between the two communities, especially differences involving infant baptism, pacifism, the church's relation to the state, and the importance of tradition and a magisterium. *Called Together to Be Peacemakers* indicates that much further study must precede any attempt to resolve these significant—perhaps fundamental—differences, and I am inclined to agree. Instead of belaboring these obvious (though important) disagreements, I would like to reflect for a moment on what the presentation of these differences between the dialogue partners here might suggest.

When a detailed Catholic discussion of the magisterium is juxtaposed to a developed Mennonite account of the radical witness of the church, one has to wonder whether something is being communicated (perhaps inadvertently) about what really matters to each group. Of course, Catholicism does not intend to value the magisterium more than the mission of the church in the world, and I am confident that the Catholic contributors to this document understand the role of the magisterium to be important precisely because the magisterium serves that mission. They also might well defend their attention to the magisterium as necessary in this sort of ecumenical dialogue because it involves key differences between Catholics and other Christians. Still, this strikingly different focus in discussion of the nature of the church—magisterium versus mission—might help to remind Catholics to keep our priorities straight. We must be clear that the magisterium exists to serve rather than to distract from (or replace!) the church's mission to the world.

Ensuring that the magisterial structure fulfills its promise to serve the mission of the church is, I believe, a significant challenge for Catholicism today, and one that I cannot hope to resolve here. Nevertheless, I would warn against the temptation to develop a magisterial authoritarianism in order to provide a putatively Catholic version of the communal witness that Mennonites (at their best) achieve. The appropriate contribution of lay experience and insight, indeed the proper lay vocation, is demeaned to the extent that pope or bishop simply dictate the specific forms of the laity's public witness. Further, Catholicism's dynamic universalism, which seeks to include as much legitimate diversity as possible, would be contradicted. Such a united witness, determined from above, is also not likely to be very prophetic or even particularly appropriate to the various circumstances in which Catholics live. Perhaps even more disturbingly, succumbing to the temptation to become yet another authoritarian collective would undermine the ancient and biblical proclamation of the freedom of the Christian, and would undermine Catholic opposition to social and political structures that deny the value of the individual person. Surely we need an ecclesial witness that fosters rather than stifles our different experiences and insights.

This is another instance of a problem that is practical as well as theoretical. I suspect that we will realize the promise of the magisterium to strengthen and to unify the witness of the Catholic communities only through much careful attention to ecclesiological practice as well as theory, as these have developed in the Catholic Church and in comparison with the structures and experiences of other Christian communities, such as the Mennonites. In other words, we need even more of the careful attention to Catholic history as well as the greater openness to the insights of other Christians that this Mennonite-Catholic dialogue has modeled.

Conclusion

As Christians, Mennonites and Catholics agree that we are called to be a new people, a people set apart, not to be removed from the world but to serve the world by bringing it the peace of Christ, a peace that allows differences to come together as enrichments of the greater community. The work of this Mennonite-Catholic dialogue group has furthered this peace by enabling Catholics and Mennonites more easily and joyfully to recognize each other as fellow Christians who labor (sometimes together and sometimes separately) for the same goal of peace with justice. In setting forth our fundamental commitments, we are challenged and challenge each other to live those commitments more fully and consistently—to be the church we proclaim ourselves to be.

There is much we might continue to learn from each other, especially if the dialogue expands to include more examination of our different ecclesial practices as sources of valuable insights. We have been blessed with a Mennonite-Catholic dialogue that appropriately included a spirit of penitence, and we must continue to face one another with humility, in Christian confidence that awareness of our sin is a gift of grace. We should also bear in mind that our ultimate hope relativizes all theological agreements and disagreements, because as the book of Revelation indicates, there will be no churches to divide or to unite us in the end. Instead, God will be immediately present to us all, joining us in the intimate communion of which our churches today provide only a foretaste.

PART 4

Sacraments and Ordinances

The Catholic Church and the Mennonite Church agree that baptism and the Lord's Supper have their origin and point of reference in Jesus Christ and in the teachings of Scripture. Both regard the celebration of these sacraments/ordinances as extraordinary occasions of encounter with God's offer of grace revealed in Jesus Christ. They are important moments in the believers' commitment to the body of Christ and to the Christian way of life. Catholics and Mennonites see the sacraments/ordinances as acts of the Church.

Called Together to Be Peacemakers, paragraph 128

Catholics and Mennonites agree that the risen Christ is present at the celebration of the Eucharist/Lord's Supper. Christ is the one who invites to the meal; he is present in the faithful who are gathered in his name; and he is present in the proclaimed Word.

Called Together to Be Peacemakers, paragraph 134

Chapter 9

"This Is My Body"

The Real Presence of Christ in the Eucharist and the Call to Be Peacemakers

Elizabeth T. Groppe

In the fall of 2004, a traveling exhibit on the human cost of the Iraq war came to Cincinnati, the city where I live.[1] A stroll across the academic mall at Xavier University became a walk through a field of black boots placed with careful precision in rows across the grass, each pair a symbol of a young man or woman from the United States military killed in the aftermath of the US invasion. Clustered below trees on the edges of the mall were piles and piles of sandals, sneakers, leather shoes, high heels, and baby booties symbolizing the death of an untold number of Iraqi civilians. Documents and photographs from Iraq were on display in the university library, including a love letter from a solider to his bereaved fiancée and a photo of the body of a small Iraqi child covered almost entirely in blood.

The city of Ur, in the land we now know as Iraq, was the birthplace of Abraham (Gen 11:26-28), the man who placed the body of another child on an altar in preparation for an act of sacrifice (Gen 22). The command of God spared Abraham's son Isaac, and the Christian exegetical tradition has interpreted this Genesis story both as a prohibition of child sacrifice and a prefiguration of the death and resurrection of Jesus Christ. Catholics celebrate this paschal mystery in the sacrament of the Eucharist, which the Second Vatican Council described as a "sacrament of love" and "the source and summit of the Christian life."[2]

---

[1] The exhibit "Eyes Wide Open" is sponsored by the American Friends Service Committee. See http://www.afsc.org/eyes.

[2] Vatican II: *Sacrosanctum Concilium* 47 and *Lumen Gentium* 11. In this chapter, references to the council are from *Vatican Council II: The Basic Sixteen Documents*, ed. Austin Flannery, OP (Northport, NY: Costello, 1996).

Called Together to Be Peacemakers, the Report of the International Dialogue, identifies numerous areas of significant congruence between Catholic eucharistic theology and Mennonite understandings of the practice of the Lord's Supper, as well as important and obvious differences concerning the character of Christ's presence. As I review these theologies and elaborate on the Catholic theology of eucharistic real presence, I give particular attention to the relationship between the Eucharist and the practice of peacemaking. As I have reflected on *Called Together*, one cluster of questions in particular has troubled me: *Why does the strong Catholic theology of Christ's real presence in the Eucharist often fail to bear fruit in a practice of peacemaking comparable in strength and consistency to that of our Mennonite brothers and sisters? What liturgical and ecclesial practices might strengthen Catholics in our vocation to become the Body of Christ that we receive?*

Roman Catholic Eucharistic Theology

The Eucharist is the source and summit of Catholic life, the sacrament of our communion with God, one another, and all creation. With Catholics, Mennonites affirm that the celebration of the Eucharist and the Lord's Supper recalls the suffering, death, and resurrection of Jesus Christ. Both traditions hold that in this celebration, we acknowledge our sinfulness and receive God's grace made available to all through the paschal mystery. From this grace comes forgiveness, nourishment of the Christian life, strengthening for mission, and growth in our conformity to the body of Christ that we might be ministers of reconciliation, peace, and justice for the world. Both Catholics and Mennonites approach the event as a foretaste of the heavenly banquet and celebrate in the spirit of eschatological hope.[3] The most obvious point of contention between Mennonites and Catholics is the question of whether the Eucharist is a symbol of Christ's suffering, death, and resurrection or the real presence of Christ.[4]

---

[3] *Called Together to Be Peacemakers*, Report of the International Dialogue, par. 133.

[4] "For Mennonites," *Called Together* explains, "the Lord's Supper is primarily a sign or symbol that points to Jesus' suffering, death, and resurrection, and that keeps this memory alive until His return" (138). For Catholics, in contrast, "in the sacrament of the Eucharist 'the body and blood, together with the soul and divinity, of our Lord Jesus Christ and therefore, the whole Christ is truly, really, and substantially contained' under the species of bread and wine which have been consecrated by an ordained bishop or presbyter" (139). This is the language of the Council of Trent, reiterated in the 1994 Catechism of the Catholic Church (par. 1374).

These need not be mutually exclusive approaches. In a survey of early Christian eucharistic theologies, Paul Jones echoes Jaroslav Pelikan in his conclusion that the theologians of the church's first three centuries approached the Eucharist with an appreciation for both its symbolism and its realism. Justin Martyr used an incarnational analogy to emphasize that the food blessed with the Word of God becomes the flesh and blood of Jesus Christ, while Clement and Origen placed more emphasis on the figurative and symbolic character of the bread and wine.[5] In a neo-Platonic culture that assumed things visible to our eyes participate in a spiritual reality that transcends sense experience, no one interpreted the Eucharist as merely a sign, even when countering the accusation that Christian liturgies were an occasion for cannibalism.[6] Indeed, John McKenna notes, it is a remarkable fact that in the diversity of traditions and theologies that emerged as Christianity grew and developed in both East and West, "there was no dispute over Christ's presence for the first eight centuries."[7] The primary focus of theological attention was the communion shared by those who partake of the Eucharist and its potential to transform and unite the communicants in Christ's body.

Landmarks in the development of the tradition include Bendictine monk Paschasius Radbertus' ninth-century treatise *De Corpore et Sanguine Domini* (On the Body and Blood of the Lord), which affirmed that the Eucharist is both a sign and image of the true body and blood of Christ, as evidenced in accounts of bleeding hosts. Emperor Charles the Bald found this approach excessively realistic and commissioned the monk Ratramnus to write another treatise, which distinguished the body of Christ that was crucified on Calvary from the Eucharist that is a true sacrament of Christ's body. Another notable historical landmark is the eleventh-century exchange between Berengarius of Tours and Lanfranc of Canterbury. Berengarius, pressured to confess at the Syond of Rome (1059) that after consecration the bread and wine are "the true body and blood of our Lord Jesus Christ—and that these are truly, physically, and not merely sacramentally, touched and broken by the hands of the priests and crushed by the teeth of the faithful," authored

---

[5] Paul H. Jones, *Christ's Eucharistic Presence: A History of the Doctrine* (New York: Peter Lang, 1994), 25–33; Jaroslav Pelikan, *The Christian Tradition: A History of the Development of Doctrine* (Chicago: University of Chicago, 1971), 1:28, 167–71.

[6] On this point see William R. Crockett, *Eucharist: Symbol of Transformation* (New York: Pueblo Publishing Company, 1989), 78–88.

[7] John McKenna, "Eucharistic Presence: An Invitation to Dialogue," *Theological Studies* 60, no. 2 (1999): 302.

De Sacra Coena (On the Sacred Meal), which stated that the priest breaks not the body of Christ but the sacrament of Christ's body. Lanfranc responded in his *Liber de Corpore et Sanguine Domini* (On the Body and Blood of Our Lord) that the earthly elements on the Lord's table are changed in an unspeakable and incomprehensible manner into the essence of Christ's body. In this dispute, Nathan Mitchell explains, Catholic theology was striving to find a way to articulate that "the Eucharist is real without being crudely realistic, and symbolic (sacramental) without being unreal."[8]

Thomas Aquinas (1225–74) articulated this with great care in the *Summa Theologiae*, a comprehensive account of the sacramental economy as a means to our healing from sin and participation in the divine nature.[9] Aquinas described the sacrament of the Eucharist as a sign that refers to something other than itself, the sacred reality that is being signified (the *res sacra*). In this sense, the Eucharist is a symbol and figure of Christ's body. At the same time, the bread and wine contain the crucified Christ "not merely in signification or figure, but also in very truth."[10] That the Eucharist is Christ's true corporeal presence is a mystery of Christ's love, through which Christ assumed for our salvation a body of our nature and continues to abide with us in our state of pilgrimage (John 6:57).[11] When Christ says of the bread and wine through the instrument of the priest "This is my Body" and "This is my blood," bread and wine truly become the body and blood of Christ, not in the way a human agent changes one form to another (e.g. flour to bread) but through God's divine power by which "the whole substance of the bread is changed into the whole substance of Christ's body, and the whole substance of the wine into the whole substance of Christ's blood."[12] The language of "substance" (*substantia*) has a physicalist sense to our twenty-

---

[8] Nathan Mitchell, OSB, *Cult and Controversy: The Worship of the Eucharist Outside Mass* (New York: Pueblo, 1982), 151. Berengarius' *De Sacra Coena* is not available in English translation. For Lanfranc's work, see *Lanfranc of Canterbury "On the Body and Blood of Our Lord" and Guitmund of Aversa "On the Truth of the Body and Blood of Christ in the Eucharist,"* trans. Mark G. Vaillancourt (Washington, DC: Catholic University of America Press, 2009).

[9] On Aquinas' sacramental theology, see Liam G. Walsh, OP, "Sacraments," in *The Theology of Thomas Aquinas*, eds. Rik van Nieuwenhove and Joseph Wawrykow (Notre Dame, IN: University of Notre Dame Press, 2005), 326–64.

[10] Aquinas, *Summa Theologiae* (ST), IIIa, q. 75, a.1, ad. c. All quotations are from the Benziger Brothers edition, translated by the Fathers of the English Dominican Province.

[11] Ibid. The other reasons he identified are the perfection of the new law and the perfection of faith.

[12] Ibid., a. 4, ad. c.

first century ears, but for Aquinas the substance of Christ's body and blood is a supernatural reality perceptible in faith only to the spiritual eye or the intellect.[13] Christ is present in the Eucharist both in sign *and* in truth, but this true corporeal presence is supernatural rather than local or sensual, a spiritual gift that enables us to grow in grace and virtue. As a sacrament of Christ's presence, the Eucharist "is the sign of supreme love."[14]

When the Council of Trent articulated its own Eucharistic theology, the context was one of polemics against the Reformers: "If anyone should maintain that the sacrament of the Eucharist does not truly, really, and substantially contain the body and blood of our Lord Jesus Christ, but (that these) are only there as in a sign or a symbolic form, let him be excommunicated." Trent directed these strong words against Zwingli, Oecolampodius, and the Sacramentarians who believed that the mass had become an illegitimate instrument of exclusive ecclesiastical power and that notions of Christ's presence were too crudely material.[15] Trent affirmed that there is a real conversion (*conversio*) of bread and wine into the body and blood of Christ and that this conversion is most suitably (*aptissime*) expressed by the term "transubstantiation."[16]

In the twentieth century, the tradition continued to develop. Kantian philosophy, existentialism, quantum theory, uneasiness with Aristotelian terms remote from modern thought, ecumenical dialogue, and the rediscovery of the symbolic in the work of theologians such as Paul Tillich and Karl Rahner invited new approaches to eucharistic theology.[17] Among these are theologies that employ phenomenology and personalist philosophy. Edward Schillebeeckx, for example, used a phenomenology of the nonduality of body and soul to articulate a theology of personal encounter in which the visible bread and wine disclose the real presence of the Body of Christ. There is

[13] Ibid., q. 76, a. 7, ad. c.
[14] Ibid., q. 75, a. 1, ad. c.
[15] On Zwingli, see Thomas N. Finger, *A Contemporary Anabaptist Theology* (Downers Grove, IL: Intervarsity Press, 2004), 185.
[16] Council of Trent: DS, 1651.
[17] For surveys of these developments, see Edward J. Kilmartin, SJ, "Sacramental Theology: The Eucharist in Recent Literature," *Theological Studies* 32, no. 2 (1971): 233–77; Edward J. Kilmartin, SJ, "The Catholic Tradition of Eucharistic Theology: Towards the Third Millennium," *Theological Studies* 55, no. 3 (1994): 405–57. For Rahner's theology of symbol, which may have potential to build bridges between the Catholic and Mennonite traditions, see "The Theology of the Symbol," trans. Kevin Smyth, *Theological Investigations* 5 (London: Darton, Longman & Todd, 1974): 221–52.

a need, he wrote, for a eucharistic realism that is sacramental rather than physicalist.[18]

Whether one formulates the Catholic theology of eucharistic presence with the language of Aquinas, Trent, or Schillebeeckx, the tradition has at its heart the conviction that the Eucharist is not only a sign that calls the paschal mystery to mind but also an encounter with the incarnational reality of Christ's profound and enduring love: "This is my body, which is given for you" (Luke 22:19). The Catholic tradition emphasizes that this real presence of Christ is not conditioned by the character of the priest nor that of the assembly. The priest who iterates Christ's words and invokes the Spirit in the prayer of *epiclesis* is simply an instrument of God's grace. In technical terms, the grace of the sacrament is given not *ex opere operantis* ("from the work of the worker") but *ex opere operato* ("from the work worked"). Although the sacrament is complete only when those who partake of the Body of Christ respond in grace to the love they have received, the reality of Christ's love is not contingent on our response. It is precisely this theology of Christ's presence as a gift neither conditioned nor constructed by the collective community, writes Jean Luc-Marion in response to critiques of Roman Catholicism, that guards against idolatrous worship.[19]

Several features of contemporary Catholic eucharistic theology bear highlighting in the context of this Mennonite-Catholic dialogue. First, the theology of Christ's eucharistic presence can be expressed in language other than that of "transubstantiation," a term that historically has been an obstacle to interdenominational understanding. Anabaptists, writes Thomas Finger,

---

[18] Edward Schillebeeckx, OP, *The Eucharist*, trans. N. D. Smith (New York: Sheed and Ward, 1968). See also his *Christ the Sacrament of the Encounter with God*, trans. Paul Barrett, Mark Schoof, and Laurence Bright (New York: Sheed and Ward, 1963).

[19] Jean-Luc Marion, *God Without Being*, trans. Thomas A. Carlson (Chicago: University of Chicago Press, 1991), 161–82. Liam Walsh notes in his article "Sacraments" that the position that sacraments give grace *ex opere operato* "was a smart way of expressing the objective value of a properly celebrated sacrament, over against the value of any other exercise of piety in the church (such as prayers offered for people) that depends on the subjective goodness, or lack of goodness, of the one who performs it. It was never meant to suggest that subjective dispositions were of no account in sacraments, either in the minister or, more particularly, on the part of the one who receives the sacrament. It was taken as obvious that, without exercising faith and charity, the recipient could gain no saving grace from a sacrament, for all its objective reality. The limitation of the expression *ex opere operato* is that is says nothing about the reason why sacraments have their objective reality. And it carries the risk of suggesting that the rite has some inherent power that works independently of all personal factors" (364, n. 46. Cf. p. 358).

have affirmed Christ's presence through the Spirit[20] but "employed concepts that apparently denied Christ's presence (e.g., the bread is only bread)" in order "to deny the notions of presence they know, because these seemed too crudely material."[21] Schillebeeckx emphasizes that Trent left open the possibility that one can speak of the eucharistic *conversio* in terms other than the council's own chosen language of transubstantiation, and the official Vatican response to the World Council of Churches' Commission on Faith and Order report *Baptism, Eucharist, and Ministry* (1982) expressed an openness to "possible new theological explanations as to the 'how' of the intrinsic change."[22]

Second, although Catholicism emphasizes that Christ is "present . . . most of all in the Eucharistic species" (SC 7), the Catholic tradition also recognizes other modes of eucharistic presence. The Second Vatican Council affirmed that Christ is present also in the person of the minister, the word of Scripture, and the church united in prayer and song (SC 7).[23] Judith Marie Kubicki notes that this conciliar approach recovers the ethos of the apostolic and patristic eras in which Christ's presence in the Eucharist is inseparable from Christ's presence in the gathered *ecclesia*.[24]

Finally, Catholic theology today emphasizes that the real presence of Christ in the Eucharist finds its full meaning in the transformation of the communicants who are, in turn, to be a witness to Christ's love in our broken world.[25] The full mystery of the body and blood of Christ is that "you are beginning to receive what you have also begun to be," as Augustine exhorted his congregation, "provided you do not receive unworthily."[26] A renewed

[20] At the conclusion of a historical survey of the theology of the Lord's Supper, he writes: "If *sacramental* means expression of invisible, spiritual grace through visible, material channels, Anabaptists appear quite sacramental so far." Finger, *Anabaptist Theology*, 107.

[21] Ibid., 197.

[22] Schillebeeckx, *Eucharist*, 41–53; Edward J. Kilmartin, "The Official Vatican Response to BEM: Eucharist," *Ecumenical Trends* 17 (1988): 39.

[23] See also *Catechism of the Catholic Church*, par. 1373; Michael G. Witczak, "The Manifold Presence of Christ in the Liturgy," *Theological Studies* 59, no. 4 (1998): 681–90.

[24] Judith Marie Kubicki, CSSF, "Recognizing the Presence of Christ in the Liturgical Assembly," *Theological Studies* 65, no. 4 (2004): 821–26.

[25] See, for example, Bernard Cooke, *Sacraments and Sacramentality* (Mystic, CT: Twenty-Third Publications, 1983), 168–212; James L. Empereur and Christopher Kiesling, *The Liturgy that Does Justice* (Collegeville, MN: Liturgical Press, 1990), 109–30; David N. Power, OMI, "Eucharistic Justice," *Theological Studies* 67, no. 4 (2006): 856–79.

[26] Augustine, Sermon 228B, in *Sermons* III / 6, *The Works of Saint Augustine: A Translation for the 21st Century*, ed. John E. Rotelle, trans. Edmund Hill (New Rochelle, NY: New City Press, 1993), 262.

emphasis on this dimension of sacramental theology opens possibilities for building bridges with the Mennonite theology of the Lord's Supper, which does "not dismiss the effectual power of the ordinance to bring change to the participants and to the community of faith."[27] *Called Together to Be Peacemakers* attests that Mennonites experience a power and closeness in their sharing of the Lord's Supper and that they leave the service changed by a spiritual presence.[28]

The Eucharist and the Practice of Peacemaking

The risen Christ greeted the disciples with a sign of peace (Luke 24:36; John 20:19, 26), and the Catholic tradition has found in Christ's eucharistic presence a source of strength to resist war. Cyprian of Carthage (ca. 200/210–58) stated in his treatise *On the Goodness of Patience* that "after the reception of the Eucharist the hand is not to be stained with the sword and bloodshed."[29] Saint Basil (ca. 330–79) wrote that anyone who has shed blood in warfare should abstain from the Eucharist for three years.[30] Even after the church moved from the predominantly pacifist ethos of its early centuries to an accommodation with warfare, some eucharistic restrictions were placed on arms bearing and participation in military activity. The Council of Chalcedon (451) decreed that clerics and monks should not take up military service; those who did so and failed to repent were subject to excommunication.[31] According to the Council of Lerida (524), clerics who served at the altar, distributed the Body of Christ, and touched the vessels of the divine service were not to spill any human blood, not even that of an enemy.[32] Councils in Macon (583) and Bordeaux (660) prohibited clerics from bearing arms, and the Council of Saint-Jean-de-Lone (ca. 670–73) included bishops in this prohibition.[33] A canon of the eleventh council of Toledo (675) prohibited

---

[27] *Called Together*, par. 126.

[28] Ibid.

[29] Cyprian of Carthage, *Liber de Bono Patientiae*, 14, trans. Louis Swift, *The Early Fathers on War and Military Service* (Wilmington, DE: Michael Glazier, 1983), 48. Cf. Carol Frances Jegen, "The Eucharist and Peacemaking: Sign or Contradiction?" *Worship* 59, no. 3 (1985): 204.

[30] Migne, PG, xxxii, 681, trans. C. John Cadoux, *The Early Christian Attitude to War: A Contribution to the History of Christian Ethics* (New York: Seabury, 1972), 261.

[31] Canon 7, in Charles Joseph Hefelé, *Histoire des Conciles d'après les documents originaux* (Paris: Letouzey et ané, 1908), II.1:788–89.

[32] Ibid., II.2:1063.

[33] Ibid., III.1:203 and 273.

priests from participating in any proceedings involving bloodshed.[34] The First National Germanic Council (742) did allow clerics to bear arms in warfare, except for "those who celebrate the holy mass or carry relics."[35]

Thomas Aquinas articulated the theological basis for the canons and conciliar rulings that barred celebrants of the Eucharist from participation in bloodshed. Once ordained, he explained, a man should not participate in military activity, for the disquieting character of warfare prevents contemplation of divine things and warfare violates the priest's sacramental representation of Christ. "Wherefore it is unbecoming for them to slay or shed blood, and it is more fitting that they should be ready to shed their own blood for Christ, so as to imitate in deed what they portray in their ministry. . . . [I]t is altogether unlawful for clerics to fight." [36] Today a long tradition of exempting military chaplains from combat continues, and this, Carol Frances Jegen comments, "is basically a question of eucharistic celebration."[37]

In our own era, there has been renewed attention to the eucharistic imperative to peacemaking. Virgil Michel, a leader of the preconciliar liturgical movement in the United States, emphasized that "the Eucharist as the sacrament of the mystical Body of Christ, or of the perfection of love, is preeminently the sacrament of the peace of Christ."[38] War, he continued, is an evil that tears apart Christ's Mystical Body and the Eucharist is the foundation of the regeneration of a society that has been fragmented by injustice and bloodshed. Vatican II's Pastoral Constitution on the Church in the Modern World (*Guadium et Spes*) decried the savagery of war and enjoined Christians to cooperate with others in securing a peace based on justice and charity, while the Dogmatic Constitution on the Church (*Lumen Gentium*) emphasized the universal call to holiness—a theology that challenges a two-tier morality that prohibits priests from bloodshed but allows laity to participate in warfare.[39] "The Mass," the US Catholic bishops stated in 1983, "is a unique means of seeking God's help to create the conditions

[34] Ibid.

[35] Ibid., III.2: 822

[36] Ibid., ST, II–II, q. 40, a. 2, ad. c.

[37] Jegen, "The Eucharist and Peacemaking," 202. On clerical pacifism see also Kenneth Kemp, "Personal Pacifism," *Theological Studies* 56, no. 1 (1995): 23–25.

[38] Virgil Michel, OSB, *The Christian in the World* (Collegeville, MN: Liturgical Press, 1939), 179. See also Tobias L. Winright, "Virgil Michel on Worship and War," *Worship* 71, no. 5 (1997): 451–62.

[39] *Vatican Council II: Gaudium et Spes*, pars. 77–90; *Lumen Gentium*, pars. 39–42.

essential for true peace in ourselves and in the world."[40] The *Compendium of the Social Doctrine of the Church* issued by the Pontifical Council for Justice and Peace described the Eucharist as "a limitless wellspring for all authentic Christian commitment to peace."[41] In 2005, the XI Ordinary General Assembly of the Synod of Bishops issued a message to the people of God entitled "The Eucharist: Living Bread for the Peace of the World."[42] At the Synod, bishops shared moving stories about the peacemaking power of the Eucharist,[43] and the Synod included among their *propositiones* this statement: "All who partake of the Eucharist must commit themselves to peacemaking in our world scarred by violence and war, and today, in particular, by terrorism, economic corruption and sexual exploitation."[44] Pope Benedict XVI highlighted this point in his 2007 postsynodal apostolic exhortation *Sacramentum Caritatis*.[45]

Across the globe, Catholics are engaged in peacemaking action. *Called Together to Be Peacemakers* highlights the contributions of national and diocesan justice and peace commissions, the Pontifical Council for Justice and Peace, and the Caritas network.[46] One could add many other examples, such as the indispensable leadership of Bishop Jaime Sin and the Catholics of the Philippines in the successful nonviolent resistance to the attempted election fraud of dictator Ferdinand Marcos,[47] the work of Pax Christi International,[48]

---

[40] US Conference of Catholic Bishops, *The Challenge of Peace: God's Promise and Our Response*, par. 295.

[41] Pontifical Council for Justice and Peace, *Compendium of the Social Doctrine of the Church* (USCCB: Washington, DC: 2004), par. 519.

[42] Available at http://www.vatican.va/roman_curia/pontifical_councils/justpeace /documents/rc_pc_justpeace_doc_20060526_compendio-dott-soc_en.html.

[43] There is no public record of these stories, but Pope Benedict wrote: "During the Synod sessions we heard very moving and significant testimonies about the effectiveness of the Eucharist in peacemaking. In this regard, *Propositio* 49 states that: 'Thanks to eucharistic celebrations, peoples engaged in conflict have been able to gather around the word of God, hear his prophetic message of reconciliation through gratuitous forgiveness, and receive the grace of conversion which allows them to share in the same bread and cup.'" Benedict XVI, *Sacramentum Caritatis*, n. 242.

[44] The *propositiones* are confidential, but some, including this one (*propositio* 48) are cited by Pope Benedict XVI in *Sacramentum Caritatis*.

[45] Benedict XVI, *Sacramentum Caritatis*, par. 89.

[46] *Called Together*, par. 154.

[47] Ma. Christine A. Astorga, "Culture, Religion, and Moral Vision: A Theological Discourse on the Filipino People Power Revolution of 1986," *Theological Studies* 67, no. 3 (2006): 567–601.

[48] See http://www.paxchristi.net/international/eng/index.php.

the Community of Sant'Egidio,[49] or the efforts of the Catholic Peacebuilding Network.[50]

Becoming What We Receive

Catholics have borne powerful witness to the call to peacemaking that is rooted in the life, death, and resurrection of Jesus Christ that we celebrate in the eucharistic sacrament. At the same time, we must honestly face our historic failures to fully become the Body of Christ that we receive. Catholics participated in pogroms against Jews, crusades against Muslims, and acts of violence against the indigenous peoples of the Americas that accompanied European colonialism. After nearly two millennia of Christian civilization, the continent of Europe became, in the twentieth century, a theater of total war and genocide in which Catholics killed not only Jews and Protestants but also other Catholic communicants. In World War I, Catholic France, Belgium, and Italy (on the Allied side) fought Catholic Austria. "Members of the body of Christ," William Temple lamented, "are tearing one another, and His Body is bleeding as it once bled on Calvary, but this time the wounds are dealt by His friends. It is as though Peter were driving home the nails and John were piercing the side."[51] In the 1980s, baptized men and women killed one another in the civil wars that sundered the small nations of Nicaragua, El Salvador, and Guatemala, which were overwhelmingly Catholic in the aftermath of the sixteenth-century Spanish conquest of Central America.

In our own day, Pope John Paul II exemplified Catholic peacemaking in his diplomatic efforts to counsel the Bush administration against the catastrophic invasion of Iraq in which we are still engaged.[52] Yet while the Vatican called the US plans immoral and illegal, polls showed American Catholics in favor of war by a margin of two to one.[53] When the United States did invade Iraq, the Vatican continued to advocate peace, but this had little effect on

[49] See http://www.santegidiousa.org/ on the US branch on this international Catholic lay association.

[50] See http://cpn.nd.edu.

[51] William Temple, *Christianity and War*, Papers for War Time No. 1 (London: Oxford University Press, 1914), 3.

[52] John Paul II, "The International Situation Today," Address to the diplomatic corps accredited to the Vatican, *Origins* 32, no. 33 (January 30, 2003): 544; "There Is Still Room for Peace," (address before midday angelus, *L'Osservatore Romano* March 17–18, 2003), 12.

[53] Richard Major, "Stars and Stripes or Keys of Peter," *The Tablet* (March 22, 2003): 4.

participation in the war by Catholic members of the military.[54] Meanwhile, at the parish level, it was difficult to talk or even pray about the war and its victims. In one Cincinnati parish, a pastor vetoed inclusion of a prayer for enemies in a bulletin insert on the grounds that this particular selection from a series of prayers provided by the US Conference of Catholic Bishops would be too controversial. On two occasions, my husband, a professor of social ethics, was invited to speak to local parishes about Catholic social teaching on war and peace, but in both cases the invitation came with the proviso, "we do not want you to speak about Iraq. That would be too controversial."

Meanwhile, many Mennonites stand clear in their opposition to the war and some have supported or participated in the Iraqi delegations of the Christian Peacemaker Teams.[55] Although Mennonites are relatively few in number, Gerald Schlabach observes, they have a remarkable track record of building relationships with "enemy" nations, working behind the scenes in international mediation, and initiating projects to defend populations subject to human rights abuses.[56]

Given Catholicism's theology of the real presence of Christ in the sacrament of the Eucharist, one would expect our record on peacemaking to be at least as strong as that of the Mennonite tradition. Yet our Mennonite sisters and brothers are more consistent in their resistance to war and development of alternative means of response to human injustice and conflict. Why is this the case? Mennonites are members of a peace church within the Anabaptist tradition and a principled opposition to war is part of their religious identity. Yet, as *Called Together to Be Peacemakers* notes, the just war tradition that dominates Catholic thinking on issues of war and peace does insist that war must be strictly a last resort.[57] The starting point of the Catholic ethic is a presumption *against* war,[58] and the conditions set forth for engagement in

---

[54] John Michael Botean, Bishop of the [Eastern Rite] Romanian Catholic Diocese of Saint George in Canton, Ohio, is one bishop who did call publicly for conscientious objection. The text of his letter is available at http://www.catholicpeacefellowship.org/nextpage.asp?m=2033.

[55] See http://www.cpt.org.

[56] Gerald W. Schlabach, "Practicing Just Policing," in *Just Policing, Not War: An Alternative Response to World Violence*, ed. Gerald W. Schlabach (Collegeville, MN: Liturgical Press, 2007), 99.

[57] *Called Together*, par. 157.

[58] The US Catholic Bishops stated in their 1983 pastoral *The Challenge of Peace* that both the just war and pacifist traditions share a "strong presumption against war" and for peace (pars. 70, 80, 83, 120). Margaret R. Pfeil explains that although an explicit

warfare are so stringent that a 1991 editorial in the Vatican-approved news-
paper *La Civiltà Cattolica* suggested that no war fought with modern means
can meet the just war criteria.[59] In 2003, Archbishop Renato Martino, president of the Pontifical Council for Justice and Peace, stated that the church's
position on warfare is moving toward a "quasi-abolitionist stance."[60]

This development in Catholic social teaching is not well-known among
Catholics. Moreover, we have not adequately understood or practiced the
vocation to peacemaking that is implicit in our celebration of the Eucharist.
Many young Catholics at Xavier University do not even associate the Eucharist with peacemaking. In an informal survey of 71 Catholic students,
most stated that the Eucharist is the Body and Blood of Christ. Some spoke
of real presence or even transubstantiation. Yet only one student explicitly
identified eucharistic reception with the mission of peacemaking.[61] Even
those who do make this association may not have sufficient support to live

---

affirmation of the presumption against the use of force is a relatively recent addition to
the just war lexicon, it has resonance with the broader tradition. See her chapter "Whose
Justice? Which Relationality?" in *Just Policing, Not War*, 111–29.

   [59] Editorial, "Coscienza cristiana e guerra moderna," *La Civiltà Cattolica* 142.3385
(1991): 3–16. An English translation by William Shannon appears as "Modern War and
Christian Conscience," *Origins* 21.28 (December 19, 1991): 450–55.

   [60] Cited in John L. Allen, Jr., "Pope's 'Answer to Rumsfeld' Pulls no Punches in
Opposing War," *National Catholic Reporter* (February 14, 2003): 3–4. In May 2003, Cardinal Ratzinger (now Pope Benedict XVI), stated in an interview that "There were not
sufficient reasons to unleash a war against Iraq. To say nothing of the fact that, given
the new weapons that make possible destructions that go beyond the combatant groups,
today we should be asking ourselves if it is still licit to admit the very existence of a 'just
war.'" See http://www.zenit.org/article-7161?l=english (September 18, 2011).

   [61] Ten respondents did say that reception of the sacrament means we must live like
Jesus, eight said it means we must make moral choices and resist sin, three said it means
we must live like God, and two spoke of the need to follow the laws of the church.
Whether or not the students understood these responses to imply an ethic of peacemaking would need to be determined by further questioning. In an alternate version of the
survey administered to another sixty-four students, I followed the question on the meaning of the Eucharist with the very direct question "does Eucharistic celebration have
any implications for Catholic ethics and practice in regard to issues of war and peace?"
When the question was posed in this manner, 45 percent did affirm a relation between
the Eucharist and peacemaking. Some explained that the Eucharist is a sacrament of
unity, while others emphasized that it should make us more like Christ. Twenty percent,
however, responded negatively, and another 15 percent answered with a question mark
or did not respond at all. One student who stated that the Eucharist is the real presence
of Christ said that the Eucharist has "no specific implications" for the ethics of war and
peace. Another said, "I don't understand how the Eucharist deals with war and peace."

out the eucharistic vocation to peacemaking. A striking feature of the Mennonite practice of the Lord's Supper is their strong emphasis on a real sharing of goods and a mutual commitment to costly discipleship. Encounter with Mennonites who exercise this discipleship reminds us that we are indeed called to become what we receive.

To this end, I suggest four liturgical and ecclesial practices that could strengthen our fidelity to the vocation to peacemaking rooted in Christ's love: the inclusion of explicit references to Christ's practice of nonviolence and call to discipleship within the eucharistic prayers; contextualization of the sacrificial language of the Eucharist in this nonviolent practice; the development of eucharistic prayers that take the form of lamentation; and the development of ecclesial education and training in the practice of active nonviolence, grounded in contemplative prayer.

1. Making Explicit the Nonviolence of Christ within the Eucharistic Prayer

The four eucharistic prayers most commonly used in the postconciliar Catholic liturgy do include multiple references to peace.[62] Eucharistic Prayer I (the Roman Canon) asks God to give "peace and unity" to the holy Catholic Church and to "grant us your peace in this life." Catholics exchange with one another a sign of peace prior to reception of the Eucharist, and the rite of dismissal includes the prayer, "Go in peace to love and serve the Lord."[63] Yet our history attests that these prayers and practices alone are not enough to impress upon all Catholics the mission to peacemaking implicit in eucharistic reception.

Scripture readings contextualize the eucharistic prayer. The Sermon on the Mount, however, and Christ's exhortation to love our enemies, are read in the Sunday liturgy only once in a three-year cycle. The same is true of the prophet Isaiah's vision of the peaceable kingdom.[64] In a culture such as ours

---

[62] Among the additional eucharistic prayers approved for use in the United States are two prayers for reconciliation that have a strong explicit theology of peace.

[63] For a full account of references to peace in the eucharistic liturgy, see the Pontifical Council for Justice and Peace, *Compendium*, n. 1102; Tobias Winright, "Gather Us In and Make Us Channels of Your Peace: Evaluating War with an Entirely New Attitude," in *Gathered for the Journey: Moral Theology in Catholic Perspective*, eds. David Matzko McCarthy and M. Therese Lysaught (Grand Rapids, MI: Eerdmans, 2007), 294–96.

[64] Isaiah 2:1-5 and Isaiah 11:1-10 are read on the first and second Sunday of Advent in lectionary Year A. Matthew 5:1-12a and 5:38-48 are read on the fourth and seventh Sunday of ordinary time in lectionary Year A.

that popularizes images of Jesus the warrior,[65] we need a stronger formation in the messianic teaching and practice of Jesus Christ and the Christian vocation to a peacemaking discipleship. To this end, Fr. Emmanual McCarthy recommends that we include in our eucharistic *anamnesis* an explicit affirmation of Christ's nonviolence. He proposes that we pray not simply "on the night before he died, he broke bread" but rather: "on the night before he died, rejecting violence, loving his enemies, and praying for his persecutors, he bestowed upon his disciples the gift of a New Commandment: Love one another. As I have loved you, so you also should love one another."[66]

2. Contextualizing the Sacrifice of the Eucharist in the Nonviolent Practice of Christ

In the Roman Catholic tradition, the Eucharist is both a memorial of Christ's unique sacrifice and a sacramental act that makes this sacrifice present, inviting members of Christ's Body to unite their own sacrifices to that of the cross.[67] Our interpretation of the sacrificial language is shaped not only by the gospels but also by association with events in our historical and cultural memories. Among the memories of North African Catholics in the fourth century was the martyrdom of Marcellus, who threw down his soldier's belt before the standards of the Roman legion and declared that he would serve Christ.[68] Today, however, the sacrificial symbols of the Eucharist meet a historical memory that typically associates the image of the cross with combat and death on a battlefield. In Germany soldiers are honored with the Iron Cross, in Britain with the Victoria Cross, in Russia with the Saint George Cross, and in France with the Cross of the League

[65] David D. Kirkpatrick, "Return of the Warrior Jesus," *New York Times* (April 4, 2004).

[66] Emmanual Charles McCarthy, "The Nonviolent Eucharistic Jesus: A Pastoral Approach," http://www.centerforchristiannonviolence.org/data/Media/NV_Eucharist _PastoralApproach_01d.pdf.

[67] On differences in Protestant and Catholic perspectives on the Eucharist and sacrifice, see David N. Power, *The Sacrifice We Offer: The Tridentine Dogma and its Reinterpretation* (New York: Crossroad, 1987). On the meaning of sacrifice from a trinitarian theological framework as distinct from sacrifice as understood in the history of religion, see Robert Daly, "Sacrifice Unveiled or Sacrifice Revisited: Trinitarian and Liturgical Perspectives," *Theological Studies* 64, no. 1 (2003): 24–42.

[68] Alban Butler, *Lives of the Saints*, ed. Herbert Thurston, SJ, and Donald Attwater, vol. 4 (Westminster, MD: Christian Classic, 1981), 220–21.

of Honor.[69] In World War I, Catholic soldiers on both sides of the trenches understood themselves to be participants in Christ's sacrifice.[70] In 1942, Catholic bishops in Hitler's Germany sent a letter to Catholic soldiers on the Russian front exhorting, "give up your life in the cross of the Lord as an expiatory sacrifice for our sins and the redemption of our people." [71]

There is no question that the suffering of those who lie dying in agony on battlefields is part of the suffering that Christ enters through the mystery of the cross. At the same time, we must recognize a fundamentally important theological distinction between Christ's sacrifice on the cross and the death of an armed soldier. The paschal mystery of Christ's death and resurrection is God's definitive triumph over the power of sin and death, the eschatological beginning of a new creation. War, in contrast, in the words of Pope John Paul II, is "a defeat for humanity"—a continuation of our fallen condition.[72] To sacrifice one's life bearing no sword or weapon is an eschatological action in the way that the sacrifice of an armed solider is not. This is not to say that in our terribly fallen world a Christian can never be justified in taking up a weapon to defend the innocent.[73] It is rather to emphasize that one who takes up arms cannot act in conformity to Christ in the same way as one who resists evil nonviolently. As the Eastern Orthodox tradition emphasizes, even if one kills another person only to prevent a greater evil, there are still damaging spiritual consequences to this act, which falls short of the norm of Christ-like love.[74]

René Girard's analysis of human history leads him to the conclusion that our willing sacrifice of human persons is a primal response to social rivalry and a means of creating social order. He believes that the history of human sacrifice climaxes with Christ's revelation of the illegitimacy of this

---

[69] Jürgen Moltmann, "The Cross as Military Symbol for Sacrifice," trans. Ingeborg Larsen, in *Cross Examinations: Readings on the Meaning of the Cross Today*, ed. Marit Trelstad (Minneapolis: Fortress, 2006), 260.

[70] See Richard Schweitzer, *The Cross and the Trenches: Religious Faith and Doubt among British and Amerian Great War Soldiers* (Westport, CT: Praeger, 2003); Annette Becker, *War and Faith: The Religious Imagination in France, 1914–1930* (New York: Berg, 1998).

[71] Cited in Moltmann, "The Cross as Military Symbol," 262.

[72] John Paul II, "The International Situation Today," 544.

[73] I know of even some Mennonites who maintain that some kind of international police force should bear and if necessary employ arms to protect the innocent and prevent genocide.

[74] See Philip LeMasters, "Peace in Orthodox Liturgy and Life," *Worship* 77, no. 5 (2003): 408–25.

practice; the victim immolated on the altar of social and political necessity is disclosed in Christ as the innocent lamb before whom all the mythologies of sacrificial violence unravel. Christians, he acknowledges, have been slow to recognize the meaning of our own revelation, but it remains embedded in the very structure of the Gospel, and the Holy Spirit, the advocate (*parakletos*) of the victim, is actively working to discredit all the gods of violence.[75]

We might hear the voice of the *parakletos* more readily if the eucharistic prayers contextualized their language of sacrifice in affirmations of the nonviolent practice of Jesus Christ, challenging our cultural assumptions about the social and even soteriological power of violence. The priest might pray, for example: "we offer to you, God of glory and majesty, this holy and perfect sacrifice *of Christ who in love renounced violence and called us to do likewise*, the bread of life and the cup of eternal salvation."[76] Or "Lord, may this sacrifice, *of Christ who loved even the enemy*, advance the peace and salvation of all the world."[77] These prayers would heighten our awareness of the difference between the sacrifice of Christ and the death of a soldier on a battlefield. "If Christian worship is finally and essentially praise and thanksgiving," David Power observes, "this is because Christians have received in Christ a way of salvation which breaks the vicious circle of evil."

3. Incorporating Lamentation into our Eucharistic Prayers

We live, writes Power, among the ruins of human culture and community. The sharper our sense of the difference between Christ's peaceable kingdom and our world of children maimed by landmines, women raped in warfare, soldiers and civilians scarred by posttraumatic stress, and soils and waters poisoned by toxins and radioactive materials, the greater the need to incorporate lamentation into the eucharistic liturgy. Through the prayers of lamentation in the Hebrew Bible, the people Israel came to God with their anguish and grief and named the betrayal of promises and the absence of *shalom*. Lamentation is the prayer both of Rachel who has lost her children (Jer 31:15) and of the sinner who has turned from the ways of God (Ps 51). For a people

---

[75] René Girard, *The Scapegoat*, trans. Yvonne Preccero (Baltimore: John Hopkins University Press, 1986), 207. See also Gil Baillie, *Violence Unveiled: Humanity at the Crossroads* (New York: Crossroad, 1995).

[76] Eucharistic Prayer I in *Sacramentary* (Collegeville, MN: Liturgical Press, 1985), with addition in italics.

[77] Eucharistic Prayer II in ibid., with addition in italics.

who are suffering, lamentation is a way of bearing the unbearable by turning pain and loss over to God—a way of voicing rage that if left to fester, readily turns to vengeance.[78] For one who is complicit in the pain of others or inured to their suffering, lamentation can rend open our hearts and begin a process of conversion.[79] Forms of systematic sin that obscure God's glory "have to be named in sorrow or bewailed," Power explains, "in order to open the way to the event of God in eucharistic remembrance."[80] Without lament, Walter Brueggeman emphasizes, praise and doxology can become acts of denial.[81]

David Power's eucharistic blessing for a time of calamity would be an appropriate prayer for a time of war. Here is just one excerpt:

> How long, O God, shall you allow death and evil to prevail over your people? Our voices are stilled by the pain that we behold on the faces of those so doomed. Be comforted, you say, but where is comfort? Peace, you proclaim, but where is peace? Receive my truth, you ask, but where is truth? . . . We praise you for Jesus Christ, for he is the one in whose suffering your judgment speaks and in whose fire we are baptized. In him we have been promised another rule, a compassionate presence, even amid strife and suffering and in hours of darkness.[82]

In the subsequent prayer of remembrance, Power proposes extending the intercessions to include those dead in the calamity at hand. In our present context, we could name not only the American men and women killed by insurgents in Iraq and Afghanistan but also the Iraqi and Afghani people killed by our bombs or by the destruction of infrastructure and the chaos that followed the invasion. In Iraq alone, the number of men, women, and children who have died is estimated to number over six hundred thousand. The US government does not include these persons in its tallies of war death statistics.[83] Our eucharistic liturgies should remember and mourn them.

---

[78] See Walter Brueggemann, "Voice as Counter to Violence," *Calvin Theological Journal* 36 (2001): 22–33.

[79] Denise M. Ackermann, *After the Locusts: Letters from a Landscape of Faith* (Grand Rapids, MI: Eerdmans, 2003), 117–21.

[80] David N. Power, OMI, *The Eucharistic Mystery: Revitalizing the Tradition* (New York: Crossroad, 1994), 336. See also "When to Worship Is to Lament" in Power, *Worship: Culture and Theology* (Washington, DC: Pastoral Press, 1990), 155–73.

[81] Walter Brueggemann, "Lament as Antidote to Silence," *Living Pulpit* 11 (October–December 2002): 24.

[82] Power, *Eucharistic Mystery*, 336–37.

[83] See Gilbert Burnham, Riyadh Lafta, Shannon Doocy, Les Roberts, "Mortality After the 2003 Invasion of Iraq: A Cross-Sectional Cluster Sample Survey," *The Lancet* (Octo-

4. Integrating Contemplation and Nonviolent Action in Catholic Formation

In a reflection on the possibility of sacramental encounter with God in our postmodern world, Paul Levesque emphasizes that mysticism and the *via negativa* must become common practices rather than the discipline of the few.[84] The loss of a sense of transcendence in the sacraments is, in his analysis, concomitant with modernity's removal of God from nature, leaving human beings as the sole masters and makers of meaning. Absent the cultural support for a theology of neo-Platonic participation or a sacramental consciousness, the Eucharist can appear to be little more than human words and gestures or a magical act disconnected from our daily lives. In response to this crisis of meaning, Levesque calls for a recovery of the inner life, following the path of darkness and unknowing in mystics such as Origen, Gregory of Nyssa, Pseudo-Dionysius, and Jan van Ruusbroec.

Just as there is little social support for sacramental consciousness in our postmodern world, so too is there little cultural support for nonviolence in our increasingly militaristic society. Patrick McCormick observes that recourse to violence is so deeply embedded in our culture that "the vast majority of American Catholics and Christians approach the moral analysis of every call to arms with a strong presumption in favor of war."[85] If the Eucharist is to be the foundation of an effective counterculture, it must be celebrated with the reverence, beauty, and joy of the Spirit that has the power to move our hearts. The exercise of contemplative disciplines such as centering prayer and eucharistic adoration support sacramental practice and give us the inner strength to resist the violence and militarism of our culture.[86] Building on this foundation in liturgy and prayer, catechesis and adult education programs can train Catholics in peacemaking and the practice of nonviolent resistance; parishes and dioceses can organize peacemaking initiatives and nonviolent action for justice at the local, national, and international levels;

---

ber 11, 2006). Published online at: http://www.thelancet.com/journals/lancet/article/PIIS0140-6736(06)69491-9/fulltext. For more recent analysis see Ronald Osborn, "Still Counting: How Many Iraqis Have Died?" *Commonweal* 138 (February 11, 2011): 10–14.

[84] Paul J. Levesque, "The Possibility of Encountering God in Postmodernity: A Return to Apophatic Theology," in *The Presence of Transcendence: Thinking 'Sacrament' in a Postmodern Age*, eds. Lieven Boeve and John C. Ries (Leuven: Peeters, 2001), 107–201.

[85] Patrick T. McCormick, "Violence: Religion, Terror, War," *Theological Studies* 67, no. 1 (March 2006): 159.

[86] Joyce Ann Zimmerman, "Eucharistic Adoration and *Missio*," *Liturgical Ministry* 13 (Spring 2004): 88–95.

and the church can support Catholic members of the military who exercise selective conscientious objection.

Conclusion

The Catholic tradition brings to our dialogue a sacramental theology of the real presence of Christ whose love overcomes even the bonds of sin and death. "This is my body, given for you." Warfare, notes war correspondent Chris Hedges with reference to Sigmund Freud's analysis of *eros* and *thanatos*, is a potent social force with erotic allure. War has the power to inspire sacrifice and unite society under the shadow of a common threat, forging bonds between the members of military units and civilian supporters. This apparent unity, however, is based on a polarizing opposition against an enemy and exists in the shadow of the possibility of annihilation.[87] It has, nonetheless, an attraction that cannot be effectively countered with moral injunction but only by the power of true *eros* and authentic communion.[88] The Eucharist has this power. It has sustained Dorothy Day, Oscar Romero, and many others unknown to us in acts of profound love and nonviolence.

Our Mennonite sisters and brothers do not share Catholicism's theology of Christ's real presence in the Eucharist *ex opere operato*. Yet contemporary developments in Catholic eucharistic theology such as an openness to the use of terms other than "transubstantiation," along with an emphasis on the Eucharist's invitation to the transformation of the communicants, may open new possibilities for bridge-building between the Catholic and Mennonite traditions. In this dialogue, Catholics offer to Mennonites a strong sacramental theology that testifies to the incarnational and unconditioned love of Christ. The Mennonite practice of the Lord's Supper challenges us, in turn, to exercise more consistently our eucharistic vocation to peacemaking. The gap between our strong sacramental theology and our historic failures to resist war to the same degree as our Mennonite brothers and sisters is cause for reexamination of our ecclesial practice. The incorporation of explicit

---

[87] Chris Hedges, *War is a Force that Gives Us Meaning* (New York: Public Affairs, 2002).

[88] After probing the complicity of German Christians in Hitler's rise to power, Eugen Drewermann concluded that the churches failed to counter the deep fears of the populace that Hitler manipulated. The church will become an instrument of peace, he argued, not by simply moralizing against war but by mediating God's love in a manner powerful enough to counter the fears that haunt the human psyche. See Matthias Beier, *A Violent God-Image: An Introduction to the Work of Eugen Drewermann* (New York: Continuum, 2004).

reference to Christ's nonviolence and call to discipleship in our eucharistic rites, the development of eucharistic prayers of lamentation, the cultivation of contemplative practices, and an ecclesial commitment to the practice of nonviolent resistance and peacemaking may help us to better exercise our vocation to become the Body of Christ that we receive.

Chapter 10

Surprising, Widening Sacramentality in the Anabaptist-Mennonite Tradition

Thomas Finger

I want to begin by expressing my profound appreciation for *Called Together to be Peacemakers*. One possible drawback of commenting on a document like this is that the task requires me to do more than emphasize its strengths. My most significant comments may well come at points where I have something more or different to say. It is possible, then, that this evaluation may sound more critical of *Called Together* than I really intend.

To avoid this impression, "let me make one thing perfectly clear," as Richard Nixon was wont to say. The task of this conference, as I understand it, is not mainly to evaluate a past document, but to continue the process that set in motion—to carry out the recommendation of paragraph 144: that Catholics and Mennonites further explore the relationships between their understandings of sacraments and ordinances. Consequently, whenever I propose that something might be said differently than the way *Called Together* says it, I will intend this not as a judgment about what the authors should have said in 2003, but as a proposal about what Catholics and Mennonites might say today. If any of us can see a bit further than the document's authors, it is because we are sitting on their shoulders.

Comprehensive Sacramentality

Let me begin, then, by suggesting that we explore Catholic and Mennonite understandings further by considering the broadest notion of "sacrament" that *Called Together* uses. The document initially describes the Catholic notion of "sacrament" as something wider than church rituals. Accordingly, it is "the mysterious manner in which God has used the agents of his creation for his self-communication."[1] Both the Catholic and Mennonite sections of the document insist that their subject matter extends far beyond church rituals, and encompasses all of life. "There is scarcely any proper use of material things which cannot thus be directed towards the sanctification of men and the praise of God."[2]

Nevertheless, as the Mennonite perspective unfolds under the heading of "Ordinances," these are immediately described as church rituals. With this, the broader perspective recedes. The Sacrament/Ordinance contrast, of course, is a helpful, traditional way of illuminating many similarities and differences, and is quite appropriate in a document like this. I want to suggest, however, that further comparisons might come to light if we begin from that overall perspective on reality that Catholics call "sacramental" and ask whether a similar perspective exists among Mennonites.

A Catholic Orientation

Let me propose that we describe the Catholic notion of sacraments, at least provisionally, in a classical, more broadly Christian way as the communication of divine, invisible, spiritual grace through creaturely, visible, material channels.[3] Sacraments, so defined, extend far beyond the church and its rituals. Almost any physical object, process, or human action can potentially become sacramental. Further, since divine grace is dynamic, such sacraments will not be separate objects or actions but will participate in, or be instruments of, that eschatological process by which God is bringing heaven and earth, humans and all creatures, ever more closely together. Catholic sacramental theology, since at least the Second Vatican Council, often extends far beyond the church or its usual theological vocabulary and seeks to conceptualize sacramental reality in more basic, broader terms.[4] One current emphasis might be called "anthropological," in the sense that it asks what human subjects are doing when they dispense, receive, and gather

---

[1] *Called Together to be Peacemakers*, par. 112.

[2] Ibid., par. 113. This section (pars. 111–44) is repeatedly interlinked with "The Nature of the Church" (pars. 70–110).

[3] Some points below are more fully developed in my article "Sacramentality" (Mennonite-Catholic Theological Colloquium, 2006) available at http://www.bridgefolk.net /theology/colloquia.

[4] For a detailed overview, see David Power, "Sacramental Theology: A Review of the Literature," *Theological Studies* 55, no. 4 (Dec. 1994): 657–746. For a briefer selection of Catholic views pertinent to Mennonites, see "Sacramentality," 3–10.

around sacraments. Karl Rahner, for instance, defined humans as symbol-making creatures, and developed his sacramental theology from a general analysis of symbols.[5] Other sacramental theologians draw on communication theory,[6] on Juergen Habermas' theory of communicative action, and on social psychology, depth psychology, cultural anthropology, ethnology, and philosophy of language.[7]

Another major emphasis is sociopolitical. According to Leonardo Boff, the Latin American liberation theologian, the entire universe is sacramental, and "Sacramental language is essentially evocative, self-involving, and performance-oriented. Sacraments refer to sacred moments and places in order to disclose the sacredness of everyday life, and to engage participants in acts of redemption here and now."[8] Latin American and feminist theologians argue that fixed, traditional, repetitive sacramental practices can support systemic social exploitation. Many feminists want sacraments to be "freed from ideologies, opened to new inspiration, encompassing new experiences, and nourished by new memories."[9]

Some current Catholic theologians are concerned, however, that investigations of sacramentality's anthropological and sociopolitical significance often stress its human and material side at the expense of its divine and spiritual dimension.[10] It is important to add, therefore, that not a few sac-

[5] Karl Rahner, *Theological Investigations,* vol. 4 (New York: Seabury, 1974), esp. 224–30, 234–42. For a simpler account of this general approach, see Bernard Cooke, *Sacraments and Sacramentality* (Mystic, CT: Twenty-Third, 1983).

[6] Esp. Alexander Ganoczy, *An Introduction to Catholic Sacramental Theology* (New York: Paulist, 1984).

[7] A major effort to incorporate many of these disciplines is Donald Gelpi, *Committed Worship: A Sacramental Theology for Converting Adult Christians,* vol. 1: *Adult Conversion and Initiation;* vol. 2: *The Sacraments of Ongoing Conversion* (Collegeville, MN: Liturgical Press, 1993).

[8] Power, "Sacramental Theology" (1994), 10. See esp. Boff, *Sacraments of Life, Life of the Sacraments: Story Theology* (Washington: Pastoral, 1987). Juan Luis Segundo, the Latin American liberation theologian, investigates the role of sacraments in forming base communities. He describes how sacramental liturgy can liberate people from structures of injustice and oppression. *The Sacraments Today* (Maryknoll, NY: Orbis, 1974).

[9] Power, "Sacramental Theology," 18; see esp. Mary Collins, "Principles of Feminist Liturgy" in Marjorie Procter-Smith and Janet Walton, eds., *Women at Worship* (Louisville, Westminster/Knox 1993), 9–26.

[10] Esp. Dennis Martin, "Two Trains Passing in the Night: a response to Thomas Finger" and "Sacramentality," available at http://www.bridgefolk.net/theology/colloquia. Martin apparently does not notice that I express the same concerns. He critiques me for selecting "a handful of contemporary self-proclaimed Catholic *theologians*" (2) "whose

ramental theologians begin, systematically, from more traditional starting points such as the liturgy,[11] the Trinity,[12] or (as we shall soon see in more detail) from Christ himself, conceived as the *primordial sacrament*[13] and/or from the church itself as the *primary sacrament*.[14]

A Mennonite Orientation

Because the Anabaptists rejected Catholic and even much Protestant sacramentality in their church life, it is often said that they and their descendants were "antisacramental." However, if we approach this issue from the perspective we have adopted, we must first ask whether a similar overarching perspective on divine activity, human life, and indeed the whole creation, informs the life-orientation, or *Lebenspraxis*, of most Mennonites. I propose that it does, although it is far more often apprehended intuitively than it is articulated theologically. Mennonites, beginning with their Anabaptist forebears, have insisted at least as much as any Christian movement that divine grace must inform every concrete activity and relationship. Their emphasis on following Jesus "literally" originated, I believe, not so much from ethical idealism as from the conviction that God's Spirit was so active in their material world that such a concrete, detailed, all-encompassing *praxis* was possible. Such a perspective, which envisions our entire material world

---

positions were condemned in *Mysterium Fidei*" (3, by Pope Paul VI) and for bypassing "the definitive magisterial statements of the Catholic Church." (4) If these theologians are so "marginal," why are they and many similar ones prominently featured in David Power's 89-page survey? I consider more traditional and magisterial statements important. But sufficient consideration of them in "Sacramentality" or the present essay would require lengthy discussion of intra-Catholic issues and obscure my purpose. Martin seems to demand that if Mennonites wish to dialogue, they must be thoroughly acquainted with traditional Catholic sacramentology. Yet he pays no real attention to my presentation of Anabaptism and dismisses the movement pejoratively (7–8).

[11] Power, "Sacramental Theology," 1–3, 23.

[12] E.g., by Edward Kilmartin, *Christian Liturgy: Theology and Practice*, vol. 1 *Systematic Theology of Liturgy* (Kansas City: Sheed & Ward, 1988), esp. 172–97; also Catherine Mowry LaCugna, *God For Us: The Trinity and the Christian Life* (San Francisco: Harper, 1991), 111–42.

[13] See, e.g., Cooke 1983; Eduard Schillebeeckx, *Christ the Sacrament of Encounter with God* (New York: Sheed & Ward, 1963), 19–39.

[14] *Called Together* calls Christ the "source-sacrament" and the church the "fundamental sacrament" (par. 112).

being open to and being repeatedly transformed by divine Spirit, might even be called "super-sacramental."

However, even when it is recognized that Anabaptists/Mennonites retained some kind of sacramental perspective, it is often supposed that they secularized it—that is, they expelled it from the church and relocated it in the world. If they did, their understandings of ecclesiology and of specific sacraments/ordinances would stress the human and material dimensions far more than divine and spiritual ones. To consider this possibility, we must now ask, how far the similarities I have mentioned extend into Anabaptist/ Mennonite Church life? And how different or similar might their views and Catholic views in these areas be?

Sacramentality and the Church

Called Together shows that while Mennonites usually identify "ordinances" narrowly with church rituals, the Catholic "sacraments" express more fully the church's overall nature. As I have mentioned, some Catholic theologians today call Christ in his incarnation—the fullest, most decisive entry of divine, spiritual reality into the creaturely, material world—the *primordial sacrament*, and the church the *primary sacrament*, which originated from Christ. This *primary sacrament* is then further expressed, or actualized, through the seven specific sacraments. Might Mennonites have taught something similar?

It is interesting to note why Menno Simons rejected the efficacy of "signs and symbols" in church ritual—precisely because Jesus is "the true Sign of all signs" and "the true sign of grace." [15] Menno's colleague, Dirk Philips, insisted that the church's covenant with God was "bound to no external symbol" because "Jesus Christ alone . . . is the only and true sign of faith." [16] In these statements, Menno and Dirk were rejecting Catholic sacramentality as they understood it, because it obscured what Catholics today can call the primordial sacrament—not because they objected to calling church rituals sacraments, for they sometimes used this word. Moreover, while historian C. Arnold Snyder can call the Anabaptist movement as a whole "antisacramen-

[15] In John Wenger, ed., *The Complete Writings of Menno Simons* (Scottdale, PA: Herald, 1956), 686.

[16] In Cornelius Dyck, William Keeney, Alvin Beachy eds., *The Writings of Dirk Philips* (Scottdale, PA: Herald, 1992), 102. God, moreover, "surrendered Jesus Christ, his only Son, into death for us (John 3:16) as a sure sign of divine grace" (102).

tal" when he refers to its general rejection of Catholic ritual,[17] he summarizes its positive ecclesiology under the heading, "The Church as Sacrament."[18]

I think, then, that many Mennonites would resonate with the contemporary Catholic way of deriving church sacraments (or ordinances, if they prefer) first from Christology, and then through ecclesiology—all within the wider framework of creation and God's comprehensive, salvific, eschatological process. I, for one, can agree entirely with paragraph 112 of *Called Together*, which outlines the *Catholic* understanding of sacraments. Many of my Mennonite friends and colleagues, I think, would view it similarly (except perhaps for the "sacrament" terminology).

Let us consider, next, how Anabaptists and Mennonites have viewed specific sacraments/ordinances. Will we find further similarities with Catholic understandings, or much more "secular" interpretations?

According to Snyder, all historic Anabaptists engaged in four basic practices.[19] Two of these, baptism and the Lord's Supper, were rituals that all other churches performed (though Anabaptists conducted baptism very differently, of course). But the other two Anabaptist practices were rooted in everyday life. Discipline, which might better be called "mutual discipling," comprised the many ways in which Anabaptists encouraged, accompanied, admonished, and sometimes corrected each other as they sought to follow Jesus through the ordinary tasks of life. Anabaptist discipline bears some resemblance to the Catholic sacrament of reconciliation (formerly called penance) today.[20]

The fourth common Anabaptist practice, economic sharing, carried radical implications for their lives in the world. Some Anabaptists, most notably the Hutterites, surrendered all their private property and formed communities of production and consumption. Most others shared their goods with others when needed—which, in a lower-class, persecuted movement, was very often. However, these last two practices (discipline and economic sharing) were closely intertwined with the first two (baptism and the Lord's Supper).

[17] C. Arnold Snyder, *Anabaptist Theology and History: An Introduction* (Kitchener, ON: Pandora, 1995), 85–86. By "anti-sacramentalism" Snyder means the view "that neither priests nor sacraments were capable of conveying God's grace" (85).

[18] Ibid., 351–64.

[19] Ibid., 90–93, 373–74.

[20] See James Dallen, *The Reconciling Community* (New York: Pueblo, 1986), esp. 258–60.

These two everyday, more "worldly" practices, were also celebrated in church rituals and were ecclesial as well.[21]

For example, believers' baptism, where the candidates and the congregation commit themselves to each other, formed the basis for mutual accountability, or discipline.[22] Since the Lord's Supper should be celebrated by those at peace with God and their neighbors, discipline often preceded it.[23] Further, the Supper re-presented Jesus' giving of himself for the communicants. This moved them to give their lives, if need be, and also their goods, for each other. In this way, the Supper provided a basis for economic sharing; distribution of goods often followed it.[24] Sharing could also be connected with baptism, perhaps because it was expected as a normal result.[25]

In none of these instances did the features of discipline and economic sharing dilute the personal and spiritual significance of baptism and the Lord's Supper, or replace them with "worldly" meanings. Instead, these features expressed, or expanded, the inherent significance of these two rituals. Historic Anabaptists were neither "secularizing" sacramentality, nor transferring it from the church to the world, as is sometimes said,[26] but linking the church with broader material reality in their own way.

To determine whether or how Mennonites might be "sacramental," it is not enough, I submit, to take some list of approved sacraments, such as the Catholic seven, and ask how many of them Mennonites practice. We should focus on the relationships among the divine and the human, and the

[21] For a Catholic view of the relationship between worship and life in the world, see Margaret Pfeil "Liturgical Asceticism: Where Grace and Discipleship Meet" her response to my article, "Sacramentality," available at http://www.bridgefolk.net/theology/colloquia.

[22] Wayne Pipkin and John Yoder, eds., *Balthasar Hubmaier* (Scottdale, PA: Herald, 1989), 127; cf. 85–86, 239, 389, 413–15; Conrad Grebel and Friends, "Letters to Thomas Muentzer" in George Williams and Angel Mergal, eds., *Spiritual and Anabaptist Writers* (Philadelphia: Westminster, 1957), 80.

[23] This was widely practiced in Swiss Anabaptism and by Pilgram Marpeck. See Thomas Finger, *A Contemporary Anabaptist Theology* (Downers Grove, IL: InterVarsity, 2004), 210, 214.

[24] Taught by Hubmaier, Hans Schlaffer, Marpeck, and Philips (Finger, "A Contemporary Anabaptist Theology," 236–42).

[25] Hans Hut, "The Mystery of Baptism" in Daniel Liechty, ed., *Early Anabaptist Spirituality* (New York: Paulist Press, 1994), 72.

[26] Dennis Martin interprets me as saying that they did, and castigates Anabaptists for succumbing to "a new (modern) view of nature and grace" without responding to the very different view of Anabaptism that I develop (7–8).

spiritual and the material, in Mennonite faith and life as a whole. We should then ask: in what primary ways do Mennonites express these?

We can continue this process by searching neither for sacraments nor ordinances as usually defined, but for "sacrament*als*," a broader term that includes these and other physical expressions of faith, such as footwashing, which Mennonites have often practiced.[27]

Speaking of footwashing, Bridgefolk members can attest to its powerful *sacramental* significance, especially at times when we have not celebrated the Eucharist together. And what about singing? The classical definition of sacrament, a "visible" sign of invisible grace, predisposes us to consider only the visual. But "visible" certainly means "perceptible." It includes audible expressions, such as singing, and also the taste of bread and the touch of water.

Before leaving this topic of sacramentality and the church, I should acknowledge that I have so far pointed more towards possible Catholic-Mennonite similarities than towards differences. For balance, I should also identify what many Mennonites would consider some main differences.

The major reason why many Mennonites resist "sacrament" language, as I see it, is that they suppose, first, that such words refer solely to church rituals and second, that these rituals are supposed to impart divine grace automatically and directly, even to passive participants. For Mennonites, however, God's grace will not transform people unless they respond in some way, which must be ultimately consistent with Jesus' life and teachings.[28]

This objection, of course, is to a stereotyped construal of the Catholic *ex operere operato*. But crude as this construal may be, it still persists widely. Yet I find the *ex operere operato* principle barely mentioned in *Called Together.* Further, I find no real discussion of another long-disputed notion, the Eucharist as a sacrifice.[29] Consequently, while *Called Together* unearths some unexpected Catholic-Mennonite similarities, I find it nearly silent on several important disagreements that our continuing explorations should consider.

Second, while most Mennonites could probably consider Christ as something like the primordial sacrament establishing the church, they would

---

[27] Among early Anabaptists, however, only the Dutch practiced it in a consistent, somewhat "sacramental" manner (cf. Snyder, 375).

[28] See Margaret Pfeil's generally positive response to this point in "Liturgical Asceticism," 2–3.

[29] "Responding to the Call: Reflections on *Called Together to be Peacemakers*" finds this omission "striking," (Toronto Mennonite Theological Centre, 2007) 4, par. 18; Dennis Martin strongly criticizes its near omission of sacrifice (3, 5–6) and of *ex operere operato* (4–5).

question phrases such as, "The sacraments are *constitutive* of the very reality of the Church;"[30] that the Eucharist is the "source . . . of the whole life of the Church;" or that the bread is the "source" and not simply the "sign of *koininia/communion* in the one body."[31] Mennonites, who prioritize ethical living and communal relationships, find it difficult to think of a ritual, no matter how important, actually *constituting* the church.

Many Mennonites might agree, at least unreflectively, with the declaration by Anabaptist theologian Balthasar Hubmaier that "the church is built on our faith . . . not we on the faith of the church."[32] Nevertheless, Hubmaier hardly meant *sola fide*.[33] Neither did he mean to replace an objective basis for the church simplistically with a merely subjective one. For Hubmaier, like other Anabaptists,[34] considered correct administration at least of baptism, the Supper, and discipline to be essential to any true church. In rejecting the priority of "the faith of the Church," Hubmaier implicitly critiqued infant baptism but not the notion that the church and its primary practices precede individual congregations and Christians, and were instituted by God.

In any case, many Mennonites today could view the church, established by the primordial sacrament Jesus Christ, as the primary sacrament that, through Christ, establishes certain practices that are essential to its life and mission. But much like Menno Simons and Dirk Philips, they probably would not call these practices "constitutive" or "sources" of ecclesial reality. Rather they would call Christ the sole Source who constitutes the church and whatever efficacy its sacraments or ordinances might have.

Particular Sacraments

Although I have sketched some broad meanings of baptism and the Lord's Supper for Catholics and historic Anabaptists, let us consider some further implications of *Called Together* for their practice today.

---

[30] *Called Together to be Peacemakers*, par. 114; cf. par. 82 (italics mine).

[31] Ibid., par. 117; cf. par. 106 on ordination, par. 116 on baptism, par. 138 on the Eucharist.

[32] *Balthasar Hubmaier*, 247.

[33] Ibid., 70, 375.

[34] Ibid., 239, 375; Walter Klaassen and William Klassen, trans., *The Writings of Pilgram Marpeck* (Scottdale, PA: Herald, 1978), 292, 300, 340; *The Writings of Dirk Philips*, 218–19, 301, 345; *The Complete Writings of Menno Simons*, 501–2, cf. 539, 239, 375.

Baptism

Called Together identifies Catholic practice almost entirely with infant baptism and Mennonites with believers or adult baptism. However, some Catholic theologians argue, in light of the post–Vatican II *Rite of Christian Initiation for Adults*, that the adult ritual is actually the normative Catholic form, while infant baptism might be called a "benign abnormality."[35] *The Shape of Baptism*, a book by one of these theologians, Aidan Kavanagh, is the best treatment of believers' baptism that I know. These theologians predict that Catholic congregations that emphasize it will become more like ideal "believers' churches"—far more active in evangelism, catechesis, and the formation of committed, articulate members.

Admittedly, Catholic interest in believers' baptism was greater in the '70s and '80s than it is today. Yet it is entirely absent from *Called Together*. Moreover, one main Catholic argument for believers' baptism was its widespread practice in the second and third centuries.[36] But the Mennonite section in *Called Together* does not mention this era, while the Catholic section only draws support for infant baptism from it (par. 116). Nonetheless, *Called Together* recommends further joint exploration of these centuries (par. 143). I recommend not only this but also a comparison of Mennonite and Catholic arguments for *believers'* baptism.

Called Together also omits the common Mennonite practice of dedicating infants or children. This ritual conveys many benefits often attributed to infant baptism. The congregation receives children who are commended to its nurture—or, could Mennonites perhaps say, who are incorporated into "the faith of the church," as paedobaptist churches sometimes do? If so, discussion of this concept might help Mennonites and Catholics clarify their understandings of baptism and faith. In any case, an account of dedication, in my view, would be indispensable for any comprehensive understanding of children's participation in Mennonite churches and for evaluating the perception that Mennonites, because they reject infant baptism, consider children and children's experiences unimportant (the document recommends this topic for further discussion in par. 141).

---

[35] Aidan Kavanagh, *The Shape of Baptism* (Collegeville, MN: Liturgical Press, 1978), 10: this does not mean that infant baptism is wholly invalid, although "The data of neither scripture nor tradition can be made to support infant baptism as the pastoral norm."

[36] Ibid., 35–78.

We might also ask whether older children who eventually expect to be baptized participate in the church much as did catechumens in the first centuries. Further, Mennonite views on infant baptism might be understood more precisely by asking why some congregations occasionally admit people baptized as infants to membership on confession of faith alone.[37]

Eucharist

Admittedly, many Mennonites have understood the Lord's Supper simply as a memorial, and its elements simply as signs pointing to the past. Nonetheless, numerous Anabaptist authors, Mennonite confessions, and other musical, liturgical, and written sources mention participatory and transformative dimensions that one might compare usefully with Catholic understandings. Many Mennonites experience Christ's presence in communion. But they do not locate this presence mainly where traditional theology has sought it—in the elements, in the words pronounced, or in the communicant's subjectivity.

Instead, I propose, communion's most distinctive feature for early Anabaptists and many later Mennonites can be designated the "communal presence of Christ."[38] Such a presence, of course, extended in a way to the elements, the words, and each communicant's experience—but that was because Jesus was present in and among the whole gathered body, throughout the entire service. Such a notion resonates with much current Catholic worship and theology. Vatican II identified "full and active participation by all the people" as "the aim to be considered" in the liturgy "before all else."[39] Many Catholic theologians stress that Christ is present not simply in the elements or the words of institution, but throughout the Service of the Word and the Service of the table, in the prayers, the hymns, the kiss of peace, and all else that occurs.

Anabaptist/Mennonites intertwine this communal dimension with the sharing of goods and of personal concerns, which can occur during the service. Current Catholic theologians also underline these social and economic dimensions.[40] According to some, bread and wine recall the labor and the pro-

[37] "Responding to the Call" recommends further exploration of this issue, along with the implications of the RCIA and the Mennonite understanding of children's place in the church (3, par. 14); cf. Thomas Finger, *A Contemporary Anabaptist Theology*, 182–84.

[38] Finger, *A Contemporary Anabaptist Theology*, 196–97, 201–4.

[39] Walter Abbot, ed., *The Documents of Vatican II* (New York: Guild, 1966), 144.

[40] Cooke, 168–212; James Empereur and Christopher Kiesling, *The Liturgy that Does Justice* (Collegeville, MN: Liturgical Press, 1990), 109–30.

cesses needed to produce and distribute them.[41] Sharing the elements and the overall experience overcomes barriers of status, ethnicity, wealth, and class.[42]

Some Catholic theologians integrate this communal dimension with the memorial dimension. According to David Power, reference to the cross is not simply to a single event, but to the overall narrative, which includes the cross. Remembering this narrative recalls the kind of person Jesus was—how he lived, what he taught, who opposed him, why he died.[43] This can impress upon us the whole way of Jesus and the importance of following him, as Mennonites emphasize, but as some Catholic sacramental theologians are saying much better.

It appears, then, that Mennonites and Catholics could learn much by comparing the Anabaptist/Mennonite emphasis on Christ's communal presence, on its social and economic aspects, and on the Supper's memorial dimension with contemporary Catholic expressions of and reflections on these.

Finally, when contemporary Catholics emphasize Christ's presence through-out the liturgy, they intimate that he is present not so much in specific things or words as he is in actions. Catholics and Mennonites can learn more about this from Anabaptism's most profound theologian, Pilgram Marpeck. The transformation of the human by the divine, and of matter by Spirit, was central to his theology. Like other Anabaptists, Marpeck avoided what he considered the crude, materialistic notion of transforming the *substances*, or *essences*, of Christ's body and blood literally into the *essences* of bread and wine. But he still wanted to show why bread, wine, and water are not arbitrary signs that simply point, but crucial features of the sacraments themselves.

Marpeck did so by insisting that the Supper (like baptism) was not a *thing* but an *activity*. The elements' significance lies not in their *nature* but in their overall *function*.[44] One major function was to bring Jesus' risen reality into the congregation's present life. This continued that transformation of matter by Spirit that had begun in Jesus' life. The Lord's Supper, in other words, was itself an agent, even a component, of matter's continuing transformation by Spirit.

---

[41] Philippe Rouillard, "From Human Meal to Eucharist," in Kevin Seasoltz, ed., *Living Bread, Saving Cup* (Collegeville, MN: Liturgical Press, 1987), 109–30.

[42] David Power, *The Eucharistic Mystery* (New York: Crossroad, 1995), 28.

[43] Ibid., 44, 298, 304–16.

[44] *The Writings of Pilgram Marpeck*, 170–71, 269, 277, 283; Marpeck, *Pilgram Marbecks Antwort auf Kaspar Schwenckfeld's Beurteilung des Buches der Bundesbezeugnis von 1542* (Vienna: Carl Fromme, 1929), 453–56, 465.

Bread and wine, then, actually participated in that transformation. Marpeck concluded that they belong to the sacrament's *essence*. He did not mean that the elements' material essences alter, but that they, precisely in their materiality, are essential to that process, or *activity*, called the Lord's Supper.[45] Without these elements, such a ritual could not *be* the Lord's Supper. For the Supper not only symbolizes matter's transformation by Spirit but also actualizes it, makes it happen. In this activity, then, its material elements are being transformed as the Supper takes place—not, however, *ontologically*, but in their *activity*, in their *functions*. These elements, then, are *essential* for conveying Jesus' risen life, through his Spirit, to the congregation, even though their creaturely *essences* remain the same.

Not long ago, some Catholic theologians advocated a theory that seems similar to me, called "transignification." They proposed that sacramental elements do change—but in their signification, or in what they signify, and in the way they perform this. A loaf of bread, for instance, usually signifies, or functions as, a means of bodily nourishment. But when the risen Jesus employs it, through the actions of a Christian community, to convey his invisible, divine presence, the bread takes on a quite different function or signification (though it still provides some nourishment). We can say that it "is" Christ's body, for all intents and purposes.

Whereas Marpeck taught that a sacramental element, through its function, can become essential to a rite, transignification proposes that a radical change in function transforms the element itself.

Support for transignification among Catholic theologians has declined for several decades, perhaps more than it has for believers' baptism. Pope Paul VI critiqued transignification for not really affirming an ontological change in the elements, as required in Catholic doctrine.[46] Nevertheless, transignification may provide a way for Mennonites to make sense of affirming "this *is* the body (or blood) of Christ," as many of us do in practice. Combined with Marpeck's sacramental theology, it might provide resources for further Catholic-Mennonite discussion.

---

[45] "[N]ot the element . . . but the activity . . . not water, bread and wine . . . but baptism and the Supper" are "one essence with the inner" (Marpeck 1929, 137, cf. 114, 121, 124, 127, 456, 458; Marpeck 1978, 195, 196).

[46] Pope Paul VI, *Mysterium Fidei* (London: Catholic Truth Society, 1965), par. 46. It is not "allowable to discuss the mystery of transubstantiation without mentioning . . . the marvelous conversion of the whole substance of bread into the Body and the whole substance of the wine into the Blood of Christ, speaking rather only of what is called 'transignification'" (par. 11, cf. par. 14).

Despite all the Catholic-Mennonite similarities above, *Called Together* claims that for Mennonites, ordinances and their elements are simply signs or symbols that point beyond themselves (pars. 120, 139). Yet this document itself cites Mennonite confessions that treat baptism "not only as a sign that points" but as an action that produces "effectual change" and as a "*means* of . . . regeneration and renewal;"[47] and also some Mennonite confessions that speak of the Lord's Supper as an act that bestows "effectual power . . . to bring change" as "the gathered body of believers shares in the body and blood of Christ."[48] I mention this not to poke holes in this excellent text, but to suggest these participatory and transformative dimensions, which many Mennonites experience, as a topic for further exploration.

Sacraments and Eschatology

As I have moved from a broad vision of sacramentality towards specific sacraments, one main feature of this vision may have been partially dimmed. This is that sacraments are not separate objects or actions, but participate together in, and are instruments of, that eschatological process that is bringing God, human beings, and all creatures more closely together. Sacraments not only recall past events and convey present realities but also point towards the future.

It is interesting that *transignification* can also be called *transfinalization*. This means that all the eucharistic actions and elements are caught up into the kind of final unity with God that will someday pervade all creation. In this way, eucharistic transformation affects not only humans but all creation. This new creation, which is "not yet" fully present, becomes "already" present in this way.[49]

To be sure, sacramental actions and elements transform only small portions of creation. But through them, I believe, God's Spirit and God's kingdom are already truly present—though not yet fully present. As such, sacraments not only fill us with divine grace and communal joy but increases our hunger for more. Rightly appropriated, sacraments send us together into the wider creation, to hope and work for its greater transformation by grace.

In this way, the church is an *eschatological sacrament*, to use a favorite term of Catholic liberation theologians. That is, the church is a visible manifestation of the future that God desires for all humans and other creatures. To

---

[47] *Called Together to be Peacemakers*, par. 123.

[48] Ibid., par. 126; this is recognized in "Responding to the Call" (4, par. 17).

[49] Joseph Powers, *Eucharistic Theology* (New York: Herder & Herder, 1967), 115–16, 131–39.

be sure, it is a partial and partly distorted manifestation, but nevertheless a real manifestation of God's intention.

Called Together notes that Catholics and Mennonites both stress *visibility*—stress the need to express and live their faith in clearly perceptible ways (pars. 97, 109). Many members of both communions seek to render God's grace and kingdom increasingly visible and actual in the world, looking forward to the time when "the earth will be filled with the knowledge of the glory of the Lord as the waters cover the sea" (Hab 2:14). Though some sacramental issues divide Mennonites and Catholics, I hope we all can consider ourselves participants in the *eschatological sacrament*—as fortunate recipients of the dynamic divine grace that impels us towards the future, that grace that through us, and sometimes in spite of us, spills over into the whole creation.

PART 5

Our Commitment to Peace

The Church is called to be a peace church, a peacemaking church. This is based on a conviction that we hold in common. We hold that the Church, founded by Christ, is called to be a living sign and an effective instrument of peace, overcoming every form of enmity and reconciling all peoples in the peace of Christ. We affirm that Christ, in his Church, through baptism, overcomes the differences between peoples. By virtue of their baptism into Christ, all Christians are called to be peacemakers. All forms of ethnic and inter-religious hatred and violence are incompatible with the gospel, and the Church has a special role in overcoming ethnic and religious differences and in building international peace. Furthermore, we agree that it is a tragedy when Christians kill one another.

Called Together to Be Peacemakers, paragraph 175

We agree that the Gospel's vision of peace includes active non-violence for the defence of human life and human rights, for the promotion of economic justice for the poor, and in the interest of fostering solidarity among peoples. Likewise, peace is the realization of the fundamental right to live a life in dignity, and so have access to all means to accomplish this: land, work, health, and education. For this reason, the Church is called to stand in solidarity with the poor and to be an advocate for the oppressed. A peace built on oppression is a false peace. . . . We hold the conviction in common that reconciliation, nonviolence, and active peacemaking belong to the heart of the Gospel.

Called Together to Be Peacemakers, paragraphs 178–79

Mennonites and Catholics share the common conviction that worship and prayer belong to the core of Christian peace work.

Called Together to Be Peacemakers, paragraph 185

Chapter 11

Pax Christi and the Gospel of Peace

Making the Case for the Abolition of War in the Twenty-First Century

Bishop Gabino Zavala

My task today is to comment on the document *Called Together to Be Peacemakers*[1]—the fruit of five years of international dialogue between the Catholic Church and the Mennonite World Conference—and specifically the section entitled "Our Commitment to Peace." It is a wonderful document and reflects how much Catholics and Mennonites share in common, in particular their "common commitment to peacemaking . . . rooted in our communion with 'the God of peace' (Rom 15:33) and in the church's response to Jesus' proclamation of 'the gospel of peace' (Eph 6:15)."[2]

I want to affirm the value of this dialogue. In a very concrete way, we are helping each other through this dialogue to be who we are and who we are called to be. Our engagement as Catholics with your Mennonite tradition and your witness as a peace church inspires us Catholics to be who we truly are, by being deeply rooted in the gospel of peace and by bearing witness to the peace of Christ in the world. As the report of our journey describes so well, *together* we are called to be peacemakers.

I speak today as Bishop President of Pax Christi USA. The very story of how Pax Christi began speaks to the heart of reconciliation and forgiveness,[3] which is at the heart of the gospel of peace and peacemaking. It is also fun-

[1] *Called Together to Be Peacemakers: Report of the International Dialogue between the Catholic Church and Mennonite World Conference, 1998–2003.*

[2] Ibid., par. 145.

[3] A longer version of this story is available on the Pax Christi International website: www.paxchristi.net.

damental to our deep and mutual desire for unity as Christians. It all began in France during the Second World War, a context in which terrible things were happening throughout Europe.

Pax Christi really grew from two seeds of inspiration. The first was a bishop—Pierre-Marie Théas, Bishop of Montauban in the South of France. During the war he was one of the only bishops to protest against the deportation of Jews from France. In a pastoral letter to be read throughout his diocese in 1942, he wrote: "I give voice to the outraged protest of Christian conscience, and I proclaim . . . that all men, whatever their race or religion, have the right to be respected by individuals and by states."

One evening in 1944, Bishop Théas spoke in his cathedral against the deportation of Jews and of young French men who were being sent to forced labor camps. The next day he was arrested and spent several weeks in a prison camp at Compiegne. While he was there the other prisoners asked him to lead them in prayer and reflection. He chose to preach on "Love your enemies" and suggested that they should pray for their jailers. This provoked a strong reaction. They found it so hard to accept. When Bishop Théas had the chance to celebrate mass in the camp, he offered it for Germany and its people. Bishop Théas was released a few weeks later and went back to his diocese, but that prison episode affected him deeply and gave him an understanding of how difficult and demanding true reconciliation between enemies would be.

The second Pax Christi seed of inspiration was a teacher, wife, and mother—Marthe Dortel-Claudot—who also lived in the South of France. She was involved in her local parish and was a very prayerful person. During the winter of 1944, as Christmas approached, Marthe found herself thinking about the suffering of the German people. She wrote in her journal: "Jesus died for everyone. Nobody should be excluded from one's prayer." She prayed that Germany would be healed of the spiritual and moral effects of twelve years of Nazism. Encouraged by her parish priest, she formed a small group who prayed with her for the rebuilding of Germany and for peace. Among the first to join her were a war widow, the daughter of a deportee, and some Carmelites.

The next step was to try to find a bishop to give the project official church support. The first person she asked refused. But in March of 1945, she went to see Bishop Théas. He was, of course, exactly the right person to understand her vision. He agreed to help, provided his archbishop approved. So the next day Madame Dortel-Claudot visited the Archbishop of Toulouse and obtained his support. When she returned to Montauban with this news,

Bishop Théas accepted the leadership of the new "Crusade of Prayer" for Germany. The project was given the name Pax Christi.

This vision of reconciliation, which these two people (Madame Dortel-Claudot and Bishop Théas) had experienced, was a strong inspiration in the early days of Pax Christi. It remains a key aspect of our spirituality, and an essential part of the gospel of peace that resonates so deeply with Catholics and Mennonites alike.

What We Share

Let me briefly outline what, according to our dialogue, we share together:

We share a common story: "We understand peace through the teachings, life, and death of Jesus Christ. In his mission of reconciliation he remained faithful unto death on the cross, and his fidelity was confirmed in the resurrection. The cross is the sign of God's love of enemies."[4]

We share a common mission: "The Church is called to be a peace church, a peacemaking church. This is based on a conviction we hold in common. We hold that the Church, founded by Christ, is called to be a living sign and an effective instrument of peace, overcoming every form of enmity and reconciling all peoples in the peace of Christ (Eph 4:1-3)."[5]

We share a common vision: "We affirm together that peace, in the sense of the biblical word *shalom*, consists of well being, wholeness, the harmony and rightness of relationships. As inheritors of the biblical tradition, we believe that justice, understood as right relationships, is the inseparable companion of peace."[6]

And we share a common witness: "We both agree that discipleship, understood as following Christ in life in accordance with the teaching and example of Jesus, is basic to the Christian life. The earthly existence of Jesus is normative for human well being (John 13:1-17; Phil 2:1-11). The decisions Jesus made and the steps he took leading to his crucifixion reveal the centrality of love, including love of enemy, in human life (Matt 5:38-48)."[7]

There is so much we share, including our desire to respond faithfully to Jesus' prayer "that we may all be one" (John 17:21),[8] as well as our commit-

---

[4] *Called Together*, par. 174.
[5] Ibid., par. 175.
[6] Ibid., par. 177.
[7] Ibid., par. 180.
[8] Ibid., par. 98.

ment "to bring the Good News of salvation to all nations by proclaiming the Gospel in word and in deed to the ends of the earth" (Isa 2:1-5; Matt 28:16-20; Eph 4:11f).[9]

We should, of course, acknowledge our differences where we diverge— around our understanding of the nature of the church, sacraments and ordinances, and how we live out our commitment to peace. But we also acknowledge a willingness to engage in fruitful dialogue, and to learn from each other. Where we converge, we are already growing in a sense of dwelling in that unity for which Jesus prayed and are participating in prayer for Christian unity, reflection on mission, peace and justice initiatives, and faith formation.[10]

Especially moving is the final section of the document, "Toward a Healing of Memories," along with the steps required to continue that process. Let us recall together the steps that *Called Together* names:

- a purification of memories . . . facing those difficult events of the past that give rise to divergent interpretations of what happened and why[11]
- a spirit of repentance . . . asking God's forgiveness as well as forgiveness from each other[12]
- ascertaining the degree to which we have continued to share the Christian faith despite centuries of separation[13]
- fostering new relationships . . . so that future generations may look back to the twenty-first century with positive memories of a time in which Mennonites and Catholics began to serve Christ together.[14]

In response, I would like to offer a portion of the prayer John Paul II offered during the Jubilee Year 2000, on the Day of Pardon:

> On the night before his passion, your Son prayed for the unity of those who believe in Him . . . [nonetheless] believers have opposed one another, becoming divided, and have mutually condemned one another and fought against one another . . . [Therefore] we urgently implore

[9] Ibid., par. 96.
[10] Ibid., par. 214.
[11] Ibid., par. 192.
[12] Ibid., par. 198.
[13] Ibid., par. 207.
[14] Ibid., par. 211.

your forgiveness and we beseech the gift of a repentant heart, so that all Christians, reconciled with you and with one another, will be able, in one body and in one spirit, to experience anew the joy of full communion."[15]

Making the Case for the Abolition of War in the Twenty-First Century

I have entitled my talk, "Pax Christi and the Gospel of Peace: Making the Case for the Abolition of War in the Twenty-First Century." I have borrowed part of the title, in fact, from an essay by Stanley Hauerwas et al. Hauerwas is a moral theologian deeply influenced by the late Mennonite theologian John Howard Yoder, both of whom taught here at Notre Dame.[16]

I admit the title is a bit challenging, but we cannot deny that our deepest longings and aspirations move us toward this goal for peace. In fact, the abolition of war forms the opening of the United Nations Charter: "We, the people of the United Nations, [are] determined to save succeeding generations from the scourge of war . . . and to live in peace with one another as good neighbors." The times require great imagination and great courage.

Particularly when we look at the state of the world today, and begin to measure our humble efforts for peace against such a stark reality of war and violence, we tend to grow discouraged and may be tempted to give up hope in ever seeing the day when war is finally abolished. Yet history is full of surprises. Who could have predicted that nonviolent movements for democracy would usher in the end of the Cold War, or that dialogue between archenemies in South Africa would lead to the end of apartheid?

Surely, others before us were discouraged and tempted to lose hope, for example, amid the long struggles to abolish slavery and torture. Why should the struggle to abolish war be any different? We know that there are more people enslaved today than in any other time in the world's history. Torture, too, continues to be practiced, as we know very well from the photos and stories that have been broadcast to the world from Abu Ghraib and Guantanamo. Still, it was a very significant step to abolish the moral and legal justifications for both slavery and torture, and it would be a very significant step to do the same regarding the practice of war.

[15] Ibid., par. 200.
[16] Stanley Hauerwas, Linda Hogan, and Enda McDonagh, "The Case for Abolition of War in the Twenty-First Century," *Journal of the Society of Christian Ethics* 25, no. 2 (2005): 17–35.

I believe there are good grounds for hope in this struggle to finally abolish war. The witness of the Mennonites and other peace churches over the past several centuries is a reason for hope. The teachings of the Catholic Church since the Second Vatican Council give rise to hope. Particularly eloquent and urgent have been the pleas of popes, from Paul VI's impassioned plea to the General Assembly of the United Nations in 1965—"Never again war! No, never again war!"[17]—to John Paul II's repetition of that plea in his encyclical *Centesimus Annus* in 1991,[18] and later his Jubilee message on the World Day of Peace in 2000: "War is a defeat for humanity!"[19]

In each of these instances, we take a step in the Catholic Church's unconditional embrace of what it means to be an authentic peace church, rooted in the gospel of peace, and the passion, death, and resurrection of Our Lord and Savior, Jesus Christ. Marking this emphasis in the Catholic Church today is an increased use of the just war theory to restrain modern warfare and a "seismic shift"[20] to nonviolence as a public witness for peace, both key elements in making the case for the final abolition of war.

Difficult questions remain: *What about Rwanda? What about Darfur?* Hauerwas and colleagues frame our challenge this way:

> If we are to advocate abandonment of war as an instrument of national and international policy, including on occasions that are likely to be justified according to the just war criteria, we need to advance a morally compelling and politically persuasive alternative to "military interventions for humanitarian purposes." . . . These emergencies, such as the unfolding disaster in the Darfur region of Sudan or the 1994 genocide in Rwanda, press against the limits of our appeal because of the apparent need to wage war to protect human life and prevent atrocity.[21]

We cannot lightly dismiss this objection. In fact, some of us, committed as we are to pacifism or nonviolence, may share these concerns. So it is incumbent upon us to put forth convincing reasons, and even more, convincing alternatives to war, including "alternatives to military interventions for humanitarian purposes."

[17] Paul VI, Address to the General Assembly of the United Nations (October 4, 1965).

[18] John Paul II, *Centesimus Annus*, 52.

[19] John Paul II, World Day of Peace (January 1, 2000).

[20] Drew Christiansen, SJ, "After September 11: Catholic Teaching on War and Peace," *Origins* 32, no. 3 (May 30, 2002).

[21] Hauerwas et al., "The Case for Abolition of War," 29.

The response by Hauerwas and his colleagues to these objections is convincing, though it does not guarantee an effective alternative:

> Military interventions in situations of political instability themselves take a very high toll on civilians, especially those [persons] the interventions are intended to protect . . . More worrying still—and contrary to the assumptions of concerned citizens worldwide—there is ample evidence that military interventions of this kind tend to intensify and prolong conflict rather than resolve it.[22]

I thought of our current situation in Iraq as I read these words. What then, do Hauerwas and colleagues propose as an alternative?

> To be clear, our argument is not against the idea of intervening across sovereign borders *per se*, but the use of military means to do so. In our view, approaches that emphasize the incremental process of resolving conflict nonviolently by containing aggression, addressing grievances (real or imagined), and building local political capacity provide a more appropriate frame of reference for the resolution of humanitarian crises. Militarism has such a grip on contemporary humanitarianism, however, that such a suggestion seems naïve at best and a recipe for disengagement at worst. . . . Yet military operations in these situations are compelling only because of earlier failures: failure to give political support for implementation of peace agreements; failure to mount appropriate political, economic, or diplomatic interventions; failure to support indigenous peace activists and political reformers; and, most of all, failure to commit in advance the significant resources required to deal with the complex synergy of violence and poverty that is at the heart of most of these conflicts.[23]

These are words of realism, with which I think we can agree, and they point in the direction of what some have called "preemptive peace."[24] But

---

[22] Ibid., 30. Hauerwas et al. add, "Observers estimate, for example, that between 6,000 and 8,000 civilians were killed during Operation Rescue Hope in Somalia. In addition, the number of refugees and internally displaced persons that arise from the escalation that inevitably results from military interventions run to tens, sometimes hundreds of thousands. . . . Moreover, introduction of an additional armed group (albeit with humanitarian goals) often merely adds another set of belligerents to an already overmilitarized situation" (30).

[23] Hauerwas et.al., "The Case for Abolition of War," 30.

[24] The term was used in a Pax Christi USA consultation July 31, 2003: "Pre-emptive Peace: Beyond Terrorism and Justified War." See also Ben Schennink, "Pre-emptive War or Pre-emptive Peace? The U.S. National Security Strategy: A Challenge to the Peace

for such alternatives to succeed, they require transformations at the local, regional, and international level. In addition to local peace initiatives, international structures must be in place to support those local initiatives. These are elements essential to the task of peacemaking with which Catholics agree.

In 1993, for example, the National Conference of Catholic Bishops in the United States issued a document, *The Harvest of Justice is Sown in Peace*, on the occasion of the tenth anniversary of *The Challenge of Peace*. In it we put forward the following elements essential to peacemaking: strengthening global institutions, securing human rights, assuring sustainable and equitable development, restraining nationalism and eliminating religious violence, building cooperative security, and shaping responsible US leadership in the world.[25]

Still, the challenge remains: to make the case as churches for the abolition of war in the twenty-first century. I will attempt to do my part, from the perspective and witness of Pax Christi, a movement for peace and justice in the Catholic Church. Whether I am successful, you may judge. But I want us to set our sights high. Too often, I believe, we lack hope because we lack imagination; and we lack imagination because we fail to trust more in Divine Providence and the Holy Spirit who continues to speak through the prophets and through a prophetic church.

If we had to rely on our own efforts alone, I would be the first to be discouraged; but we are not alone. The church, in addition to being the People of God, the Body of Christ, the Temple of the Holy Spirit, is also the communion of saints. We are surrounded today by a "cloud of witnesses," those saints and martyrs and prophets who have gone before us and who continue

---

Movement." Advisory report for Pax Christi Netherlands; and Bryan Massingale, STD, "The Security We Seek: Whose Security? At What Cost? To Whom? A Catholic Perspective" (keynote address to the Roundtable Symposium, February 8, 2003).

[25] National Conference of Catholic Bishops, *The Harvest of Justice is Sown in Peace: A Reflection of the National Conference of Bishops on the Tenth Anniversary of The Challenge of Peace* (November 17, 1993). In addition to the elements essential to peacemaking, the document addresses a number of special problems, including nuclear disarmament and proliferation, demilitarization, economic sanctions, humanitarian intervention, and global responses to regional conflicts. A more recent statement by the since-renamed US Conference of Catholic Bishops, *Living with Faith and Hope After September 11,* issued November 14, 2001, in the section "Pursuing Justice and Peace After September 11," specifically addresses the Israeli-Palestinian conflict, Iraq, Sudan, the scandal of poverty, human rights, weapons of mass destruction and the arms trade, and strengthening the UN and other international institutions.

to encourage and intercede for us in our humble and faithful labors to work for justice and for peace. Let us not disappoint them, nor disappoint each other. Let us not disappoint those who yearn to hear the words of peace spoken in a prophetic fashion, those who are victims of war and those who mourn the victims. Let us not disappoint the children growing up today, the hope of future generations. Let us err on the side of the impossible, because for God, nothing is impossible.

The Journey of the Catholic Church to Nonviolence

At the beginning of my remarks today, I referred to *Called Together to Be Peacemakers* and what Catholics and Mennonites share in common—namely, "a common commitment to peacemaking. . . . rooted in our communion with 'the God of peace' (Rom 15:33) and in the church's response to Jesus' proclamation of 'the gospel of peace' (Eph 6:15)."[26]

As we have noted, there is much that Catholics and Mennonites share in common. But what about our divergences? These are important to name as well. Unless we understand and name our differences, we will not be able to move toward that unity to which Jesus calls us. *Called Together to Be Peacemakers* names three:

A *first* divergence has to do with diverging understandings of the role of the state:

> While Catholics and Mennonites regard political authority as part of the God-given moral order of the universe . . . Catholics understand the social nature of humanity to be blessed by Christ's life and teaching . . . Because of their long history of persecution and discrimination, Mennonites have tended to mistrust the state. They still tend to be critical of Christian involvement in government because of the use of violence and the possible corruption of power.[27]

I do not believe these are irreconcilable differences between Catholics and Mennonites. In fact, since the end of the Cold War and the emergence of the United States as the single super-power in the world, many Catholic theologians have taken a more critical look at the way states have exercised their political power, and the way just war theory has been interpreted to

---

[26] *Called Together*, par. 145.
[27] Ibid., par. 186.

enable states to go to war. This was true after the Persian Gulf War in 1991[28] and especially after the most recent Iraq war.[29]

In light of the Iraq war, some theologians have called for a new category to be added to the just war theory, namely that which governs the aftermath of war (*jus post bellum*). While that is certainly welcome, given the present conundrum about exit strategy in Iraq and the responsibilities of postwar reconciliation and reconstruction, I think additional reflection needs to be done on the responsibilities of Christians and of the church in the face of an unjust war.

To give a concrete example: John Paul II and the US bishops cautioned against going to war with Iraq on the basis of the just war criteria; once warfare began, the church could have done more to encourage in a public way a stronger nonviolent response, including conscientious objection to the war, nonviolent initiatives for peace, and a commitment to postwar reconciliation. This is certainly in line with a more positive assessment that the church has given to the role of civil society in peacemaking.

---

[28] After the Persian Gulf War in 1991, Catholic moral theologian John Langan, SJ, pointed to three criticisms of this reliance on just war theory: "First, the pacifist theses that the theory is theologically unacceptable and is incompatible with basic Christian values; second, the view that the theory effectively leaves out of consideration some aspects of either the particular situation or the general character of modern warfare that need to be considered if a satisfactory and conclusive verdict on the morality of a given war is to be reached; third, the view that the theory contains so many indeterminate elements and potentially contradictory considerations that we should not be surprised that applying it does not yield a determinate result." John Langan, SJ, "The Just-War Theory After the Gulf War," *Theological Studies* 53, no. 1 (1991): 95–112. Text cited is on p. 99.

[29] After the US invasion of Iraq in 2003, Catholic moral theologian David DeCosse claimed that the American government's use of deception in making its case for the Iraq War to the American people revealed a deficit in the integration of democratic ideas into Catholic conceptions of just war theory, and called for the following steps to be taken: "When addressing issues of war, Catholic thought should rely more consciously on the political model of a free society articulated in a document like *Dignitatis Humanae* . . . [rather than] pre-modern models of political authority . . . and pay increasing attention to the rights, responsibilities, and virtues of democratic citizens in time of war. . . . Catholic thought should be bolder in assessing claims from the perspective of the possibly deceived . . . [and] the criterion of legitimate authority should specifically include a requirement for truthful speech to citizens about going to war. A political authority that failed to fulfill such a requirement would fail the *jus ad bellum* test of legitimacy." David E. DeCosse, "Authority, Lies, and War: Democracy and the Development of Just War Theory," *Theological Studies* 67 (2006): 378–94. Text cited is on pp. 393–94.

A *second* divergence noted by the document has to do with nonviolence and just war:

> Mennonites include nonviolence as an essential component of discipleship in the sense that in principle they refuse to use violence in all situations. In situations of conflict, however, both Catholics and some Mennonites acknowledge that when all recourse to nonviolent means has failed, the state or international authorities may use force in defense of the innocent. For Mennonites, however, Christians should not participate in this kind of action. For Catholics, Christians ought to be committed "as far as possible, to live in peace with everyone" (Rom 12:18) and to encourage their governments to resolve disputes peacefully, but Christians may take up arms under legitimate authority in exceptional circumstances for the defense of the innocent.[30]

Here, too, I think Catholics and Mennonites are moving toward a convergence. Already at the beginning of his papacy, on a visit to Ireland, John Paul II reiterated his judgment about the destructiveness of violence as a means to resolve conflict:

> Violence is never a proper response. With the conviction of her faith in Christ and with the awareness of her mission, the Church proclaims "that violence is evil, that violence is unacceptable as a solution to problems, that violence is unworthy of man. Violence is a lie, for it goes against the truth of our faith, the truth of our humanity. Violence destroys what it claims to defend: the dignity, the life, the freedom of human beings."[31] Rather, what the world needs more is "the witness of unarmed prophets."[32]

Especially with the end of the Cold War, and the example of nonviolent movements in Eastern Europe that effectively put an end to Communism, the theme of nonviolence comes to the fore in Catholic social teaching. Reflecting on the events of 1989 in *Centesimus Annus*, Pope John Paul II wrote:

> It seemed that the European order resulting from the Second World War and sanctioned by the Yalta agreements could only be overturned

[30] *Called Together*, par. 187.

[31] Address at Drogheda, Ireland (September 29, 1979), 9. See Pontifical Council for Justice and Peace, *Compendium of the Social Doctrine of the Church*, 496.

[32] John Paul II, Address to the Pontifical Academy of Sciences (November 12, 1983), 5. See Pontifical Council for Justice and Peace, *Compendium of the Social Doctrine of the Church*, 496.

by another war. Instead, it has been overcome by the nonviolent commitment of people who, while always refusing to yield to the force of
power, succeeded time after time in finding effective ways of bearing
witness to the truth. This disarmed the adversary . . . Once again I thank
God for having sustained people's hearts amid difficult trials, and I pray
that this example will prevail in other places and other circumstances.
May people learn to fight for justice without violence, renouncing
class struggle in their internal disputes and war in international ones.[33]

The clearest message of this movement away from war as a means to resolve
conflict and towards nonviolence appears in Pope John Paul II's powerful
renunciation of war made at the time of the first Persian Gulf War in 1991.
In another passage from *Centesimus Annus* that was often repeated in later
papal statements, he declared:

I myself, on the occasion of the recent tragic war in the Persian Gulf,
repeated my cry: "Never again war! No, never again war, which destroys the lives of innocent people, teaches how to kill, throws into
upheaval even the lives of those who do the killing and leaves behind
a trail of resentment and hatred, thus making it all the more difficult
to find a solution of the very problems which provoked the war . . .
It must never be forgotten that at the root of war there are usually real
and serious grievances: injustices suffered, legitimate aspirations frustrated, poverty and the exploitation of multitudes of desperate people
who see no real possibility of improving their lot by peaceful means.
For this reason, another name for peace is development. Just as there
is a collective responsibility for avoiding war, so there is a collective
responsibility for promoting development."[34]

Finally, *Called Together to Be Peacemakers* speaks of nonresistance as a *third*
divergence between Catholics and Mennonites:

For Mennonites, non-resistance is part of the new way of Jesus (Matt
5:38-41). There is an expectation that Christians are called to adhere
to the principles of ethics implied in the 'new way,' and that through
the power of the Holy Spirit and the encouraging support of the Christian community, it is possible to walk the way faithfully. For Catholics,
non-resistance is 'a counsel of perfection,' and Catholics, as well as all
people of good will, are required to resist grave public evil nonviolently,

[33] *Centesimus Annus*, 23.2.
[34] Ibid., 52.

if at all possible, but in exceptional circumstances by limited use of force exercised by public authorities.[35]

Here, too, I do not believe differences between Catholics and Mennonites are irreconcilable. For Mennonites, nonresistance, when understood in the context of discipleship, takes on the characteristic of nonviolent resistance to evil and active love in the service of justice and the good. This is certainly a very Catholic understanding of discipleship, and one to which we could give our whole-hearted assent.

The *Confession of Faith in a Mennonite Perspective* declares:

> The same Spirit that empowered Jesus also empowers us to love enemies, to forgive rather than to seek revenge, to practice right relationships, to rely on the community of faith to settle disputes, and to resist evil without violence (Matt 5:39; 1 Cor 6:1-16; Rom 12:14-21). Led by the Spirit, and beginning in the church, we witness to all people that violence is not the will of God . . . We give our ultimate loyalty to the God of grace and peace, who guides the church daily in overcoming evil with good, who empowers us to do justice, and who sustains us in the glorious hope of the peaceable reign of God.[36]

And for Catholics, nonresistance, understood in this way as nonviolent resistance to evil and active nonviolent love, is redemptive. As John Paul II wrote in *Centesimus Annus*:

> It is by uniting his own sufferings for the sake of truth and freedom to the sufferings of Christ on the cross that man is able to accomplish the miracle of peace and is in a position to discern the often narrow path between the cowardice which gives in to evil and the violence which, under the illusion of fighting evil, only makes it worse.[37]

Where Catholics and Mennonites disagree is as to whether there are exceptions to nonresistance. Mennonites do not admit exceptions. The same *Confession of Faith* says this clearly: "As disciples of Christ, we do not prepare for war, or participate in war or military service." Pax Christi would accept this understanding of discipleship whole-heartedly. But the teaching of the Catholic Church still allows for exceptions, in *exceptional* circumstances.

[35] *Called Together*, par. 188.
[36] *Called Together*, par. 181.
[37] *Centesimus Annus*, 25.

Even with these exceptions, Catholic social teaching judges war to be "a defeat for humanity," and insists that it can only be undertaken with "deep regret." The Catholic Church also recognizes the right to conscientious objection to war, though it has not been so conscientious in recognizing the *duty* not to participate in an unjust war. Some have even urged broadening the understanding of conscientious objection beyond a "solitary witness" to encourage a more pastoral and even political witness as civilian initiatives and social movements for peace.[38]

Here I think both Catholics and Mennonites can collaborate by offering an effective witness to peacebuilding as a step toward abolishing war and offering concrete alternatives for peace. As Mennonites increasingly view nonresistance Mennonites in positive terms as nonviolent resistance to evil and active love in the service of justice and the good, the differences between Catholics and Mennonites begin to narrow considerably.

On the first day of the twenty-first century, the World Day of Peace, John Paul II spoke eloquently of the challenge of peace before us and the urgency to abolish war:

> In the century we are leaving behind, humanity has been sorely tried by an endless and horrifying sequence of wars, conflicts, genocides and "ethnic cleansings" which have caused unspeakable suffering: millions and millions of victims, families and countries destroyed, an ocean of refugees, misery, hunger, disease, underdevelopment and the loss of immense resources . . . The twentieth century bequeaths to us above all else a warning: wars are often the cause of further wars because they fuel deep hatreds, create situations of injustice and trample upon people's dignity and rights . . . War is a defeat for humanity. Only in peace and through peace can respect for human dignity and its inalienable rights be guaranteed.[39]

Building Foundations for Inclusive Security

Let me conclude my talk with the declaration of the last General Assembly of Pax Christi International, held in 2004 at Seton Hall University in New Jersey and attended by representatives from forty-five nations around the world. I think it serves as a fitting conclusion to the challenge we face as the church to make the case for abolishing war in the twenty-first century—and

[38] Response of Michael Baxter, CSC, and Mary Evelyn Jegen, SND de Namur, to the Pax Christi USA consultation held in 2003.

[39] John Paul II, Message on the World Day of Peace, (January 1, 2000).

to boldly and prophetically articulate another vision. It is titled "Building Foundations for Inclusive Security:"

The General Assembly of Pax Christi, the international Catholic peace movement, gathered May 19–22, 2004 for the first time in the United States, speaks from deep experience in many countries where poverty, lack of access to a decent job or a dignified life—and too often, war and terrorism—have been institutionalized, threatening the present and future security of entire peoples and nations.

From Colombia to Cambodia, Israel and Palestine to El Salvador, the Philippines to the Horn of Africa, Guatemala to the DR Congo, India and Pakistan to the Sudan and northern Uganda—and from so many other corners of the world we have heard the cry of our peoples. Their suffering has pierced our hearts.

With them we seek a world at peace where the dignity of each person, social and economic justice and the integrity of the whole creation are the heart of the matter—a world profoundly opposed to that sought by terrorists and by the "war on terrorism." We seek a world shaped by inclusive human security and the globalization of solidarity.

This is a new and dangerous moment in human history due to acts of terror and the war on terrorism itself. We are less secure each day. The United States and other states supporting the war on terrorism bear much responsibility for this. Other countries, especially in Europe, have great difficulties in charting another course.

The war on terrorism is polarizing our world. Awesome, insidious power of the U.S. is used to overwhelm governments and interfere in the right of people to participate in the decisions that affect their lives.

On theological, ethical and political grounds, Pax Christi condemns the U.S.-driven war on terrorism, the concept of preventive war, and the weakening or abandonment of multiple mechanisms for international cooperation and the rule of law.

The war on terrorism and the policies behind it have unleashed a new spiral of violence, expanding military buildup and spending, undermining the international disarmament agenda and efforts to make our world free from nuclear weapons and to prevent the development and proliferation of weapons of mass destruction. Small arms control efforts are stymied. Remilitarization in many of our societies and scandalous increases in military spending have been at the expense of the poor and social programs. New U.S. nuclear weapons are on the horizon.

The abuse of prisoners by U.S. and allied personnel has shocked the world and made visible the horrors of torture. The war on terrorism spawns more terrorism, feeding fundamentalist ideologies and leading to a false clash of civilizations. Fear is orchestrated and so-called enemies abound; few are welcome to cross borders; the dominant culture and particular models of democracy and economic life are being imposed.

Ulterior motives must be unmasked. The interests of an elite few and their exclusive access to natural resources are being pursued in lieu of inclusive human security.

We believe there is a need for deep changes in individual and collective lifestyles, especially in the North; for education that promotes attitudes of tolerance and respect for other cultures; for a deep reconstruction of the value system and worldview that undergird the rush to war; and for a transparent, accountable, and democratic form of global governance.

We are people of faith; we believe that *another world is possible*, and we commit ourselves to helping birth it. We echo the cry of Pope John Paul II that "war is always a defeat for humanity." With the United States Conference of Catholic Bishops, we believe that forgiveness in international politics is an alternative in the path toward peace.

We will support efforts to strengthen international law and international institutions, especially the United Nations. Truly effective, cooperative arrangements, including policing and other civil measures to address terrorism, must replace the failed policy of relying on military measures to achieve justice and secure peace.

We see signs of hope on the horizon—right relationships being built and rebuilt, the gradual globalization of solidarity. The World Social Forum could be one such sign of hope in which we intend to take a more active role—and there are many more in each of our countries where people are organizing for social, economic and ecological justice.

We commit our movement to articulate and promote a vision for peace and security grounded in the Gospel.

We will build right relations with each other and with people from around the world, promoting the inclusion of women, interfaith and cross-cultural dialogue and collaboration. We honor and embrace all faith traditions seeking to build justice and peace.

As citizens of the world we call on the U.S. government to repudiate preventive war and the war on terrorism as it is now being waged. We make a special call to stop the abuse and torture of prisoners in Iraq, Afghanistan and Guantanamo. We call on all governments to pursue peace by ensuring inclusive human security and the global common good in full cooperation with the family of nations and all peoples.

We call on the U.S. and the U.K. to cease all offensive military actions in Iraq and allow the United Nations to assume appropriate responsibility for enabling a just and peaceful transition to Iraqi authority.

As Christians we call our churches to the prophetic task in these dangerous times of speaking truth to power and to the challenging pastoral task of helping us reclaim Gospel values, nurture justice and right relationships and participate in the transformation of the world.

Chapter 12

The Gift of the Other

Toward Mutual Transformation

Duane K. Friesen

I am grateful to participate in this growing dialogue between Roman Catholics and Mennonites on peacemaking. In 1976–77 our family was privileged to spend a sabbatical year at the Ecumenical Institute at Saint John's University and Abbey. I sensed a deep kinship between the Anabaptist and Roman Catholic tradition that year as our family worshiped together with Catholics and participated in the prayer life of the Abbey. The spirituality of that setting deeply shaped my book on peacemaking and international conflict. In the concluding chapter I wrote:

> At the heart of the Roman Catholic mass is the sign of peace. Before the congregation shares in the bread together, the people express their love for each other and petition each other for peace and unity in the church and with all humanity . . . Bread, the universal stuff of human sustenance, so simple and so basic, when broken and shared in a group of people, becomes a symbol of nourishment, of solidarity, and of communion. The eating together of a common meal is an all-embracing gesture of friendship and love, understood the world over.[1]

It is in the spirit of this deep kinship with the Roman Catholic tradition, our common solidarity in the Body of Christ, that I would like to probe further our common call to be peacemakers.

In responding to the report of the international dialogue between Mennonites and Roman Catholics, 1998–2003, there are two different, though complementary, ways to engage this dialogue. On the one hand, we could focus on our

---

[1] Duane K. Friesen, *Christian Peacemaking and International Conflict: A Realist Pacifist Perspective*, foreword by Stanley Hauerwas, Christian Peace Shelf Selection (Scottdale, PA: Herald Press, 1986), 247.

differences—our diversity, and the gift that each offers as we share with each other within the mystery of our distinctiveness and individuality within the One Body of Christ. On the other hand, we can focus on the convergences between our traditions—how both of us are being transformed by this dialogue as we are nurtured by our common unity in Christ. I am choosing to emphasize the second approach, all the while being clear that we need to avoid a homogenization that does not respect the mystery of difference. Thus I have titled my presentation, "The Gift of the Other: Toward Mutual Transformation." For over the last thirty years I have found that my growing experience and knowledge of the Roman Catholic tradition has transformed my understanding and interpretation of my own Anabaptist-Mennonite heritage. In what follows I will identify three areas where I believe our dialogue with Roman Catholics can transform Mennonites in ways that allow us to modify, change, develop, and grow our own tradition so that we become faithful as Christian peacemakers and, thus, move our two traditions toward further convergence.

Three Areas of Transformation of the Mennonite Tradition

1. Theological Interpretation of Political Authority
and Participation in Government

I wish to focus on two sections of the *Called Together to be Peacemakers* document that correctly and honestly report—I believe—on historical divergences between the Roman Catholic and Anabaptist tradition. First, however, I must object to the tendency in the document to reify the Swiss "origin" of the Anabaptism by failing to reflect adequately on the diversity on political authority at the beginning of the movement. Nor does the document adequately represent how the Anabaptist tradition has grown and been transformed. We tend to overemphasize the "protestant principle" by going back to our beginnings for first principles. I would like to see us acknowledge the "authority" of a growing and developing tradition.

Note paragraph 186 of the text, which refers to "the way [the two traditions] tend to diverge on the question of participation in government . . . They [Mennonites] still tend to be critical of Christian involvement in government because of the use of violence involved and the possibility of the corruption of power." The summary of the Mennonite critique of Constantinianism in paragraph 165 calls for the church to "distance itself from the state," and criticizes a theology "too tightly tied to state structures" that fails to take Jesus seriously as a norm for political ethics.

I do not disagree with these points as such. However, the text does not balance its report on Mennonite suspicion of the state with the views of some Anabaptists who have a more positive view of the state. Nor does it report on changes in Mennonite theology and practices since the sixteenth century that reflect a more positive role for Christian participation in government. Let me suggest, then, that Mennonites might "grow" our tradition in ways that could lead to more convergence with Roman Catholic views. Mennonites can do this without giving up the store; in fact, we can become more faithful followers of Christ. Let me support this main thesis with four subpoints.

The first subpoint invites us to consider the authority of our own historical tradition. Our own Mennonite history reflects a more nuanced understanding of participation in political structures than is reflected in the statements from the document I quoted. Given the limitations of time, I can only cite several examples:

First, two examples from the beginnings of the Anabaptist movement. Along with many others, John Rempel has noted that even though Menno Simons "was a separatist in his emphasis on a disciplined church, he developed Christian norms for a 'just society' and 'just rulers,' holding those terms before magistrates of the day. A magistrate who acted justly, and, for example, did not take human life, could be counted a Christian."[2] However, Menno's theory of Christians participating nonviolently in the creation of a just society remained largely untested. Pilgrim Marpeck, on the other hand, was at the same time a convinced Anabaptist and a career civil servant. Rempel summarizes Marpeck this way: "Although his writings are occasional and not systematic, in practice Marpeck held together faithfulness and responsibility."[3]

The separatist stance of article 6 of the 1527 Schleitheim Confession of Faith was one view among a variety of Anabaptist views of the Christian's relationship to government. By the end of the sixteenth century, a "separatist" consensus had emerged, one born in the crucible of persecution. In the context of greater tolerance in later centuries, however, we can observe a variety of views on political authority emerge, along with greater openness to quite a variety of types of participation in systems of public order and security. We can see this in the way Mennonites in Holland, Germany,

[2] Duane K. Friesen and Gerald W. Schlabach, eds., *At Peace and Unafraid: Public Order, Security and the Wisdom of the Cross* (Scottdale, PA: Herald Press, 2005), 355.
[3] Ibid., 357.

Russia, Canada, and the United States have responded in a variety of different contexts.

Canadians, for example, have had a more positive view of the state than US Mennonites, and have participated even actively in politics, at both local and national levels. Likewise, in the recent book that Gerald Schlabach and I have edited, *At Peace and Unafraid: Public Order, Security, and the Wisdom of the Cross*, we include an essay by Judith Gardiner, a Mennonite who is an active member of the Labour Party who has twice been elected a councilor for the London borough of Tower Hamlets. In another essay, Alfred Neufeld, explores the implications of the decision of the president in Paraguay in 2003 to invite four Mennonite professionals into his cabinet in order to give his anticorruption campaign nonpartisan credibility. Colombia offers yet another case study, and a particularly interesting one, because the political involvement of Colombian Mennonites has developed in a context of extreme violence and repression. Our research team met with Ricardo Esquivia who told us the problem with Columbia is its lack of "institutionality," by which he means the structures of public order and law that can protect and sustain life. In her essay, Alix Lozano described ways in which the Colombian Mennonite Church is working "'in favor of the city,' above all in matters that are concerned with public peace, justice, and order."[4]

Ted Grimsrud argues that Mennonites in the United States are called to a prophetic stance in critiquing the violence and illusions of "American Empire," while at the same time actively participating in democratic institutions to shape the common good. Tim Wichert, a Canadian Mennonite lawyer, argues in another essay that Mennonites

> should recognize and use humans rights law as a key tool in the pursuit of public peace, justice, and order. . . . A traditional Mennonite focus on the dignity of all people, working among suffering people, and building relationship forms an excellent basis for developing a human rights paradigm that builds on the notions of presence and accompaniment. But this is just a first step, and must lead to a more complete pursuit of justice through protection and persuasion as well.[5]

My second subpoint is that since the sixteenth century, Mennonite theological thinking has also evolved toward a much more nuanced understanding of political authority and a greater openness to political participation at many levels.

---

[4] Ibid., 299.
[5] Ibid., 345.

Increasingly operative in Mennonite thinking is a view of political authority that draws upon an interpretation of the "principalities and powers" language of the Bible. Political and economic systems are not merely fallen, for they are also God's creation. The redemptive work of the church includes the redemption of the powers so that they might fulfill their function to serve the "peace of the city." A more robust Mennonite political theology can also draw upon the biblical wisdom tradition, symbolized by the stories of Esther and Joseph, whose creativity from within their positions of power enabled them to serve justice and the common good. Mennonites must do more than offer a negative critique of Constantinianism; they must address the issues that Constantinianism raises in a positive way: How *do* Christians contribute to justice and peace in the lands where we dwell? With a more nuanced Mennonite view of political authority, shaped by recent biblical theology, a Mennonite peace theology may increasingly converge with the Roman Catholic view that sees it as the responsibility of the church to concern itself with the common good. Mennonites can do this even as we continue to caution against Constantinian compromises in which the church sometimes feels compelled to do evil that good may come.

A third subpoint is that Mennonites and Roman Catholics can both benefit from the concept of subsidiarity. Mennonites have been too theologically preoccupied with "the state," and this has resulted in a too-negative view of political participation. Our history demonstrates that Mennonites have participated in political systems of law and public governance at many different levels—ranging from family systems, city councils, nongovernmental organizations, professions like law and social work, to democratic processes of decision making at state and national levels, to regulatory agencies that protect the public welfare and the environment, along with prophetic witness on issues of war and peace, human rights, international law, and many other policy issues.

A fourth subpoint is that Mennonites and Roman Catholics could state more clearly and forcefully the importance of being multilingual in our commitment to peacemaking. *Called Together to Be Peacemakers* is strong in identifying our "first" language as Christians—the narrative that shapes our common identity as Christians in the story of Jesus' life, teaching, death, and resurrection—as the grounding of our common witness as the Body of Christ. But the document might wisely employ at least four other languages as well: prophetic witness that unmasks the powers and names evil for what it is; the language of Christian vocation by which we seek to apply our primary commitment to our daily lives in the world of work as public servants;

the language of democratic discourse by which we engage in conversation with fellow citizens who do not share our first language; and the language of "middle axioms" by which we seek to address authorities who may be indifferent or even hostile to Christian principles. It is at this "middle axiom" level that pacifist Mennonites might discern together with just-war Roman Catholics how best to utilize just war criteria in order to judge whether a particular war meets or does not meet the criteria of just war. For example, even as pacifists, many Mennonites could have agreed with the pope that Iraq did not even meet the criteria of a just war.

To summarize: the Mennonite tradition has developed more positive views of political authority than are evident in *Called Together*, along with an increasing active participation in political life to shape the common good. There is a growing and developing convergence between Roman Catholics and Mennonites here.

2. Public Order and Security in Response to Grave Public Evils

Paragraph 157 of *Called Together*, in the section on "Catholic perspectives on peace," raises issues that are the greatest challenge to the pacifist tradition, in an area that we Mennonites have only recently begun to address theologically and practically. In that section we read: "All Catholics bear a general obligation to actively resist grave public evil." It is in this section that the "limited use of force as a last resort (the Just War)" is developed as a component of Roman Catholic peace theology.

Then again in paragraph 187 on "Nonviolence and War," in the section on "divergences," we read the statement: "both Catholics and some Mennonites acknowledge that when all recourse to nonviolent means has failed, the state or international authorities may use force in defense of the innocent. For Mennonites, however, Christians should not participate in this kind of action."

Since this paragraph is titled, "nonviolence and war," I assume that the phrase "may use force in defense of the innocent" opens the door for both Roman Catholics and some Mennonites to approve of war by the state or an international authority. It seems to me that the statement in this paragraph is weak because it may leave the door open for a too-easy justification of war. The statement would be stronger if both Mennonites and Roman Catholics were to distinguish more carefully between "policing" and "war." Let me briefly outline several key features of policing that John H. Yoder, Glen Stassen, myself, and others have identified.

A. Policing is a discriminate use of force, applied only to the offending party.
B. The use of force is subject to review by higher authorities within a system of law.
C. The authorized force is within a society where an offender knows the laws apply to both enforcers and offenders.
D. Safeguards exist to contain police force lest it be used on the innocent.
E. Police power is a monopoly of force by an existing political authority and is thus usually sufficient to overwhelm the offender such that resistance is pointless. Most arrests are made without any violence.

War, by contrast, is a blunt instrument that inevitably brings about the killing of noncombatants, lacks a timely systematic review of whether the force used is legitimate, usually operates without all sides accepting the jurisdiction of a common legal authority, and involves large-scale killing and destruction because no one actor has a monopoly of force. Multiple actors each have and employ their own weapons in a cause each believes is justified. War leads to the escalation of violence that is very difficult to contain and end.

I believe that after 9/11 it would have been much wiser if the United States would have appealed to the world to respond to the terrorist attack on the World Trade Center as a "crime against humanity" rather than with a "war against terror." It seems to me that since 9/11, war has served only to recruit more terrorists and escalate terrorism. The more successful responses to terrorism (one example is in Great Britain) have operated within a law enforcement model—careful gathering of intelligence, the foiling of terrorist plots, and the arrest and trial of terrorists within the framework of the rule of law. The wars in Afghanistan and Iraq have only increased terrorism, and the treatment of prisoners as "enemy combatants" has only discredited the United States as a society that respects human dignity and the rule of law.

Could both Mennonites and Roman Catholics agree to distinguish more clearly between just policing and war? If so, I think we might find possible areas of convergence between the two traditions around a paradigm of "just policing." Gerald Schlabach has suggested movements in both traditions that may point to convergences that we could not have anticipated, given the perennial historical tension between just war and pacifism.[6] Propelling

---

[6] See Gerald W. Schlabach, "Just Policing: How War Could Cease to Be a Church-Dividing Issue," *Journal of Ecumenical Studies* 41, no. 3–4 (Summer–Fall 2004): 409–30;

many of the changes from the Mennonite side, I think, is the conviction that many of us share with Roman Catholics, namely that "all bear a general obligation to actively resist grave public evil." Mennonites, for example, have participated with other historic peace churches in the World Council of Churches ecumenical dialogue that led to the approval by the churches of the document, "The Responsibility to Protect," at the Port Alegre, Brazil, General Assembly meetings in 2006.[7]

From the Roman Catholic side, there are grave doubts that war can address these issues of grave public evil. War is simply too blunt an instrument to address the problem of evil without perpetuating the very evils it seeks to prevent. So can the Roman Catholic position develop toward a position that is just "just policing," as Gerald Schlabach has suggested and, thus, provide a paradigm that is an alternative to the institution of war? The principle of noncombatant immunity that is already intrinsic to the just war theory should work to restrain warfare; does this not point in the direction of just policing? And could not Mennonites acknowledge that a "legitimate" use of force by the state is acceptable within a policing paradigm? Such a limited acknowledgment of force is supported by the exegesis of Romans 13. As John H. Yoder has argued in *The Politics of Jesus*, "the sword" is the symbol of judicial authority (not the instrument of capital punishment, nor a weapon of war).[8]

This possible convergence on just policing does not eliminate the debate about the justification of lethal force, but it does move both our traditions in the direction of convergence toward policing as an alternative to war. I think we together could make a significant contribution to the public policy debate about how to respond to terrorism.

3. Shared Practices of Just Peacemaking

In paragraph 170 of *Called Together*, Mennonites state that "in some places in the world, Mennonites are moving in their theology and practice from

---

and Gerald W. Schlabach, ed., *Just Policing, Not War: An Alternative Response to World Violence*, (Collegeville, MN: Liturgical Press, 2007).

[7] World Council of Churches, *Vulnerable Populations at Risk: Statement on the Responsibility to Protect* (approved by the 9th assembly, Porto Alegre, Brazil: February 14–23, 2006), doc. no. PIC 02–2, available at http://www.oikoumene.org/resources/documents/assembly/porto-alegre-2006/1-statements-documents-adopted/international-affairs/report-from-the-public-issues-committee/responsibility-to-protect.html.

[8] John H. Yoder, *The Politics of Jesus*, 1st ed. (Grand Rapids: William B. Eerdmans, 1972), 206.

'nonresistance' to active peacemaking and to a position of just peacemaking." Just peacemaking theory emerged in the 1990s as a group of Christian scholars sought to identify how a measure of peace had broken out unexpectedly with the end of the Cold War; they eventually identified ten practices that just-war and pacifist Christians could both identify as normative, even when they came to these practices on the basis of somewhat different principles.[9] I would like to see us say more strongly that we support this direction, and that it is a direction that our peace theology supports. In fact, *Called Together* demonstrates that Roman Catholics and Mennonites already share many of the ten practices of just peacemaking. At numerous points the document suggests convergence, though future dialogues could spell out several of the just peacemaking practices more explicitly and identify others that its authors did not mention. In what follows, I am using the practices of just peacemaking as a kind of "report card" to assess how we are doing.

Just Peacemaking Practices

The just peacemaking practices are organized into three normative categories. The first four practices emphasize *peacemaking initiatives*, practices that generate a process of nonviolent conflict resolution as an alternative to violence.

Practice 1: Nonviolent Direct Action

Called Together makes several references to the commitment of both Mennonites and Roman Catholics to nonviolence.[10] Nonviolent direct action is a peacemaking practice that addresses "grave moral evil" and we have begun to develop a historical consciousness of numerous instances of successful nonviolent transformation. It seems to me that *Called Together* might have stated this practice much more directly and explicitly in the section on convergences between the two traditions. One of the important dimensions of many nonviolent movements is a spirituality and ethic of sacrificial love and

---

[9] See Glen Stassen, ed., *Just Peacemaking: The New Paradigm for the Ethics of Peace and War*, rev. ed. (Cleveland: Pilgrim Press, 2008); and Duane K. Friesen and Glen H. Stassen, "Just Peacemaking," in *Transforming Violence: Linking Local and Global Peacemaking*, ed., Robert Herr and Judy Zimmerman Herr, foreword by Konrad Raiser (Scottdale, PA: Herald Press, 1998).

[10] See *Called Together to Be Peacemakers*, paragraphs 152 and 157 in the Roman Catholic section, and paragraphs 168 and 170 in the Mennonite section.

Part 1: Peacemaking Initiatives
1. Support nonviolent direct action.
2. Take independent initiatives to reduce threat.
3. Use cooperative conflict resolution.
4. Acknowledge responsibility for conflict and injustice and seek repentance and forgiveness.

Part 2: Justice
5. Advance democracy, human rights, and religious liberty.
6. Foster just and sustainable economic development.

Part 3: Love and Community
7. Work with emerging cooperative forces in the international system.
8. Strengthen the United Nations and international efforts for co-operation and human rights.
9. Reduce offensive weapons and weapons trade.
10. Encourage grassroots peacemaking groups and voluntary associations.

suffering, both which were evident in the movements that Martin Luther King Jr. and Mahatma Gandhi led. Both Roman Catholics and Mennonites emphasize Jesus' nonviolent cross as a model for discipleship.[11] Catholics and Mennonites are especially well situated to contribute toward a spirituality and ethic of sacrificial love and voluntary suffering in the practice of nonviolent direct action.

Practice 2: Take Independent Initiatives to Reduce Threat

Unfortunately, *Called Together* does not mention this practice explicitly, though it could be a center piece of convergence between Roman Catholics and Mennonites. I recommend the work of Glen Stassen who has demonstrated the parallels between transforming initiatives in Jesus' teaching in the Sermon on the Mount and practices of peacemaking that have been successfully utilized even by actors of nation states.[12]

[11] Ibid., par. 180, subsection on "Discipleship and Peace."
[12] For Stassen's work on the Sermon on the Mount see Glen Harold Stassen and David P. Gushee, *Kingdom Ethics: Following Jesus in Contemporary Context* (Downers Grove, IL: InterVarsity Press, 2003); and Glen H. Stassen, *Living the Sermon on the Mount: A Practical Hope for Grace and Deliverance* (San Francisco: Jossey-Bass, 2006).

Both the Roman Catholic and Mennonite sections of *Called Together* support practice 3, cooperative conflict resolution.[13]

Practice 3: Cooperative Conflict Resolution

The theological foundation of this practice appears in the convergence section:

> We affirm that Christ, in his Church, through baptism, overcomes the differences between peoples. By virtue of their baptism into Christ, all Christians are called to be peacemakers. All forms of ethnic and inter-religious hatred and violence are incompatible with the gospel, and the Church has a special role in overcoming ethnic and religious differences and in building international peace. Furthermore, we agree that it is a tragedy when Christians kill one another.[14]

Practice 4: Acknowledge Responsibility for Conflict and Injustice and Seek Repentance and Forgiveness

Both Roman Catholics and Mennonites provide the theological underpinning for the centrality of forgiveness.[15] What is missing is the practice of repentance and forgiveness in the relationships between political actors. We have learned that acknowledging responsibility for injustice and willingness to forgive can transform relationships, even on the national or international stage. One significant example is the leadership of Bishop Tutu in the South African Truth and Reconciliation Commission.[16]

The second category in just peacemaking theory emphasizes *justice* itself, and the two normative practices that the theory identifies are the ones that *Called Together to Be Peacemakers* identifies most frequently.

Practice 5: Advancing Democracy, Human Rights, and Religious Liberty

Advancing democracy, human rights, and religious liberty appear in paragraphs 151, 153, 160, and 169 of *Called Together*, as well as the convergence section (176 and 177).

---

[13] *Called Together*, pars. 155, 168, and 169.

[14] Ibid., par. 175.

[15] Ibid., pars. 150, 151, and 166.

[16] See Donald W. Shriver, *An Ethic for Enemies: Forgiveness in Politics* (New York: Oxford University Press, 1995); and Walter Wink, *When the Powers Fall: Reconciliation in the Healing of Nations* (Fortress Press, 1998).

Practice 6: Supporting Just and Sustainable Economic Development

Supporting just and sustainable economic development is implicit in references to concern for the poor and the marginal (paragraphs 151, 166, and 171), and in the convergence statement in paragraph 178. This paragraph offers one of the best statements of the entire document, in my judgment, as it forcefully and explicitly emphasizes practices 5 and 6 (of 10) of just peacemaking:

> We agree that the Gospel's vision of peace includes active non-violence for the defense of human life and human rights, for the promotion of economic justice for the poor, and in the interest of fostering solidarity among peoples. Likewise, peace is the realization of the fundamental right to live a life in dignity, and so have access to all means to accomplish this: land, work, health, and education. For this reason, the Church is called to stand in solidarity with the poor and to be an advocate for the oppressed. A peace built on oppression is a false peace.

The third category of just peacemaking practices—love and community—finds theological grounding in many places in the document.

Practices 7 and 8: Working with the International System

Only in the Roman Catholic section is there implicit reference to *practice 7, work with emerging cooperative forces in the international system*, and passing reference to *practice 8, strengthen the United Nations and international efforts for cooperation and human rights* (paragraphs 149, 153). Our very existence as churches—transnational bodies with transnational networks that transcend divisions between nations and within nations—testifies to our contribution to the emerging forces within the international system toward cooperation. We could affirm practice 7 even more strongly; we could also say more forcefully that our churches support a strengthened United Nations, as well as a strengthened system of international law that supports human rights and protects the natural environment. The document emphasizes our commitment to the protection of the natural environment (paragraphs 171 and 173). Together we can speak more prophetically against the tendency toward unilateralism by the United States, its failure to sign or live up to several very important international treaties, among them the Kyoto Treaty on global warming and treaties recognizing the authority of the International Criminal Court.

Practices 9 and 10: Weapons Reduction; Grassroots Community

The document nowhere addresses *practice 9, reducing offensive weapons and the weapons trade*, but both traditions give strong support to *practice 10, encouraging grassroots peacemaking groups and voluntary associations.* By virtue of our very existence as church bodies, associations, and institutions within a differentiated pluralistic political and international order, we are committed to practice 10. Paragraphs 154 and 169 make explicit how we encourage and work through grassroots peacemaking groups and voluntary associations in our work of peacemaking.

To summarize, five of the practices (1, 3, 5, 6, and 10) are explicitly named and emphasized in *Called Together to Be Peacemakers*; three of the practices are named but not developed explicitly (4, 7, and 8); and two are not named (2 and 9). Nonetheless, I believe that theological and ethical foundations are present so that all of these practices could be identified or further developed. Would it be possible for Roman Catholics and Mennonites to go on record as supporting the ten practices of just peacemaking?

Conclusion

Let me conclude by reflecting on two gifts that that I have received through my Mennonite tradition but that most challenge and test my commitment to peacemaking.

The first is the gift of an ethic of risk. The way of nonviolence is an ethic of risk. It is a commitment to a way of living that believes that ends and means are integrally connected. Peace is the way to peace. It is grounded in an eschatological hope, that the way of the Lamb that was slain is ultimately the way of victory over evil. Our great temptation is to sacrifice an ethic of means for the sake of a good end.

If means and ends are integrally connected, then the practice of peacemaking in an imperfect world is grounded in the conviction that the practice of nonviolence is not only faithful but also effective. Yet there is no *guarantee* of success. Nonviolence does fail, especially in the short run. Do we then abandon nonviolence? To live nonviolently and practice nonviolence is a commitment to a hopeful vision. It requires a redirection of our energies, resources, and talents. It is the risk we live. It is the risk of this gift that we Christians can offer to the world. This is the Gospel, the good news.

But the choice between nonviolence and violence is not between a utopian hope and hard-nosed realism. The reliance on violent force is its own kind of utopianism. The justification of violent force is ultimately based on a utilitarian calculus of success—that the use of force as a last resort is the only way to protect the innocent from harm, and that violent force will likely result in greater good than harm.

The commitment to violence force is thus an "ethic of risk" also. A good outcome is not guaranteed. We are usually not able to predict consequences. The behavior of adversaries changes outcomes that we thought were so predictable. We usually fail to anticipate negative outcomes. Our pride and power create the illusion that we are in control. Just because we have tried everything else, why should we assume that violence as the "last resort" will work?

Our challenge is therefore to risk nonviolence instead. We can use our imagination, energy, intellectual, and economic resources to develop a cultural of nonviolence. If we continue to hold out war as a last resort, that commits us to plan for it, organize our society to prepare for it, and to use vast intellectual and economic resources for war rather than in building a culture of peace. What could happen if the Christians of the world were to commit ourselves to an alternative ethic of risk that invests in building a culture of nonviolence?

The second gift is the gift of the power of weakness. One of the greatest challenges that US Christians face is how to live with integrity in our relationship with Muslims. Many Muslims in the world cannot "see" Jesus because the Gospel of love and peacemaking we preach has become so prostituted by the links of the Christian faith to one Western empire after another, and now to an American empire, symbolized by the Iraq War and Guantanamo Bay. The challenge for us is to rediscover the heart of our faith, the power of the cross. Our strength as Christians is paradoxically the weakness of the cross. I conclude, therefore, by highlighting the most important convergence between Mennonites and Roman Catholics, identified in paragraph 174:

> We understand peace through the teachings, life and death of Jesus Christ. In his mission of reconciliation he remained faithful unto death on the cross, and his fidelity was confirmed in the resurrection. The cross is the sign of God's love of enemies.

PART 6:

Toward a Healing of Memories

The healing of memories involves several aspects. It requires a purification of memories so that both groups can share a picture of the past that is historically accurate. This calls for a spirit of repentance—a penitential spirit—on both sides for the harm that the conflicts have done to the body of Christ, to the proclamation of the Gospel, and to one another. Healing the memories of divided Christians also entails the recognition that, despite conflict, and though still separated, they continue to hold in common much of the Christian faith. In this sense they remain linked to one another. Moreover a healing of memories involves the openness to move beyond the isolation of the past, and to consider concrete steps toward new relations. Together, these factors can contribute to reconciliation between divided Christians.

Called Together to Be Peacemakers, paragraph 191

We believe that another fundamental part of the healing of memories is the call to foster new relationships. The significant elements of our common understanding of basic Christian faith ascertained in this dialogue may provide a sufficient theological foundation on which to build. Our experience of re-reading history conjointly suggests that looking together at those periods in which our conflicts initially took place may shed new light on the past and foster a climate for better relationships in the future. For centuries our communities lived with the memories generated from the conflicts of the sixteenth century and in isolation from one another. Can we not increase our efforts to create new relationships today so that future generations may look back to the twenty-first century with positive memories of a time in which Mennonites and Catholics began increasingly to serve Christ together?

Called Together to Be Peacemakers, paragraph 211

Chapter 13

Catholic and Mennonite

A Journey of Healing

Gerald W. Schlabach

E nglish teachers and editors tell us not to mix metaphors. Well, it is a good thing Jesus got to us before they did. To project the Kingdom of God or to explain God's love for the lost, Jesus unabashedly gave us multiple metaphors and parables. A mustard seed, yeast, a treasure hidden in a field. A lost coin, a lost sheep, a prodigal son. For the mystery of God's work, we seem positively to require mixed metaphors. Our job is to collate them and gain a fuller picture by connecting their dots.

Part three of *Called Together to be Peacemakers* offers us, with its very title, one metaphor for our most basic of ecumenical tasks: "the healing of memories." "Bridgefolk," the name of the grassroots organization for dialogue and unity between Mennonites and Roman Catholics, offers another image—the bridging of peoples. I would like to collate these two images by exploring yet another image—scars—and the function they play in the healing of actual bodies, wherever the painful separation of flesh has occurred.

In a faith so incarnational as Christianity, the healing of memories in the broken body of Christ will remain merely gnostic if it is not enfleshed through the bridging of folk.[1] And when severed flesh comes together, scars are the bridge, while scar formation is a sign of returning health. Yet even in the healthiest of recovering bodies, scars remain.

And scars remind. Even when memories heal, in other words, the body writes new memories onto its very flesh. Often such scars continue to itch.

---

[1] In speaking of "the bridging of folk" or "bridge people," I am referring not just to participants in the Bridgefolk movement or organization but to others like them as well, who seek to bridge multiple traditions.

For some, this can be a calling, to incarnate the healing of memories, to be the scars that close gaping wounds in the body of Christ, and, frankly, to itch.

Bridge people, I argue, ought neither to *be* nor to be *seen* as distractions in an otherwise clean bilateral process of ecumenical dialogue. Nor should their "double belonging" be taken merely as the product of postmodern messiness. To be sure, something can be unsettling about both still-forming scars and folks who remain "on a journey." But in the incarnational faith we call Christianity, no healing of memories will be complete—or really even begin—without someone there to enflesh the rejoining of separated parts.

Bridging

Almost every year, someone participating in a Bridgefolk conference either plays with the image of a bridge or asks whether the metaphor really works. Bridgefolk began in the late 1990s as Ivan Kauffman and I began to wonder if we were in the presence of a nascent, still-inchoate, movement. Through friendship and word of mouth, we were learning of a striking number of Mennonites drawn to Catholic liturgical or contemplative traditions, and of Catholics drawn to Mennonite traditions of service and peacemaking. Hoping to figure out what was going on, we soon invited Marlene Kropf and Weldon Nisly to join us in planning an unadvertised retreat bringing together twenty-five Catholics and Mennonites to tell their stories, pray, and discern. More as an act of generic description than one of poetry or theology, we simply called it a bridging retreat.

So what sort of bridge is this? someone wonders. Yes, a few of the folk in Bridgefolk have "crossed-over," changing their primary ecclesial identity from one church to the other. Yet those of us who have done so are not the sort of "converts" who are *burning* their bridges by renouncing the values or legitimacy of the church communities that formed them. In any case, far more often, ours is a bridge that facilitates hospitality and exchange, allowing once-estranged Christians in these two traditions to meet as friends, find inspiration in one another's charisms, learn from one another's practices, but then return home, back across the bridge, enriched.

If the first bridging metaphor—crossing over—is too triumphalistic, however, the second—amiable exchange—may be too benign. For it fails to account for either the pain or the joy that many of the folk in Bridgefolk have experienced. On the one hand, some have felt at times like homeless refugees no longer fully at home in either tradition, grateful to find shelter *under* the Bridgefolk bridge, yet painfully aware that such a home can only be makeshift and provisional at best. On the other hand, some of us are interchurch couples or individuals with dual membership, trying to find creative, comfortable ways actually to live *on* the bridge. Bridges aren't supposed to become the site for permanent homes, right? Except that in rare cases they do, as with the charming Ponte Vecchio in Florence.

Still, the last thing we in Bridgefolk leadership want to imply is that ours is an actual church home. A home away from home—maybe. An ecclesial movement, as Rome approvingly labels certain kinds of groups—gladly. But not a church. And only even a bridge between our churches so long as few better options exist for being simultaneously Mennonite and Catholic. Thus the common prayer that has been our one shared "rule of life" since 2001 actually does not speak at all of a bridge *between* Catholics and Mennonites. Rather, it speaks of a bridge to somewhere that neither Christian community is currently fully at, a bridge to God's "coming Kingdom," a bridge "to that future of unity and peace which You ever yearn to give to your Church, yet ever give in earnest through Your Church as You set a table before us." Gratefully we later learned that both Cardinal Walter Kasper (head of the Pontifical Council for Promoting Christian Unity) and then-Cardinal Joseph Ratzinger (now Pope Benedict) named exactly this to be the proper goal of ecumenism—not that long-separated Christians move closer to one another but that together we grow closer to Christ.[2] What exactly the far end of that bridge will look like thus remains to be discovered.

Healing

I do not know whether even my closest friends or colleagues have noticed. But every once in a while, in moments of distraction, I reach across my chest and scratch an itch. Nine years ago, I had surgery to remove a lymph node that had become impacted with the infection from cat scratch disease. I will spare you the gorier details but this much seems necessary: The wound that surgery leaves in a case like this cannot simply be closed and sutured. It must remain open to be regularly cleaned and dressed until it heals and closes from the inside, lest a new and far more systemic infection occur. Healing cannot be rushed. The wound requires patient, loving attention, in my case

[2] Walter Cardinal Kasper, "Current Problems in Ecumenical Theology," *Reflections* 6 (Spring 2003): 64–65; Joseph Ratzinger, *Church, Ecumenism, and Politics: New Essays in Ecclesiology* (New York: Crossroad, 1988), 87.

at the hands of my long-suffering wife. And then, as with any scar tissue, an itch may persist, even after healing is complete, as I can attest.

That scars abide in the body of Christ, even where healing occurs, should not surprise us. Christianity is a faith of realistic hope, not cheery optimism. At its very center, after all, is a gruesome cross that we not only must behold but recognize as our own doing. It is precisely because we can look into the face of suffering and shame that we find the courage to believe, in the words of Julian of Norwich, that "all will be well, and all will be well, and all manner of things will be well." After all, even the resurrected body of Jesus continues to bear the visible wounds of suffering (John 20:27).

Scars function in at least three ways. I have already mentioned the first: Scars are the place where the body's separated flesh comes together. In ways small yet nonetheless decisive for the health of the whole, they bridge. Second, scars are places that mark the eschatological "already" and "not yet" of our own resurrected bodies and—more to the point—of the perfectly healed, reunited, resurrected body of Christ. If even in resurrection, scars may still be visible, then those scars that continue to ache in the still-healing body of Christ are a sure reminder of the Church's "not yet." Yet even so, even now, we may celebrate an "already." The grace that is the wonder of the human body is capable of amazing healing, even in the meantime.

Third and finally, scars are a place that functions to set an agenda for the body. Scars in the process of healing marshal energy and resources from throughout the body at those locales whose recovery is critical for the well-being of the whole. And even after healing is complete, scars want to be scratched. They incite other parts of the body to pay attention. They itch. So that even as the body of Christ *heals* its memories, the scars that remain also continue to *provoke* memory, itching, and calling for further action.

To illustrate the healing-yet-still-itching role of Catholic and Anabaptist-Mennonite bridge people in the body of Christ, I would like to share an imagined conversation. Let me defer for now the question of whether and where such a conversation might actually take place.

To make the conversation easy to follow, I will call the Mennonite Anna B. and the Catholic Cathy. Anna is a deacon in her local congregation and is pursuing a master's degree in spiritual direction. Cathy works full time as social justice coordinator in her local parish. They have been friends for a number of years, and when *Called Together to be Peacemakers* came out they initiated a study of the document, bringing together members of both communities. The study is just about to wrap up and they are meeting at a coffee shop to debrief and discuss what to do next.

□ □ □

"Hey, I thought our last session on the healing of memories went well," says Anna as they sit down at a corner table. "What a relief!"

"That we're done?" asks Cathy with surprise. "I'm going to miss meet–"

"No, not that. What a relief that we really are both Christians! The document says so! Mennonites and Catholics are allowed to see one another as brothers and sisters in Christ [par. 210]."

Catching on, Cathy chuckles. "Of course you and I knew that already. It's a shame that it took our high-level delegations five years to reach the same conclusion!"

"Or five hundred years," Anna interrupts.

"Yeah, I know," agrees Cathy. "I'm just sort of teasing them in absentia. They *did* have a lot of issues to work through. Still do, I guess. But at least we're moving beyond mutual condemnation, as Cardinal Kasper put it [par. 202]. They really came a long way in facing 'those difficult events of the past.' I mean, most of us Catholics don't even know that we used to persecute groups like the Mennonites. *I* didn't, and I work on human rights issues! I can really understand what they mean by 'the healing of memories.'"

"Or 'purification of memories,'" suggests Anna.

"Whatever. The document uses the terms interchangeably, doesn't it?"

"No, not whatever," Anna insists. "I've been thinking some more about this since our last meeting. I don't think they're quite the same. It's one thing to clear up a misunderstanding. That's purification. It's like cleaning a wound. But that doesn't mean the wound is healed yet. Especially"—Anna's voice grows quieter—"when the wound gets reopened every once in a while."

Cathy is a bit taken aback: "What do you mean?"

"Well, it's hard enough to face difficult events of the past, but what about events of the present?"

"I'm not sure I follow you," says Cathy, still puzzled. "Persecution is long past. Vatican II committed Catholics to the principle of religious liberty. We discussed all this, you know. And the Catholic Church's growing commitment to peace and nonviolence—I wish it were happening faster, but it *is* happening!"

"Not at the table," says Anna, with more resignation than bitterness. "Suddenly at the last minute I'm not seen as a sister in Christ after all. Or if I am, I'm second class."

"Oh, I'm sorry. That. Of course," says Cathy. "You know how torn I feel about that. You're welcome to participate in the Eucharist as far as I'm concerned. But, well, I'm just not the only one concerned. You know me. I get as frustrated as anyone that change takes so long in the Roman church. But that's part of what it means to be a Catholic—to move together as a worldwide body. So the Eucharist isn't only about you, me, and Jesus. It's also our fullest expression of visible church unity, so where unity is incomplete, well, I suppose it's better to be honest. I mean—Geez, I can't believe I'm defending the rules! Maybe it feels different to me because we Catholics are so good at finding exceptions to rules. I'm sorry if I was insensitive."

"It's okay," Anna assures her friend. "On one level, I get it too. You know how much I've come to love the liturgy. When I attend other Protestant services now and they have open communion, sometimes it feels a little too cheap and nonchalant. Even at my own Mennonite congregation, we've finally agreed to celebrate the Lord's Supper once a month, but one time we do it one way, then next time another way. So I'm torn too. If it weren't for the thorn of your all-male priesthood, I could almost start to *appreciate* your rules!"

"*Their* all-male priesthood," Cathy interjects, and they both laugh.

"So as I was saying, it's okay. I get it. I guess."

"Well, that wasn't very convincing," Cathy notes.

Anna pauses, trying to decide whether it is worth the risk of going on. "I get it—until we get to that one line: 'Happy are those who are called to His supper.' You welcome me as a friend and sister. The liturgy, it . . . I guess I would say it enfolds me. But then at the last minute, am I called to this supper or not? Am I a sister in Christ or not? All I know is that I'm *not* quite 'happy' at this supper. In the very moment of welcome I'm turned away because I'm a second-class Christian. It isn't even enough that I sincerely pray the next line: 'I am not worthy to receive you, but only say the word and I shall be healed.' Jesus can say the healing word but I'm not worthy just because I'm not a Catholic?"

"Well," says Cathy, "here's where *I'm* the one who sort of gets it and sort of doesn't." She hesitates, then stammers: "You could . . . I mean . . . Look, we've had this study group for nine months without anyone trying to convert anyone else, and I'm not starting now. But if the Eucharist is coming to mean so much to you, you *could* become Catholic. I'm not saying you should, y'know. It's just that, well, I don't think it's quite fair to say that the church is turning you away."

"Oh come on, you know why I can't do that," says Anna. "You've told me your own frustrations as a woman working within the structures of the church. Do you really think you'd join if you weren't a 'cradle Catholic?'

You say the church is moving toward a stronger commitment to peace and nonviolence, but only slowly. Do you really expect it to give up its just war teaching—ever? . . . Don't worry that you've stepped over the line; I appreciate your honesty. But I have to be honest too: I just don't know how I could be part of a church like that. Still too Constantinian. Still way too patriarchal—"

"Still the whore of Babylon?" Cathy interrupts.

"No, I didn't say *that*!"

"But you did say that the Roman Catholic Church still hasn't changed enough, is still not good enough. Not worthy. Isn't that just a politer way of saying what Protestants have been saying for almost 500 years?"

Both friends are silent for a minute. At last Anna finds a way to connect her thoughts and feelings with those of her friend: "Well, it's tricky, this business of worthiness and recognition. I guess both our churches find ways to turn each other away at the last minute."

"But only say the word—"

"and I shall be healed."

"At least we have *this* table."

"Yeah—want some more coffee? I don't think our work is over yet!"

❏ ❏ ❏

So could some version of this conversation actually take place? In the hallway outside this meeting? In the cafeteria at our Bridgefolk gatherings? On the tearful late-night bed of a Mennonite-Catholic marriage?

No and yes. I have been in all of these places, marveling both at growing trust among friends and sudden breakthroughs of insightful candor. But I have yet to hear a conversation *quite* this blunt. Except for one place—my own Mennonite-Catholic head. There, I hear it often. And though I can't know for sure, I suspect that versions of this conversation replay regularly in the minds and hearts of others who have found some sort of way to be simultaneously Mennonite and Catholic. The conversations are not just intellectual matters either—much less gnostic—for they take on their poignancy and depth precisely because we are keeping our bodies planted in both communities, continuing to serve and be present rather than leaving one for the other. The pain of estrangement we once felt may have abated. But an itch lingers on. If we are scar tissue in the body of Christ, that itch keeps us longing and working for less painful, ever healthier ways to bring together divided flesh in the body of Christ.

Dialogue

So I am arguing that bridge people play a critical role in the ecumenical healing of divisions. I am seeking to name spaces within the ecumenical movement where grassroots dialogue can and does play a role. I will close by envisioning some possible next ways in which Mennonites and Catholics acting together can contribute to Christian unity in fresh and creative ways. These arguments inevitably imply that ecumenical dialogue and progress will suffer from certain limitations if they only proceed through high-level encounters, and I mean to explicate some of these limitations shortly. But let me be clear: none of this aims to detract in any way from the immense gratitude that grassroots bridge people owe to the classical ecumenical movement functioning on more official levels.

A first affirmation: Historically, the impulse for ecumenical endeavors has sprung from what matters most—*missio Dei*, God's own outreach to the needy world that God loves and the call of God's Church to participate in this mission. As it took shape among Protestants in the early twentieth century, the classical ecumenical movement was virtually indistinguishable from the missionary movement then in its heyday. The disunity of churches obstructed a clear presentation of the gospel, after all, and young churches that did form in new regions of the world often found North Atlantic denominational structures a confusing puzzle at best.

Later, when the Catholic Church made its decisive commitment to ecumenical dialogue at the Second Vatican Council, that context was no mere coincidence. The larger purpose of the council was to reinvigorate the church so that it might better communicate the Gospel in the modern world.[3] As he opened the council, Pope John XXIII expressed his hope that it was "bringing together the Church's best energies" to prepare the church to proclaim "more favourably the good tidings of salvation."[4]

For their part, Mennonites have discovered an ecumenical mandate precisely as they have engaged in mission and service around the world. Integral to the corporate culture of the relief, development, and peacebuilding organization Mennonite Central Committee, for example, is a commitment to "work with the church" whenever possible in any given region or locale. But

---

[3] Giuseppe Alberigo, ed., *History of Vatican II*, 5 volumes, English version ed. Joseph Komonchak (Maryknoll, NY: Orbis Books, 1996), I:2–3.

[4] Pope John XXIII, *Gaudet mater ecclesia* (opening speech to the Second Vatican Council, 1962).

since this can hardly involve Mennonite partners alone (given the relatively small size of the worldwide Mennonite communion, if nothing else) MCC has in practice inculcated a strikingly catholic ecclesiology—far more than Anabaptist-Mennonite theology has quite known how to name.

A second affirmation unfolds to become multiple affirmations: We can be grateful for a diversity of charisms among multiple ecumenical dialogues and do not need to celebrate one at the expense of others. Naturally, each dialogue takes on the character and primary concerns of its respective dialogue partners. The international dialogue between Mennonites and Catholics took up a number of issues but two or three were particularly urgent for the relationship between these two communities—the memory of sixteenth-century persecution, the contemporary call to peacemaking, and (extending from both) the relation of church and state, both historically and today. It is not that other matters are unimportant.[5] Yet obviously we cannot take on every issue at once. That every dialogue has its own charism is thus a great gift. Mennonites and Catholics in dialogue together are freer to drill down into their own matters of urgency knowing that others who have the concern and competence to focus on different issues are doing so.[6] So in the diversity of ecumenical charisms, we owe great debts to one another; each frees others to pursue their respective callings.

While gratefully acknowledging the legacy of classical ecumenism, however, we must honestly name certain limitations. The "we" here refers especially to

[5] The Mennonite-Catholic dialogue also gave some attention to ecclesiology and sacraments or ordinances, though in my judgment with less creativity. And there are certainly Mennonites for whom the papacy or Mariology is an obstacle, or who assume that Catholics believe in justification through works—just as there are Catholics who will wonder how far Mennonite-Catholic dialogue can proceed until Mennonites recognize the charism of office as realized through the sacrament of holy orders.

[6] Pentecostals and Baptists have discussed with Catholics the role of Mary in God's economy of salvation. Anglicans and Eastern Orthodox know they can never recover formal unity with the Roman church until they come to terms on the Petrine ministry of the bishop of Rome. The Faith and Order process mainly among Protestant churches has taken on a host of issues through the years but the title of a 1982 watershed document names the most important—"Baptism, Eucharist and Ministry." (World Council of Churches, *Baptism, Eucharist and Ministry*, adopted by Faith and Order at its plenary commission meeting in Lima, Peru in 1982, Faith and Order Paper, no. 111 [Geneva: World Council of Churches, 1982].) And of course we can all be grateful for the breakthrough achieved in 1999 with the concord between Lutherans and Catholics concerning justification by grace through faith. The World Methodist Conference has incidentally illustrated my point here by officially signing on to the Lutheran-Catholic concord.

those who come from, or are sensitive to, the so-called free church tradition. As the late John Howard Yoder persistently argued throughout his career, however generous particular ecumenists have hoped to be, the very structure of ecumenical dialogue has too often served to marginalize the free churches.[7] Arguably, any assumption that high-level negotiators representing their churches might deliver blocks of Christians into new configurations is covertly Constantinian at worst or question-begging at best.[8] If free churches instead understand church authority to proceed "from below"—or better, from Christ "above" who distributes a wide diversity gifts among all believers[9]—then the very shape of the ecumenical table dare not preclude their full participation.

Even when heirs to the Radical Reformation have found a place at the ecumenical table, Yoder also reminded us, the classical agenda encoded in the formula of "Faith and Order," has tended to assume that matters of doctrine and church structure were "confessional issues" and their resolution what is most essential for greater church unity, but that ethics and discipleship are secondary.[10] Thankfully, ecumenists are increasingly recognizing that the heirs of the Radical Reformation have a rightful claim to the argument that these too are "confessional" matters. If Yoder were alive, however, he

---

[7] See for example John Howard Yoder, "On Christian Unity: The Way from Below," *Pro Ecclesia* 9, no. 2 (Spring 2000): 165–83.

[8] Perhaps the word "Constantinian" is too loaded, since some will reply that the authority of church officials to negotiate on behalf of their communities owes nothing to political authorities (now, anyway) and everything to the apostolic mandate that has constituted an authoritative magisterium in Christ's church. But such a reply only underscores Yoder's point: A key ecclesiological point is being begged. That is, the very position that needs proving is serving as the premise of the argument.

[9] I am alluding here to Yoder's interpretation of Ephesians 4:7-13, which provided the overarching image and title for Yoder's argument that all Christians share in the church's mission, John Howard Yoder, *The Fullness of Christ: Paul's Revolutionary Vision of Universal Ministry* (Elgin, IL: Brethren Press, 1987).

[10] Thus, even those of us who fully accept the Trinitarian structure of Nicaea and Chalcedon as an irreplaceable framework for Christian unity have reason to wonder: Why have Johannine formulae such as "I and my Father are one" or "whoever sees me sees the one who sent me" underwritten the metaphysics of the creeds but failed to underscore, historically, a nonviolent ethic of discipleship? After all, when Jesus himself spoke most explicitly of his Father's character, pointing out that God makes rain to fall on just and unjust alike, this served to underscore that we too must love our enemies and respond to their aggression with creative nonviolence. So too, one would think that the more Christians agree on the saving power of Jesus' cross and resurrection, the more they would see that Christ-like suffering service on behalf of others is the true power that truly secures our lives even now in history, not domineering violence.

would still be pressing the question of whether their full recognition does not require a more radically thoroughgoing review of the Faith and Order agenda itself—a reshaping of the table, as it were.

The experience of Bridgefolk suggests at least two other limitations to classical ecumenism. First, classical ecumenism has not accounted very well for postmodern fluidity of identity and is only beginning to do so now. The standard agenda of ecumenical dialogue has taken up matters of doctrine and polity with a certain assumption that long-standing historical positions continue to have purchase in the respective Christian communities. Far be it from me as a professional theologian to suggest otherwise; one of our perennial tasks as theology professors is to convince undergraduates that ideas of centuries past continue to shape our lives. But let us be honest: This very pedagogical task is more urgent than ever precisely because students and parishioners alike feel unprecedented freedom to mix and match, try on a succession of identities, and forge patterns of double belonging. The obvious danger here is an individualistic "cafeteria Christianity." Yet leading ecumenists themselves imply gratitude for the larger possibilities that the postmodern condition opens up, whenever they recognize the power of "spiritual ecumenism"—the way that formally divided Christians overcome old suspicions and develop mutual appreciation whenever they work together for the common good, pray common prayers, sing together, and so on. Though ecumenists may celebrate spiritual ecumenism more than they bemoan cafeteria Christianity, what all of us have trouble accounting for is how we can have one without the other. The fluidity of postmodern identity seems both to lubricate ecumenical conversation and to allow people to slide over hard questions that will haunt us later if we hope to move any closer to full communion.

Which brings me to a final limitation. If our only hope and model of ecumenical progress is a painstakingly negotiated solution to every church-dividing issue between every estranged Christian community, then the ecumenical horizon will ever recede. Patience is a key Christian virtue, of course, and eschatological tension is good theology. But a Christian has only one lifetime to live out his or her earthly vocation and live into the path of discipleship Christ has placed before us. Perhaps some of us have succumbed to the vice of impatience and are trying to hurry the eschaton. But when we find that full participation in the sacraments and ample communion with Christians through the ages and around the globe is necessary to sustain lives of nonviolent discipleship—in other words and for example, when we find our Christian identities *already* taking on both a Catholic and a Mennonite shape—then forgive us our itches, but we wonder how long we must wait for a *not yet* that seems more tragically unnecessary than properly eschatological. Our plea is not for premature solutions to the serious issues that Christians must face after centuries of division and mistrust. Our plea is to concentrate on moving together toward Christ rather negotiating our way toward each other. Concretely, our plea is for fresh models aiming not so much to resolve historic differences as to transcend them.

Vision

So a reshaped table, hosting a search for fresh models, must somehow make a place for the lessons of grassroots ecumenical dialogue and the voice of bridge people who may not represent one church or another officially, but who bear in their own bodies the healing scars of their struggles for reconciliation. As my brief review of Yoder has already implied, learning to accommodate messy grassroots modes of discernment and decision making will be critical for *any* dialogue that includes the free church tradition, anyway. One can understand the puzzle someone like Cardinal Kasper faces when he surveys the exponential expansion of "evangelical, charismatic and above all Pentecostal communities," when he recognizes that the horizon of church unity will only recede further if older churches cannot find ways to converse with these new ones, but when he also finds it nearly impossible to identify representatives of these communities who hold corresponding decision making positions that allow them to serve as conversation partners.[11] Yet the puzzle underscores the need. And fortunately, learning to converse with a nonhierarchical world communion such as the Mennonites offers practice for talking with other groups whose dynamics are more akin to the Radical Reformation than the magisterial Reformation.

What may not be so obvious is that it is eminently appropriate for a group like Bridgefolk to emerge in the context of ecumenical conversation involving Mennonites. Mennonite ecclesiology expects discernment to take place throughout the gathered body according to the model of 1 Corinthians 14, whereby even the words of the most gifted leader must be tested by the local assembly. When Catholics are attracted to Mennonites, one of the draws is sometimes this participatory pattern of church life. Thus, if Bridgefolk did not exist, it would probably have to be invented.

---

[11] Walter Kasper, Cardinal, "The Current Ecumenical Transition," *Origins* 36, no. 26 (7 December 2006): 411–13.

Here, though, we must cross-reference another major challenge that Cardinal Kasper has identified in the current ecumenical landscape. Kasper notes that the ecumenical scene is simultaneously fragmenting and reconnecting through new kinds of ecclesial networks and unpredictable new forms. Uncertain whether it is proper for the pontifical council he heads to enter into dialogue with these energetic yet unofficial groups, Kasper nonetheless voices gratitude for their commitment and seems intrigued that they come knocking.[12]

The challenge Kasper is identifying as he paints this picture is one that others associate with postmodernity. It is the phenomenon that paradoxically couples greater awareness of the role of traditions and community identity with greater fluidity of identities. The postmodern condition brings many dangers, of course. Elsewhere I have argued that too often it is little more than a pose for a kind of *hyper*modernity;[13] identities found and shaped in this way are too easily gnostic, individualistic, and unaccountable to any real and stable community. And yet we must have the courage to recognize opportunity here too.

Postmodernity has loosened rigid identity configurations that long kept peoples, cultures, and churches distrustful, estranged, and unable to exchange gifts. Postmodernity has thus allowed for fresh, creative, once-unthinkable conversations. It is reshaping our identities whether we welcome its changes or not. For those who welcome its opportunities self-critically, it makes once unthinkable identity configurations possible. Ivan Kauffman frees us from obsessing over whether postmodernity is simply producing "cafeteria Christians" when he proposes that the postmodern age is actually misnamed. At least for Christians, our age *is*, in fact, the "ecumenical age," says Kauffman. For the realization is dawning: Everyone needs the gifts that everyone else has to offer.

Still, how to have the benefits of our postmodern (a.k.a. ecumenical) age while minimizing its dangers? My appeal is to church officials and in its essence it is really quite simple: Give bridge people better ways to be

---

[12] Ibid., 412–13.

[13] Gerald W. Schlabach, "The Vow of Stability: A Premodern Way Through a Hypermodern World," in *Anabaptists & Postmodernity*, eds. Susan Biesecker-Mast and Gerald Biesecker-Mast, foreword by J. Denny Weaver, The C. Henry Smith Series, vol. 1 (Telford, PA: Pandora Books US, 2000), 301–24; Gerald W. Schlabach, "Stability Amid Mobility: The Oblate's Challenge and Witness," *American Benedictine Review* 52, no. 1 (March 2001): 3–23.

accountable; help them make "double belonging" into something more than their own improvised idiosyncrasies.

Though no fully canonical model yet exists for double belonging to both the Roman Catholic Church and some other Christian communion, models and categories do already exist. Some are the precedents of centuries, in fact, while others have only recently emerged.

Already before anyone had begun to imagine such a thing as a "Catholic Mennonite" or "Mennonite Catholic" identity, certain hybrid categories existed in both traditions—ecclesial models and patterns that defy easy pigeonholing according to a Troeltschian typology of "church" and "sect," or that otherwise allowed for "double belonging" long before anyone had coined the term:

- On the one hand, monasteries and religious orders had long embodied dynamics within the big tent of Catholic Christendom that contemporary "believers churches" see as essential for authentic Christianity—mature adult commitment, thoroughgoing discipleship, both taking primary shape in accountably local Christian communities.

- On the other hand, when Radical Reformation communities emerged, critics from the magisterial Reformation intriguingly wrote them off as married monastics. Later historians have seconded the observation. Rather than resist the designation, some of us now embrace it as a reminder of Anabaptism's Catholic roots.

- For centuries, recognition of alternative rites has been one way for the Roman church to maintain or restore communion with local churches whose histories have followed a divergent trajectory, resulting in non-Roman liturgies and polities that can nonetheless claim ancient precedent.

- Another kind of hybrid polity began to emerge in Latin America already prior to Vatican II—base ecclesial communities drawing together small groups led by lay leaders the church itself had trained. Though base communities have sometimes suffered from political struggle in both society and the church, leaving them with a tarnished reputation among conservative prelates, we do well to recall that base communities began as the bishops' own solution to some of their pastoral challenges.

- Meanwhile and with little controversy, Mennonites in North America have sometimes resolved pastoral problems resulting from their own history of division by allowing congregations to affiliate with more than one denomination. In a few cases, the second (or third!) affiliation has not even been Mennonite.

- And overseas, Mennonite mission agencies have won recognition as leaders in their willingness to work with African independent churches and others without any expectation of denominational affiliation. Add to this the many examples of MCC collaboration with Catholic bodies in Latin America, the Philippines, etc., and the result is a striking range of creative affiliations across the continuum running from "low" to "high church."

Still other models have been emerging in ways that seem to respond even more obviously to postmodern pastoral needs and dynamics. Not surprisingly, all of them have figured into the journeys of at least a few of the folk in Bridgefolk:

- One way that some Mennonites (and many other non-Catholics, of course) have found to connect with Catholic traditions has been as Benedictine oblates and through similar "third order" affiliations.
- Though not well known in North America, the Vatican has been looking to "ecclesial movements" to play a leading role in the revitalization of Christianity, especially in Europe. The theological tendencies of ecclesial movements cover a broad range of Catholicism, from traditionalist Opus Dei, to ecumenically generous Focolare, to socially activist Sant'Egidio. The polity of ecclesial movements is hybrid not only because they are emphatically lay-led but also because, in some cases, they admit non-Catholics into their membership.
- Although formal recognition of non-Roman rites is reserved for traditions with a claim to ancient precedent and apostolic continuity, a case can be made that at least one community and its liturgy has received informal or de facto recognition as a rite—the Taizé community centered in France. Founded by French Protestants soon after World War II in order to promote and embody Christian unity, Taizé has developed its own interchurch liturgy and enjoyed warm relations with the Vatican. At the funeral of Pope John Paul II, officiating Cardinal Joseph Ratzinger—soon to be Pope Benedict XVI—offered Taizé's aging leader Brother Roger the Eucharist while the world's cameras rolled. At Brother Roger's own funeral a few months later, Cardinal Kasper officiated. In a church that is highly attuned to ritual meaning, and that prefers to let policy and doctrinal development settle through received practice before ratifying them through canonical pronouncement, surely these were quite deliberate signals.

- Such historic developments still can take decades to play out, so individuals who seek to identify with one tradition without renouncing their formative tradition must continue to improvise. A few have, in fact, made formal dual affiliations. In my own case, for example, I was confirmed in the Catholic Church at Pentecost 2004 but have maintained associate membership in a Mennonite congregation as well. In Bridgefolk we are aware of at least a half dozen people who have worked out similar patterns. Crucially, they have often done so with the knowledge, support, or even the encouragement of both congregational and parish leadership.

So there you have at least ten models and precedents. Perhaps they are not all equally fruitful. Nor do all of them operate at the same level. If anything, one of the challenges I am trying to address is the very disparity that leaves some unheralded Christians to improvise patterns of double belonging amid warnings that they are breaking the rules, while warm and generous relationships develop, for example, between Vatican officials and the leadership of Taizé.

Nonetheless, even those precedents that are least accessible to Catholic Mennonites, such as official recognition of non-Roman rites or lay associations of the faithful, remind us that when Rome wants to reconcile with a long-estranged Christian community or recognize a movement of the Spirit emerging "from below," it finds a way. Likewise, when Mennonites want to cooperate with Christians of other churches whom Mennonite historiography or theology once labeled "fallen," or when Mennonites' own denominational structures fail to match their lived relationships, they find workarounds.

Now, I have no idea when, if ever, Mennonites as a community will consider moving toward visible unity with the Catholic Church. Mennonite World Conference leaders are on record assuring doubtful constituents that this is not the purpose of its dialogue with the Vatican. Realistically, I am sure that the only possible purpose of the dialogue at this point is simply to reduce mistrust. And yet anyone who joins in lamenting the scandal of Christian disunity in the face of Jesus' prayer "that all may be one" is of necessity looking toward a day when matters will be otherwise.

My suggestion is this: If and whenever such a day comes closer, it could actually be easier for Mennonites and some other "free churches" to move toward visible unity than for churches of the magisterial Reformation. Such a claim will no doubt seem counterintuitive to those who assume that the radical Reformation constituted a double estrangement—first from Rome and then from Luther or Calvin. Historians and theologians have been rebutting this for at least three decades by noting certain ways in which Anabaptists remained more Catholic than Protestant in both doctrine and practice.[14] But a further point needs attention, this time with regard to polity.

The greater asymmetry between so-called high and low churches could actually be an advantage. The magisterial Reformation contested Roman claims of apostolic succession in various ways, of course, but did so, in part, by pitting another hierarchical authority over against that of bishop and pope—namely the prince or city council. The resulting principle, *cuios regio eius religio* or the regent's religion is the region's religion, was if anything *hyper*-Constantinian. There has been a territorial element in Christianity since Saint Paul wrote letters to churches in specific regions and the seer of Patmos wrote to their "angels," but even after Constantine, ecclesiastical jurisdiction was not necessarily a zero-sum game until the Reformation. Just as feudalism, whatever its flaws, involved more fluid, overlapping, and federated jurisdiction than would soon be the case within the nation-state system so, too, did medieval Catholicism allow bishops and monasteries, and then itinerant religious orders, to all operate at different levels in the same territory.

With the disestablishment of all churches in North America and of many others elsewhere, we have moved into yet another cultural and political context, of course. But here is a way to notice the continuing legacy of zero-sum territorial ecclesiology: Someone who called herself both Lutheran and Catholic would sound like an unlikely oxymoron, even on this side of the 1999 concord on justification. Someone who called himself both Mennonite and Lutheran would sound like he is on a postmodern journey. But someone who is both a Franciscan and a Catholic, however, would be altogether unremarkable.

So what about Mennonite Catholics? There is a reason why this does not need to be either impossible or merely postmodern—a reason why one day it could even become unremarkable. Mennonites insist on the need for Christian faith to express itself in communities of local accountability. Catholics insist on the need for every local expression of Christian faith to be accountable to apostolic tradition and to the global church by way of affiliation with its visible representatives. But these two claims can, in principle, be complementary

---

[14] Groundbreaking in this regard was Walter Klaassen, *Anabaptism: Neither Catholic Nor Protestant* (Waterloo, Ontario, Canada: Conrad Press, 1981); Klaassen reportedly remarked later that he wished he had named the book "Anabaptism: Both Catholic and Protestant."

rather than competing. For the two foci work at different levels and do not necessarily compete for the same territory.

In fact, many of the precedents I have listed are already beginning to take contemporary expression.

- At a personal level, I already find that the easiest way for me to explain how I can be a Mennonite Catholic is to say I am both in much the same way that a Franciscan or a Benedictine is both.
- At a local level, Bridgefolk groups are emerging in a few locales in ways that are sociologically akin to base communities.
- At a wider level, Bridgefolk as a whole probably qualifies already as an ecclesial movement.
- If an entire Mennonite congregation were to seek entrance into Catholic communion,[15] it seems plausible to expect it could work out a juridical relationship with its bishop roughly analogous to that of a Benedictine monastery.
- And meanwhile, as I have already noted, Taizé seems to be in the process of becoming a de facto Protestant Catholic rite.

Conclusion: Brother Roger

But perhaps someone has wondered why I keep mentioning Taizé. To be sure, the music of the Taizé community has quickly found a beloved place in Mennonite hymnody, while individual Mennonites have found visits to the Taizé community deeply transformative. But admittedly, Mennonites have no special role or connection with Taizé.

Or perhaps someone else will object that my call for some way to formally recognize patterns of accountable double belonging invites an open season of ecclesial poaching. Rightly, one of Cardinal Kasper's biggest stated worries about responding to "individual groupings" who knock on his door seeking dialogue outside of official denominational channels is precisely this. "It is a delicate issue," he has said. "Obviously we do not wish to be involved in any dishonest double-dealing; we want to have absolutely nothing to do with any form of proselytism" and must always respond with "a high degree of transparency toward our partners in other churches."[16]

---

[15] I know the leaders of one Mennonite congregation have at least played with this idea.

[16] Kasper, "The Current Ecumenical Transition," 413.

So why mention Taizé? Because it not only represents one of the most hopeful signs of Vatican openness to fresh and creative models but also suggests exactly how to avoid ecclesial poaching. Vatican recognition of Taizé as a Protestant "rite" may only be quasi and de facto at this point. But it is far enough along for us to see the potential of allowing individual Christians and grassroots groups to practice double belonging in accountable ways—precluding mere "cafeteria" grazing by individuals on the one hand, and distancing church policy from ecclesial poaching on the other hand.

It turns out that when Taizé's aging leader Brother Roger received communion from soon-to-be Pope Benedict XVI at the funeral of John Paul II, it was neither his first Roman Catholic Eucharist, nor was it merely a concession to a wheelchair-bound nonagenarian with an irresistible smile. A few months after the papal funeral, Brother Roger also died in a senseless public stabbing by a mentally ill woman visiting Taizé; a year later, stories began to emerge that way back in 1972, Brother Roger had actually "converted" to Catholicism. The claim was misleading, as the community quickly clarified.[17]

If "conversion" meant renouncing his Protestant origins, no, Brother Roger had not converted, and those who interpreted his journey this way had not "grasped the originality of Brother Roger's search." Yes, however, Brother Roger had first received communion in 1972 from the then-Bishop of Autun, Mgr. Armand LeBourgeois, upon his profession of faith according to the Creed. "From a Protestant background," explained his community, "Brother Roger undertook a step that was without precedent since the Reformation: entering progressively into a full communion with the faith of the Catholic Church without a 'conversion' that would imply a break with his origins."

The journey was anything but private. In 1980 Brother Roger explained it at a meeting in Saint Peter's Basilica, no less, in the presence of Pope John Paul II: "I have found my own identity as a Christian by reconciling within myself the faith of my origins with the mystery of the Catholic faith, without breaking fellowship with anyone." As his successor Brother Alois has explained: "He was not interested in an individual solution for reconciliation but, through many tentative steps, he sought [a] way [that] could be accessible for others."

---

[17] The report first emerged in the newsletter of a traditionalist Catholic organization, and was picked up by the French daily *Le Monde* in an article of 6 September 2006. The Taizé community issued a clarification on that same day, which I quote in the paragraph that follows.

Some of those others are some of us. Personally, I found it little short of astounding to learn these details about Brother Roger. For since my confirmation as a Catholic at Pentecost 2004, I had resisted the label "convert" and instead explained myself in words that are a close theological match to his: "I am a Mennonite who has come into full communion with the Catholic Church." But although I cannot speak for everyone in Bridgefolk, my deepest hope is for a day when such strictly individual self-definitions and solutions will not be necessary at all.

Surely this too was the hope of soon-to-be Pope Benedict XVI when he offered Brother Roger the Eucharistic host before a watching world, knowing that he was sending a signal, given that few others knew that the Taizé leader had come into full communion years before, though in an unconventional way. Surely this, too, was the hope of Cardinal Walter Kasper when he officiated at Brother Roger's funeral mass. For in a church so ritually attuned as the Catholic Church, these are not just expressions *of* hope but signals *calling forth* hope.

And in Christianity, hope takes on flesh.

Enfleshed, scarred, but thus healing and still itching, yes, we do go knocking at doors.

Chapter 14

Response to "Catholic and Mennonite

A Journey of Healing"

Abbot John Klassen, OSB

I wish to thank Gerald for his thoughtful and insightful reflection on the "healing of memories," which is such a fundamental element of ecumenical transformation. For the purposes of this response I wish to focus on three elements. First, I wish to comment on Gerald's choice of the metaphor of a wound that leads to a scar. Second, I wish to comment on the historical problem we face in all ecumenical dialogue between the Roman Catholic Church and Christian churches that emerged from the Reformation. Third, I wish to comment on the ecclesial model for communion between the Mennonite Church and the Catholic Church.

First, I think that the metaphor of wound/scar is well chosen. It is an accessible and imaginative way to describe the complicated and hurtful relationship between Mennonites and Catholics as a result of the rupture at the time of the Reformation. If one keeps in mind the metaphor of the Body of Christ, which Paul articulates in 1 Corinthians 12, one can see how the metaphor of wound describes the dysfunctional relationship between Mennonites and Catholics from the time of the Reformation until the present, along with the need for true healing. Gerald describes a particular wound that cannot be immediately closed and sutured but must be kept open, irrigated with saline solution to prevent infection, and allowed to heal from the inside out. By analogy, the memories of torture and killing that Mennonites carry cannot simply be forcibly repressed. If treated in this manner, they will live on in "the body," cause a low-grade infection, stimulate other symptoms of ill health, and percolate to the surface at the worst possible moments.

In fact, the memories of these events must be purified—that is, Mennonite and Catholic scholars need to reconstruct events as carefully as possible and free them from polemic and from both exaggeration or minimization.[1] We can learn much from the healing of memories for survivors of atrocities in our own time[2] or from survivors of sexual abuse. When survivor and offender can come to a mutual acknowledgement of "what happened," healing is more likely for both parties. However, as Gerald notes, no matter how much healing occurs, the body remembers: for any serious wound, a scar remains—a scar that is sensitive to cold or to changes in barometric pressure, or that itches. As theologian Thomas Ryan notes in his response to the recent Vatican statement, "Responses to Some Questions Regarding Certain Aspects of the Doctrine on the Church," the downside of this [Vatican] statement is that "since the point of the exercise was to clarify the language earlier used, the same words which landed with a thud in earlier renderings reopened old wounds when brought forth once again."[3]

Second, I wish to comment on the historical problem we face in all ecumenical dialogue between the Roman Catholic Church and Christian churches which emerged from the Reformation. If the only model for full communion in the Body of Christ is through the Catholic Church's understanding of apostolic succession, then full communion in the future will be virtually impossible to achieve. For one thing, this view of communion leads one to the assumption that the only meaningful dialogue is between upper-echelon leaders in each church. As Gerald astutely suggests, there are spaces in ecumenical dialogue for grassroots efforts such as Bridgefolk, which focus on the mission of the Body of Christ. That mission is nothing less than the proclamation of the Reign of God to a world that longs to know how to work for justice, how to go about making peace, how to live each day in the presence of God. Dialogue at the grassroots level provides a forum for exploring and extending our sense of sacramentality. For example, what happens if we explore the historical and theological significance of footwashing as a sign of full communion? This sacrament does not depend on apostolic succession but it may have been the sacrament of baptism into Christ for at least some Johannine communities.[4] How we live the Gospel

---

[1] *Called Together to be Peacemakers: Report of the International Dialogue Between the Catholic Church and the Mennonite World Conference (1998–2003)*, paragraphs 190–93.

[2] Cf. Desmond Tutu, *No Future Without Forgiveness* (New York: Doubleday, 1999).

[3] Thomas Ryan, CSP, "The Doctrine on the Church: Intramural Debate and Extramural Reactions," http://www.catholic-thoughts.info/catholic_life/CDFAspectsOf DoctrineJune2007.html.

[4] See Martin F. Connell, "Nisi Pedes, Except for the Feet: Footwashing in the Communities of John's Gospel," *Worship* 70, no. 6 (November 1996): 517–31.

and pray with each other, how we are reconciled, how we bring joy and hope to our world, and how we give each other mutual support are important ecumenical contributions because they give concreteness to our statements of belief. As we have noted in our Bridgefolk gatherings, full communion between Mennonites and Catholics would lead to a new reality in which both are transformed for the sake of mission, for the sake of peacemaking, for the sake of bringing the Reign of God into the world.

Third, I wish to comment on the ecclesial model for communion between the Mennonite Church and the Catholic Church. Gerald suggests that the Mennonite Church might well live in a manner analogous to a religious order within the Catholic Church, in full communion but with the relative independence of an order such as the Benedictines. There is much in me that resonates strongly with this, and not just because I am a Benedictine. For example, this is a hard time to be in the Catholic Church if you are either a homosexual person or a woman. The environment of a religious community buffers a person, at least a bit, from the political tugs and pulls that sometimes operate in the church's hierarchy. Religious communities, especially those founded before the Reformation, have a place in the church that canon law respects and protects. At the same time there is account-ability to a Vatican congregation. The community or congregation has its own constitution and governance, as well as a liturgical tradition that is in dialogue with the larger tradition of liturgy and prayer within the church. Right now one can be a Benedictine and Catholic in good standing, even as one admits that it pinches being Catholic, for all kinds of reasons. I suspect that this kind of situation could work for a Mennonite community as well, given the right arrangements and clarity in the relationship.

There were many other fine elements in Gerald's paper, such as the dia-logue between Anna B. and Cathy, and his observations on the implications of a postmodern situation for ecclesial life. I hope they will jumpstart further conversation.

Chapter 15

Response to "Catholic and Mennonite

a Journey of Healing"

Mary H. Schertz

Thank you, Gerald, for this thoughtful reflection. Although not often applied to academic papers, the word that comes to mind is "compassion." What you model, in life as well as in this piece, is empathy. The bridge on which you stand may not be the most comfortable location. But the fruit of the Spirit—that interaction between your spirit and the Holy Spirit—is increased understanding between the Mennonite and the Catholic traditions—traditions that have both nurtured and continue to nurture you.

What may be even more worth noting is that this empathy you model is not unusual in either Bridgefolk or the Catholic Mennonite theology conferences that have occasionally taken place alongside Bridgefolk. This particular manifestation of ecumenical dialog has been profoundly relational. The Bridgefolk mantra, "proceed through friendship," has been much more than either a slogan or an ideal. We have spent considerable time in each other's institutional "homes." We have shared deeply of joy and sorrow—we have laughed uproariously and wept unashamedly. This ongoing conversation may not be as grassroots as it could be or should be, but it has been, in its regional as well as its continental forms, wider and deeper than many ecumenical discussions. It has proceeded through friendship and, in that respect, the table *has been* and *is being* reshaped in ways that open up hospitable space for the elephant and the mouse to enjoy each others' company. The model of friendship may not be a novel model of ecumenical dialogue but I am aware that friendship is, in itself, a spiritual discipline. I do not think that it is exactly an accident that those sustaining the dialog, those showing up year after year, are Catholics and Mennonites formed in communal traditions.

I have two comments on the paper, and then a text.

First, I appreciated the candor of the conversation between Anna B. and Cathy. You are correct, I think, that Bridgefolk discussions rarely get quite that nitty-gritty, although I do remember one late night, off-campus conversation at Eastern Mennonite University a couple of years ago about "the Pope," among other topics, which came close!

The part of the exchange that I found most poignant had to do with the ministries of women. I am sure that I have thought and said the sentiments critical of the Catholic Church that you put into Anna B's mouth, Gerald. But I think I want to repent and call us, especially Catholic and Mennonite women, to more thoughtful dialog on the issue. Only relatively recently have Mennonite women become fully free to minister—in the last thirty years or so. Furthermore, in that struggle, I think Mennonite women acted more Catholic than Mennonite. Mennonites have schismed on many issues—but not that one. I can testify that we were tempted, sometimes, to just walk out and become Methodists, but in fact we did not. We argued with the Mennonite *hierarchy* and we studied theology and, having studied theology, we pointed out the sins of the Mennonite *patriarchy* and we often got tired and went on women-only retreats. But mostly we waited, not necessarily patiently, for the church to change. I know this point is not a major one for this paper, but I think it would be both fascinating and instructive to look at how the two traditions receive and work with internal challenges to its truth and practice. I also think it would be both fascinating and instructive to get more women and people of color involved in these conversations, but that is not a new concern for anyone here.

My second comment has to do with your catalog of the ways Mennonites and Catholics are finding to connect, which I found both evocative and hopeful. I have witnessed some of these models and participated in others. We, as Catholic and Mennonite brothers and sisters, have been blessed and enriched in ways that we could not have imagined before embarking on this journey. As you say, when we want to connect or find it useful to connect, we find a way—from grassroots Mennonite Central Committee workers to the Vatican itself.

Your most radical idea, of course, is the intriguing musing about Mennonites, or some Mennonites anyway, as a Catholic congregation or order, similar to the Benedictines or Franciscans. That we can sit here today as a group of Catholics and Mennonites and discuss this idea calmly might serve as an historical marker of some sort. I cannot imagine that such a thing would have been possible ten years ago—or even five or six years ago when Bridgefolk began meeting at Collegeville. As I played with this notion during the past few days, one of the questions I asked myself has been, *what of my basic beliefs I would need to rethink in order to become this sort of Mennonite Catholic?* My answer was, *maybe none*. I have not met him or her yet but conceivably there is a Catholic somewhere in the world who already agrees with me on every point of doctrine. That is not to say that I agree with every teaching point of the Catholic Church. But then, I have been discovering, neither do all Catholics. Such Mennonite Catholics would likely find themselves located somewhere on the margins of the greater Catholic world, but as a social location that is neither that uncommon nor particularly uncomfortable for solely Mennonites.

Although, with Gerald, I am unsure when or how Mennonites would ever move toward visible unity with the Catholic Church, I think it is helpful to think about it. Such a move would likely require further attentions to some tensions that have emerged in Bridgefolk as well as elsewhere. These tensions may not be resolvable. Indeed they may be more in that category of paradox, which some at this meeting have urged us to embrace. Briefly, however, let me name a few.

One such tension is the question of authority, especially with regards to the Bible and the church. Mennonites have become less naïve about *sola scriptura* and Catholics are rediscovering and reclaiming the Bible. We could have some lively conversation on biblical interpretation and the authority of the church to interpret Bible, which not only would be helpful to this ecumenical dialog but would be of use to each of our traditions internally as well.

Another area of attention and exploration has to do with truth and love. In an earlier conversation on martyrdom in our traditions, Catholic historian Brad Gregory condemned the *persecution* of Anabaptists but then went on to explain the care for the truth that impelled the *prosecution* of Anabaptists. At one point in that conversation, Mennonite theologian James Reimer—to the surprise of his fellow Mennonites who know him as fairly creedal—said emphatically that for Mennonites, love *is* truth. That conversation merits further consideration.

A third tension has to do with the definition of love. During one of our Bridgefolk conferences on peacemaking, I was starting to wonder if there were any disagreements at all in this group of Mennonites and Catholics. Then we got to the wrap-up session on Sunday morning and suddenly it became very clear that for Mennonites, love is love of the enemy, and for Catholics, love is love for the defenseless. It was also pretty clear that these two perspectives need each other desperately—but it was Sunday morning and we were getting ready to leave. I would also like to revisit that one.

Finally, in addition to the shape of the conference table there is also the perennial question of the shape of the communion table. Mennonites talk about Jesus being truly present in their celebration of communion. Catholics talk about the real presence of Christ in the Eucharistic event. So close, so far; we meet, we miss.

In conclusion, a text. (As the only biblical scholar on the program, what did you expect?)

In 1 Peter 3:7, Christian husbands are admonished to honor their wives, lest their prayers be hindered. For five hundred years, we have not honored each other and I believe that our prayers have been hindered. For all our thriving as parallel communities of faith, we have in some ways both been hobbled. The monks at Collegeville often bow first to the cross over the altar and then to each other. We have, as Mennonites and Catholics, both been bowing to the cross in our respective ways. Now we are learning how to turn and bow to the other. According to 1 Peter we should not be surprised to find that in finding each other we are also finding Christ in a new way. We are experiencing in these conversations another of the variegated graces of God of which 1 Peter also speaks. Whether we ever, as Gerald puts it, move toward visible unity, it is obvious that we can never return to our former hostility. We are indeed grateful for you, Gerald, and for those incessant arguments going on in your Mennonite Catholic head. Thank you.

After having worked with each other over these five years, we, Catholic and Mennonite members of this dialogue, want to testify together that our mutual love for Christ has united us and accompanied us in our discussions. Our dialogue has fortified the common conviction that it is possible to experience reconciliation and the healing of memories. Therefore we beseech God to bestow divine grace upon us for the healing of past relationships between Mennonites and Catholics, and we thank God for present commitments to reconciliation within the body of Christ. Together we pray that God may bless this new relationship between our two families of faith, and that the Holy Spirit may enlighten and enliven us in our common journey on the path forward.

Called Together to Be Peacemakers, paragraph 215

Appendix A

Called Together to Be Peacemakers

Report of the International Dialogue between the Catholic Church and Mennonite World Conference
1998–2003

Table of Contents

PREFACE

1. In the spirit of friendship and reconciliation, a dialogue between Catholics and Mennonites took place over a five-year period, from 1998–2003. The dialogue partners met five times in plenary session, a week at a time. At the first four sessions, at least two papers were presented by each delegation as the joint commission explored their respective understandings of key theological themes and of significant aspects of the history of the church. At the fifth session the partners worked together on a common report.

2. This was a new process of reconciliation. The two dialogue partners had had no official dialogue previous to this, and therefore started afresh. Our purpose was to assist Mennonites and Catholics to overcome the consequences of almost five centuries of mutual isolation and hostility. We wanted to explore whether it is now possible to create a new atmosphere in which to meet each other. After all, despite all that may still divide us, the ultimate identity of both is rooted in Jesus Christ.

3. This report is a synthesis of the five-year Catholic-Mennonite dialogue. The Introduction describes the origins of the dialogue within the contemporary inter-church framework, including other bilateral dialogues in which Catholics and Mennonites have participated in recent decades. It identifies specific factors that led up to this particular dialogue. The Introduction then states the purpose and scope of the dialogue, names the participants, and conveys something of the spirit in which the dialogue was conducted. It concludes by naming the locations at which each of the annual dialogue sessions took place, and states the themes that were discussed at each session.

4. Three chapters follow the Introduction. The first of these, "Considering History Together", summarizes the results of our common study of three crucial eras (and related events) of history that have shaped our respective traditions and have yielded distinctive interpretations. These are 1) the rupture of the sixteenth century, 2) the Constantinian era, and 3) the Middle Ages as such. The aim of our study was to re-read history together for the purpose of comparing and refining our interpretations. Chapter I reports on our agreed-upon evaluations as well as some differing perspectives on the historical eras and events that were selected and examined.

5. In the second chapter, "Considering Theology Together", we report on our common and differing understandings of the Church, of Baptism, of the Eucharist or the Lord's Supper, and of peace. In each case, we state the historic theological perspectives of the Catholic Church and of the Mennonite Churches.[1] This is followed by a summary of our discussion on major convergences and divergences on each theme. Of particular significance is our theological study and comparison of our respective peace teachings. The Mennonites are one of the "Historic Peace Churches"[2], which means that the commitment to peace is essential to their self-definition. The Catholic Church takes the promotion of unity—and accordingly peace—as "belonging to the innermost nature of the Church".[3] Is it possible, therefore,

---

[1] The words "church" is used in this report to reflect the self-understandings of the participating churches, without intending to resolve all the ecclesiological issues related to this term. Mennonites and Catholics do not share a common understanding of the Church.

[2] The term "Historic Peace Churches", in use since about 1935, refers to Mennonites, Quakers (Society of Friends), and Church of the Brethren. For an orientation to the Historic Peace Churches, see Donald Durnbaugh, ed., *On Earth Peace: Discussions on War/Peace Issues between Friends, Mennonites, Brethren and European Churches 1935–1975* (Elgin: The Brethren Press, 1978).

[3] "Pastoral Constitution on the Church in the Modern World", *Gaudium et spes*, 42.

that these two communities can give witness together to the Gospel which calls us to be peacemakers in today's often violent world?

6. Chapter III is entitled "Toward a Healing of Memories". In a sense, every interchurch dialogue in which the partners are seeking to overcome centuries of hostility or isolation is aimed at healing bitter memories that have made reconciliation between them difficult. The third chapter identifies four components that, we hope, can help to foster a healing of memories between Mennonites and Catholics.

7. The members of this dialogue offer this report, the results of our work, to the sponsoring bodies in the hope that it can be used by Mennonites and Catholics not only within their respective communities but also as they meet together, to promote reconciliation between them for the sake of the Gospel.

INTRODUCTION

The Origin of These Conversations

8. Since the beginning of the twentieth century, separated Christian communions have come into closer contact, seeking reconciliation with each other. Despite ongoing divisions, they have started to cooperate with one another to their mutual benefit and often to the benefit of the societies in which they give witness to the Gospel. They have engaged in theological dialogue, exploring the reasons for their original divisions. In doing so, they have often discovered that, despite centuries of mutual isolation, they continue to share much of the Christian heritage which is rooted in the Gospel. They have also been able to clarify serious differences that exist between and among them in regard to various aspects of the Christian faith. In short, in modern times we have witnessed the emergence of a movement of reconciliation among separated Christians, bringing with it new openness to one another and, on the part of many, a commitment to strive for the unity of the followers of Jesus Christ.

9. Many factors have contributed to this contemporary movement. Among them are conditions and changes in the modern world. For example, the destructive power of modern weapons in a nuclear age has challenged Christians everywhere to reflect on the question of peace in a totally new way—and even to do so together. But the basic inspiration for dialogue between separated Christians has been the realization that conflict between them impedes the preaching of the Gospel and damages their credibility. Indeed, conflict between Christians is a major obstacle to the mission given by Jesus Christ to his disciples. It is difficult to announce the good news of salvation "so that the world may believe" (*Jn* 17:21) if those bearing the good news have basic disagreements among themselves.

10. Since the Second Vatican Council (1962–1965), the Catholic Church has been engaged in a wide variety of ecumenical activities, including a number of international bilateral dialogues. There has been dialogue between the Catholic Church and the Orthodox Church, the Coptic Orthodox Church, the Malankara Orthodox Churches, the Assyrian Church of the East, the Anglican Communion, the Lutheran World Federation, the World Alliance of Reformed Churches, the World Methodist Council, the Baptist World Alliance, the Christian Church (Disciples of Christ), the

Pentecostals, and the Evangelicals. There have been consultations with the World Evangelical Alliance and Seventh Day Adventists. Also, since 1968 Catholic theologians have participated as full voting members of the multilateral Commission on Faith and Order of the World Council of Churches.

11. Mennonite World Conference (MWC) has previously held international bilateral dialogues with the World Alliance of Reformed Churches and with the Baptist World Alliance. Also, together with the Lutheran World Federation and the World Alliance of Reformed Churches, MWC sponsors the multilateral dialogue on the "First, Second and Radical Reformations", also known as the "Prague Consultations". MWC and the Lutheran World Federation have agreed to international conversation beginning in 2004. Mennonite World Conference member churches in France, in Germany, and in the United States have held bilateral dialogues with Lutheran churches in those countries.

12. Though Mennonites and Catholics have lived in isolation or in tension for centuries, they too have had increasing contact with each other in recent times. On the international level, they have met each other consistently in a number of interchurch organizations. For example, representatives of the Mennonite World Conference (MWC) and the Pontifical Council for Promoting Christian Unity (PCPCU) meet annually at the meeting of the Conference of Secretaries of Christian World Communions (CS/CWC), a forum which has for more than forty years brought together the general secretaries of world communions for informal contacts and discussion. There have been numerous other contacts on national and local levels.

13. More recently some Catholics and Mennonites have begun to invite one another to meetings or events each has sponsored. On the international level, Pope John Paul II invited Christian World Communions, including the Mennonite World Conference, to participate in the Assisi Day of Prayer for Peace, held in October 1986. The MWC Executive Secretary, Paul Kraybill, attended that meeting. The MWC invited the PCPCU to send an observer to its world assembly in Calcutta in January of 1997. Msgr. John Mutiso Mbinda attended on behalf of the PCPCU and brought a message from its President, Edward Idris Cardinal Cassidy, in which the Cardinal expressed the "sincere hope that there will be other contacts between the Mennonite World Conference and the Catholic Church". After the international Mennonite-Catholic Dialogue began in 1998, MWC was among those Pope John Paul II invited to send representatives to events in Rome related to the Jubilee Year 2000. The Mennonite co-chairman of this dialogue, Dr. Helmut Harder, attended a jubilee event at the Vatican in 1999 on the subject of inter-religious dialogue. More recently, accepting the invitation of Pope John Paul II to leaders of Christian World Communions, Dr. Mesach Krisetya, president of the MWC, participated in the Assisi Day of Prayer for Peace, January 24, 2002. Moreover, to name one example from a national context, the National Conference of Catholic Bishops in the USA,[4] in the course of writing its pastoral statement on peace in 1993 [*sic;* actual date 1983], sought the expertise of persons from outside the Catholic Church, including that of Mennonite theologian John H. Yoder.

---

[4] Now called the United States Conference of Catholic Bishops.

14. The possibility and desirability of an international Catholic-Mennonite dialogue came into view in the context of informal contacts during meetings of the CS/CWC. The question was first raised in the early 1990s in a conversation between Dr. Larry Miller, Executive Secretary of the MWC, Bishop Pierre Duprey, Secretary of the PCPCU, and Msgr. John A. Radano, also of the PCPCU. During ensuing annual CS/CWC meetings, Msgr. Radano and Dr. Miller continued to informally discuss the possibility of an international dialogue. Two particularly compelling reasons for dialogue were the awareness that contemporary historical studies point to medieval sources of spirituality which Catholics and Mennonites share, and the conviction that both believe peace to be at the heart of the Gospel. There was also a sense that, as in other relationships between separated Christians, there is need for a healing of memories between Mennonites and Catholics. In 1997 the leaders of both communions responded positively to a proposal that a Mennonite-Catholic dialogue should take place on the international level. The dialogue, envisioned initially for a five-year period, began the following year, organized on the Catholic side by the PCPCU and on the Mennonite side by the MWC.

Purpose, Scope, and Participants

15. The general purpose of the dialogue was to learn to know one another better, to promote better understanding of the positions on Christian faith held by Catholics and Mennonites, and to contribute to the overcoming of prejudices that have long existed between them.

16. In light of this purpose, two tracks were followed during each of the annual meetings. A contemporary component explored the positions of each side on a selected key theological issue. A historical track examined the interpretation of each dialogue partner with reference to a particular historical event or historical development that caused or represented separation from one another in the course of the history of the Church.

17. In order to implement the study of these two tracks, MWC and PCPCU called on papers from participants who brought historical or theological expertise and understanding to the events, the themes, and the issues that effect relationships between Catholics and Mennonites.

18. Mennonite delegation members were Dr. Helmut Harder (co-chairman, Canada), systematic theologian and co-editor of "A Confession of Faith in Mennonite Perspective"; Dr. Neal Blough (USA/ France), specialist in Anabaptist history and theology; Rev. Mario Higueros (Guatemala), head of the Central American Mennonite seminary with advanced theological studies at the Salamanca Pontifical University in Spain and numerous contacts with Catholics in Latin America; Rev. Andrea Lange (Germany), Mennonite pastor and teacher, especially on themes related to peace church theology and practice; Dr. Howard J. Loewen (USA), Mennonite Brethren theologian and expert in the confessional history of Anabaptist/ Mennonites; Dr. Nzash Lumeya (D.R. Congo/USA), missiologist and Old Testament specialist; and Dr. Larry Miller (co-secretary, USA/France), New Testament scholar and Mennonite World Conference Executive Secretary. Dr. Alan Kreider (USA), historian of the early church, joined the group for the annual session of the dialogue in the year 2000.

19. On the Catholic side, participants included the Most Reverend Joseph Martino, (co-chairman, USA), a church historian and Auxiliary Bishop of Philadelphia, located in an area which includes many communities of the Anabaptist tradition; Rev. Dr. James Puglisi, SA (USA/Italy), Director of the Centro Pro Unione and specialist in liturgy and sacraments; Dr. Peter Nissen (The Netherlands), church historian and authority on relations between Catholics and Anabaptists in the sixteenth century; Msgr. John Mutiso Mbinda (Kenya/Vatican City), PCPCU staff member who participated in the 1997 MWC world assembly meeting in Calcutta and whose work brings him into regular contact with international Christian organizations where Mennonites participate at times; Dr. Joan Patricia Back (United Kingdom/Italy), on the staff of Centro Uno, ecumenical secretariat of the Focolare Movement, whose communities around the world have contacts with many Christian groups, including Mennonites; Rev. Dr. Andrew Christiansen, SJ (USA), an expert in social ethics whose work in matters of peace both on the academic and the practical levels have brought him into contact and conversation with Mennonite scholars; and Msgr. Dr. John A. Radano (co-secretary, USA/Vatican City), Head of the Western Section of the PCPCU who has participated in various international dialogues.

20. The atmosphere in the meetings was most cordial. Each side presented its views on the theological issues as clearly and forcefully as possible, seeking to foster an honest and fruitful dialogue. As the conversation partners heard the other's views clearly stated, it was possible to begin to see which parts of the Christian heritage are held in common by both Mennonites and Catholics, and where they have strong differences. In presenting their respective views on history, dialogue members did not refrain from allowing one another to see clearly the criticism each communion has traditionally raised against the other. At the same time, dialogue participants did this with the kind of self-criticism that is needed if an authentic search for truth is to take place. The constant hope was that clarifications in both areas of study, historical and theological, might contribute to a healing of memories between Catholics and Mennonites.

21. Prayer sustained and accompanied the dialogue. Every day of each meeting began and ended with prayer and worship, led by members of the delegations. On Sundays, dialogue participants attended services in a Mennonite or a Catholic congregation, depending on which side was hosting the meeting that year. During the week, the host side arranged a field trip to sites associated with its tradition. These services and trips contributed to the dialogue by helping each partner to know the other better.

Locations and Themes of Annual Meetings

22. The first meeting took place in Strasbourg, France, October 14–18, 1998. Each delegation made presentations in response to the question, "Who are we today?" A second set of papers helped to shed light on the reasons for reactions to each other in the sixteenth century. At the second meeting, held in Venice, Italy, October 12–18, 1999, the discussion in the theological sessions focussed on the way each communion understands the church today. The historical track explored the Anabaptist idea of the restitution of the early church, as well as the medieval roots of the Mennonite

tradition of faith and spirituality. At the third meeting, November 24–30, 2000, held at the Thomashof, near Karlsruhe, Germany, the contemporary discussion turned to an area of possible cooperation between Mennonites and Catholics today, with the theme formulated as a question: "What is a Peace Church?" In the historical sessions, each presented an interpretation of the impact of the "Constantinian shift" on the church. In the fourth meeting, at Assisi, Italy, November 27 to December 3, 2001, each delegation presented its views on Baptism and the Eucharist or Lord's Supper. The historical part of that meeting focussed on the view of each on the relationship between church and state in the Middle Ages. At the fifth meeting, October 25–31, 2002, in Akron, Pennsylvania, members worked on the final report of the dialogue. Drafting meetings in March, May and June, 2003 provided occasions to refine the report in preparation for its submission.

Note: A list of the papers presented at the dialogue sessions, together with their authors, appears as an *Appendix* at the end of this report.

I

CONSIDERING HISTORY TOGETHER

A. Introduction: A Shared Hermeneutics or Re-reading of Church History

23. A common re-reading of the history of the church has proven to be fruitful in recent inter-church dialogues.[5] The same is true for our dialogue. Mennonites and Catholics have lived through more than 475 years of separation. Over the centuries they developed separate views of the history of the Christian tradition. By studying history together, we discovered that our interpretations of the past were often incomplete and limited. Sharing our insights and our assessments of the past helped us gain a broader view of the history of the church.

24. First of all, we recognized that both our traditions have developed interpretations of aspects of church history that were influenced by negative images of the other, though in different ways and to different degrees. Reciprocal hostile images were fostered and continued to be present in our respective communities and in our representations of each other in history. Our relationship, or better the lack of it, began in a context of rupture and separation. Since then, from the sixteenth century to the present, theological polemics have persistently nourished negative images and narrow stereotypes of each other.

---

[5] Cf. the following samples from bilateral dialogues: 1) "Towards a Common Understanding of the Church: Reformed/Roman Catholic International Dialogue, Second Phase (1984–1990)", chapter 1, "Toward a Reconciliation of Memories", and chapter 3, "The Church We Confess and our Divisions in History", *Information Service* 74 (1990/III), pp. 93–102, pp. 106–115; 2) *The Joint Declaration on the Doctrine of Justification*, signed by the Lutheran World Federation and the Catholic Church (1999), *Information* Service 103 (2000/I–II), pp. 3–6; 3) "Les entretiens luthéro-mennonites (1981–1984)", *Cahiers de Christ Seul*, No. 16 (1984); 4) *Bericht vom Dialog VELKD/Mennoniten: 1989 bis 1992*, Texte aus der VELKD, 53 (Hannover: Lutherisches Kirchenamt der VELKD, 1993).

25. Secondly, both our traditions have had their selective ways of looking at history. Two examples readily come to mind: the interplay of church and state in the Middle Ages, and the use of violence by Christians. We sometimes restricted our views of the history of Christianity to those aspects that seemed to be most in agreement with the self-definition of our respective ecclesial communities. Our focus was often determined by specific perspectives of our traditions, which frequently led to a way of studying the past in which the results of our research were already influenced by our ecclesiological starting-points.

26. The experience of studying the history of the church together and of re-reading it in an atmosphere of openness has been invaluable. It has helped us gain a broader view of the history of the Christian tradition. We have been reminded that we share at least fifteen centuries of common Christian history. The early church and the church of the Middle Ages were, and continue to be, the common ground for both our traditions. We have also discovered that the subsequent centuries of separation have spelled a loss to both of us. Re-reading the past together helps us to regain and restore certain aspects of our ecclesial experience that we may have undervalued or even discounted due to centuries of separation and antagonism.

27. Our common re-reading of the history of the church will hopefully contribute to the development of a common interpretation of the past. This can lead to a shared new memory and understanding. In turn, a shared new memory can free us from the prison of the past. On this basis both Catholics and Mennonites hear the challenge to become architects of a future more in conformity with Christ's instructions when he said: "I give you a new commandment, that you love one another. Just as I have loved you, you also should love one another. By this everyone will know that you are my disciples, if you have love for one another" (*Jn* 13:34-35). Given this commandment, Christians can take responsibility for the past. They can name the errors in their history, repent of them, and work to correct them. Mennonite theologian John Howard Yoder has written: "It is a specific element in the Christian message that there is a remedy for a bad record. If the element of repentance is not acted out in interfaith contact, we are not sharing the whole gospel witness".[6]

28. Such acts of repentance contribute to the purification of memory, which was one of the goals enunciated by Pope John Paul II during the Great Jubilee of the Year 2000. The purification of memory aims at liberating our personal and communal consciences from all forms of resentment and violence that are the legacy of past faults. Jesus asks us, his disciples, to prepare for this act of purification by seeking personal forgiveness as well as extending forgiveness to others. This he did by teaching his disciples the Lord's Prayer whereby we implore: "Forgive us our trespasses as we forgive those who trespass against us" (*Mt.* 6:12). The purification of one's own memory, individually and as church communities, is a first step toward

---

[6] John Howard Yoder, "The Disavowal of Constantine: An Alternative Perspective on Interfaith Dialogue", in: *The Royal Priesthood: Essays Ecclesiological and Ecumenical* (Grand Rapids: Wm. B. Eerdmans, 1994), pp. 242–261, esp. p. 251.

the mutual healing of memories in our inter-church dialogues and in our relation-ships (cf. Chapter III).

29. To begin the process of the healing of memories requires rigorous historical analysis and renewed historical evaluation. It is no small task to enter into

> "a historical-critical investigation that aims at using all of the informa-tion available, with a view to a reconstruction of the environment, of the ways of thinking, of the conditions and the living dynamic in which those events and those words were placed in order in such a way to ascertain the contents and the challenges that—precisely in their diversity—they propose to our present time".[7]

Proceeding carefully in this way, a common re-reading of history may help us in purifying our understanding of the past as a step toward healing the often-painful memories of our respective communities.

B. A Profile of the Religious Situation of Western Europe on the Eve of the Reformation

30. On the eve of the Reformation, Christian Europe entered a time of change, which marked the transition from the medieval to the early modern period.[8] Up to 1500, the Church had been the focal point of unity and the dominant institution of European society. But at the dawn of the early modern period its authority was challenged by the growing power of the first modern states. They consolidated and centralised their political authority and sovereignty over particular geographical areas. They tried to strengthen their power over their subjects in many aspects of human life. For centuries, secular rulers considered themselves responsible for religion in their states. But now they had new means at their disposal to consolidate such authority. This sometimes brought them into conflict with the Church, for instance in the area of ecclesiastical appointments, legal jurisdiction, and taxes.

31. The rise of the early modern states led to a decline of the consciousness of Christian unity. The ideal of a unified Christendom (*christianitas*) that reached its climax in the period of the Crusades was crumbling. This process had been stimu-lated already by the events of the fourteenth and fifteenth centuries. At that time there was the so-called Babylonian Captivity of the papacy (1309–1377), when the residence of the Popes was in Avignon (in present day south-eastern France). Then

---

[7] *Memory and Reconciliation: the Church and Faults of the Past*, 4.1, International Theo-logical Commission, Vatican City, December, 1999.

[8] For paragraph 30 and following, cf. Thomas Brady, Jr., Heiko A. Oberman, and James D. Tracy, eds., *Handbook of European History, 1400–1600: Late Middle Ages, Renais-sance, and Reformation* (Leiden/NY/Cologne: E.J. Brill, 1994), 2 vols., reprinted Grand Rapids, 1996; John Bossy, *Christianity in the West, 1400–1700* (New York/Oxford: Ox-ford University Press, 1985); John W. O'Malley, ed., *Catholicism in Early Modern Europe* (St. Louis: Center for Reformation Research, 1988); Robert Bireley, *The Refashioning of Catholicism, 1450–1700: A Reassessment of the Counter Reformation* (New York/London: Macmillan, 1999).

followed the so-called Great Western Schism (1378–1417), when the papal office was claimed by two or even three rival Popes.

32. At the same time, a divided Europe was experiencing massive social and economic changes. The sixteenth century was a period of enormous population growth. Historians estimate that the European population grew from 55 million in 1450 to 100 million in 1650. This growth was of course prominent in the urban settlements, although the majority of the population still lived in rural areas. Population growth was also accompanied by economic expansion, which mainly benefited the urban middle classes. They became the main carriers of ecclesiastical developments in the sixteenth century, both in the Reformation and in the Catholic renewal. But at the same time economic expansion was accompanied by a growing gap between rich and poor, especially in the cities but also in rural areas. Social unrest and upheaval became a familiar phenomenon in urban society, as peasant rebellions were in rural villages. To some extent this social unrest also contributed to the soil for the Radical Reformation.[9]

33. During this period, the cultural elite of Europe witnessed a process of intellectual and cultural renewal, identified by the words "Renaissance" and "Humanism". This process showed a variety of faces throughout Europe. For instance, in Italy it had a more 'pagan' profile than in northern Europe, where 'biblical humanists' such as Erasmus and Thomas More used humanist techniques to further piety and biblical studies. Meanwhile in France Humanism was mainly supported by a revival of legal thought. The core spirit of the Renaissance, which took its roots in Italy in the fourteenth century, is well expressed in the famous words of the historian Jacob Burkhardt as 'the discovery of the world and of humankind'. These words indicate a new appreciation for the world surrounding humanity. They also herald a new self-consciousness characterized by recognition of the unique value and character of the individual human person. Humanism can be considered as the main intellectual manifestation of the Renaissance. It developed the study of the ancient classical literature, both Latin and Greek. But it also fostered the desire to return to the roots of European civilization, back to the sources (*ad fonts*) and to their values. Within Christianity, this led to an in-depth study of Scripture in its original languages (Hebrew and Greek), of the Church Fathers, and of other sources of knowledge about the early church. It led as well to the exploration of other sources of knowledge about the early church. Humanism also entailed an educational program, which mainly reached the expanding urban middle classes. It fostered their self-consciousness,

---

[9] The term, "Radical Reformation", was introduced by the historian George Hunston Williams in his famous book of the same title, *The Radical Reformation*, 3rd edition (Kirksville: Sixteenth Century Journal Publishers, 1992). By "Radical Reformation" we mean that sixteenth century movement which rebelled not only against the Catholic Church at that time but also against the classical Reformers. It consisted of varied groups such as the leaders of the Great Peasants' War (1524–1525), the Anabaptists, the Spiritualists, Evangelical Rationalists, Unitarians and Schwenckfelders. Others label these groups as the 'Left Wing of the Reformation.'

preparing them to participate in government and administration and to take on certain responsibilities and duties in church life and in ecclesiastical organization.

34. On the eve of the Reformation, church life and piety were flourishing. For a long time both Catholic and Protestant Church historians have described religious life at the end of the Middle Ages in terms of crisis and decline. But today the awareness is growing that these terms reflect a retrospective assessment of the situation of the Middle Ages that was determined by inadequate criteria. There is a growing tendency, both among Catholic and Protestant historians, to give a more positive evaluation of religious life around the year 1500.[10] Many consider this period now to be an age of religious vitality, a period of 'booming' religiosity. They perceive the Reformation and the Catholic Reform not only as a reaction against late medieval religious life, but also and principally as the result and the fruit of this religious vitality. Certainly there were abuses among the clergy, among the hierarchy and the papacy, and among the friars. There were abuses in popular religion, in the ecclesiastical tax system, and in the system of pastoral care and administration. Absenteeism of parish priests and bishops and the accumulation of benefices were among the indicators of the problem.

35. Yet this was hardly the whole story. Religious life was at the same time characterized by a renewed emphasis on good preaching and on religious education, especially among the urban middle classes. There was a strong desire for a more profound faith. Translations of the Bible appeared in the major European vernacular languages and spread through the recently invented printing press. Religious books dominated the book market. The many confraternities that were founded on the eve of the Reformation propagated a lay spirituality. These confraternities served the social and religious needs of lay people by organizing processions and devotions, by offering prayer services and sermons, and by propagating vernacular devotional books. They also provided care and help for the sick and the dying, and for people caught in other kinds of hardships. Zealous lay movements like the so-called *Devotio Moderna*[11] as well as preachers and writers from several religious orders propagated a spirituality of discipleship and of the 'imitation of Christ.' Many of the religious orders themselves witnessed reform movements in the fifteenth century, which led to

---

[10] For instance, see Bernd Moeller's famous article *"Frömmigkeit in Deutschland um 1500"*, *Archiv für Reformationsgeschichte* 56 (1965), pp. 5–30, translated several times, for example, as "Piety in Germany Around 1500", in: Steven E. Ozment, ed., *The Reformation in Medieval Perspective* (Chicago: Quadrangle Books, 1971), pp. 50–75. See also Eamon Duffy, *The Stripping of the Altars: Traditional Religion in England 1400–1580* (New Haven/ London: Yale University Press, 1992).

[11] *Devotio Moderna* or 'Modern (= New, Contemporary) Devotion' is the name of a movement of spiritual renewal that laid great emphasis on the inner life of the individual and on the imitation of Christ. It was inspired by the deacon Geert Grote (1340–1384), and had its origins in the Low Countries, but during the fifteenth century it was spread all over Western Europe. See R.R. Post, *The Modern Devotion* (Leiden: E.J. Brill, 1968); G. Epinay-Burgard, *Gérard Grote (1340–1384) et les débuts de la dévotion moderne* (Wiesbaden: F. Steiner, 1970); John van Engen, *Devotio Moderna: Basic Writings* (New York: Paulist Press, 1988).

the formation of observant branches. These groups desired to observe their religious rule in the strict and original way in which their founder intended it to be followed.

36. The Church in general also witnessed reform movements whose goal was to free the Christian community from worldliness. From simple believers to the highest church authorities, Christians were called to return to the simplicity of New Testament Christianity. These reforms, which affected people at every level of society and church, criticized the pomp of the church hierarchy, spoke against absenteeism among pastors, noted the lack of good and regular preaching, and called into question the eagerness of church leaders to purchase church offices. These late medieval reform movements envisioned ideals that a century or two later would become common in the Protestant Reformation, the Radical Reformation, and the Catholic Reform as well.

37. Of course, a certain externalism and even materialism and superstition were also present in late medieval popular piety. These were in evidence especially in the many devotions, in processions and pilgrimages, and in the veneration of saints and relics. But at the same time the performance of these many forms of religious behaviour reflects a strong desire for salvation, for religious experience, and a zeal for the sacred. In the sixteenth century, the Protestant Reformation, the Radical Reformation, as well as the Catholic Reform benefited significantly from these yearnings for a higher spirituality.

C. The Rupture between Catholics and Anabaptists

Origins

38. The separation of the Anabaptists from the established Church in the sixteenth century is to be understood in the larger context of the first manifestations of the Reformation. The respective Anabaptist groups had varied origins within diverse political, social, and religious circumstances.[12] Anabaptist movements first originated within the Lutheran and Zwinglian reformations in Southern Germany and Switzerland during the 1520's. In the 1530's, Anabaptist (Mennonite) movements in the Netherlands broke more directly with the Catholic Church. These ruptures had to do with understandings of baptism, ecclesiology, church-state relationships and social ethics. The latter included the rejection of violence, the rejection of oath taking, and in some cases the rejection of private property. For all at that time, but especially for the leaders in church and state, this must have been a very confusing situation. There were diverse and sometimes conflicting currents within the Anabaptist movement and within the Radical Reformation, for instance concerning the use of the sword. Nevertheless, all the Anabaptist movements, contrary to the main reformers such as Luther, Zwingli, and Calvin, agreed on the conviction that, since infants are not able to make a conscious commitment to Christ, only adults can be baptized after having repented of their sins and having confessed their faith. Since Anabaptists did not consider infant baptism valid, those Christians who were baptized as infants needed to be baptized again as adults. Anabaptist groups

---

[12] Cf. James M. Stayer, Werner O. Packull, and Klaus Deppermann, "From Monogenesis to Polygenesis: The Historical Discussion of Anabaptist Origins", *Mennonite Quarterly Review* 49 (1975), pp. 83–122.

shared other convictions with related streams of the Radical Reformation. While the first Anabaptists often saw themselves in harmony with the ideals and theology of Luther and Zwingli, their rejection of infant baptism and other theological or ethical positions led both Protestants and Catholics to condemn them.

39. These condemnations should also be understood in relation to the disasters of the Peasants' War (1524–25) and the "kingdom of Münster" in Westphalia (1534–35). For Catholic rulers, the Peasants' movement was a clear sign of the subversive nature of Luther's break with Rome. To defend himself against such accusations, Luther (and other reformers) blamed the Peasants' War on people called "Enthusiasts" or "Anabaptists". It is difficult to sort out historically the origins of Anabaptism in the context of the popular movement commonly designated as the "Peasants' War". The early years of the Reformation were quite fluid, and historians now recognize that movements or churches designated as "Lutheran", "Zwinglian", or "Anabaptist", were not always clearly recognizable or distinct from each other, especially up until the tragic events of 1524–1525. Nevertheless, the radical experiment of the kingdom of Münster, where in 1534–35 the so called Melchiorites (followers of the Anabaptist lay preacher Melchior Hoffman) established a violent and dictatorial regime in order to bring about the "Day of the Lord", confirmed both Catholic and Protestant authorities in their fear of the Anabaptist movement as a serious threat to church and society. Whereas many Anabaptist groups were faithful to their principles of non-violence and pacifism, some groups nevertheless allowed the use of the sword in the establishment of the Kingdom of God.[13] As a result, the term "Anabaptist", employed in both Catholic and Protestant polemics, came to connote rebellion and anarchy. Often it was deemed that Anabaptist groups who claimed to be non-violent were only so because they lacked power. Rulers thought that if the occasion arose, violence would once again be used by Anabaptists.

40. Given the close relationship between church and state, the practice of rebaptizing those who were already baptized as infants had an extremely provocative effect in the sixteenth century. For the Catholic Church and the emerging Protestant Churches, it could only be considered heretical. The practice of rebaptism had already been condemned in the early fifth century as reflected in Augustine's polemics against the Donatists, a separatist movement in North Africa, who rebaptized all recruits from the established Church.[14] For the state, a law of the Roman emperors Honorius and Theodosius of 413 determined severe penalties for the practice of rebaptism. In 529, the emperor Justinian I, in reproducing the Theodosian edict in his revision of Roman law, specified the penalty as capital punishment.[15] On the basis of this ancient imperial law against the Donatists, the Diet of Speyer in 1529 proclaimed the death penalty for all acts of "rebaptism".

---

[13] Cf. James M. Stayer, *Anabaptists and the Sword*, 2nd edition (Lawrence, KS: Coronado Press, 1976).

[14] Cf. William H.C. Frend, *The Donatist Church: A Movement of Protest in Roman North Africa* (Oxford: The Clarendon Press, 1952).

[15] Cf. *Code of Justinian*, book I, tit. 6,2.

Images of Each Other

41. Mennonites and Catholics have harboured negative images of each other ever since the sixteenth century. Such negative images must of course be put into the context of early modern Catholic and Protestant polemical theology. Nevertheless both Catholics and Protestants condemned and persecuted the Anabaptists, and the Anabaptists considered the Protestant Reformers to be as reprehensible as the Catholic Church they had left.

42. Anabaptists shared many of the common Reformation images of the Catholic Church. Along with other Protestant reformers, Anabaptists accused Catholics of works righteousness and of sacramental idolatry. They saw the Reformation as a prelude to the end of time, and viewed the Pope as the Antichrist. Anabaptists soon left the Reformation camp, criticizing both Catholics and Protestants for what they saw as very unhealthy relationships with political power. They considered the Church to be fallen. This fall was associated with the Emperors Constantine and Theodosius and the fact that Christianity was officially proclaimed as the only religion of the Roman Empire. They saw infant baptism as the culminating sign of a religion that forced people to be Christians independent of any faith commitment. In the eyes of the Anabaptists, such Christianity could not be ethically serious nor produce the fruits of discipleship. Persecution and execution of Anabaptists increased the level of polemics and fostered negative images. Anabaptists saw Catholic religion as being based on ceremonies, works, tradition and superstition. Priests were characterized as ignorant, lazy and evil. The *Martyrs' Mirror*, compiled by a Dutch Mennonite in the seventeenth century, tells the stories of many Anabaptist martyrs. It puts them in the context of the faithful church throughout the centuries. Through narrative and engravings, this very important book for Mennonites portrays Catholics and Protestants as persecutors, torturers and executioners. As the centuries went on, Mennonites often lacked direct knowledge about the Catholic Church and her history, but they retained their earlier views.

43. For Catholics, Anabaptists represented the logical outcome of Protestant heresy and schism. When Luther left the Catholic Church, he rejected the only legitimate Christian authority of the time. This opened up the door to numerous and contradictory readings of Scripture as well as to political subversion. Alongside traditional Catholic objections to "Protestantism", the rejection of infant baptism and the practice of rebaptizing dominated the early Catholic theological reaction against Anabaptism. Catholics saw Anabaptists as ignorant people whose theologians did not know Latin. For example, they charged that the Anabaptist theologian, Dr. Balthasar Hubmaier, was an agitator, an enemy of government and an immoral person. For a long time, even into the twentieth century, Catholic writers associated the most peaceful followers of Menno Simons with the radical Melchiorites of Münster. In fact, Catholic theologians had limited knowledge of the history of Anabaptism. They saw Anabaptists as restoring old heresies that had been condemned long ago. All this was complicated by the fact that during the sixteenth century, Catholic theologians were writing against people whom the state, at the request of both Catholic and Protestant princes, had already condemned to death at the Diet of Speyer (see para. 40 above), and who therefore lived outside the protection of the law.

An Ecclesiology of Restitution

44. The question of the apostolic nature of the church created a major ecclesiological divide between Anabaptists and Catholics during the sixteenth century. From the early centuries on, Christians of both East and West had understood apostolic succession via the office of bishops as ensuring the transmission of the faith and therefore the transmission of the apostolic nature of the church throughout the ages. Sixteenth century Anabaptists, on the contrary, rejected the idea of an apostolic continuity guaranteed by the institutional Church. They began to speak of the "fall" of the Church and described it as a sign of her unfaithfulness. This unfaithfulness implied the necessity of a restitution of the "apostolic" church. The Catholics and most of the magisterial reformers considered infant baptism to be an apostolic tradition, practised from the beginning of the church. Anabaptists, on the contrary, saw the general acceptance of infant baptism, together with the close political ties between church and empire (Constantine and Theodosius), as the major signs of apostasy from the apostolic vision of the faithful church and therefore as evidence of the "fall". For the Anabaptists, correspondence with the New Testament writings on ethical and doctrinal issues became the test for measuring apostolic Christianity. Faithfulness was defined not as maintaining institutional continuity, but as restitution of the New Testament faith. In their view, the restoration and preservation of the apostolic church required them to break away from the institutional church of their day. Continuity was sought not through the succession of bishops, but rather through faithfulness to the apostolic witness of Scripture and by identification with people and movements. For example, the Waldensians and the Franciscans were considered by the Anabaptists as faithful representatives of true Christianity throughout the course of their long history.[16]

Persecution and Martyrdom

45. One of the results of the division among Christians in the sixteenth and seventeenth centuries, given the approach to judicial matters and punishment at that time, was persecution and martyrdom.[17] Given the close relationship between religion and society, the establishment of the principle *cuius regio, eius religio* (the religion of the ruler is to be the established religion of a region or a state) at the Peace of Augsburg in 1555 contributed to the already strongly negative sentiments between separated Christians. It introduced a type of society where one specific Christian confession (Catholic, Lutheran, and later Reformed) became the established religion of a given

---

[16] Extended efforts to describe this continuity can be found in *The Chronicle of the Hutterian Brethren*, translated and edited by the Hutterian Brethren (Rifton, NY: Plough Publishing, 1987); and in Thieleman J. van Braght, *Bloody Theater or Martyrs' Mirror*, translated from the Dutch Edition of 1660 by Joseph Sohm, 5th English edition (Scottdale: Herald Press, 1950).

[17] Brad S. Gregory, *Salvation at Stake. Christian Martyrdom in Early Modern Europe* (Cambridge/London: Harvard University, 1999), esp. chapter 6 on Anabaptists and Martyrdom and chapter 7 on Roman Catholics and Martyrdom.

territory. This type of society, the so-called confessional state, was characterized by intolerance towards persons of other Christian confessions. Due to this specific and particular political situation, martyrdom became a common experience for Christians of all confessions, be it Catholic, Lutheran, Reformed, Anglican or Anabaptist.

46. Mennonites suffered greatly in this period, both in Protestant and in Catholic states. Many governments did not tolerate Radical Reformation dissidents, including pacifist Anabaptists. According to recent estimations, approximately 5,000 persons were executed for their religious beliefs in the course of the sixteenth century. Of these, between 2,000 and 2,500 were Anabaptist and Mennonite men and women, the majority of them in Catholic territories, who were convicted of heresy.[18] Anabaptists could hardly find any stable political haven in sixteenth century Europe. In some countries the persecution of Mennonites would last for centuries. In some states they were discriminated against and subjected to social and political restrictions even into the twentieth century, especially because of their principled attitude of conscientious objection.

47. For Anabaptists and Mennonites, discipleship indeed implied the openness to oppression, persecution, and violent death. The danger of persecution and martyrdom became a part of the Mennonite identity. As the Mennonite scholar Cornelius Dyck has written, "the possibility of martyrdom had a radical impact on all who joined the group—on their priorities, status and self-consciousness".[19] Mennonites held their martyrs in highest regard. They sang of their faithful testimony and celebrated their memory by collecting their stories in martyrologies, such as *Het Offer des Heeren* (The Sacrifice unto the Lord) and Thieleman Jans van Braght's *Martelaers Spiegel* (*Martyrs' Mirror*), which is still read today within the global Mennonite church.

48. Catholics never suffered any persecution at the hands of Mennonites.[20] Nevertheless, in the consideration of the Anabaptist and Mennonite experience of martyrdom and persecution, it is important to note that, in their post-medieval history, Catholics have also known this experience. In some territories where the Reformed and Lutheran confession was established, and also in England after the

---

[18] James M. Stayer, "Numbers in Anabaptist Research", in C. Arnold Snyder, ed., *Commoners and Community: Essays in Honour of Werner O. Packull* (Waterloo: Herald Press, 2002), pp. 51–73, esp. pp. 58–59. Anabaptist and Mennonite martyrs then constituted about 40 to 50 percent of all the religious martyrs of the sixteenth century.

[19] Cornelius J. Dyck, "The Suffering Church in Anabaptism", *Mennonite Quarterly Review* 59 (1985), p. 5.

[20] Cf. Brad S. Gregory, *op. cit.*, p. 319. While there are no known instances of Mennonites persecuting or executing Catholics in the sixteenth or seventeenth centuries, Catholic soldiers may have been victims of the violence of the siege of Münster in Westphalia (1534–1535). Whether or not this is an instance of Anabaptist persecution of Catholics is an unresolved question of our discussions. For Catholics, this incident raises the possibility of Catholic deaths at the hands of Anabaptists. For Mennonites, both the Schleitheim confession (1527) and Menno Simons' critiques during and after these events have founded a consistent Mennonite rejection, from that time until the present, of what happened at Münster and all efforts at theologically justifying such actions.

establishment of the Church of England, Catholics were subject to persecution and to the death penalty. A number of them, especially priests, monks and nuns, were brutally martyred for their faith. Persecution of Catholics and violation of religious freedom continued in some countries for centuries. For a long while, the practice of the Catholic faith was not allowed publicly in England and in several Lutheran countries such as in Scandinavia and in the Dutch Republic. Catholics were able to practice their faith openly in these countries only by the end of the eighteenth or the beginning of the nineteenth century. In some cases discrimination against the Catholics lasted into the twentieth century. During those restrictive years, both Catholics and Mennonites in several countries were constrained to live a hidden life.

Areas of Future Study

49. When conflict occurs within an institution and separation ensues, discourse easily takes on the nature of self-justification. As Mennonites and Catholics begin discussion after centuries of separate institutional existence, we need to be aware that we have developed significant aspects of our self-understandings and theologies in contexts where we have often tried to prove that we are right and they are wrong. We need tools of historical research that help us to see both what we have in common as well as to responsibly address the differences that separate us. Mennonites now have almost five centuries of accumulated history to deal with, along with a growing experience of integration into the established society. Catholics, on the other hand, increasingly find themselves in situations of disestablishment where they are faced with the same questions as Mennonites were facing as a minority church in an earlier era. These facts could help both traditions to be more open to the concerns of the other, and to look more carefully at the fifteen centuries of commonly shared history as well as the different paths each has taken since the sixteenth century. Our shared history of fifteen centuries, built upon the foundation of the patristic period, reminds us of the debt that Western Christianity owes to the East, as well as of the rich and varied theological, cultural, spiritual and artistic traditions that flourished in the Middle Ages.

50. Contemporary historical scholarship speaks of the "Left Wing of the Reformation" or of the "Radical Reformation". Less polemical and less confessional historical perspectives demonstrate that there were many different theologies and approaches among the Reformation dissidents. Not only were there Anabaptists, Spiritualists, and Rationalists among those called "Enthusiasts" or "Schwärmer". There were also different kinds of Anabaptists and Spiritualists. Present day Mennonites find their origins in the non-violent Anabaptist groups of Switzerland, southern Germany and the Netherlands. Both Catholic and Mennonite scholars now have become aware of the complicated situation of the sixteenth century rupture within Christianity. They also acknowledge that the rupture between the Catholic Church and the Anabaptist groups should be studied and understood within the broader framework of the social, political and religious conflicts of the sixteenth century. The oppression and persecution of Anabaptists and Mennonites need to be perceived and evaluated within the framework of a society that resorted to violent 'solutions' rather than to dialogue.

51. Further joint studies by Catholic and Mennonite historians would deepen our knowledge and awareness of the complexity of our histories. Catholics would do

well to acquaint themselves with the history of the extreme diversity of the radical movements. This would help prevent continual historical misrepresentations of Mennonites. At the same time, Mennonites need to rethink how difficult it must have been in the sixteenth century to sort out the differences among those who had rejected both Rome and Luther. Those who now call themselves Mennonites came to a doctrinal understanding of non-violence only after the Peasants' War (1527 at Schleitheim in the case of the Swiss Anabaptists) and after Münster (1534–1535 in the case of the Dutch Anabaptists).

52. The common experience of martyrdom and persecution could help both Catholics and Mennonites to reach a renewed understanding of the meaning of martyrdom in the painful division of the Christian church in the early modern period, given the close relationship between religion and society at that time. A common study of the history of sixteenth century martyrdom and persecution can help Catholics to appreciate and esteem the Mennonite experience of martyrdom and its impact on Mennonite spirituality and identity. Mennonites could benefit from a study of the Catholic Church's minority status in many countries since the Reformation period and from the knowledge that Catholics have also had the experience of being persecuted over the centuries.

D. The Constantinian Era

53. After having studied the sixteenth century together, it became clear to our dialogue group that further joint historical work was necessary on two other periods. In the Reformation period conflicting understandings of these periods of history were a major reason for separation. The following sections reflect our consideration of both the Constantinian era and the later medieval period.

A Joint Reading of Events and Changes

54. By 'Constantinian era,' 'change' and 'shift,' we refer to the important developments that took place from the beginning of the fourth century onward. Mennonites and other radical reformers often refer to these changes as the 'Constantinian Fall'.[21] In 313, the Roman emperor Constantine issued the Edict of Milan which allowed Christianity to exist without persecution alongside other religions. He also required all buildings, cemeteries, and other properties taken in earlier persecutions to be returned to the church. In 380, the emperor Theodosius I decreed Christianity as the official religion of the Empire by raising the Nicene Creed to imperial law. At this point, religions other than Christianity no longer had legal status in the Roman Empire, and they often became the objects of persecution. Due to these changes, the Church developed from a suppressed church (*ecclesia pressa*) to a tolerated church (*ecclesia tolerata*), and then to a triumphant church (*ecclesia vincens*) within the Roman Empire.[22]

---

[21] Cf. Walter Klaassen, "The Anabaptist Critique of Constantinian Christendom", *Mennonite Quarterly Review* 55 (1981), pp. 218–230.

[22] Cf. Gerhard Ruhbach, ed., *Die Kirche angesichts der Konstantinischen Wende* (Darmstadt: Wissenschaftliche Buchgesellschaft, 1976); Robin Lane Fox, *Pagans and Christians*

55. In the fourth and fifth centuries, Christianity became a respected religion, with greater freedom to fulfill its mission in the world. Churches were built and worship took place without fear of persecution. The Gospel was preached throughout the world with the intention of evangelising culture and society under favourable political circumstances. But during the same period, civil rulers sometimes exercised authority over the Church and often asserted the right to control ecclesiastical affairs. And, in some instances, though not without resistance from the Church, they convened synods and councils and controlled various kinds of ecclesiastical appointments, especially those of the bishops in the main cities of the empire. The Church accepted the favours and the benevolent treatment by the state. The power of the state was used to enforce Christian doctrines. To some extent Christians even accepted the use of violence, for instance in the defence of orthodoxy and in the struggle against paganism although some did resist this use of violence. In the ensuing centuries of the Middle Ages, this arrangement led in some cases to forced conversion of large numbers of people, to coercion in matters of faith, and to the application of the death penalty against 'heretics'.[23] Together we repudiate those aspects of the Constantinian era that were departures from some characteristic Christian practices and deviations from the Gospel ethic. We acknowledge the Church's failure when she justified the use of force in evangelism, sought to create and to maintain a unitary Christian society by coercive means, and persecuted religious minorities.

56. A common rereading of the history of the early Church by Mennonites and Catholics has been fostered by at least two recent developments. First of all, the social environment and societal position of both the Catholic Church and the Mennonite churches have changed. In many parts of the world Mennonite churches have left their position of isolation that was often imposed by others. Thus Mennonites are experiencing the challenges of taking up responsibilities within society. At the Second Vatican Council (1962–1965), the Catholic Church 1) affirmed freedom of religion and conscience for all, 2) opposed coercion in matters of religion, and 3) sought from the state for itself and all communities of believers only freedom for individuals and for communities in matters of religion.[24] The Catholic Church thus renounced any desire

---

(New York/London: Knopf, 1987); Jochen Bleicken, *Constantin der Große und die Christen* (München: Oldenbourg, 1992); Michael Grant, *Constantine the Great. The Man and his Times* (New York: Prentice Hall, 1994); T.G. Elliott, *The Christianity of Constantine the Great* (New York: Fordham University Press, 1997).

[23] Cf. Ramsey MacMullen, "Christianity Shaped through its Mission", in: Alan Kreider, ed., *The Origins of Christendom in the* West (Edinburgh: T&T Clark, 2001), pp. 97–117; Gilbert Dagron, Pierre Riché and André Vauchez, eds., Évêques moines et empereurs (610–1054), *Histoire du christianisme*, vol. 4 (Paris: Desclée, 1993), p. 637; Michel Rouche, *Clovis* (Paris: Fayard, 1996), p. 143; W.R. Cannon, *Histoire du christianisme au Moyen Âge: de la chute de Rome à la chute de Constantinople* (Paris: Éditions Payot, 1961), p. 8; Jacques le Goff and René Rémond, eds., *Histoire de la France religieuse*, vol. 1 (Paris: Éditions du Seuil, 1988), p. 179.

[24] See Vatican Council's "Declaration on Religious Freedom", *Dignitatis humanae*, especially 6–7, 12–13, also 2, 4, 9 and *Gaudium et spes*, 41 and 42.

to have a predominant position in society and to be recognized as a state church.[25] In the following decades, the Catholic Church strenuously defended the principle of religious freedom and of the separation of church and state. In his encyclical *Centesimus Annus* (1991), Pope John Paul II stated that religious freedom is the "source and synthesis" of other human rights. Secondly, the 1999 document, "Memory and Reconciliation", published by the International Theological Commission, challenges us to study the history of the Church, and to recognize the faults of the past, as a means of facilitating the reconciliation of memories and the healing of wounds.

57. Both our traditions regret certain aspects of the Constantinian era, but we also recognize that some developments of the fourth and fifth centuries had roots in the early history of the church, and were in legitimate continuity with it. Mennonites have a strong negative interpretation of the Constantinian change. Catholics have a strong sense of the continuity of the Church during that period and through the ages. But both of us also recognise that past eras were very different from the present, and we also need to be careful about judging historical events according to contemporary standards.

Areas of Future Study

58. We can agree that through a reading together of sources of the early church, we are discovering ways of overcoming some of the stereotypes that we have had of each other. The *ressourcement* (return to the sources) that the Catholic church engaged in when preparing for the Second Vatican Council, enriched Catholicism, and a parallel movement is beginning in contemporary Anabaptism.[26] With the use of early Christian sources we can affirm new ways of understanding the question of continuity and of renewal in history. We can both agree that the study of the Constantinian era is significant for us in that it raises important questions regarding the mission of the church to the world and its methods of evangelisation.

59. Various aspects of post-Constantinian Christendom have different meanings in our respective traditions. Catholics would see matters such as the generalization of infant baptism, the evolution of the meaning of conversion, as well as Christian attitudes toward military service and oath taking as examples of legitimate theological developments. Mennonites consider the same phenomena as unfortunate changes of earlier Christian practice and as unfaithfulness to the way of Jesus. Catholics understand the establishment of a Christian society during the Middle Ages, which attempted to bring all social, political, and economic structures into harmony with the Gospel, to have been a worthy goal. Mennonites remain opposed to the theological justification of such an endeavour, and are critical of its results in practice.

---

[25] Cf. *Gaudium et spes* 76 which states: "The Church, by reason of her role and competence, is not identified in any way with the political community nor bound to any political system. . . . The Church and the political community in their own fields are autonomous and independent from each other".

[26] Alan Kreider, *The Change of Conversion and the Origin of Christendom* (Harrisburg: 1999); Idem, *The Origins of Christendom, op. cit.*

Mennonites also tend to identify and locate the continuity of the church during this period, in people and in movements that were sometimes rejected as heretical by the Catholic Church. To be sure, they also see continuity in reform movements within the medieval church.

60. Mennonites can affirm the position on religious liberty that was adopted in the Second Vatican Council's "Declaration on Religious Freedom" (*Dignitatis humanae*) in 1965. A key quote from the "Declaration" reads as follows:

> "This Vatican Council declares that the human person has a right to religious freedom. This freedom means that all men are to be immune from coercion on the part of individuals or of social groups or of any human power, in such wise that no one is to be forced to act in a manner contrary to his own beliefs, whether privately or publicly, whether alone or in association with others, within due limits" (*Dignitatis humanae*, 2).

This quotation and the entire text reflects in many ways the position that was taken by sixteenth century Anabaptists. Such Anabaptists as Balthasar Hubmaier[27] or Pilgram Marpeck[28] questioned the use of coercion in relation to religious pluralism and criticised the use of political means against those who believe differently or who have no religious beliefs at all. This same declaration signifies that the Catholic Church renounces the claim to be a "state" church in any and every context. Protestants are no longer addressed as heretics, but as separated sisters and brothers in Christ, even while there are continuing disagreements, and while visible unity has not yet been achieved. It was this "Declaration" as well as other important documents of the Second Vatican Council that contributed significantly to dialogues such as this one. In light of these changes, new possibilities for relating to one another are becoming possible.

61. Catholics affirm that the "Declaration on Religious Freedom" represents a development in doctrine that has strong foundations in Scripture and tradition.[29] The "Declaration" states that:

> "In the life of the People of God, as it has made its pilgrim way through the vicissitudes of human history, there has at times appeared a way of

---

[27] "But a Turk or heretic cannot be overcome by our own doing, neither by sword nor by fire, but alone with patience and supplication, whereby we patiently await divine judgment", Balthasar Hubmaier, "On Heretics and Those Who Burn Them", in: H. Wayne Pipkin and John Howard Yoder, eds., *Balthasar Hubmaier: Theologian of Anabaptism*, Classics of the Radical Reformation, 5 (Scottdale: Herald Press, 1989), p. 62.

[28] "All external things including life and limb are subjected to external authority. But no one may coerce or compel true faith in Christ . . . ", Pilgram Marpeck, "Exposé of the Babylonian Whore", in: Walter Klaassen, Werner Packull, and John Rempel, *Later Writings of Pilgram Marpeck and his Circle*, vol. I (Kitchener: Pandora Press, 1999), p. 27.

[29] Cf. Walter Kasper, "The Theological Foundations of Human Rights", *The Jurist* 50 (1990), p. 153.

acting that was hardly in accord with the spirit of the Gospel, or even opposed to it. Nevertheless, the doctrine of the Church that no one is to be
coerced into faith has always stood firm."[30]

Mennonite readings of medieval history doubt such a claim. They state that major
theologians, Popes, ecumenical councils, emperors and kings justified persecution theologically. They supported the punishment of heretics by the state, and in some instances,
from Theodosius onward, the Church forced the 'christianisation' of large numbers of
people. The continuity of the tradition and the differing interpretations of the development
of doctrine in this respect, as well as the different ways of evangelisation, need further
joint study. Nonetheless, the contemporary Catholic position on this question allows
for significant progress in dialogue, and for mutual comprehension and collaboration.

62. Catholics and Mennonites have different interpretations of the historical
development of the practice of infant baptism in Christianity. Catholics understand
the baptism of children as a long-held tradition of the Church in the East and in the
West, going back to the first centuries of Christianity. They refer to the fact that liturgical documents, such as "The Apostolic Tradition" (ca. 220) and Church Fathers
such as Origen and Cyprian of Carthage, speak about infant baptism as an ancient
and apostolic tradition. Mennonites, on the other hand, consider the introduction of
the practice of infant baptism as a later development and they see its generalization
as the result of changes in the concept of conversion during the Constantinian era.
The historical development of the practice of baptism in relation to the changing
position of the Christian Church in culture and society needs to be studied together
more thoroughly by both Catholic and Mennonite scholars.

E. Toward a Shared Understanding of the Middle Ages

Reviewing our Respective Images of the Middle Ages

63. In looking repeatedly at church history in the Middle Ages, both Catholic and
Mennonite historians are becoming aware of the fact that their images of the medieval
church may be one-sided, incomplete, and often biassed. These images need careful
revision and amplification in the light of modern scholarship. To Catholic historians
it is becoming clear that the Middle Ages were not as deeply christianised as the nineteenth century image of the 'Catholic Middle Ages' wanted to see them.[31] To Mennonite
historians it is becoming clear that the Middle Ages were not as barbaric and decayed
as their restitutionist view depicted them. The period between the early church and the
Reformation era is considered now to be much more complex, varied, many-voiced and
many-coloured than the denominational images of this period wanted us to believe.

64. Therefore, for both our traditions, it is important to see the 'other' Middle Ages,
namely those aspects of the period that are often lacking in the image that is popular
and widespread in our respective religious communities. For Catholics, besides the

---

[30] *Dignitatis humanae,* 12.
[31] John Van Engen, "The Christian Middle Ages as an Historiographical Problem",
American Historical Review 91 (1986), pp. 519–552.

positive aspects of the Christian civilization of the Middle Ages, it is important to see the elements of violence, of conversion by force, of the links between the church and secular power, and of the dire effects of feudalism in medieval Christendom. For Mennonites, besides the negative aspects, it is important to see that Christian faith also served as a basis for criticizing secular powers and violence in the Middle Ages. Several reform movements, led by monasteries (for example, Cluny), but also by the Popes (notably, the Gregorian Reform), tried to free the Church from secular influences and political dominance.[32] Unfortunately, they succeeded only to a very limited extent. Other movements, often led by monks and ascetics, but also by Popes and bishops, tried to restrict the use of violence in medieval Christianity, and sought to protect the innocent, the weak and the defenceless. Again, their efforts were met with very limited success. Nevertheless, within the often-violent society of medieval Christendom there was an uninterrupted tradition of ecclesiastical peace movements.[33] All these movements and initiatives reminded the medieval church of her vocation and her mission: to proclaim the Kingdom of God and to promote peace and justice. Their pursuit of the freedom of the Church from secular domination was also a pursuit of the purity of the Church. Similar concerns took shape in the Free Churches of the sixteenth century.

Medieval Traditions of Spirituality and Discipleship and the Roots of Anabaptist-Mennonite Identity

65. Moreover, the medieval church reveals an ongoing tradition of Christian spirituality, of discipleship (*Nachfolge*), and of the imitation of Christ. From the early monastic tradition up to the mendicant friars of the High Middle Ages, and from the movements of itinerant preachers up to the houses of Sisters and Brethren of the Common Life, medieval Christians were in search of what the challenge of the Gospel might mean for their way of living.[34] They tried to discover how their personal relationship with Jesus might change their lives. The concept of conversion gained a new and real meaning to them. They were not Christians merely out of habit or by birth.

66. Both Catholic and Mennonite historians have recently made clear that at least a part of the spiritual roots of the Anabaptist-Mennonite tradition is to be found in this medieval tradition of discipleship.[35] Key concepts of the Anabaptist-Mennonite

---

[32] Christopher M. Bellitto, *Renewing Christianity. A History of Church Reform from Day One to Vatican II* (New York: Paulist Press, 2001).

[33] Ronald G. Musto, *The Catholic Peace Tradition* (Maryknoll, NY: Orbis Books, 1986).

[34] Bernard McGinn, et al., *Christian Spirituality* (New York: Crossroad, 1985–1989), 3 vols.

[35] Kenneth Ronald Davis, *Anabaptism and Asceticism: A Study in Intellectual Origins* (Eugene: Wipf and Stock, 1998); C. Arnold Snyder, "The Monastic Origins of Swiss Anabaptist Sectarianism", *Mennonite Quarterly Review* 57 (1983), pp. 5–26; C. Arnold Snyder, *The Life and Thought of Michael Sattler* (Scottdale/Kitchener: Herald Press, 1984); Peter Nissen, "De Moderne Devotie en het Nederlands-Westfaalse Doperdom: op zoek naar relaties en invloeden", in: P. Bange a.o. eds., *De Doorwerking van de Moderne Devotie.*

identity, such as yieldedness (*Gelassenheit*), discipleship (*Nachfolge*), repentance (*Buss-fertigkeit*), and conversion were developed through the Middle Ages in all kinds of spiritual traditions. They are found in the Benedictine and the Franciscan tradition, in the tradition of German mysticism, and in that of the "Modern Devotion". Medieval and post-medieval Catholic spirituality, on the one hand, and Anabaptist and Mennonite spirituality, on the other, are essentially in harmony, with respect to their common objective: holy living in word and deed.

67. Recent scholarship has also shown that the early Anabaptist-Mennonite tradition, as well as others such as the Lutheran tradition, used the same catechetical basis as did medieval Christianity. Both traditions considered the Lord's Prayer, the Apostles' Creed and the Ten Commandments to express and represent the essence of Christian faith and doctrine. In this sense, early Anabaptist sources stood in a clearly identifiable medieval tradition. As their medieval predecessors had done, Anabaptist leaders considered these three texts to be essential elements of Christian knowledge. They accepted conventional catechetical presuppositions of the medieval tradition and used them as a prerequisite and a preparation for baptism.[36]

Areas of Future Study

68. Mennonites and Catholics share the need for a fuller appreciation of the variety of medieval Christianity. They are both engaged in (re-)discovering unknown aspects of their common past, the 'other' Middle Ages. Nevertheless, they still have a differing appreciation of their common medieval background. Mennonites might tend to evaluate certain spiritual movements in the Middle Ages as rare exceptions that prove the rule, whereas Catholics might be inclined to consider them as the normal pattern of medieval Christianity. Mennonites and Catholics might reach a deeper understanding of their common background by reading and studying the history of medieval Christian spirituality together. Finally, further scholarly research is important in the field of the relationship between medieval traditions of discipleship and the early Anabaptist-Mennonite tradition. Can Anabaptist-Mennonite piety indeed be understood as a non-sacramental and communitarian transformation of medieval spirituality and asceticism?

Windesheim 1387–1987 (Hilversum: Verloren, 1988), pp. 95–118; Dennis D. Martin, "Monks, Mendicants and Anabaptist: Michael Sattler and the Benedictines reconsidered", Mennonite Quarterly Review 60 (1986), pp. 139–164; Dennis D. Martin, "Catholic Spirituality and Anabaptist and Mennonite Discipleship", Mennonite Quarterly Review 62 (1988), pp. 5–25.

[36] Russell Snyder-Penner, "The Ten Commandments, the Lord's Prayer and the Apostles' Creed as Early Anabaptist Texts", *Mennonite Quarterly Review* 68 (1994), pp. 318–335.

II

CONSIDERING THEOLOGY TOGETHER

69. In addition to the foregoing historical considerations, we presented the respective beliefs that Catholics and Mennonites hold on several common themes, and we sought to ascertain the extent to which our theological points of view converge and diverge. Our theological dialogue was motivated by the commonly acknowledged biblical mandate, which calls for believers in Christ to be one so that the world may believe in the unity of the Father and the Son (*Jn* 17:20-23), and for the Church to pursue the goal of "speaking the truth in love" (*Eph* 4:16) and "building itself up in love" (*Eph* 4:17). In the course of five years of dialogue, we identified and discussed several theological topics: the nature of the Church; our understandings of baptism; of the Eucharist and the Lord's Supper; and our theologies of peace. Our dialogue has been deep and wide ranging, and yet we were not able in this brief period to cover all aspects of the chosen topics or to identify all the issues that require careful consideration. Nonetheless we believe that our mutual consideration of theological issues was significant. We hope that our method of engaging one another can provide a model for the future of dialogue together wherever Catholics and Mennonites engage one another around the world.

A. The Nature of the Church

70. The decision to discuss the nature of the Church came quite naturally. The Catholic-Mennonite dialogue is a conversation between officially nominated representatives of the Catholic Church and the Mennonite World Conference, which is the world communion of Mennonite related churches. Since appropriate dialogue begins with personal introductions, it seemed right that each of us should introduce ourselves in terms of our identity as church bodies. Fortunately, over the years both have given major attention to their respective understandings of the Church. It also seemed right to us that if we were to dialogue fruitfully with each other, we should attempt to define the relationship between us in terms of the common ground we occupy as well as the theological issues that separate us. This could set the stage for drawing conclusions, and for dialogue at some future time on outstanding issues.

A Catholic Understanding of the Church

71. For Catholics, "the Church is in Christ like a sacrament or as a sign and instrument both of a very closely knit union with God and of the unity of the whole human race".[37] The Church comprises both "a divine and a human element".[38] A variety of Biblical images have been employed to express the reality of the Church (for example, church as servant, as spouse, as community of the reconciled, as communion, and so forth).

---

[37] Dogmatic Constitution on the Church, *Lumen gentium,* 1.
[38] *Lumen gentium,* 8.

72. From among this variety, three images in particular come to the fore. First the Church is understood to be the people of God, namely a people God planned to assemble in the holy Church who would believe in Christ. "Already from the beginning of the world the foreshadowing of the Church took place. It was prepared in a remarkable way through the history of the people of Israel and by means of the Old Covenant".[39] The Church is therefore seen to be in continuity with the Chosen People who were assembled on Mount Sinai and received the Law and were established by God as his holy people (*Ex* 19). Nonetheless a new and culminating point in salvation history comes about with the saving death and resurrection of Christ and with the coming of the Holy Spirit at Pentecost. Those who follow Christ are, as stated in 1 Pet 2:9ff., "a chosen race, a royal priesthood, a holy nation, God's own people, in order that they may proclaim the mighty acts of him who called you out of darkness into his marvellous light. Once you were not a people, but now you are God's people". Thus the Church is given the vocation of participating in God's plan for all peoples to bring the light of salvation which is Christ to the ends of the earth.

73. A second image associated with the Church is that she is the body of Christ in and for the world. Perhaps the most profound expression of this reality is to be found in the Pauline use of the image of the body where the term *ekklesia* is realised in the Eucharistic assembly, being the body of Christ for the world (*1 Cor* 11). Once again there is a clear continuity with the idea of the universal mission of Israel carried out through the presence of Christians who belong to the body of Christ in the world. Paul reminds us that Christ reconciled the world to God, thereby bringing about a new creation whereby all who are in Christ are ambassadors for Christ, "since God is making his appeal through us . . . be reconciled to God" (*2 Cor* 5:20).

74. A third image is that of the Church as the temple of the Holy Spirit (cf. *Eph* 2:19-22; *1 Cor* 3:16; *Rom* 8:9; *1 Pet* 2:5; *1 Jn* 2:27; 3:24). The Church is seen as the temple of the Spirit because she is to be the place of perpetual worship of God. Filled with the Holy Spirit, the Church renders continual praise and adoration of God. Christians through their baptism become living stones in the edifice of the Temple of the Holy Spirit. According to the "Dogmatic Constitution on the Church",

". . . the Church prays and likewise labours so that into the People of God, the Body of the Lord and the Temple of the Holy Spirit, may pass the fullness of the whole world, and that in Christ, the head of all things, all honour and glory may be rendered to the Creator, the Father of the universe".[40]

Just as the Trinity is one, in the diversity of persons, so too is the Church one though many members. For Catholics this unity is expressed above all in the sacrament of the Eucharist (*1 Cor* 10:17), where the realization of the unity of the Spirit in the bond of peace is actualized. As is said in the letter to the Ephesians:

[39] *Lumen gentium*, 2.
[40] *Lumen gentium* 17. Cf. Rom 12

"There is one body and one Spirit . . . but each has been given a grace according to the measure of Christ and . . . the gifts were given . . . to equip the saints for the work of ministry, for the building up of the body of Christ, until all of us come to the unity of the faith and of the knowledge of the Son of God, to maturity, to the measure of full stature of Christ" (cf. *Eph* 4:4-13).

75. Catholics express the mystery of the Church in terms of the inner relation that is found in the life of the Trinity, namely *koinonia* or communion. Communion with God is at the heart of our new relationship with God. This has been described as "peace or communion" and is the reconciliation of the world to God in Jesus Christ (*2 Cor* 5:19).[41] This gift of peace/communion is given to us through the one unique mediator between God and humanity, Jesus Christ. This makes Jesus Christ the paradigm of communion. He is the cornerstone upon which rests the edifice of the Church; he alone is the head of the body and we the members. This edifice is constructed as the "household of God, built upon the foundation of the apostles and prophets with Christ Jesus as the cornerstone" (*Eph* 2:20).

76. One is truly incorporated into Christ and into the Church through the sacrament of baptism, and fully integrated into the economy of salvation by receiving confirmation and Eucharist.[42] Through these sacraments, new members are received into the body of Christ and assume co-responsibility for the life and mission of the Church shared with their brothers and sisters.

77. Catholics likewise believe that the apostles, in showing their solicitude for that which they had received from the Lord, have chosen worthy men to carry on this task of transmitting the faithful witness of Christ down through the ages. Thus the apostolic continuity of the Church is served by the apostolic succession of ministers whose task is to preach the Word of God both "in season and out", (*2 Tim* 4:2), to teach with sound teaching and to preside over the building up of the body of Christ in love. The "Dogmatic Constitution on Divine Revelation", *Dei verbum* states clearly the value of the revealed Word of God for believers when it says that "by divine Revelation God wished to manifest and communicate both himself and the eternal decrees of his will concerning the salvation of mankind".[43] Vatican II further recognizes the role of the apostles in this transmission[44] and the role of the faithful people of God in the truthful transmission of the faith when it says that

"the whole body of the faithful who have an anointing that comes from the holy one (cf. *1 Jn* 2:20, 27) cannot err in matters of belief. This characteristic is shown in the supernatural appreciation of the faith (*sensus fidei*)

---

[41] Cf. Decree on the Church's Missionary Activity, *Ad gentes*, 3.

[42] Cf. The Decree on Ecumenism *Unitatis redintegratio*, 22 and the Pontifical Council for Promoting Christian Unity, "Directory for the Application of the Principles and Norms of Ecumenism" (March, 1993), 92.

[43] Dogmatic Constitution on Divine Revelation *Dei verbum*, 6.

[44] Cf. *Dei verbum*, 7.

of the whole people, when 'from bishops to the last faithful' they manifest a universal consent in matters of faith and morals".[45]

78. Furthermore, Catholics believe that sacred Scripture and sacred Tradition make up a single deposit of the Word of God. This single deposit has been entrusted to the Church. The "task of giving an authentic interpretation of the Word of God has been entrusted to the living teaching office of the Church. . . . Its authority in this matter is exercised in the name of Jesus Christ".[46] The "teaching office" (Magisterium) is exercised by the bishops in communion with the Bishop of Rome, the Pope. Since the Magisterium is not superior to the Word of God,[47] the teaching office of the Pope and bishops is at the service of the Word of God and forms a unity with Tradition and Scripture and teaches only that which has been handed down to it. In his encyclical on the Catholic Church's commitment to ecumenism, *Ut unum sint*, John Paul II identified this point as one of the five areas for further discussion:

> "It is already possible to identify the areas in need of fuller study before a true consensus of faith can be achieved: 1) the relationship between Sacred Scripture, as the highest authority in matters of faith, and Sacred Tradition, as indispensable to the interpretation of the Word of God. . . "[48]

79. The Bishop of Rome has the office of ensuring the communion of all the Churches and hence is the first servant of unity. This primacy is exercised on various levels, including vigilance over the handing down of the Word, the celebration of the Liturgy and the Sacraments, the Church's mission, discipline and the Christian life. He also has the duty and responsibility to speak in the name of all the pastors in communion with him. He can also—under very specific conditions clearly laid down by the First Vatican Council—declare *ex cathedra* that a certain doctrine belongs to the deposit of faith. Furthermore,

> "religious submission of mind and will must be shown in a special way to the authentic magisterium of the Roman Pontiff, even when he is not speaking *ex cathedra*; that is, it must be shown in such a way that his supreme

---

[45] *Lumen gentium*, 12.

[46] *Dei verbum*, 10.

[47] Cf. *Dei verbum*, 10.

[48] The other points are: "2) the Eucharist, as the Sacrament of the Body and Blood of Christ, an offering of praise to the Father, the sacrificial memorial and Real Presence of Christ and the sanctifying outpouring of the Holy Spirit; 3) Ordination, as a Sacrament, to the three-fold ministry of the episcopate, presbyterate and deaconate; 4) the Magisterium of the Church, entrusted to the Pope and the Bishops in communion with him, understood as a responsibility and an authority exercised in the name of Christ for teaching and safeguarding the faith; 5) the Virgin Mary, as Mother of God and Icon of the Church, the spiritual Mother who intercedes for Christ's disciples and for all humanity" (*Ut unum sint*, 79).

magisterium is acknowledged with reverence, the judgments made by him
are sincerely adhered to, according to his manifest mind and will".[49]

By thus bearing witness to the truth, he serves unity.[50]

80. The Church (the faithful and the ordained) therefore has the obligation to be
a faithful witness of that which she has received in word (teaching/preaching) and
deed (holy living). This is possible through the anointing that has been received by
the Holy Spirit (*1 Jn* 2:20f.). The Church lives then under the Word of God because
she is sanctified in truth by that same word (cf. *Jn* 17:17), and being made holy she
may then sanctify the world in truth. The Catholic Church confesses that the Church
is indeed holy because she is purified by her Lord and Saviour Jesus Christ, and she
has been given the Holy Spirit, the Advocate, to plead the just cause of God before
the nations. The followers of Jesus must conquer the spirit of this world with the
Spirit of the beatitudes. This is the continuation of Jesus' mission to "prove the world
wrong about sin and righteousness and judgment" (*Jn* 16:8ff.). This is possible only
with the aid of the Holy Spirit, the Advocate.

81. When Catholics speak of the one Church of God, they understand her to be
realized "in and formed out of particular Churches"[51] and that she is concretely real
in the Catholic Church.[52] For the ecclesiology of Vatican II, the universal Church is
the body of particular churches from which (*in et ex quibus*) the one and only Catholic
Church comes into being,[53] but the local churches also exist in and out of the one
Church,[54] shaped in its image.[55] The mutual relationship between the communion of
particular churches and the one church, just described, means that the one Church
and the diversity of particular churches are simultaneous. They are interior to each
other (perichoretic). Within this perichoresis the unity of the Church has priority over
the diversity of the local churches, and over all particular interests as is really very
obvious in the New Testament (*1 Cor.* 1:10ff.). "For the Bible, the one Church corresponds to the one God, the one Christ, the one Spirit, the one baptism (cf. Eph 4:5f.)
and lives according to the model of the early community of Jerusalem (Acts 2:42)".[56]

82. A particular church is that portion of the people of God that is united around
the bishop whose mission is to proclaim the Gospel and to construct the Church

---

[49] *Lumen gentium*, 25.

[50] Cf. *Ut unum sint*, 94.2.

[51] *Lumen gentium*, 23.1.

[52] Cf. *Lumen gentium*, 8.

[53] Cf. *Lumen gentium*, 23, 2; see also, Decree on the Ministry of Bishops, *Christus
dominus*, 11 and Congregation for the Doctrine of the Faith, in "Some Aspects of the
Church Understood as Communion", *Communionis notio*, pp. 7f.

[54] Cf. *Communionis notio*, 9.

[55] Cf. *Lumen gentium*, 23.

[56] Walter Cardinal Kasper, "Present Situation and Future of the Ecumenical Movement", prolusio of the plenary meeting of the Pontifical Council for Promoting Christian
Unity, *Information Service* 109 (2002/I–II), p. 18.

through the sacraments—in particular through baptism and the Eucharist.[57] The communion of particular churches is presided over by the Bishop of Rome, the successor of Peter to whom was entrusted the care for confirming and strengthening the faith of his brothers. Together with the bishops, the Pope governs the Catholic Church in its mission to proclaim the Good News of the kingdom of God and the gift of salvation in Jesus Christ that God offers freely to all of humanity.

83. In the past "catholicity" was understood to mean: extending over the whole world. While this aspect is true, there is a deeper meaning that indicates, in spite of the diversity of expression, there is the fullness of the faith, respect for the gifts of the Spirit in their diversity, communion with other apostolic Churches and faithful representation to human cultures.[58] "Driven by the inner necessity of her own catholicity", the Church's universal mission "strives ever to proclaim the Gospel to all" and demands the particularity of the churches. Hence the Church is to speak all languages and embrace all cultures.[59] In addition the Church is to imitate the incarnation of Christ who linked himself to certain social and cultural conditions of those human beings among whom he dwelt.[60] In this context catholicity of the Church is a call to embrace all legitimate human particularities.[61] The catholicity of the Church therefore consists in the recognition of the same apostolic faith that has been incarnated in diverse cultures and places throughout the world. In spite of the diversity of its expressions and practices in its celebration, the Catholic faith is understood to be the same faith contained in the Scriptures, handed on by the apostles, and confessed in the creeds today.

A Mennonite Understanding of the Church

84. In Anabaptist-Mennonite theology the Church is understood as the community of faith endowed with the Spirit of God and shaped by its response to the grace of God in Christ. Three biblical images of the Church are basic to a Mennonite perspective. First, the Church is the new *people of God*.[62] While the concept of peoplehood indicates the continuity of the Church with the people of faith of the Old Testament (*Gal* 2:15-21), the initiative of God in Jesus Christ marks a new beginning. In Christ, God called "a chosen race, a royal priesthood, a holy nation, God's own people . . . out of darkness into his marvellous light" (*1 Pet* 2:9). The life, death and resurrection of Christ established the good news that people of all races and classes and genders are invited through the grace of God to belong to the people of God (*Gal* 3:28). The Church, as a family or household of faith (*Gal* 6:10;

---

[57] Cf. *Christus dominus*, 11.

[58] Cf. *Lumen gentium*, 13.3 and the Pontifical Council for Promoting Christian Unity's "Directory for the Application of the Principles and Norms of Ecumenism" (March 25, 1993), 16.

[59] Cf. *Ad gentes*, 1, 4.

[60] Cf. *Ad gentes*, 10.

[61] Cf. *Ad gentes*, 22.

[62] Cf. Harold S. Bender, *These Are My People: The New Testament Church* (Scottdale/Kitchener: Herald Press, 1962), pp. 1ff.

Eph 2:19), adds to its characterization as people of God. Hospitality is a mark of the household of faith, as members of the household welcome all who join the family, care for one another, and together share their spiritual and material resources with those in need (*Jas* 2:14-17).

85. Secondly, the *body of Christ* is an important biblical image for an Anabaptist-Mennonite understanding of the Church.[63] Reference to Christ in this figure points to the foundation (*1 Cor* 3:11) and head (*Col* 1:18) of the Church. Members of the Church are incorporated as a body into Christ. The image of the body has its background in the Hebrew concept of corporate personality. Corporate personality implies commitment to Christ as a body of believers (*Rom* 12:15; *Eph* 4:1-16), which in turn implies a commitment to one another as members of the Church. Members of the body are called to be holy as Christ is holy: "The church, the body of Christ, is called to become ever more like Christ, its head, in its worship, ministry, witness, mutual love and care, and the ordering of its common life".[64]

86. A third image of the Church, important for Anabaptist-Mennonites, is the *community of the Holy Spirit*.[65] A defining moment occurred when the risen Christ "breathed on [the disciples] and said to them, 'Receive the Holy Spirit. If you forgive the sins of any, they are forgiven them; if you retain the sins of any, they are retained'" (*Jn* 20:22-22). The endowment of the disciples with the Holy Spirit mandated his followers to become a forgiving community. A further step in the formation of the apostolic community took place when, after the outpouring of the Spirit at Pentecost, the first converts "devoted themselves to the apostles' teaching and *koinonia* (fellowship, community), to the breaking of bread and the prayers" (*Acts* 2:42). The early church understood itself as the "new Messianic community in which the main feature is the Holy Spirit's renewed presence with God's people".[66] As such, the Spirit plays a crucial role in the functioning of the body of Christ, as the giver of spiritual gifts to its members (*1 Cor* 12:4-11) and as the creator of the oneness of the body (*1 Cor* 12:12ff). Given the multi-faceted composition of the Church, it is a formidable task for the community to "maintain the unity of the Spirit in the bond of peace" (*Eph* 4:3). The Spirit provides the power to vie for the Church's oneness and to maintain its ethical focus on the "more excellent way" (*1 Cor* 12:31; cf. *1 Cor* 13; *1 Pet* 1:2) of love.

87. Besides these three images which follow the trinitarian formula, a Mennonite understanding of the Church is illumined by various descriptions. The first of these is *fellowship of believers*. The Anabaptist movement established the idea that the Church is comprised of all who, by their own free will, believe in Jesus Christ and obey the Gospel. Submission to Christ implies mutual accountability to one another in congregational life (*1 Cor* 12:25; *Jas* 2:14-17; *1 Jn* 3:16). This includes the task of

---

[63] Cf. Bender, *ibid.*, p. 23ff.

[64] *Confession of Faith in a Mennonite Perspective*, 9 (Scottdale/Waterloo: Herald Press, 1995), p. 39.

[65] Cf. Norman Kraus, *The Community of the Spirit* (Grand Rapids: Wm. B. Eerdmans, 1974); Bender, *op. cit.*, pp. 42ff. Bender's terminology, "The Holy Community", is practically interchangeable with the image of the "community of the Holy Spirit".

[66] Kraus, *op. cit.*, p. 24.

reproving and forgiving as well as guiding and affirming one another in accordance with the biblical mandate to engage in "binding and loosing" on behalf of Christ (*Mt* 16:19; 18:15-22; *Jn* 20:19-23).[67] Further, the Mennonite concept of the Church requires the separation of church and state, with the clear understanding that the Christian's primary loyalty is to Jesus Christ. For example, in matters of warfare, allegiance to the Christ as Lord takes precedence over the demands of the state. Important to the original impetus of the Anabaptist movement was the idea of "a covenantal people" called out from among the nations to be a reconciling community internally[68] as well as "salt and light" in the world (*Mt* 5:13-16). Mennonites depict themselves as being 'in the world but not of the world' (*Jn* 17:15-17).

88. Mennonites understand the Church as a *community of disciples.* As was the case for New Testament believers, the acceptance of salvation made visible in baptism and in identification with the people of "the Way" (*Acts* 9:2), marks their resolute intention to be instructed in the way of Jesus of Nazareth, and to seek to follow the Master as his first disciples had done. Discipleship (*Nachfolge*) is integral to the Anabaptist-Mennonite understanding of faith, as exemplified in a quote from the Anabaptist Hans Denck (1526): "The medium is Christ whom no one can truly know unless he follow him in his life, and no one may follow him unless he has first known him".[69] Mennonite historians and theologians have identified discipleship as one of the most important legacies of the Anabaptist movement for the continuing Mennonite vision of the Church and the vocation of its members. A recent confession of faith states: "The church is the new community of disciples sent into the world to proclaim the reign of God and to provide a foretaste of the church's glorious hope".[70]

89. Mennonites understand the Church as a *people in mission.* The Anabaptists took seriously Christ's commission to "be my witnesses . . . to the ends of the earth" (*Acts* 1:8).[71] Following a period of self-preservation in the seventeenth and eighteenth centuries, the latter nineteenth century brought with it a renewal of the missionary spirit. Today the Church understands its very being as missional. That is, the call to proclaim the Gospel and to be a sign of the kingdom of God characterizes the Church and includes every member of it. Mission activity is carried out in a peaceful manner without coercion, and includes the ministries of evangelism, social service, and advocacy for peace and justice among all people.

90. The Mennonite Church is a *peace church.* Peace is essential to the meaning and message of the Gospel and thus to the Church's self-understanding. The Church submits to the Prince of Peace, who calls for the way of peace, justice and non-resistance, and

---

[67] Cf. John Howard Yoder, *Body Politics* (Nashville: Discipleship Resources, 1997), ch. 1.

[68] Cf. F.H. Littell, *The Anabaptist View of the Church : A Study in the Origins of Sectarian Protestantism*, second edition, revised and enlarged (Boston: Beacon Press/Starr King Press, 1958), pp. 37ff.

[69] Walter Klaassen, ed., *Anabaptism in Outline* (Scottdale/Kitchener: Herald Press, 1981), p. 87.

[70] *Confession of Faith in a Mennonite Perspective*, 9, *op. cit.*, p. 42.

[71] Cf. R. Friedmann, *The Theology of Anabaptism* (Scottdale: Herald Press, 1973), pp. 149ff.

who exemplifies the way of non-violence and reconciliation among all people and for all God's creation. The peace church advocates the way of peace for all Christian churches. One important correlate of the Church's identity as a peace church is the Church's claim to be a 'free' church. Mennonites believe that freedom is an essential gift of the Spirit to the Church (*2 Cor* 3:17). Church membership entails a free and voluntary act whereby the person makes a free and uncoerced commitment to faith. The separation of church and state along with the refusal to engage in violence against enemies is an implication of freedom of conscience and of the liberating power of the Gospel.

91. Mennonites understand the Church as a *servant community*. Jesus came to serve, and he taught his disciples the way of servanthood (*Mk* 10:43-45). In Anabaptist-Mennonite theology, the Sermon on the Mount (*Mt* 5-7) is taken seriously as the operative ethical agenda for all who confess Christ as Saviour and Lord. The Spirit endows believers with varieties of gifts for building up the body of Christ and sharing its message in the world (*1 Cor* 12). In the Church some, both men and women, are called to serve in leadership ministries. These may include offices such as pastors, deacons and elders, as well as evangelists, missionaries, teachers and overseers. Patterns of leadership vary from place to place and from time to time as they already did in the apostolic Church (*Acts* 6:1-6; *Eph* 4:11; *1 Tim* 3:1-13). The "priesthood of all believers" is understood to encourage all believers as "priests" to lead a holy life and to give honour to God by serving one another in the Church and in a needy world.

92. The Church is a *communion of saints*. In Anabaptist-Mennonite thought, reference to "saints" includes all who believe in Jesus Christ and seek to follow him in holy living. The Church in its particular setting shares the calling to sainthood "together with all those who in every place call on the name of our Lord Jesus Christ, both their Lord and ours" (*1 Cor* 1:2; cf. also *Rom* 15:26; *1 Cor* 14:33; *Heb* 14:24; *Rev* 22:21). The communion of saints includes the "cloud of witnesses" (*Heb* 12:1) of the past who have endured faithfully to the end. Sainthood is not based on ethical merit, but is accorded those who have persevered to the end, "looking to Jesus the pioneer and perfecter of our faith" (*Heb* 12:2). Anabaptists already claimed the depiction of the Church as a fellowship of saints of 'catholic' or 'universal' nature in the early stages of the movement. The Anabaptist theologian, Balthasar Hubmaier, made this explicit in "A Christian Catechism" of 1526, where he wrote that

> "through this baptism for the forgiveness of sins the person, in open confession of his faith, makes his first entry and beginning in the holy, catholic, Christian Church (outside of which there is no salvation) . . . and is at that time admitted and accepted into the community of the saints".[72]

Much later, in the twentieth century, we find a similar standpoint as, for example, in the *Mennonite Brethren Confession of Faith* of 1902, which states:

> "Although the members of [the Church of Jesus Christ] belong to all nations and ranks scattered here and there throughout the world and are divided

---

[72] Denis Janz, *Three Reformation Catechisms: Catholic, Anabaptist, Lutheran* (New York/ Toronto: The Edwin Mellen Press, 1982), p. 134.

in denominations, yet they all are one and among one another brethren and members and exist as one body in Christ their head, who is the Lord, Chief, Shepherd, Prophet, Priest and King of the church".[73]

Convergences

93. *Nature of the Church.* Catholics and Mennonites agree on conceiving of the Church as the people of God, the body of Christ, and the dwelling place of the Holy Spirit, images that flow from the Scriptures. Catholics and Mennonites agree that the Church is called into being, is sustained, and is guided by the triune God who nourishes her in "the grace of the Lord Jesus Christ, the love of God, and the communion of the Holy Spirit" (*2 Cor* 13:13).

94. *Foundation of the Church.* We agree that the Church is "built upon the foundation of the apostles and prophets, with Christ Jesus himself as the cornerstone" (*Eph* 2:20. cf. *1 Cor* 3:11). Catholics and Mennonites agree and teach that the faith of the Church is founded on the authority of the Scriptures, which bear witness to Jesus Christ, and is expressed in the early creeds of the Church, such as the Apostles' Creed and the Nicene-Constantinopolitan Creed.[74] Both Catholics and Mennonites affirm the Scriptures as the highest authority for the faith and life of the Church.[75] Both affirm the inspiration of the Holy Spirit in the formation of the Scriptures. Catholics speak of such divinely revealed realities as are contained and presented in Sacred Scripture as having been committed to writing under the inspiration of the Holy Spirit.[76] Mennonites speak similarly of the Scripture as God's word written.[77]

95. *Incorporation into the body of Christ.* We agree that the invitation to be God's faithful people is offered to all in the name of Jesus Christ. Through baptism we become members of the Church, the body of Christ.[78] The generous gifts of the Spirit, given to the

---

[73] Howard J. Loewen, *One Lord, One Church, One Hope, and One God: Mennonite Confessions of Faith* (Elkhart, IN: Institute of Mennonite Studies, 1985), p. 166.

[74] Cf. *Dei verbum,* 10–20; *Confession of Faith of the General Conference of Mennonite Brethren Churches,* 2 (Winnipeg/Hillsboro: Kindred Productions, 1999); *Confession of Faith in a Mennonite Perspective,* 4, *op. cit.,* p. 21. According to Rainer W. Burkart, secretary of the MWC Faith and Life Council, "statements of faith from the Mennonite and Brethren in Christ tradition often borrow language that can be found in the Apostles' and Nicene Creeds, and some view the Apostles' Creed as a foundational text for understanding the essentials of the faith. Many Mennonite and Brethren in Christ confessions follow the traditional creedal order . . .", Courier, *A Quarterly Publication of the Mennonite World Conference* 12, 4 (1997), p. 3.

[75] Although for Catholics this is never without relationship to "Sacred Tradition as indispensable to the interpretation of the Word of God", *Ut unum sint,* 79.

[76] Cf. *Dei verbum,* 11.

[77] For example, John C. Wenger, *God's Word Written* (Scottdale: Herald Press, 1966); *Confession of Faith in a Mennonite Perspective,* 4, *op. cit.,* p. 42.

[78] On the relationship between incorporation into the Church and baptism, see para. 76 and 115–116 for the Catholic position and para. 92 and 121–124 for the Mennonite position.

community of faith, enable each member to grow in a lifelong process of Christlikeness. The Eucharist and the Lord's Supper respectively draw believers together in the Church by nurturing their communion with the triune God and with one another.

96. *Mission of the Church*. Mennonites and Catholics agree that mission is essential to the nature of the Church. Empowered and equipped by the Holy Spirit, whose coming was promised by Jesus Christ, it is the mission of the Church to bring the Good News of salvation to all nations by proclaiming the Gospel in word and in deed to the ends of the earth (cf. *Is* 2:1-4; *Mt* 28:16-20; *Eph* 4:11f.). The 1995 *Confession of Faith in a Mennonite Perspective* states: "We believe that the church is called to proclaim and to be a sign of the kingdom of God".[79] We also agree that the Church's mission is carried out in the world through every follower of Jesus Christ, both leadership and laity.[80] A dimension of the mission of the Church is realized when the Church is present among people of all nations. Thereby the divinely destined unity of humanity as one people of faith is called into being from peoples of many tongues and nations (*Eph* 4:4-6; *Phil* 2:11).[81] Mission requires that Christians seek to become "one" for the sake of their witness to Jesus Christ and to the Father (*Jn* 17:20-21), and that they make "every effort to maintain the unity of the Spirit in the bond of peace" (*Eph* 4:3).[82] It belongs to the mission of the Church to present Jesus Christ to the world and to extend the work of Christ on earth.

97. *Visibility of the Church*. We agree that the Church is a visible community of believers originating in God's call to be a faithful people in time and place. The visible Church was prefigured by the formation of the Old Testament people of God, and was renewed and expanded as the one new humanity, through the blood of Christ (*Gen* 12:1-3; *Eph* 2:13-15; *1 Pet* 2:9-10). Together we value the Biblical image of the Church as "the light of the world" and as "a city built on a hill" (*Mt* 5:14). Accordingly, the visibility of the Church is evidenced when, in word and deed, its members give public witness to faith in Christ.[83]

98. *Oneness of the Church*. Together with other disciples of Christ, Catholics and Mennonites take seriously the Scripture texts that call Christians to be one in Christ. We confess that our witness to the revelation of God in Christ is weakened when we live in disunity (*Jn* 17:20-23). Together we hear the call to "maintain the unity of the Spirit in the bond of peace" (*Eph* 4:3). Together we ask: What does it mean for the churches to confess "one Lord, one faith, one baptism, one God and Father of all" (*Eph* 4:5-6)? Together we pray the Lord's Prayer, imploring God to increase his kingdom among us.

99. *Church as Presence and Promise of Salvation*. Catholics and Mennonites agree that the Church is a chosen sign of God's presence and promise of salvation for all creation. Catholics speak of this by affirming that the Church is "the universal

---

[79] *Confession of Faith in a Mennonite Perspective*, op. cit., 4, p. 28.

[80] Cf. *Lumen gentium*, 17, 33; "Decree on the Apostolate of the Laity", *Apostolicam actuositatem*, 2–4; *Dordrecht Confession (1632)*, Art. V, Loewen, op. cit., p. 64.

[81] Cf. *Unitatis redintegratio*, 7.

[82] *Unitatis redintegratio*, 12.

[83] Cf. Klaassen, op. cit., p. 102.

sacrament of salvation at once manifesting and actualizing the mystery of God's love for humanity".[84] Mennonites express the promissory character of the Church by proclaiming that "in God's people the world's renewal has begun",[85] and that "the church is the new community of disciples sent into the world to proclaim the reign of God and to provide a foretaste of the church's glorious hope".[86] We agree that the Church is still underway toward its heavenly goal, and we believe that God will sustain the faithful Church unto the realization of its glorious hope.[87] Here and now the Church manifests signs of its eschatological character and thus provides a foretaste of the glory yet to come.

100. *Ministry of the Church.* We agree that ministry belongs to the whole Church, and that there are varieties of gifts of ministry given for the good of all. We also agree that chosen leaders, ordained and lay,[88] are essentially servants of God's people, called "to equip the saints for the work of ministry, for building up the body of Christ" (*Eph* 4:12).

101. *Holiness and Discipleship.* Catholics and Mennonites have a common zeal for the Christian life of holiness, motivated by devotion to Jesus Christ and the word of God, and actualized in a spirituality of discipleship and obedience (*Mt* 5-7; *Rom* 12; *Eph* 2:6-10).[89] The gift of faith freely received provides the motivation for Christian works offered to the world as thanksgiving for the abundant grace we have been given by God. The life of discipleship and holiness is referred to and expressed variously in terms of "following Christ" (*Nachfolge Christi*), "imitation of Christ" (*imitatio Christi*), Christlikeness, and devotion to Christ.

102. *Education and Formation.* Together we affirm the necessity of Christian formation by which individuals come to an understanding and acceptance of their faith and take responsibility for its implementation in life and witness (*Phil* 2:12ff.). In Mennonite churches, Christian education is fostered in many ways: Scripture reading, preaching, pre-baptismal instruction, Sunday school for all ages, marriage preparation, study groups, day schools for children and youth, discipleship programs, Bible schools, college and seminary programs, and voluntary service assignments at home and abroad. In Catholic communities, formation takes place in preparation for the sacraments of initiation (Baptism, Confirmation and Eucharist) including the Rite of Christian Initiation for Adults and prebaptismal preparation for parents and sponsors, in homilies, in marriage preparation, in catechesis, adult education, college and seminary programs, and for some in voluntary service programs. Special formation is encouraged for the laity, and for those who become pastoral workers in the Church.[90]

---

[84] *Gaudium et spes*, 45.

[85] Cf. Douglas Gwyn *et al.*, *A Declaration on Peace* (Scottdale/Waterloo: Herald Press, 1991).

[86] *Confession of Faith in a Mennonite Perspective*, 9, *op. cit.*, p. 39.

[87] Cf. *Lumen gentium*, 48–49.

[88] For explanation of the difference between ordained and lay ministry in Catholic teaching, see para. 106.

[89] Cf. Bender, "The Anabaptist Vision", *op. cit.*, 13–17; *Lumen gentium*, 39–42.

[90] Cf. *Apostolicam actuositatem*, 28–32.

Divergences

103. *Church and the Authority of Tradition.* Catholics and Mennonites differ in their understanding of the relationship of Scripture and Tradition/tradition[91] and in their view of the authority of Tradition/tradition. Catholics speak of Scripture and Tradition as forming one sacred deposit of the Word of God, committed to the Church.[92] Sacred Tradition, coming from the Apostles, is the means by which the Church comes to know the full Canon of Sacred Scripture and understands the content of Divine Revelation. Tradition transmits in its entirety the Word of God entrusted to the apostles by Christ and the Holy Spirit. Sacred Tradition, Sacred Scripture and the teaching authority of the Church, in accord with God's most wise design, are so linked and joined together that one cannot stand without the others, and that all together and each in its own way under the action of the one Holy Spirit contribute effectively to the salvation of souls.[93] Mennonites view tradition as the post-Biblical development of Christian doctrine and practice. The Church needs constantly to test and correct its doctrine and practice in the light of Scripture itself. Tradition is valued, yet it can be altered or even reversed, since it is subject to the critique of Scripture.

104. *Incorporation into the Church.* Mennonites and Catholics differ in their understanding of who may be incorporated into the Church, and by what means. For Catholics,

> "by the sacrament of baptism a person is truly incorporated into Christ and into his church and so is reborn to a sharing of the divine life. Baptism, therefore, constitutes the sacramental bond of unity existing among all who through it are reborn. Baptism, of itself, is the beginning, for it is directed toward the acquiring of fullness of life in Christ"[94]

which takes place in the celebration of confirmation and the reception of the Eucharist. The Eucharist is the summit of initiation because it is through participation in Christ's eucharistic body that one is fully incorporated into the ecclesial body. The fact that infants cannot yet profess personal faith does not prevent the Church from conferring baptism on them, since in reality it is by and in her own faith that the Church baptizes them. For Mennonites, membership in the Church follows upon adult baptism, while children are committed to the care of God and the grace of Christ until such a time as they freely request to be baptized and are received into church membership.

105. *Structure of the Church.* For Catholics the visible Church of Christ consists of particular churches united around their bishops in communion with one another and

---

[91] When Catholics capitalize Tradition they acknowledge the close bond that exists between Sacred Tradition and Sacred Scripture as "forming one sacred deposit of the Word of God" (*Dei verbum*, 10) and not various human traditions that may develop in the course of the history of the Church.

[92] Cf. *Dei verbum*, 10.

[93] Cf. *Dei verbum*, 7–10

[94] Pontifical Council for Promoting Christian Unity, "Directory for the Application", *op. cit.*, 91.

with the Bishop of Rome as the successor of Saint Peter. For Mennonites, the primary manifestation of the Church is the local congregation and the various grouping of congregations variously named conferences, church bodies, and/or denominations.

106. *Ministry, Authority, and Leadership.* In the Anabaptist-Mennonite tradition, ministerial leaders, both men and women, are chosen and authorized by the congregation and/or by regional groups of congregations. In some Mennonite churches it is the practice to ordain leaders for life. In others, ordination is for a set period of time. Mennonites do not have a hierarchical priesthood. As 'priests of God,' all believers have access to God through faith.[95] While Catholics affirm the "common priesthood of the faithful",[96] they hold to a ministerial, hierarchical priesthood, differing from the former "not only in degree but also in essence",[97] that has roots in, and takes its authority from Christ's priesthood. With the outpouring of the Holy Spirit and the laying on of hands, the Sacrament of Orders confers on bishops, priests, and deacons gifts for the service of the Church. Both laity and clergy share in the fundamental equality of the baptized in the one people of God and in the one priesthood of Jesus Christ.[98] The differentiation of offices and roles within the Catholic Church reflects the variety of gifts given by one Spirit to the one body of Christ for the good of all (cf. *1 Cor* 12).[99]

Areas of Future Study

107. *Church and Tradition.* Further discussion is needed on our respective understandings of the relationship between Scripture as the highest authority in matters of faith, and Tradition/tradition as indispensable to the interpretation of the Word of God.[100] It is recognized that the Catholic Church has a developed understanding of Tradition in God's revelation. While Mennonites may have an implicit understanding of the role of tradition, little attention has been given to the role of tradition relative to Scripture and to the development of doctrine and ethics.

108. *Catholicity of the Church.* We agree that further study and discussion is needed on the question of the definition and implications of our respective understandings of the catholicity and universality of the Church. Mennonites believe that all who truly confess Christ as Lord, who are baptized, and follow him in life, are members of the Church universal. For Catholics, catholicity properly means the fullness of the confession of faith, respect for the gifts of the Spirit in their diversity, communion

---

[95] Cf. Marlin Miller, "Priesthood of all Believers", *Mennonite Encyclopedia*, vol. V (Scottdale/Waterloo: Herald Press, 1990), pp. 721–722. For Mennonites, the Reformation's emphasis on the 'priesthood of all believers' did not become a point of doctrine. The expression was used by some Anabaptists to support the New Testament's teaching that all believers corporately are a 'kingdom of priests,' a 'royal priesthood.'

[96] *Lumen gentium*, 10.

[97] *Ibid.*

[98] Cf. *Lumen gentium*, 10, 34.

[99] Cf. *Lumen gentium*, 12.

[100] Cf. *Ut unum sint*, 79.

with other churches, and witnessing in all human cultures to the mystery of Christ in fidelity to the Apostolic Tradition.

109. *The Church Visible and Invisible.* Agreement among us on the visibility of the Church raises the question of the meaning of visible and invisible aspects of the Church, suggested in such expressions as "cloud of witnesses" (*Heb* 12:1) and "communion of saints" as stated in the *Apostles' Creed*.

110. *Ministry.* A comparative study of ministry, ordination, authority, and leadership in our two traditions is needed.

B. Sacraments and Ordinances

111. Since differences of interpretation with respect to two traditional church practices, baptism and the Mass, triggered the rupture between Anabaptists and Catholics in the sixteenth century, it seemed right to both Catholic and Mennonite members of the dialogue that we should present our respective current understandings of these practices, and upon that basis enter into a consideration of historic points of agreement and disagreement. Below is a synopsis of what we presented to each other, and of what we identified as convergences, divergences, and areas for future study. As the discussion proceeded, we were challenged by words from Ephesians: "There is one body and one Spirit, just as you were called to the one hope of your calling, one Lord, one faith, one baptism, one God and Father of all, who is above all and through all and in all" (*Eph* 4:4-6).

A Catholic Understanding of Sacraments

112. *Sacrament* is an important concept for Catholics. This concept has been expressed in many ways throughout the long history of the life of the Church and especially with two words: *mysterion* and *sacramentum*. *Mysterion* and *sacramentum* refer to the mysterious manner in which God has used the elements of his creation for his self-communication. The Scriptures, especially the New Testament, reveal that for the Christian the place of fundamental encounter with God is Jesus Christ. Catholicism has traditionally understood that God's relationship to us is not to be understood solely in an individual way but also in a communal or corporate manner. This is basically a way of expressing the Pauline understanding of all having fallen in Adam and all having been raised (saved/justified) to new life in Christ (cf. *Rom* 5:19; *2 Cor* 5:14f.; *Acts* 17:26ff.). Linked to the notion of corporate personality is that of the ecclesial dimension of the mysteries/sacraments, in that sacraments appear as the symbolic expression of the eschatological embodiment of God through the Spirit, first in Christ (the "source-sacrament") then in the Church (the "fundamental-sacrament" of Christ). This dimension is important for the Catholic understanding of the sacraments since it is the Church, as body of Christ, which is the fundamental sacrament of God's promise and deliverance of the kingdom.[101] Just as Christ is the

---

[101] Cf. *Lumen gentium,* 48; *Phil* 2:12. In talking about the relationship of Israel to the Church, *Lumen gentium,* 9 describes the sacramental nature of the Church in this way: "Israel according to the flesh, which wandered as an exile in the desert, was already

sacrament of the encounter with God, so the Church is the sacrament of encounter with Christ, and hence, ultimately with God.

113. The Second Vatican Council speaks of the sacrament as a reality to be lived especially as the life of the Christian is linked to the Paschal mystery:

> "Thus, for well-disposed members of the faithful the liturgy of the sacraments . . . sanctifies almost every event of their lives with the divine grace which flows from the paschal mystery of the Passion, Death and Resurrection of Christ. From this source all sacraments . . . draw their power. There is scarcely any proper use of material things, which cannot thus be directed toward sanctification of men and the praise of God".[102]

The whole sacramental system in the Catholic Church evolves from the understanding of the centrality of the Paschal mystery. The Paschal mystery is the place where God reveals and grants salvation in symbolic acts and words. The Church in turn worships God through Christ, empowered by the Holy Spirit through the active participation of the faithful in word and symbolic action. Sacraments as the Council teaches are "sacraments of faith".[103] They are so in four ways: sacraments presuppose faith, nourish faith, fortify faith and express faith.

114. Vatican II offers four points of reference for sacraments which are important for their comprehension: 1) Sacraments are liturgical. As such they are located within the Liturgy of the Word[104] and within the action of the Spirit.[105] 2) Sacraments are linked to God, which means that they are the place of divine action. 3) They are linked to the Church, since the Church is where the sacraments are celebrated thanks to the priestly reality of the whole body[106] and because the Church is edified by them. The sacraments are constitutive of the very reality of the Church, and are seen as institutional elements building up the body of Christ.[107] 4) Lastly, sacraments are linked to the whole of the Christian life, since there is a strong link between the sacramental celebration and the ethic of Christian living. Hence a link is made between the Word of God proclaimed, the Word of God celebrated and the Word of God lived that engages each Christian in their daily life.

---

called the Church of God (*2 Esdr* 13:1; cf. *Deut* 23:1ff.; *Num* 20:4). So likewise the new Israel, which while living in this present age goes in search of a future and abiding city (Cf. *Heb* 13:14), is called the Church of Christ (cf. *Mt* 16:18). For he has bought it for himself with his blood (cf. *Acts* 20:28), has filled it with his Spirit and provided it with those means which befit it as a visible and social union. God gathered together as one all those who in faith look upon Jesus as the author of salvation and the source of unity and peace, and established them as the Church that for each and all it may be the visible sacrament of this saving unity".

[102] "Constitution on the Sacred Liturgy", *Sacrosanctum concilium,* 61.

[103] *Sacrosanctum concilium,* 59; *Lumen gentium,* 40.1; *Gaudium et spes,* 38.2.

[104] Cf. *Sacrosanctum concilium,* 7.

[105] Cf. *Sacrosanctum concilium,* 8.

[106] Cf. *Lumen gentium,* 11.1.

[107] Cf. *Sacrosanctum concilium,* 41.2.

115. *Baptism* for Catholics is above all the sacrament of that faith by which, enlightened by the grace of the Holy Spirit, we respond to the Gospel of Christ. Through baptism one is incorporated into the Church and is built up in the Spirit into a house where God lives. Baptism is the cleansing with water by the power of the living word that washes away every stain of sin and makes us sharers in God's own life. Those who are baptized are united to Christ in a life like his (*Col* 2:12; cf. *Rom* 6:4f.). Catholic teaching regarding baptism may be put in six points: 1) baptism is the beginning of the Christian life and the door to other sacraments; 2) it is the basis of the whole Christian life; 3) the principle effects of baptism are purification and new birth; 4) through baptism we become Christ's members and are incorporated into his Church and made sharers in its mission; 5) confirmation that completes baptism deepens the baptismal identity and strengthens us for service; and 6) lastly, as true witnesses of Christ the confirmed are more strictly obligated to spread and defend the faith by word and deed. In addition, the "Decree on Ecumenism" of the Second Vatican Council adds: "Baptism, therefore, constitutes a sacramental bond of unity linking all who have been reborn by means of it".[108]

116. Both in the churches of the East and of the West, the baptizing of infants is considered a practice of ancient tradition.[109] The oldest known ritual, describing at the start of the third century the *Apostolic Tradition*, contains the following rule: "First baptize the children. Those of them who can speak for themselves should do so. The parents or someone of their family should speak for the others".[110] The Catholic Church baptizes adults, infants and children. In each of these cases, faith is an important element. In the context of adults and children the individuals themselves make their profession of faith. In the context of infants the Church has always understood that the one baptized is baptized into the faith of the Church. It is the Church that with her faith envelopes a child who cannot now make a personal confession of faith. At the basis of this reflection is the double solidarity found in the Pauline writings, namely the solidarity in Adam and the solidarity in Christ (*Rom* 5). It is stated in the introduction to the rite of baptism of infants that

---

[108] *Unitatis redintegratio*, 22. "Directory for the Application . . .", *op. cit.*, footnote 41.

[109] Cf. Origen, *In Romanis*, V, 9: PG 14, 1047; Cf. St. Augustine, *De Genesi ad litteram*, X, 23, 39: *PL* 34, 426; *De peccatorum meritis et remissione et de baptismo parvulorum ad Marcellinum*, I, 26, 39: *PL* 44, 131. In fact, three passages of the Acts of the Apostles (16:15, 16:33, 18:81) speak of the baptism of a whole household or family. See also Irenaeus, *Adv. Haereses* II, 22, 4: *PG* 7, 784; Harvey I, 330. Many inscriptions from as early as the second century give little children the title of "children of God", a title given only to the baptized, or explicitly mention that they were baptized: Cf., for example, *Corpus Inscriptionum Graecarum*, 9727, 9801, 9817; E. Diehl, ed., *Inscriptiones Latinae Christianae Veteres* (Berlin: Weidmann, 1961), nos. 1523 (3), 4429 A. For a comprehensive study of the question of the baptism of infants within the context of the rites of Christian initiation, see Maxwell E. Johnson, *The Rites of Christian Initiation: Their Evolution and Interpretation* (Collegeville: The Liturgical Press, 1999).

[110] Hippolytus of Rome, *Apostolic Tradition*, 21.

"to fulfill the true meaning of the sacrament; children must later be formed in the faith in which they have been baptized. The foundation of this formation will be the sacrament itself, which they have already received. Christian formation, which is their due, seeks to lead them gradually to learn God's plan in Christ, so that they may ultimately accept for themselves the faith in which they have been baptized".[111]

117. *The Eucharist* is not simply one of the sacraments but it is the pre-eminent one. Vatican II states that the Eucharist is the source and the summit of the whole life of the Church.[112] Through the activity of the Holy Spirit, the atoning work of Jesus Christ is made universal and brings all things in heaven and on earth together under one head, Jesus Christ (*Eph* 1:10). The sacramental basis of this *koinonia* or communion is the one baptism through which we are baptized in the one body of Christ (*1 Cor* 12:12f.; cf. *Rom* 12:4f.; *Eph* 4:3f.) through baptism we are one in Christ (*Gal* 3:26-28). The summit of this communion is found in the Eucharist where the many become one through the participation in the one loaf and one cup (*1 Cor* 10:16f.). Therefore the *koinonia/communion* in the one Eucharistic bread is the source and sign of the *koinonia/communion* in the one body of the Church. In the Eucharist we are united to the heavenly liturgy and anticipate eternal life when God will be all in all. The Eucharist, wherein Christ is really and substantially present, sacramentally represents the sacrifice of Christ made on the cross once and for all. It is a *memorial* of his passion, death and resurrection.[113] There is a richness in understandings of what the Eucharist is for Catholics. By taking these together, we can have a fuller

---

[111] *Rite of Baptism for Children*, introduction. See also the instruction by the "Congregation of the Doctrine of the Faith", *Pastoralis actio* (October 20, 1980), 14 which states: "The fact that infants cannot yet profess personal faith does not prevent the Church from conferring this sacrament on them, since in reality it is in her own faith that she baptizes them. This point of doctrine was clearly defined by Saint Augustine: 'When children are presented to be given spiritual grace', he wrote, 'it is not so much those holding them in their arms who present them—although, if these people are good Christians, they are included among those who present the children—as the whole company of saints and faithful Christians. . . . It is done by the whole of Mother Church which is in the saints, since it is as a whole that she give birth to each and every one of them' (*Epist.* 98, 5: *PL* 33, 362; Cf. *Sermo* 176, 2, 2: *PL* 38, 950). This teaching is repeated by St. Thomas Aquinas and all the theologians after him: the child who is baptized believes not on its own account, by a personal act, but through others, 'through the Church's faith communicated to it' (in *Summa Theologica*, IIIa, q. 69, a. 5, ad 3, cf. q. 68, a. 9, ad 3). This same teaching is also expressed in the new Rite of Baptism, when the celebrant asks the parents and godparents to profess the faith of the Church, the faith in which the children are baptized (*Ordo baptismi parvulorum, Praenotanda*, 2: cf. 56)."

[112] Cf. *Lumen gentium*, 11.

[113] The term memorial (*zikkaron* in Hebrew *anamnesis* in Greek) is a technical term which is not merely the recollection of past events but the proclamation of the mighty works (*mirabilia Dei*) wrought by God for us (Ex 13:3). In liturgical celebrations these events become in a certain way present and real.

understanding of the meaning of the Eucharist. For example, the Eucharist is under-stood as a meal that realizes and manifests the unity of the community; in addition this meal is understood in relationship to the unrepeatable death of Christ on the cross. In the Eucharistic sacrifice, the whole of creation loved by God is presented to the Father through the death and resurrection of Christ. Through Christ the Church can offer the sacrifice of praise in thanksgiving for all that God has made good, beautiful, and just in creation and in humanity.[114]

118. Even though the eucharistic celebration consists of several parts, it is con-ceived of as a single act of worship. The eucharistic table is the table of both the Word of God and the body of the Lord. Vatican II taught that Christ is present in several ways in the celebration of the Eucharist. First, in the presence of the minis-ter who gathers the Church in the name of the Lord and greets them in his Spirit; second, in the proclamation of the Word; third, in the assembly gathered in God's name; and fourth, in a special way under the eucharistic elements.[115] The faithful are invited to share in the celebration of the liturgy in an active way by means of hymns, prayers and especially the reception of the eucharistic body and blood of the Risen Lord. The faithful commune at the table of the Lord by receiving both the eucharistic bread and the cup.

119. Lastly we can affirm that the Church makes a link between what is celebrated and what is lived. Therefore as St. Augustine taught, we are to become more fully that which we receive, namely the body of Christ. This means that as Paul taught First Corinthians, we must live coherently the reality that we are (cf. *1 Cor* 11:17ff.), hence the link between the Eucharist and justice, peace and reconciliation. Catholics are committed, because of this eucharistic reality, to become a living sign of Christ's peace and reconciliation for the world.

A Mennonite Understanding of Ordinances

120. The term ordinance is used instead of 'sacrament' in Anabaptist-Mennonite theology.[116] To speak of baptism and the Lord's Supper as ordinances emphasizes that the Church began and continues these practices because Christ ordained (instituted) them (*Mt* 26:26-29; *1 Cor* 11:23-26). Two ordinances are common to all Mennonite churches, namely baptism and the Lord's Supper. A third, foot washing, is practiced by some (cf. *Jn* 13:3-17).[117] On another matter of terminology, Mennonites do not

---

[114] Cf. *Catechism of the Catholic Church*, 2nd ed. rev. in accordance with the official Latin text (Vatican City: Libreria Editrice Vaticana, 2000), n. 1359.

[115] Cf. *Sacrosanctum concilium*, 7.

[116] Mennonites shied away from the use of the term 'sacrament' because they feared what they called 'sacramentalism,' the temptation to attribute miraculous power to the ritual and its elements as such. Even then, the designation 'sacrament' was used at times, as for example in Art. 26 of the *Ris Confession* (1766) which states: "That the Lord instituted this *sacrament* (italics added) with the intention that it is to be observed by His disciples in His church in all time, is plainly seen" (Loewen, *op. cit.,* p. 98).

[117] A recent outline of Anabaptist ordinances adds 'church discipline,' although it is not commonly recognized as such. Church discipline replaced the sacrament of

use the term 'Eucharist', but refer to the meal as the 'Lord's Supper', and sometimes as 'Holy Communion'. It has become common in theological and confessional writing to refer to the ordinances and to the elements of water, bread and wine, as symbols or signs. By this is meant that the ordinances and the elements point beyond themselves to their spiritual significance, and also, in the case of the Lord's Supper, to its historic memory. This report will limit itself to the ordinances of baptism and the Lord's Supper, since these were the focus of the Mennonite-Catholic dialogue.

Baptism

121. In Anabaptist-Mennonite understanding, *baptism* derives its meaning from the biblical accounts of baptisms—the baptism of Jesus (*Mt* 3:13-17; *Mk* 1:9-11; *Lk* 3:21-22; *Jn* 1:29-34) and of those baptized in Jesus' name (for example, *Acts* 2:41)—as well as biblical references to the meaning of baptism (for example, *Rom* 6:3-4; *Col* 2:12; *1 Jn* 5:7-8). Consideration of these texts leads to an understanding of water baptism as a sign that points to three interrelated dimensions of Christian initiation and formation[118]: 1) In baptism the individual bears witness before the congregation that he/she has repented of sin, has received the grace of God, and has been cleansed of all unrighteousness (*Ezek* 36:25; *Acts* 2:38). Baptism is thus the sign of a good conscience before God and the Church. 2) Water baptism signifies the outpouring of the Holy Spirit in the life of the Christian (*Acts* 2:17, 33). Baptism is thus an acknowledgement on the part of the one being baptized, of the presence of the Spirit in his/her life of faith. 3) Baptism provides a public sign to the congregation of the person's desire to walk in the way of Christ. Such a walk is sometimes referred to in Anabaptist writings as "walking in the resurrection".[119]

122. The baptismal commitment to faith and faithfulness is not an individualistic action, as baptism and church membership are inseparable. The person is "baptized into one body" (*1 Cor* 12:13), the body of Christ, the Church. The baptismal candidate's affirmation of faith is an affirmation of the faith of the Church, and an affirmation made in the context of the community of believers to which the baptized person is joined as a responsible member. The new church member declares a willingness to give and receive care and counsel and to participate in the church's life and mission. The individual relates to the Trinitarian God in a deeply personal way, and also

---

penance by following the New Testament pattern (*Mt* 18:15-18) of offering the sinner an opportunity for repentance, forgiveness, and readmission into the fellowship of the church. See C.A. Snyder, *From Anabaptist Seed* (Kitchener/Scottdale: Pandora Press/ Herald Press, 1999), pp. 28ff.

[118] Another way of outlining the meaning of baptism would be to follow an early scheme developed by the Anabaptists on the basis of 1 Jn 5:7-8, which is understood as a reference to a three-fold outline: baptism of the Holy Spirit, baptism of water, and baptism of blood. Cf. "Confession of Faith According to the Holy Word of God" (ca. 1600), 21, in Thielemann J. van Braght, *Martyrs Mirror, op. cit.*, pp. 396ff.

[119] H.S. Bender, "Walking in the Resurrection", *The Mennonite Quarterly Review*, 35 (April, 1961), pp. 11–25.

together in and with the community of believers where grace is experienced and faith is affirmed in and with the people of God.

123. Mennonite confessional statements as well as centuries of practice suggest that baptism is understood not only as a sign that points beyond the baptismal ritual to its historic and spiritual significance, but that in and through baptism the individual and the community of faith undergo effectual change. For example, the *Dordrecht Confession* (1632) says that all penitent believers are to be baptized with water "to the burying of their sins, and thus to become incorporated into the communion of the saints".[120] Here participation in the baptismal act appears to *effect* the putting away of sins. A statement on baptism in the *Ris Confession* (1766) speaks of baptism as a *means* of spiritual blessing, regeneration and renewal: "If Christian baptism is thus devoutly desired, administered, and received, we hold it in high esteem as a means of communicating and receiving spiritual blessing, nothing less than a washing of regeneration and renewing of the Holy Spirit".[121] More recent Mennonite confessional statements on baptism also reveal the expectation of *transformation* due to participation in the ordinance. The *Confession of Faith of the Mennonites in Canada* (1930), states:

> "Baptism is an incorporation (*Einverleibung*) in Christ and his church and the covenant of a good conscience with God. It signifies the burial of our old life in the death of Christ and binds the baptized to unity with Christ in a new obedient life, to follow him in his footsteps and to do what he has commanded them to do".[122]

While there is the recognition in Mennonite theology and in Mennonite confessions that 'something happens' in the very act of baptism, baptismal transformation in and through the ritual is conceivable only if and when it is verified in the faith and life of the individual undergoing baptism and of the baptizing community.

124. Mennonites practice adult baptism, sometimes referred to as 'believers baptism.' Baptism is reserved for youth and adults who freely request it on the basis that they have accepted Jesus Christ as their personal Saviour and Lord. This presupposes, on the part of the one being baptized, the ability to reason and to take personal accountability for faith, and to become a responsible participant in the life of the Church. Baptism is administered "according to the command and doctrine of Christ, and the example and custom of the apostles".[123] The person is baptized with water in the name of the Father, the Son, and the Holy Spirit. Mennonites understand baptism to include instruction in the Word of God and in the way of discipleship (*Mt* 28:19f.). The mode of baptism is either by effusion of water upon the individual (pouring or sprinkling) or by immersion of the person in water.[124]

125. The Mennonite Church observes the *Lord's Supper* in accordance with Jesus' institution of the Supper and with the teachings of the New Testament concerning

---

[120] *Dortrecht Confession*, Art. 7, Loewen, *op. cit.*, p. 65.

[121] *Ris Confession,* Art. 25, Loewen, *ibid.*, p. 97.

[122] Loewen, *ibid.*, Art. 9, p. 306.

[123] *Dordrecht Confession*, Art. 7, Loewen, *ibid.*, p. 65.

[124] Cf. *Ris Confession*, Art. 25, Loewen, *ibid.*, pp. 97f.

its meaning: 1) The Lord's Supper is a meal of remembrance whereby participants thankfully recall that Jesus suffered, died, and was raised on behalf of all people, sacrificing his body and shedding his blood for the forgiveness of sins (*Mt* 26:28; *1 Cor* 11:23-25). 2) The meal is a sign bearing witness to the new covenant established in and by the death and resurrection of Christ, and thus an invitation to participants to renew their covenant with Christ (*Jer* 31:33-35; *Mk* 14:24; *1 Cor* 11:25). 3) The Lord's Supper is a sign of the Church's corporate sharing in the body and blood of Christ, recognition that the Church is sustained by Christ, the bread of life, and thus an invitation for members of the Church to be one (*Lk* 22:19f.; *1 Cor* 10:16f.). 4) The meal is a proclamation of the Lord's death, a joyous celebration of hope in his coming again, a foretaste of the heavenly banquet of the redeemed, and an occasion for hearing anew the call to serve the Lord in sacrificial living until his return (*Lk* 22:28-30; *1 Cor* 11:26).

126. While throughout the Mennonite confessional tradition there runs a persistent emphasis on the Lord's Supper as a memorial and a sign, Mennonite confessions of faith do not dismiss the effectual power of the ordinance to bring change to the participants and to the community of faith. The *Schleitheim Confession* (1527) depicts the congregation of true believers as being "made one loaf together with all the children of God".[125] This suggests that in a spiritual sense the community becomes the loaf, the bread. Something of this power associated with the sharing of the bread itself, is felt and known when brothers and sisters claim a spiritual closeness during the communion service, and when they leave the service 'changed.' In its statement on the Lord's Supper, the *Ris Confession* identifies the presence of this spiritual power when it states: "On the part of God and Christ [the Lord's Supper] serves as a means to confirm and seal unto us in the most emphatic manner the great blessings comprehended in the gospel".[126] The *Confession of Faith in a Mennonite Perspective* (1995) states: "As we partake of the communion of the bread and the cup, the gathered body of believers shares in the body and blood of Christ and recognizes again that it's life is sustained by Christ, the bread of life".[127] The key lies not in the elements as such, but in the context as a whole, including the communion of the gathered congregation, the prayerful aspiration of each individual, and the spiritual presence that is suggested and re-presented with the aid of appropriate symbols and liturgy.[128]

127. The invitation to take part in the Lord's Supper is open to all baptized believers who are in right fellowship with the Lord and with their congregation, and who by the grace of God seek to live in accordance with the example and teachings of

---

[125] *Schleitheim Confession*, Art. 3, Loewen, *ibid.*, p. 80.

[126] *Ris Confession*, Art. 26, Loewen, *ibid.*, p. 98.

[127] *Confession of Faith in a Mennonite Perspective*, 12, *op. cit.*, p. 50.

[128] Cf. John D. Rempel, *The Lord's Supper in Anabaptism* (Scottdale/Waterloo: Herald Press, 1993). Rempel says that the Anabaptists "made the church as a community the agent of the breaking of bread. There is still a presider who symbolizes the community's order and authority. But it is the congregation that does the action. The Spirit is present in their action, transforming them so that they are reconstituted as the body of Christ. The life of the congregation, consecrated in its faith and love, consecrates the elements" (p. 34).

Christ. From the beginning of the Anabaptist-Mennonite movement, the unity of the body of believers was seen as a desired prerequisite for coming to the table of the Lord.[129] How can there be participation, it is asked, if there is not a striving for the unity of the one body of Christ? The emphasis upon preparing for the Lord's Supper by ensuring that members are in 'right' relationship with brothers and sisters in the Church is a distinctive mark of the Mennonite practice of Holy Communion.

Convergences

128. The Catholic Church and the Mennonite Church agree that baptism and the Lord's Supper have their origin and point of reference in Jesus Christ and in the teachings of Scripture. Both regard the celebration of these sacraments/ordinances as extraordinary occasions of encounter with God's offer of grace revealed in Jesus Christ. They are important moments in the believers' commitment to the body of Christ and to the Christian way of life. Catholics and Mennonites see the sacraments/ordinances as acts of the Church.

129. Mennonites and Catholics are agreed on the basic meaning and import of baptism as a dying and rising with Christ, so that "just as Christ was raised from the dead by the glory of the Father, so we too might walk in newness of life" (*Rom* 6:4). We both also emphasize that baptism signifies the outpouring of the Holy Spirit and the promised presence of the Holy Spirit in the life of the believer and the Church.

130. Catholics and Mennonites agree that baptism is a public witness to the faith of the Church, and the occasion for the incorporation of new believers into Christ and the Church. Both hold that baptism is an unrepeatable act.

131. For Mennonites and Catholics a public profession of faith is required at the time of baptism. Mennonite churches baptize upon the candidate's own confession of faith. This is also the case in the Catholic rite of adult baptism. In the case of infant baptism in the Latin Rite of the Catholic Church, it is the Church, along with the parents and the godparents, that makes the profession of faith on behalf of the child. This profession becomes personal when the child is able to reason and to affirm the faith. This is done solemnly at confirmation. In the Eastern Rite, all three sacraments are celebrated together and the sense of confirmation is the inserting of the candidate into the public witness of Christ and the reception of the grace proper to this public witness.

132. Mennonites and Catholics practice the rite of baptism as a public celebration in the congregation. Both practice baptism by effusion of water or immersion in water; and they baptize in the name of the Father, the Son, and the Holy Spirit as Jesus instructed (cf. *Mt* 28:19). In Mennonite churches, an ordained minister of the congregation administers baptism. In the Catholic Church, it is ordinarily a bishop, a priest, or a deacon who administers baptism.

133. Mennonites and Catholics agree on significant aspects of the meaning of the Lord's Supper or Eucharist: 1) Both hold that the celebration of the Eucharist/Lord's Supper is rooted in God's marvellous gift of grace made available to all people by virtue

---

[129] Cf. *Schleitheim Confession*, 3, Loewen, *op. cit.*, p. 80.

of the suffering, death, and resurrection of Jesus Christ. 2) We agree that the Lord's Supper/Eucharist recalls the suffering, the death, and the resurrection of Christ. 3) We agree that the meal provides an important occasion for the acknowledgement of our sinfulness and for receiving grace and forgiveness. 4) Both celebrate the Eucharist/Lord's Supper for the nourishing of Christian life; for the strengthening of the church's sense of mission; and for the conforming of our communities to the body of Christ in order to be ministers of reconciliation, peace and justice for the world (cf. *1 Cor* 11:17-32; *2 Cor* 5:16-21). 5) Both celebrate the Lord's Supper/Eucharist in the spirit of Christian hope, as a foretaste of the heavenly banquet anticipated in the coming kingdom of God.

134. Catholics and Mennonites agree that the risen Christ is present at the celebration of the Eucharist/Lord's Supper. Christ is the one who invites to the meal; he is present in the faithful who are gathered in his name; and he is present in the proclaimed Word.

Divergences

135. Both Mennonites and Catholics view sacraments and ordinances as outward signs instituted by Christ, but we have differing understandings of the power of signs. For Mennonites, ordinances as signs point to the salvific work of Christ and invite participation in the life of Christ. For Catholics, in addition to participating in the life of Christ, signs also communicate to those who receive them, the grace proper to each sacrament.

136. The Catholic Church advocates both infant baptism and adult baptism, and accepts Mennonite baptism, which is done with water and in the name of the Trinity, as valid. In the Mennonite Church, baptism is for those who understand its significance and who freely request it on the basis of their personally owned faith in Jesus Christ.

137. Mennonites and Catholics differ in part in their understanding of the role of a personal confession of faith as it pertains to baptism. Both agree to the necessity of the profession of faith. However, in the Catholic practice of infant baptism, a profession of faith is made on behalf of the child by the parents, the godparents, and the whole assembly. In the Mennonite churches, which do not practice infant baptism, it is required that a profession of faith and a baptismal commitment be made personally by the individual being baptized. In the Mennonite churches, the practice of making a profession of faith on behalf of a person being baptized who does not at the moment of baptism realize the basic meaning and implications of his or her baptism, is not acceptable.

138. Catholics and Mennonites diverge in their understanding of how Christ is present in the Eucharist or the Lord's Supper. For Mennonites, the Lord's Supper is primarily a sign or symbol that points to Jesus' suffering, death, and resurrection, and that keeps this memory alive until His return. For Catholics, the Eucharist is the source and the summit of the whole life of the Church in which the sacrifice, made once and for all on the cross, is made really present under the species of the consecrated bread and wine, and presented to the Father as an act of thanksgiving and praise for the wonderful work of salvation offered to humanity.

139. Mennonites and Catholics diverge in their understanding of the presence of Christ at the Eucharist/Lord's Supper. The Anabaptists rejected the idea that there was a real bodily presence of Christ in the elements of bread and wine. Mennonites today view the elements as signs or symbols that recall the significance of the death of Christ for the forgiveness of sin and for the Christian's commitment to love and discipleship. In Catholic understanding, in the sacrament of the Eucharist "the body and blood, together with the soul and divinity, of our Lord Jesus Christ and, therefore, the whole Christ is truly, really, and substantially contained",[130] under the species of bread and wine which have been consecrated by an ordained bishop or presbyter.

140. With respect to participation in the Lord's Supper, most Mennonite churches extend an open invitation for all believers to partake, who are baptized, who are in good standing in their church, and who are in right relationship with the Lord and with one another. In Catholic understanding, the ecclesial dimension of the Eucharist has consequences for the question of who may be admitted to the Eucharistic communion, since the Eucharist as the sacrament of unity presumes our being in full ecclesial communion.[131] Therefore the ecclesial dimension of the Eucharist must be taken into consideration in the question of who is admitted to the Eucharist.

Areas of Future Study

141. Discussion is needed concerning our divergent views on the role of the faith of the Church as it bears on the status of infants and children. This would include a comparative study of the theology of sin and salvation, of the spiritual status of children, and of baptism.

142. The question of recognizing or not recognizing one another's baptism requires further study.

143. It is necessary to study, together, the history of the origin and development of the theology and practice of baptism for the purpose of ascertaining the origin of infant baptism, assessing the changes brought about with the Constantinian shift, the development of the doctrine of original sin, and other matters.

144. It would be fruitful to have additional discussions of the relationship between the Catholic understanding of sacraments and the Mennonite understanding of ordinances, to further ascertain where additional significant convergences and divergences may lie.

C. Our Commitment to Peace

> *"Blessed are the peacemakers,*
> *for they shall be called the children of God" (Mt 5:8).*

145. Through our dialogue, we have come to understand that Catholics and Mennonites share a common commitment to peacemaking. That commitment is rooted in

---

[130] *Catechism of the Catholic Church*, 1374 citing the Council of Trent (1551), DS 1651.
[131] Communion with the local bishop and with the Bishop of Rome is understood as a sign and service of the unity of the Church.

our communion with "the God of Peace" (*Rom* 15:33) and in the church's response to Jesus' proclamation of "the gospel of peace" (*Eph* 6:15). Christ has entrusted to us the ministry of reconciliation. As "ambassadors of Christ" (*2 Cor* 5:20) we are called to be reconciled to God and to one another. Moved by the Spirit, we want to share with our brothers and sisters in faith, and with a wider world, our call to be instruments of God's peace.

146. We present the results of our dialogue on the question of commitment to peace in four parts: (1) a survey of distinctive aspects of our respective views of peacemaking and related Christian doctrines; (2) points of convergence; (3) points of divergence; and (4) issues requiring further exploration.

Catholic Perspectives on Peace

147. *The Church's Social Vision.* The primary way in which the Church contributes to the reconciliation of the human family is the Church's own universality.[132] Understanding itself as "a sacrament of intimate union with God and of the unity of mankind",[133] the Catholic Church takes the promotion of unity, and accordingly peace, "as belonging to the innermost nature of the Church".[134] For this reason it fosters solidarity among peoples, and calls peoples and nations to sacrifices of advantages of power and wealth for the sake of solidarity of the human family.[135] The Eucharist, which strengthens the bonds of charity, nourishes such solidarity. The Eucharist, in turn, is an expression of the charity which binds members of the community in Christ (*1 Cor* 11:17-34).[136]

148. The Church views the human vocation as essentially communitarian, that is, all human relations are ordered to unity and love, an order of love confirmed by the life and teaching of Jesus and the Spirit-filled life of the Church (cf. *Lk* 22:14-27; *Jn* 13:1-20; 15:1-17; 17:20-24).[137] This order of love is manifest in the lives of the faithful and in the community of the Church, but is not restricted to them. In fact, by virtue of creation and redemption, it is found at all levels of human society.

149. God created the human family for unity, and in Christ confirmed the law of love (*Acts* 17:26; *Rom* 13:10). Accordingly, the Church sees the growth of interdependence across the world, though not without problems due to sin, a force that can contribute to peace.[138] Thus, Pope John Paul II has written: "The goal of peace, so desired by everyone, will certainly be achieved through the putting into effect of social and international justice, but also through the practice of virtues which favour togetherness, and which teach us to live in unity . . . ".[139]

---

[132] Cf. *Acts* 2; *Lumen gentium*, 1, 9, and especially 13; *Gaudium et spes*, 42.

[133] *Lumen gentium*, 1, 4, 9, 13.

[134] *Gaudium et spes*, 42.

[135] Cf. *Sollicitudo rei socialis*, 38–40, 45; *Centesimus annus*, 52.

[136] Cf. *Sacrosanctum concilium*, 9–10; *Lumen gentium*, 3, 7; *Sollicitudo rei socialis*, 48.

[137] Cf. *Gaudium et spes*, 24–25, 32.

[138] Cf. *Lumen gentium*, 1; *Gaudium et spes*, 4, 6, 24–25; *Sollicitudo rei socialis*, 45.

[139] *Sollicitudo rei socialis*, 39. Cf. *Jas* 3:18.

150. *The Call to Holiness.* All Christians share in God's call to holiness (*1 Thess* 4:3; *Eph* 1:4).[140] This is a sanctity "cultivated by all who under God's spirit and, obeying the Father's voice . . . , follow Christ, poor, humble and cross bearing . . .".[141] As God's own people, living in the inauguration of the kingdom, we are to be "peacemakers" who "hunger and thirst for righteousness" (*Mt* 5:6) and "are persecuted for righteousness' sake" (*Mt* 5:11). We are to love one another, forgive one another, and live humbly in imitation of Jesus, who though he was "in the form of God . . . humbled himself becoming obedient unto death, even death on a cross" (cf. *Phil* 2:6, 8). We are to be generous and forgiving with everyone, as God is generous with us (*Lk* 6:37f.). In a word, as disciples of Jesus, we are instructed to "Be perfect, therefore, as your heavenly Father is perfect" (*Mt* 5:48).

151. All the commandments, as Saint Paul teaches, are summed up in the saying, "Love your neighbour as yourself" (*Rom* 13:9; cf. *Jas* 2:8; *1 Jn* 4:11f.). For Catholics, love of neighbour takes special form in love and service of the poor and marginalized; indeed, in "a preferential option for the poor". The ministry of love to the neighbour is promoted through personal and corporate works of mercy, in organized charities, as well as in advocacy on behalf of justice, human rights and peace. Lay people, bishops and Church agencies engage in such initiatives.[142] The love command likewise entails reverence and love for enemies (*Mt* 5:43; *1 Jn* 3:16).[143] Like our heavenly Father, who "makes the sun to rise on the evil and the good and sends rain on the righteous and the unrighteous" (*Mt* 5:45), we are to love our enemies, bless them, pray for them, not retaliate, and share our possessions with those who would take things from us (*Lk* 6:27-35). Furthermore, we must be prepared to establish just relations with them, for true peace is the fruit of justice, and "because justice is always fragile and imperfect, it must include and, as it were be completed by the forgiveness which heals and rebuilds troubled human relations from their foundations".[144] Finally, in the midst of conflict, the Lord gives us his peace that we may have courage under persecution (*Jn* 16:33; 20:21).

152. Nonviolence, in Catholic eyes, is both a Christian and a human virtue. For Christians, nonviolence takes on special meaning in the suffering of Christ who was "led as a sheep to the slaughter" (*Is* 53:7; *Acts* 8:32). "Making up the sufferings lacking in Christ" (*Col* 1:34), the nonviolent witness of Christians contributes to the building up of peace in a way that force cannot, discerning the difference "between the cowardice which gives into evil and the violence which under the illusion of fighting evil, only makes it worse".[145] In the Catholic view, nonviolence ought to be implemented in public policies and through public institutions as well as in personal

---

[140] Cf. *Lumen gentium*, 39.

[141] *Lumen gentium*, 41.

[142] Cf. *Gaudium et spes*, 43, 88–91; *Sollicitudo rei socialis*, 42–43, 47; *Centesimus annus*, 58; Pope John Paul II, World Day of Peace Message, 1993, "If You Want Peace, Reach Out to the Poor". Cf. *Mt* 25: 41-36; *Lk* 14:15-24; *Jas* 2:1-7.

[143] Cf. *Gaudium et spes*, 28; *Sollicitudo rei socialis*, 40; *Evangelium vitae*, 41.

[144] Pope John Paul II, "No Peace Without Justice, No Justice Without Forgiveness", World Day of Peace Message, 2000.

[145] *Centesimus annus*, 23, 25.

and church practice.[146] Both in pastoral practice and through Vatican diplomacy, the Church insists, in the face of conflict, that "peace is possible".[147] The Church also attempts to nourish a culture of peace in civil society, and encourages the establishment of institutions for the practice of non-violence in public life.[148]

153. *Peacemaking.* On the pastoral level, the Catholic theology of peace takes a positive stance. It focuses on resolving the causes of conflict and building the conditions for lasting peace. It entails four primary components: (1) promotion and protection of human rights, (2) advancing integral human development, (3) supporting international law and international organizations, and (4) building solidarity between peoples and nations.[149] This vision of peace is articulated in the whole body of contemporary Catholic social teaching beginning with Pope John XXIII's *Pacem in terris* ("Peace on Earth") forty years ago and continuing through Pope John Paul II's *Tertio millennio ineunte* ("The Third Millennium") in 2000.[150]

154. The Catholic Church's work for peace is carried out in many ways. Since the Second Vatican Council, it has largely been carried out through a network of national and diocesan justice and peace commissions and through the Pontifical Council for Justice and Peace. Their work has been especially influential in the struggle for human rights in Asia, Latin America, and some parts of Africa. Catholic human rights offices, like the Vicarate for Solidarity in Chile, Tutela Legal in El Salvador, Batolomeo Casas in Mexico, the Archdiocesan Office in Guatemala City, and the Society of Saint Yves in Jerusalem have been models for active defence of the rights of the poor, of indigenous people, and of those under occupation. Catholic relief and development agencies, especially *Caritas Internationalis* and the *Caritas* network, provide relief, development, refugee assistance and post-conflict reconstruction for divided societies. In many places, individual bishops have also played an important role in national conciliation efforts; and one, Bishop Felipe Ximenes Belo of E. Timor, won the Nobel Peace Prize for his efforts.

155. The Holy See[151] exercises "a diplomacy of conscience" through the Vatican diplomatic corps and other special representatives. This diplomatic activity consists of advocacy on behalf of peace, human rights, development and humanitarian issues. It also contributes to international peacemaking indirectly through initiatives of Catholic groups, like the Community of Sant'Egidio, and various bishops' conferences. Above all, the pope exercises a unique ministry for peace through his teaching and public statements, in his meetings with world figures, through his pilgrimages

---

[146] Cf. *Gaudium et spes*, 88–93; *Centesimus annus*, 52.

[147] Pope Paul VI, "Peace is Possible", World Day of Peace Message, 1973.

[148] Cf. *Centesimus annus*, 51–52.

[149] Cf. *Gaudium et spes*, 44, 64–65, 83–90, 32.

[150] This constructive approach to peace (that is, Pope Paul VI: "If you want peace, work for justice") is a complement to the contemporary practice of Mennonites in conflict resolution, conflict transformation and technical peace-building. It also is supportive of broader conceptions of peace-building now being promoted in both Mennonite and Catholic circles.

[151] The Holy See is the title the Catholic Church employs in international affairs.

across the world, and through special events like the Assisi Days of Prayer and the Great Jubilee Year 2000.

156. Since the Second Vatican Council, the Church has sought to view war "with a whole new attitude".[152] In the encyclical letter, *Evangelium vitae* ("The Gospel of Life"), Pope John Paul II identified war as part of the culture of death, and he found a positive sign of the times in "*a new sensitivity ever more opposed to war* as an instrument of the resolution of conflict between people, and increasingly oriented to finding effective but 'nonviolent' means to counter the armed aggressor".[153]

157. The Catholic tradition today upholds both a strong presumption against the use of force and an obligation to resist the denial of rights and other grave public evils by active nonviolence, if at all possible (cf. *Rom* 12:14-21; *1 Thess* 5:14f.). All Catholics bear a general obligation to actively resist grave public evil.[154] Catholic teaching has increasingly endorsed the superiority of non-violent means and is suspect of the use of force in a culture of death.[155] Nonetheless, the Catholic tradition also continues to maintain the possibility of a limited use of force as a last resort (the Just War), particularly when whole populations are at risk as in cases of genocide or ethnic cleansing.[156] As in the days before the U.S. war against Iraq (2003), Pope John Paul II as well as Vatican officials and bishops' conferences around the world have urged the international community to employ nonviolent alternatives to the use of force. At the same time, they have employed just-war criteria to prevent war and to promote the limitation of force and to criticize both potential and actual uses of force by governments.

158. Just-war reasoning, however, is not a simple moral calculus. Following the notion of 'right reason,' valid application of the just-war criteria depends on possessing a virtuous character. Such virtues as moderation, restraint, and respect for life are intrinsic to sound application of just-war criteria, as are Christian virtues such as humility, gentleness, forgiveness and love of enemy. Accordingly, Church teaching and application of the Just War criteria have grown more stringent in recent years, insisting that the function of the Just War Tradition is to prevent and limit war, not just legitimate it.[157]

159. The Just War today should be understood as part of a broad Catholic theology of peace applicable only to exceptional cases. War, as Pope John Paul II has said, "is never just another means that one can choose to employ for settling differences between nations".[158] The Pope's overall assessment of the evils of war made at the end of the 1991 Gulf War remains valid today:

---

[152] *Gaudium et spes*, 80.

[153] *Evangelium vitae*, 27; cf. 10–12, 39–41.

[154] Cf. *Gaudium et spes*, 78.

[155] Cf. *Centesimus annus*, 23, 25, 52.

[156] Cf. *The Catechism of the Catholic Church*, 2313; Pope John Paul II, "Address to the International Conference on Nutrition", 1992.

[157] Cf. World Day of Peace Message, 2002; *Evangelium vitae*, 41; National Conference of Catholic Bishops, "Harvest of Justice Is Sown in Peace".

[158] Pope John Paul II, "Address to the Diplomatic Corps", January 12, 2003, (making reference to the conflict then developing between the United States and the United Kingdom with Iraq).

"No, never again war, which destroys the lives of innocent people, teaches how to kill, throws into upheaval even the lives of those who do the killing, and leaves behind a trail of resentment and hatred, thus making it all the more difficult to find a just solution of the very problems which provoked the war".[159]

160. *Religious Freedom.* Jesus proclaimed the time "when true worshippers will worship the Father in spirit and in truth, for the Father seeks such as these to worship him" (*Jn* 4:26). Meek and humble of heart, Jesus "did not wish to be a political Messiah who would dominate by force but preferred to call himself the Son of Man who came to serve, and to give his life as 'a ransom for many'".[160] Today the Catholic Church repudiates the use of force in the name of the Gospel and upholds freedom of conscience in matters of religion. In accord with Vatican II's "Declaration on Religious Liberty" (*Dignitatis humanae*), Catholics affirm freedom of religion for all and repudiate the use of coercion in the spread of the Gospel.[161] The Catholic Church also repents of offenses committed "in the name of Truth" in past centuries by officials' use of the civil arm to suppress religious dissent, and she begs God's forgiveness for these violations.[162]

161. *History, Eschatology and Human Achievement.* Catholics believe that human achievement of every sort, particularly the achievements of a political society that contributes to a greater measure of justice and peace in the world, prepares humanity "to share in the fullness which 'dwells in the Lord'".[163]

"For after we have obeyed the Lord, and in his Spirit have nurtured on earth the values of human dignity, brotherhood and freedom . . . we will find them again, but free of stain, burnished and transfigured. This will be so when Christ hands over to the Father a kingdom eternal and universal: 'a kingdom of truth and life, of holiness and grace, of justice, love and peace'".[164]

At the same time sin, which is always attempting to trap us and which jeopardizes our human achievements, is conquered and redeemed by the reconciliation accomplished by Christ (cf. *Col* 1:20).[165]

Mennonite Perspectives on Peace

162. *Christological Basis of Our Peace Commitment.* For the Mennonite Church, peace has its basis in the love of God as revealed in creation, in God's story with his

---

[159] *Centesimus annus*, 52; *Evangelium vitae*, 10, 12.

[160] *Dignitatis humanae*, 11. Cf. *Lk* 22:21-27; *Mk* 10:45.

[161] Cf. *Dignitatis humanae*, 7.

[162] Cf. Day of Pardon, para. 200–202 below.

[163] *Sollicitudo rei socialis*, 31, 48.

[164] *Gaudium et spes*, 39.

[165] *Sollicitudo rei socialis*, 31.

people, and in the life and message of Jesus Christ. The biblical word *shalom* expresses well-being, wholeness, and the harmony and rightness of relationships. Justice is the inseparable companion of peace, as the prophets testify: "and the effect of justice will be peace and the result of righteousness quietness and trust forever" (*Is* 32:17).

163. God's peaceable kingdom is expressed definitively in Jesus Christ, for "he is our peace, who has made us both [Gentile and Jew] one, and has broken down the dividing wall of hostility" (*Eph* 2:14). In Christ we see that God's love is radical, loving even the enemy. The resurrection of Jesus Christ is the ultimate sign of the victory of the way of Jesus. Salvation and ethics are based on and permeated by this way of Jesus.

164. *What is a Peace Church?* A peace church is a church called to bear witness to the gospel of peace grounded in Jesus Christ. The peace church places this conviction at the centre of its faith and life, its teaching, worship, ministry and practice, calling Jesus Lord and following him in his nonresistant and nonviolent way. A peace church is nothing other than the Church, the body of Christ. Every Church is called to be a peace church.[166]

165. The earliest Swiss Anabaptists, forerunners of the Mennonites, saw the necessity of separating the church from its allegiance to the state. Only in this way could they follow the nonviolent way of Jesus and uphold their confession of Jesus as Lord, in accordance with the early Christians of the apostolic era. Their stance of nonresistance and conscientious objection to war was a choice of faith (*Mt* 5:38-41). Within this frame of thinking, "just war" considerations had no place, and the church must distance itself from the state. For this reason, a peace church says farewell to Constantinianism, the liaison of church and state. Even more, the Church resists the captivity of the church in regard to her theological thinking.[167] For Mennonites, traditional Christology is often seen to have been weakened by "Constantinianism" with the result that the normative character of the teachings of Jesus is too often depreciated in ethics and ecclesiology. In addition, theology too tightly tied to state structures has often formulated social ethics from a top down perspective, looking to political leaders for articulation of what is possible rather than focusing on what Jesus taught his disciples and how that can concretely be lived out by the body of Christ in the world.

166. *Discipleship and Peacemaking.* The teachings and the example of Christ give orientation for our theology and teaching on peace. The concept of discipleship, of following Christ in life, is central for Mennonite theology. Mennonites insist that confessing Jesus Christ as Lord means that the humanity of Christ has ethical relevance. Though the decisions he made and the steps he took leading to his crucifixion must be interpreted in the context of his times, they reveal the love of God for his followers.[168] Christian love includes love of enemy, the message of forgiveness as a gift for everybody, the concern for those at the margins of society, and the call for a new community.

---

[166] Cf. Fernando Enns, *Friedenskirche in der Ökumene. Mennonitische Wurzeln einer Ethik der Gewaltfreiheit* (Göttingen: Vandenhoek & Ruprecht, 2003).

[167] Cf. F. Enns, *Friedenskirche, op. cit.,* and John Howard Yoder, "Peace without Eschatology" in: *The Royal Priesthood, op. cit.*

[168] Cf. John Howard Yoder, *The Politics of Jesus,* 2nd rev. ed., (Grand Rapids/Carlisle: Wm. B. Eerdmans/Paternoster, 1994).

167. An ultimate theological challenge is to spell out the consequences of the cross for our teaching on peace and war. The atonement is the foundation of our peace with God and with one another. Reconciliation and nonviolence belong to the heart of the Gospel. Therefore an ethic of nonresistance, nonviolence, and active peacemaking corresponds to our faith in God. God revealed his love for humanity in Jesus Christ, who was willing to die on the cross as a consequence of his message of the Kingdom of God. Thus the cross is the sign of God's love of his enemies (*Rom* 5:10f.). In the resurrection God confirms the way of Jesus and establishes new life. The conviction that 'love is stronger than death' sustains Christians where their faith leads to suffering.

168. What kinds of attitudes and activities are the marks of a peace church? At the heart of its worship is the celebration of God's presence. Witnessing to the presence of God in this world, the Church is a community of those being reconciled. In a "Believer's Church", reconciliation is reflected in all aspects of the church's life. Its discipline orients members to reconciliation and conflict resolution. In accordance with *Mt* 18:15-22, it applies "binding and loosing" to biblical interpretation and ethical decisions. The disciples' witness to the kingdom of God includes nonviolence, active peacemaking, and the confrontation of injustice. Resistance to violence means not only refusing to take part in it, but also serving victims and confronting aggressors. The peace church seeks to love the enemy while at the same time confronting evil and oppression. It advocates justice for all. It expresses conscientious objection to war and conscientious participation in state and society.

169. Mennonites engage in peace groups in congregations, participate on peace committees on the national level, and promote international peace networks via Mennonite World Conference and Mennonite Central Committee. The conviction that peace has to be built in many steps has led Mennonites to foster voluntary service on different levels: as relief work and disaster service, as educational work and the promotion of human rights. Methods of conflict transformation and mediation have been worked out and improved. Christian Peacemaker Teams are an initiative of Mennonites and other Historic Peace Churches to intervene in situations of armed conflict and protect threatened people by being present with them and putting themselves on the line.

170. Mennonites in all parts of the world grapple with peace issues and consider such a struggle to be a core practice of the Church. For some, 'nonresistance' would describe best their stance of faith in the sense of refusing to take part in war, shunning all forms of violence and even refusing service of any kind to government. For others, nonresistance no longer characterizes their conviction; and a faith-based pacifism would be a more accurate term. In some places in the world, Mennonites are moving in their theology and praxis from 'nonresistance' to active nonviolence and to a position of just peacemaking.[169] This includes the prophetic denunciation of violence through active criticism of government politics, as for example during the Balkan War.

---

[169] Cf. Glenn Stassen, ed., *Just Peacemaking: Ten Practices for Abolishing War* (Cleveland: Pilgrim Press, 1998); Duane K. Friesen, *Christian Peacemaking and International Conflict: A Realist Pacifist Perspective* (Scottdale/Waterloo: Herald Press, 1986).

171. Another dimension of peace understood biblically is protecting the integrity of creation. A lifestyle of simplicity and of responsible use of the world's limited resources has been a typical stance for Mennonites for a long time.

> "As stewards of God's earth, we are called to care for the earth and to bring rest and renewal to the land and everything that lives on it. As stewards of money and possessions, we are to live simply, practice mutual aid within the church, uphold economic justice, and give generously and cheerfully".[170]

Convergences

172. *Creation and Peace.* Mennonites and Catholics can agree that God, "who from one man has created the whole human race and made them live all over the face of the earth" (*Acts* 17:26) has destined humanity for one and the same goal, namely, communion with God's own self. Likewise, created in the image and likeness of God, human beings are called to unity with one another, through reciprocal self-giving (cf. *Gen* 1:26; *Jn* 17:21f.).[171] Redemption, moreover, has restored to creation the peace lost by sin (*Gen* 9:1-17; *Col* 1:19f.; *Rev* 21:5). As God's new creation, Christians are called to live a new life in peace with one another and with all humankind (*2 Cor* 13:11; *Rom* 12:18).

173. We also agree that the biblical vision of peace as *shalom* entails protecting the integrity of creation (*Gen* 1:26-31; 2:5-15; 9:7-17; *Ps* 104).[172] The Church is called to witness, in the spirit of stewardship, that people may live as caretakers and not exploiters of the earth.

174. *Christology and Peace.* The peace witness of both Mennonites and Catholics is rooted in Jesus Christ "who is our peace, who has made us both one . . . making peace that he might reconcile us both to God in one body through the cross" (*Eph* 2:14-16). We understand peace through the teachings, life and death of Jesus Christ. In his mission of reconciliation he remained faithful unto death on the cross, and his fidelity was confirmed in the resurrection. The cross is the sign of God's love of enemies.[173]

---

[170] *Confession of Faith in a Mennonite Perspective*, *op. cit.*, 21. Cf. also H. S. Bender *et al.*, "Simplicity" in *Mennonite Encyclopedia*, IV, *op. cit.*, pp. 529–530.

[171] For Catholics, the model for a vision of the union of humans with one another is based theologically on the union of the Trinity (cf. *Gaudium et spes*, 24).

[172] Cf. *Confession of Faith in a Mennonite Perspective*, *op. cit.*, 21. *Sollicitudo rei socialis*, 26, 29–30, esp. 34; Pope John Paul II, "Peace with God, Peace with All Creation", World Day of Peace Message, 1990.

[173] A quote from Menno Simons expresses the close theological bond in Christology between the peaceful nature of Jesus Christ and our lives: "Christ is everywhere represented to us as humble, meek, merciful, just, holy, wise, spiritual, long-suffering, patient, peaceable, lovely, obedient, and good, as the perfection of all things; for in him there is an upright nature. Behold, this is the image of God, of Christ as to the Spirit which we have as an example until we become like it in nature and reveal it by our walk" (Menno Simons, "The Spiritual Resurrection" (c. 1536), in J.C. Wenger, ed., *The Complete Writings*

175. *Ecclesiology and Peace.* The Church is called to be a peace church, a peacemaking church. This is based on a conviction that we hold in common. We hold that the Church, founded by Christ, is called to be a living sign and an effective instrument of peace, overcoming every form of enmity and reconciling all peoples in the peace of Christ (*Eph* 4:1-3).[174] We affirm that Christ, in his Church, through baptism, overcomes the differences between peoples (*Gal* 3:28). By virtue of their baptism into Christ, all Christians are called to be peacemakers. All forms of ethnic and inter-religious hatred and violence are incompatible with the gospel, and the Church has a special role in overcoming ethnic and religious differences and in building international peace.[175] Furthermore, we agree that it is a tragedy when Christians kill one another.

176. Catholics and Mennonites share an appreciation of the Church as different from simply human organizations, and together we stand for religious freedom and the independence of the Church. The freedom of the Church from state intervention enables her to offer witness to the wider society. In virtue of their dignity as children of God, moreover, all men and women possess the right to freedom of religion and conscience. No one should be forced to act contrary to conscience, particularly in matters of religion.

177. *Peace and Justice.* We affirm together that peace, in the sense of the biblical word *shalom,* consists of well being, wholeness, the harmony and rightness of relationships. As inheritors of this biblical tradition, we believe that justice, understood as right relationships, is the inseparable companion of peace. As the prophets testify, "the effect of justice will be peace and the result of righteousness quietness and trust forever" (*Is* 32:17; cf. *Ps* 85:10, 13).[176]

---

of Menno Simons (Scottdale: Herald Press, 1956), pp. 55f. Catholic teaching on the link between peace and the redemptive work of the Lord is best seen in *Gaudium et spes*; 38: "Undergoing death itself for all of us sinners (cf. *Jn* 3:16; *Rom* 5:8), he taught us by example that we too must shoulder that cross which the world and the flesh inflict upon those who search after peace and justice". See also *Gaudium et spes*; 28 and 32.

[174] Cf. *Confession of Faith in a Mennonite Perspective,* 22, *op. cit.,* 22; *Gaudium et spes,* 42 and 78.

[175] Cf. Pope John Paul II, "To Build Peace, Respect Minorities", World Day of Peace Message, 1989; *Gaudium et spes,* 42. A widely accepted Mennonite standpoint with respect to all conflict, including international conflict, is expressed in *A Declaration on Peace: In God's People the World's Renewal Has Begun,* co-authored by Douglas Gwyn, George Hunsinger, Eugene F. Roop, John Howard Yoder (Scottdale/Waterloo: Herald Press, 1991), which states in part: "The church's most effective witness and action against war . . . consists simply in the stand she takes in and through her members in the face of war. Unless the church, trusting the power of God in whose hand the destinies of the nations lie, is willing to 'fall into the ground and die,' to renounce war absolutely, whatever sacrifice of freedoms, advantages, or possessions this might entail, even to the point of counseling a nation not to resist foreign conquest and occupation, she can give no prophetic message for the world of nations" (pp. 74f.).

[176] Cf. *Confession of Faith in a Mennonite Perspective,* 22, *op. cit., Populorum progressio,* 76–80; *Centesimus annus,* 52.

178. We agree that the Gospel's vision of peace includes active non-violence for the defence of human life and human rights, for the promotion of economic justice for the poor, and in the interest of fostering solidarity among peoples. Likewise, peace is the realization of the fundamental right to live a life in dignity, and so have access to all means to accomplish this: land, work, health, and education. For this reason, the Church is called to stand in solidarity with the poor and to be an advocate for the oppressed. A peace built on oppression is a false peace.

179. We hold the conviction in common that reconciliation, nonviolence, and active peacemaking belong to the heart of the Gospel (*Mt* 5:9; *Rom* 12:14-21; *Eph* 6:15). Christian peacemaking embraces active nonviolence in the resolution of conflict both in domestic disputes and in international ones,[177] and for resolving conflict situations. We believe that the availability of such practices to individual groups and governments reduces the temptation to turn to arms, even as a last resort.

180. *Discipleship and Peace.* Both agree that discipleship, understood as following Christ in life in accordance with the teaching and example of Jesus, is basic to the Christian life. The earthly existence of Jesus is normative for human well being (*Jn* 13:1-17; *Phil* 2:1-11).[178] The decisions Jesus made and the steps he took leading to his crucifixion reveal the centrality of love, including love of enemy, in human life (*Mt* 5:38-48). They also include the message of forgiveness as a gift for everybody, the concern for those at the margins of society, and the call for a new community. Love of neighbour is the fulfilment of the law, and love of our enemies is the perfection of love (*Rm* 13:8; *Mt* 5:43-48).[179]

181. Christian peace witness belongs integrally to our walk as followers of Christ and to the life of the Church as " the household of God" and "a dwelling place of God in the Spirit" (*Eph* 2:19, 22). Christian communities have the responsibility to discern the signs of the times and to respond to developments and events with appropriate peace initiatives based on the life and teaching of Jesus (*Lk* 19:41-44).[180] The Mennonite Church tends to initiate its witness in and through the discerning congregation:

> "Led by the Spirit, and beginning in the church, we witness to all people that violence is not the will of God. . . We give our ultimate loyalty to the God of grace and peace, who guides the church daily in overcoming evil with good, who empowers us to do justice, and who sustains us in the glorious hope of the peaceable reign of God".[181]

In the Catholic Church, peace initiatives come in many forms: from parishes, communities of faith and religious movements, from justice and peace or human

---

[177] Cf. *Confession of Faith in a Mennonite Perspective*, 22, *op. cit.*; *Centesimus annus*, 23.

[178] Cf. *Confession of Faith in a Mennonite Perspective*, 17, *op. cit.*; *Gaudium et spes*, 32.

[179] Cf. *Confession of Faith in a Mennonite Perspective*, 22, *op. cit.*; *Gaudium et spes*, 28.

[180] Cf. *Octogesima adveniens*, 4.

[181] *Confession of Faith in a Mennonite Perspective*, 22, *op. cit.*

rights commissions, from individual bishops and conferences of bishops, from the Holy Father and various offices of the Holy See.[182]

182. God revealed his love for humanity in Jesus Christ, who was willing to die on the cross as a consequence of his message of the Kingdom of God. The cross is the sign of God's love of his enemies (*Rom* 5:10f.). For both Catholics and Mennonites the ultimate personal and ecclesial challenge is to spell out the consequences of the cross for our teaching on peace and war. We acknowledge suffering as a possible consequence of our witness to the Gospel of peace. We note with joy that we have a common appreciation for martyrs, "the great cloud of witnesses" (*Heb* 12:1), who have given their lives in witness to truth.[183] Together we hold that "God's foolishness is wiser than human wisdom, and God's weakness is stronger than human strength" (*1 Cor* 1:25).

183. Mennonites and Catholics live with the expectation that discipleship entails suffering. Jesus challenges us: "If any want to become my followers, let them deny themselves and take up their cross and follow me" (*Mk* 8:34). Love is stronger than death – this faith sustains Christians where their faith leads to suffering. Catholics affirm with Pope John Paul II:

> "It is by uniting his own sufferings for the sake of truth and freedom to the sufferings of Christ on the Cross that man is able to accomplish the miracle of peace and is in a position to discern the often narrow path between the cowardice which gives in to evil and the violence which, under the illusion of fighting evil, only makes it worse".[184]

Both Mennonites and Catholics take their inspiration from Gospel texts such as Mark 10:35-45 and Luke 22:24-27, where Jesus invites his followers to offer up their lives as servants.

184. Both our communities endeavour to foster the peaceable virtues: forgiveness, love of enemies, respect for the life and dignity of others, restraint, gentleness, mercy, and the spirit of self-sacrifice. We also attempt to impart the spiritual resources for peacemaking to our members. The mission of the Church has an eschatological dimension. It anticipates the kingdom of God. The Church lives in the tension between "already now" and "not yet". Already now the Messianic time has come. But the past age has not yet come to an end; its rules and values continue to exist. In this parallel existence of the old and the new the Church has the decisive function: to foster peace and to incarnate the new order of the kingdom of God by helping its members to orient themselves according to the rules of the kingdom.

---

[182] Cf. *Gaudium et spes*, 89–90.

[183] For Mennonites, see *Martyrs Mirror, op. cit.*; for Catholics, in addition to the long liturgical tradition of commemorating martyrs and other witnesses to the faith in the course of the centuries, during the celebration of the Great Jubilee of the Year 2000, there was an ecumenical commemoration of "recent witnesses and martyrs". See also Robert Royal, *The Catholic Martyrs of the Twentieth Century* (New York: Crossroads, 2000).

[184] *Centesimus annus*, 25.

185. Mennonites and Catholics share the common conviction that worship and prayer belong to the core of Christian peace work. We celebrate what we have received from God. We cry out to God and we plead for peace. In prayer, we are renewed and by prayer we receive orientation. When we meet for ecumenical prayer services, we overcome existing divisions between us, and we experience communion with God and with one another in faith.

Divergences

186. *Church and Society*. While Catholics and Mennonites regard political authority as part of the God-given moral order of the universe, they tend to diverge on the question of participation in government. Catholics understand the social nature of humanity to be blessed by Christ's life and teaching.[185] Participation in government is honoured and encouraged as a contribution to the common good, and military service is respected.[186] At the same time, nonviolent action, conscientious objection, and resistance to immoral orders are strongly endorsed.[187] Because of their long history of persecution and discrimination, Mennonites have tended to mistrust the state. They still tend to be critical of Christian involvement in government because of the use of violence involved and the possible corruption of power.

187. *Nonviolence and Just War*. Mennonites include nonviolence as an essential component of discipleship in the sense that in principle they refuse to use violence in all situations. In situations of conflict, however, both Catholics and some Mennonites acknowledge that when all recourse to nonviolent means has failed, the state or international authorities may use force in defence of the innocent. For Mennonites, however, Christians should not participate in this kind of action.[188] For Catholics, Christians ought to be committed "as far as possible, to live in peace with everyone" (*Rom* 12:18) and to encourage their governments to resolve disputes peacefully, but Christians may take up arms under legitimate authority in exceptional circumstances for the defence of the innocent. Service in the military may be virtuous, but conscientious objection to military service is also respected. The Just War position provides tools for the prevention and limitation of conflict as well as for warranting force by political authorities. The principle of "right intention" requires that force be used only to restore the peace and to protect the innocent and not in a spirit of vengeance, a quest for domination, or out of other motives inconsistent with love of enemy.

188. Mennonites and Catholics have somewhat different views on non-resistance. Mennonites hold to non-resistance on principle without exception, while Catholics affirm non-resistance, but allow for exceptions. For Mennonites, non-resistance is part of the new way of Jesus (*Mt* 5:38-41). There is an expectation that Christians are called to adhere to the principles of ethics implied in the 'new way,' and that through the power of the Holy Spirit and the encouraging support of the Christian

---

[185] Cf. *Gaudium et spes*, 32.

[186] Cf. *Gaudium et spes*, 74, 79.

[187] Cf. *Gaudium et spes*, 78–79.

[188] Cf. *Schleitheim Confession*, 1527, VI., in Loewen, *op. cit.*, pp. 80f.

community, it is possible to walk the way faithfully. For Catholics, non-resistance is "a counsel of perfection", and Catholics, as well as all people of goodwill, are required to resist grave public evil nonviolently, if at all possible, but in exceptional circumstance by limited use of force exercised by public authorities.[189]

Areas of Future Study

189. Many questions remain to be explored. Among these are the following: 1) What is the relationship of the different Christian peace positions to the apostolic faith? 2) What place do initiatives for conflict resolution and non-violent direct action have in a Catholic theology of peace? 3) What is the relation of human rights and justice to the non-violent resolution of conflict in contemporary Mennonite theology? 4) How can we meet the challenge of developing common theological perspectives on peace that reflect the diverse voices of men and women from different contexts world wide? 5) What is the role of the Church in promoting a culture of peace in civil society and establishing institutions for the practice of non-violence in public life? 6) What is the relationship between peace, peace witness, the call to Christian unity and the unity of the human family? 7) How is ethical discernment—interpreting the signs of the times in regard to a unified and concerted Christian peace witness— carried out in Mennonite and Catholic communities on the local and global levels?

III

TOWARD A HEALING OF MEMORIES

190. Bitter memories have resulted from past conflicts and divisions between Christians and from the sufferings they have produced over ensuing centuries. Mutual hostility and negative images have persisted between separated Christians of the Catholic and Reformation traditions from the time of the divisions of the sixteenth century until today. It has therefore been the intention and hope from the beginning of this dialogue between Mennonites and Catholics that our conversations would contribute to a healing of memories.

191. The healing of memories involves several aspects. It requires a purification of memories so that both groups can share a picture of the past that is historically accurate. This calls for a spirit of repentance—a penitential spirit—on both sides for the harm that the conflicts have done to the body of Christ, to the proclamation of the Gospel, and to one another. Healing the memories of divided Christians also entails the recognition that, despite conflict, and though still separated, they continue to hold in common much of the Christian faith. In this sense they remain linked to one another. Moreover a healing of memories involves the openness to move beyond the isolation of the past, and to consider concrete steps toward new relations. Together, these factors can contribute to reconciliation between divided Christians.

---

[189] Cf. *Gaudium et spes*, 78; *Evangelium vitae*, 41; *Catechism of the Catholic Church*, 2267.

A. The Purification of Memories

192. The healing of memories requires, first of all, a purification of memories. This involves facing those difficult events of the past that give rise to divergent interpretations of what happened and why. Past events and their circumstances need to be reconstructed as precisely as possible. We need to understand the mentalities, the conditions, and the living dynamics in which these events took place. A purification of memory includes an effort to purge "from personal and collective conscience all forms of resentment or violence left by the inheritance of the past on the basis of a new and rigorous historical-theological judgment, which becomes the foundation for a renewed moral way of acting".[190] On this basis, both Catholics and Mennonites have the possibility of embarking on a sure and trustworthy way of thinking about and relating to each other that is in accordance with Christian love (cf. *1 Cor* 13).

193. Our effort to re-read church history together as Catholics and Mennonites (Chapter I) helped us begin to reconcile our divergent memories of the past. We saw that "our relationship, or better the lack of it, began in a context of rupture and separation. Since then, from the sixteenth century to the present, theological polemics have persistently nourished negative images and narrow stereotypes of each other".[191] Because of these dynamics, we have "sometimes restricted our views of the history of Christianity to those aspects that seemed to be most in agreement with the self-definition of our respective ecclesial communities".[192]

194. In our study of history we began to assess together, and in a fresh way, events or periods of history that Mennonites and Catholics have traditionally interpreted very differently from one another. For example, we have seen a more nuanced and complex picture of the Middle Ages, including the so-called "Constantinian era", than either side typically saw when explanations of those centuries were heavily influenced by post-Reformation polemics. In considering the era of the sixteenth century Reformation, we saw that although there were serious abuses and problems within the Catholic Church at that time, there were also efforts to reform the church from within. Recent studies have indicated that Christian piety was flourishing in many ways on the eve of the Reformation and that it is too simplistic to describe the Christianity of that day as in a state of crisis or decline. Recent historical studies illustrating these factors call us to continue our study of that period, and to look for fresh evaluations of the circumstances that led to the separation of Christians at the time.

195. On the question of Christian witness to peace and non-violence based on the Gospel, our study of history suggested points of reference that could open the door to mutual support and cooperative efforts between Catholics and Mennonites. For example, we observed that within the often-violent society of the Middle Ages there was, as part of the heritage of the Catholic Church, an uninterrupted tradition of ecclesiastical peace movements.[193] We saw also that even though some Anabaptist-

---

[190] *Memory and Reconciliation*, 5.1.
[191] Para. 24 above.
[192] Para. 25 above.
[193] Cf. para. 64 above.

related groups allowed the use of the sword in the establishment of the kingdom of God, many were faithful to principles of pacifism and non-violence from the beginning, and soon these positions were accepted doctrinally and held consistently by Anabaptists and Mennonites.[194] Purifying our memory on these points means that both Catholics and Mennonites need to continually struggle to maintain the Gospel's perspective on questions of peace and non-violence. And both can find resources in the earlier history of the church to assist us in shaping a Christian witness to peace in today's violent world.

196. Briefly, we believe not only that reconciliation and purification of historical memories must continue in our communities, but also that this process may lead Catholics and Mennonites to new cooperation in witnessing to the Gospel of peace.

197. On the Catholic side, statements of the Second Vatican Council reflect a purification of memory. Unlike in the past when others were blamed for ruptures that took place, the Council acknowledged the culpability of Catholics too. The Council made the admission with reference to past ruptures that "at times, men of both sides were to blame"[195] for what happened. Furthermore, in an open spirit inviting dialogue, the Council further acknowledged—and this reflects a Catholic attitude toward Mennonites today—that "one cannot impute the sin of separation to those who at present are born into these communities and are instilled therein with Christ's faith. The Catholic Church accepts them respect and affection as brothers".[196] In a similar open spirit supporting dialogue, a recent statement of the Executive Committee of Mennonite World Conference has said: "We see Christian unity not as an option we might choose or as an outcome we could create, but as an urgent imperative to be obeyed".[197]

B. A Spirit of Repentance, a Penitential Spirit

198. A healing of memories involves also a spirit of repentance, a penitential spirit. When Christians are divided and live with hostility towards one another, it is the proclamation of the Gospel that often suffers. The integrity and power of the Gospel is severely diminished in the mind of the hearer, when Christians witness to it in divergent and contradictory ways. Therefore, Christians separated from one another, including Catholics and Mennonites, have reason to ask God's forgiveness as well as forgiveness from each other. In doing so, they do not modify their convictions about the Christian faith. On the contrary, a penitential spirit can be another incentive to resolve, through dialogue, any theological divergences that prevent them from sharing together "the faith that was once for all entrusted to the saints" (*Jude* 1:3).

---

[194] Cf. para. 39 above.

[195] *Unitatis redintegratio*, 3.

[196] *Ibid.*

[197] "God Calls Us to Christian Unity", a statement adopted by the executive of Mennonite World Conference, Goshen, Indiana, July, 1998.

Catholic Delegation Statement

199. While a penitential spirit with respect to Christian divisions was reflected in the Second Vatican Council, the Catholic Church took a further step during the Jubilee year 2000, on March 12, the "Day of Pardon". In the Catholic tradition the Holy Year is a time of purification. Thus, "in order to reawaken consciences, enabling Christians to enter the third millennium with greater openness to God and his plan of love",[198] during the mass of the first Sunday of Lent, Pope John Paul led the Catholic Church in a universal prayer including a confession of sins committed by members of the Church during the past millennium, and a plea to God for forgiveness. He stated that, while "the Church is holy because Christ is her head and her spouse [and] the Spirit is her life-giving soul . . . , [nonetheless] the children of the Church know the experience of sin. . . . For this reason the Church does not cease to implore God's forgiveness for the sins of her members".[199] Two of the seven categories of sins identified as having been committed during the previous millennium, and consequently confessed that day, were "sins which have harmed the unity of the Church" and "sins committed in the service of truth".[200] At that Lenten mass, these categories of sins were presented in a generic way, without mentioning specific cases or situations.

200. During the ceremony, there was confession of "sins which have rent the unity of the body of Christ and wounded fraternal charity". On behalf of the Catholic Church, the Pope beseeched God the Father that while "on the night before his Passion, your son prayed for the unity of those who believe in him . . . , [nonetheless] believers have opposed one another, becoming divided, and have mutually condemned one another and fought against one another". Therefore, he concluded, we "urgently implore your forgiveness and we beseech the gift of a repentant heart, so that all Christians, reconciled with you and with one another, will be able, in one body and in one spirit, to experience anew the joy of full communion".[201]

201. In regard to the "confession of sins committed in the service of truth", the introductory prayer asked that each one of us recognize "that even men of the Church, in the name of faith and morals, have sometimes used methods not in keeping with the Gospel in the solemn duty of defending the truth". The prayer then recited by the Pope recalled that "in certain periods of history Christians have at times given in to intolerance and have not been faithful to the great commandment of love, sullying in this way the face of the Church, your Spouse". He then prayed, "Have mercy on your sinful children and accept our resolve to seek and promote truth in the gentleness of charity, in the firm knowledge that truth can prevail only in virtue of truth itself".[202]

---

[198] Pope John Paul II, Angelus, March 12, 2000.

[199] *Ibid.*

[200] "Universal Prayer for Forgiveness", March 12, 2000 in *Information Service* 103 (2000/I–II), p. 56.

[201] *Ibid.*

[202] *Ibid.*

202. Catholics today are encouraged to look at the conflicts and divisions among Christians in general and, in the present context, at the conflicts between Mennonites and Catholics, in light of this call for repentance expressed during the "Day of Pardon". For their part, in the spirit of the "Day of Pardon", Catholics acknowledge that even the consideration of mitigating factors, such as cultural conditioning in previous centuries, which frequently converged to create assumptions which justified intolerance, "does not exonerate the Church from the obligation to express profound regret for the weaknesses of so many of her sons and daughters".[203] Without compromising truth, Catholics in this dialogue can apply this spirit of repentance to the conflicts between Catholics and Mennonites in the sixteenth century, and can express a penitential spirit, asking forgiveness for any sins which were committed against Mennonites, asking God's mercy for that, and God's blessing for a new relationship with Mennonites today. We join our sentiments to those expressed by Walter Cardinal Kasper when he addressed the Mennonite World Conference representatives of the Catholic-Mennonite dialogue group on the occasion of their visit to Rome in November, 2001:

> "Is it not the case that we, Catholics and Mennonites, have mutually condemned one another? Each saw the other as deviating from the apostolic faith. Let us forgive and ask forgiveness. The authorities in centuries past often resolved problems in society by severe means, punishing with imprisonment or death those who were seen as undermining society. Especially, in the sixteenth century, the Anabaptists were among those who suffered greatly in this regard. I surely regret those instances when this took place in Catholic societies".

Mennonite Delegation Statement

203. The statement of the Executive Committee of Mennonite World Conference, "God Calls Us to Christian Unity", invites a spirit of repentance on the part of the MWC community of churches in relations to other Christians, including Catholics. The statement says, in part:

> "As Mennonites and Brethren in Christ, we give thanks to God for brothers and sisters of other traditions around the globe who accept the claims of Scripture and seek to live as followers of our Lord. We confess that we have not done all we could to follow God's call to relate in love and mutual counsel to other brothers and sisters who confess the name of Jesus Christ as Lord and seek to follow him. We have seen peacemaking and reconciliation as callings of all Christian disciples, but confess that we have not done all we could to overcome divisions within our circles and to work toward unity with other brothers and sisters".[204]

In regard to the sixteenth century rupture, we recognize that as the Anabaptists sought to be faithful followers of Jesus Christ, they called into question the established

---

[203] *Tertio millennio adveniente*, 1994, 35.

[204] See footnote 197 above.

churches and societies. We acknowledge that there were diverse and sometimes divergent currents within the Anabaptist movement. We believe that it was initially difficult for contemporaries to distinguish between the Anabaptists we claim as our spiritual forebears—those committed to Biblical pacifism, ready to suffer martyrdom for the cause of Christ—and those who took the sword, thinking that they were doing God's will in preparing the way for the return of Jesus. We regret Anabaptist words and deeds that contributed to fracturing the body of Christ.

204. We confess also that in spite of a commitment to follow Jesus Christ in daily life, we and others in our family of faith have frequently failed to demonstrate love towards Catholics. Too often, from the sixteenth century to the present, we have thoughtlessly perpetuated hostile images and false stereotypes of Catholics and of the Catholic Church. For this, we express our regret and ask forgiveness.

Common Statement

205. Together we, Catholic and Mennonite delegations, recognize and regret that sixteenth century Christians, including Catholics and Anabaptists, were unable to resolve the problems of the church of that time in such way as to prevent divisions in the body of Christ that have lasted to the present day.

206. Together we acknowledge and regret that indifference, tension, and hostility between Catholics and Mennonites exist in some places today, and this for a variety of historical or contemporary reasons. Together we reject the use of any physical coercion or verbal abuse in situations of disagreement and we call on all Christians to do likewise. We commit ourselves to self-examination, dialogue, and interaction that manifest Jesus Christ's reconciling love, and we encourage our brothers and sisters everywhere to join us in this commitment.

C. Ascertaining a Shared Christian Faith

207. Theological dialogue can contribute to healing of memories by assisting the dialogue partners to ascertain the degree to which they have continued to share the Christian faith despite centuries of separation. Mennonites and Catholics in this dialogue explained their own traditions to one another. This contributed to a deeper mutual understanding and to the discovery that we hold in common many basic aspects of the Christian faith and heritage. These shared elements, along with unresolved questions and disagreements, are outlined in Chapter II.

208. Catholics and Mennonites are convinced that the first responsibility of a Christian is the praise of God and that all aspects of Christian life must be rooted in prayer. Therefore in the course of the five years of this dialogue, we started and ended each day with prayer together. Together we read and reflected on the Scriptures and sang hymns. Each year we worshipped in each other's churches on Sunday in order to deepen mutual understanding of our traditions.

209. Among the important aspects of the Christian life that Catholics and Mennonites hold in common, are faith in Jesus Christ as Lord and Saviour (fully divine and fully human), the Trinitarian faith as expressed in the Apostles Creed, and numerous perspectives on the church. There is also much that we can agree on concerning baptism and the Lord's Supper as fundamental grace-filled celebrations of God's saving acts in

Christ. We share a great deal in regard to the role of the church on matters of mission and evangelism, peace and justice, and life of discipleship. Moreover, Mennonites and Catholics both face the challenge of how to communicate the faith in an increasingly secular world, and both struggle with the complexities of the relationship between church and society.

210. While recognizing that we hold basic convictions of faith in common, we have also identified significant differences that continue to divide us and thus require further dialogue. Nonetheless, and although we are not in full unity with one another, the substantial amount of the Apostolic faith which we realize today that we share, allows us as members of the Catholic and Mennonite delegations to see one another as brothers and sisters in Christ. We hope that others may have similar experiences, and that these may contribute to a healing of memories.

D. Improving our relationships

211. We believe that another fundamental part of the healing of memories is the call to foster new relationships. The significant elements of our common understanding of basic Christian faith ascertained in this dialogue may provide a sufficient theological foundation on which to build. Our experience of re-reading history conjointly suggests that looking together at those periods in which our conflicts initially took place may shed new light on the past and foster a climate for better relationships in the future. For centuries our communities lived with the memories generated from the conflicts of the sixteenth century and in isolation from one another. Can we not increase our efforts to create new relationships today so that future generations may look back to the twenty-first century with positive memories of a time in which Mennonites and Catholics began increasingly to serve Christ together?

212. Indeed, as the Introduction to this report already suggested, the building of improved relationships is beginning as Mennonites and Catholics talk to one another. On the international level, this dialogue is an important sign that the Catholic Church and the Mennonite World Conference are willing, for the sake of Christ, to strive for mutual understanding and better relationships. We believe that one should not underestimate the importance of what it means for our two families of Christians, separated for centuries, to enter into conversation.

213. Locally as well, in several parts of the world, some Catholics and Mennonites already engaged with each other in theological dialogue and in practical cooperation. In various places collaboration between the Mennonite Central Committee and Caritas or Catholic Relief Services is taking place in humanitarian causes. We hear of Mennonites working with Catholics in the USA, in the Middle East, and in India, to name but a few examples. And even though numerous local Catholic-Mennonite initiatives are unofficial and personal, they serve the wider church by helping to overcome false caricatures about and mutual prejudices of each other.

214. In light of this situation, the dialogue members encourage Mennonites and Catholics to engage each other in joint study and cooperative service. Areas of interaction could include a review of history text books on each side, participation in the week of prayer for Christian unity, mutual engagement in missiological reflection, peace and justice initiatives, some programs of faith formation among our respective members,

and 'get acquainted' visits between Catholic and Mennonite communities, locally and more widely.

Conclusion

215. After having worked with each other over these five years, we, Catholic and Mennonite members of this dialogue, want to testify together that our mutual love for Christ has united us and accompanied us in our discussions. Our dialogue has fortified the common conviction that it is possible to experience reconciliation and the healing of memories. Therefore we beseech God to bestow divine grace upon us for the healing of past relationships between Mennonites and Catholics, and we thank God for present commitments to reconciliation within the body of Christ. Together we pray that God may bless this new relationship between our two families of faith, and that the Holy Spirit may enlighten and enliven us in our common journey on the path forward.

APPENDIX A

Bibliography of Dialogue Papers and Their Authors

Strasbourg, France, October 14–18, 1998

Howard John Loewen, "The Mennonite Tradition: An Interpretation".

James Puglisi, S.A., "A Self-Description of Who We Are as Catholics Today".

Neal Blough, "Anabaptist Images of Roman Catholics during the Sixteenth Century".

Peter Nissen, "The Catholic Response to the Anabaptist Movement in the Sixteenth Century".

Venice, Italy, Oct. 12–18, 1999

Neal Blough, "The Anabaptist Idea of the Restitution of the Early Church".

Peter Nissen, "The Anabaptist/Mennonite Tradition of Faith and Spirituality and its Medieval Roots".

Helmut Harder, "A Contemporary Mennonite Theology of the Church".

James Puglisi, S.A., "Toward a Common Understanding of the Church".

Thomashof, Germany, Nov. 24 to Nov. 30, 2000

Peter Nissen, "The Impact of the Constantinian Shift on the Church: A Catholic Perspective".

Alan Kreider, "Conversion and Christendom: An Anabaptist Perspective".

Drew Christiansen, S.J., "What is a Peace Church? A Roman Catholic Perspective".

Mario Higueros, "Justice, the Inseparable Companion of Peace".

Andrea Lange, "What is a Peace Church? An Answer from a Mennonite Perspective".

Assisi, Italy, Nov. 27 to Dec. 3, 2001

Peter Nissen, "Church and Secular Power(s) in the Middle Ages".

Neal Blough, "From the Edict of Milan to Vatican II, via Theodosius, Clovis, Charlemagne and the Fourth Lateran Council or Why Some Mennonites Can't Quite Trust the 'Declaration on Religious Freedom'".

Helmut Harder, "What Anabaptist-Mennonite Confessions of Faith Say About Baptism and the Lord's Supper".

James F. Puglisi, S.A., "Contemporary Theology of the Sacraments with Particular Attention to Christian Initiation (Baptism and Eucharist)".

Appendix B

Mennonite and Catholic Contribution to the World Council of Churches' *Decade to Overcome Violence*

INTRODUCTION

An international dialogue between Catholics and Mennonites took place between 1998 and 2003, beginning with the theme "Toward a Healing of Memories", and concluding with a report entitled *Called Together to be Peacemakers* (CTBP). In the hope that, on the basis of that dialogue, Catholics and Mennonites may together offer suggestions for the World Council of Churches' *Decade to Overcome Violence* (DOV), and especially in reference to the International Ecumenical Peace Convocation (IEPC) in 2011 with which it culminates, the Pontifical Council for Promoting Christian Unity and the Mennonite World Conference sponsored a brief conference 23–25 October 2007 in consultation with the DOV office. It took place at the Centro Pro Unione in Rome. As a result we now submit some theological reflections which Mennonites and Catholics, committed to overcoming violence, may affirm together as a witness to peace in the ecumenical context. We hope these reflections can be useful to others as preparation continues for the IEPC.

We begin by identifying biblical and theological foundations of peace. These appear under the sub-headings of *Creation, Christology*, and *Ecclesiology*. Then follows a section on peace and discipleship. We conclude with some challenges and recommendations which might be considered as the focus of workshops at the IEPC.

I. BIBLICAL-THEOLOGICAL FOUNDATIONS OF PEACE

A. Creation: Peace as Gift and Promise

From the beginning of creation, the God of *shalom* "who from one man has created the whole human race and made them live all over the face of the earth" (*Acts* 17:26), has destined all humanity for one and the same goal, namely, communion with God. This harmonious relationship reminds us that since human beings are created in the image and likeness of God, we are called to a life of unity with one another through reciprocal self-giving (cf. *Gen* 1:26; *Jn* 17:21f.). Although sin has marred our harmonious relationship with God and with one another, redemption through Christ has restored to creation the possibility of peace marred by sin (*Gen* 9:1-17; *Col* 1:19f.; *Rev* 21:5). As God's new creation, Christians are called to life in peace with one another, with all humankind, and with all creation (*Acts* 10:36; *2 Cor* 13:11; *Rom* 12:18).

The depth of the *shalom* offered by Jesus is seen in his farewell address to his disciples (*Jn* 14:27-31). It is customary, in Jewish leave-taking, to offer peace as a parting gift. Jesus goes deeper by offering the gift of peace by way of a participation in his very self. The peace of Christ flows from his very being, which is united to the Father in love. The world cannot give this peace because it does not know this intimate "being-in-peace" with the author of all peace. The peace that Jesus gives is the peace infused by the spirit of the Beatitudes. This peace makes nonviolence possible, since its true claimants speak and act in accordance with the logic of the selfless love of Jesus Christ.

The biblical vision of peace as *shalom* includes the protection of the integrity of creation (*Gen* 1:26-31; 2:5-15; 9:7-17; *Ps* 104). The Church calls people to live as stewards of the earth, and not as exploiters. The gift of peace flows from the very being of a gracious God and touches all of creation. As God is generous and faithful to his promise of peace, we in turn need to receive this gift and employ it responsibly in our relationship with God, who has entrusted each other and the whole of creation to our care.

B. Christology: Jesus Christ, the Foundation of Our Peace

The peace witness of both Mennonites and Catholics is rooted in Jesus Christ. He "is our peace, who has made us both one . . . making peace that he might reconcile us both to God in one body through the cross" (*Eph* 2:14-16). We understand peace through the teachings, the life, and the death of Jesus Christ. He taught us to turn the other cheek, to love our enemies, to pray for our persecutors (*Matt* 5:39ff.), and not to use deadly weapons (*Matt* 26:52). In his mission of reconciliation, Jesus remained faithful even unto death, thereby manifesting the peace-making dimension of divine love and confirming the depth of God as a lover of humanity. Jesus' fidelity was confirmed in the resurrection.

Peace and the Cross

God revealed his love for humanity in Jesus Christ, who died on the cross as a consequence of his message of the Kingdom of God. The cross is the sign of God's love of enemies (*Rom* 5:10f.). For both Catholics and Mennonites the ultimate personal and ecclesial challenge is to spell out the consequences of the cross for our teaching on peace and war, and for our response in the face of injustice and violence.

In looking upon the cross of Christ we come to realize what the atonement means for us. As the apostle Peter wrote: "He himself bore our sins in his body on the cross, so that, free from sins, we might live for righteousness; by his wounds you have been healed" (*1 Pet* 2:24). That is, through the cross Jesus makes our peace with God who offers us the *shalom* of a new creation while we are still sinners (*Rom* 5:8).

At the same time the cross beckons us to follow in the steps of Jesus who "did not regard equality with God as something to be exploited" (*Phil* 2:6). Rather, "when he was abused, he did not return abuse; when he suffered, he did not threaten; but he entrusted himself to the one who judges justly" (2:23). Thus, "in Christ, there is a new creation" (*2 Cor* 5:17) in which we now take up our cross and follow his way of peace and righteousness.

Peace and Suffering

We acknowledge suffering as a possible consequence of our witness to the Gospel of peace. We do not live in a utopian world. Following Christ will require costly discipleship. Mennonites and Catholics live with the expectation that discipleship entails suffering. Jesus challenges us: "If any want to become my followers, let them deny themselves and take up their cross and follow me" (*Mk* 8:34). The faith that love is stronger than death sustains Christians in their suffering. Yet, we are called to suffer and to alleviate suffering rather than to compound it. Catholics affirm with Pope John Paul II:

> "It is by uniting his own sufferings for the sake of truth and freedom to the sufferings of Christ on the Cross that man is able to accomplish the miracle of peace and is in a position to discern the often narrow path between the cowardice which gives in to evil and the violence which, under the illusion of fighting evil, only makes it worse" (*Centesimus annus*, 25; cf. *Gaudium et spes*, 42 and 78).

Reflecting the same conviction, a recent Mennonite confession of faith states:

> "Led by the Spirit, and beginning in the church, we witness to all people that violence is not the will of God . . . We give our ultimate loyalty to the God of grace and peace, who guides the church daily in overcoming evil with good, who empowers us to do justice, and who sustains us in the glorious hope of the peaceable reign of God/(*Confession of Faith in a Mennonite Perspective* [Scottdale/Waterloo: Herald Press, 1995, Art. 22]).

Both Mennonites and Catholics take their inspiration from Gospel texts such as Mark 10:35-45 and Luke 22:24-27, where Jesus invites his followers to offer up their lives as servants. We note with joy our common appreciation for martyrs, "the great cloud of witnesses" (*Heb* 12:1), who have given their lives in witness to truth. Together, we hold that "God's foolishness is wiser than human wisdom, and God's weakness is stronger than human strength" (*1 Cor* 1:25). This commitment has implications for how we understand the church and what it means to be the church in the world.

C. Ecclesiology

The ecclesiological marks of the peace church derive from her message of reconciliation, her commitment to nonviolence, her freedom, her mission, her oneness, and her hope of salvation.

Peace and Reconciliation

Together Catholics and Mennonites affirm that the true vocation of the church is to be the community of the reconciled and of reconcilers. We accept this calling "from God, who reconciled us through Christ, and has given us the ministry of reconciliation" (*2 Cor* 5:18). Our similar identities as "peace churches" (Mennonite) and as a "peacemaking church" (Catholic) derive from our commitment to be followers and imitators of Jesus Christ, the Prince of Peace and Lord of the Church. By their baptismal commitment to Christ, all Christians are called to the way of peace and reconciliation.

Peace and Nonviolence

In the midst of a world that has not known how to accept or employ the peace that Jesus brings, it is the holy calling of the church to witness, by its very being, to the way of peace and nonviolence. The Church is called to be a peace church. This calling is based on the conviction we hold in common as Catholics and Mennonites, that the Church, founded by Christ, is to be a living sign and an effective instrument of peace, overcoming every form of enmity and reconciling all peoples in the peace of Christ (*Eph* 4:1-3). We hold the conviction in common that reconciliation, nonviolence, and active peacemaking belong to the heart of the Gospel (*Mt* 5:9; *Rom* 12:14-21; *Eph* 6:15). Mennonites and Catholics affirm that the power of Christ overcomes divisions between peoples (*Eph* 2:13-22; *Gal* 3:28). On this basis, the Church bears the responsibility, in the name of Christ, to work at overcoming ethnic and religious violence, and to contribute to the building of a peace culture among races and nations.

Together Mennonites and Catholics agree that the path of violence is no solution to the problem of enmity between persons, groups or nations. Christian peacemaking embraces active nonviolence in the transformation of conflict in both domestic and international disputes. Furthermore, we regard it as a tragedy and a grave sin when Christians hate and kill one another. The availability of resources for the practice of nonviolence to individual groups and governments reduces the temptation to turn to arms, even as a last resort.

Peace and Freedom

Together, Catholics and Mennonites share the conviction that the Church should be independent of society's human organizations. That is, the Church should enjoy religious freedom and self-government under the Lordship of Christ, the Prince of Peace. The freedom of the Church from state control enables her to witness without encumbrance to the wider society. In virtue of their dignity as children of God, moreover, all men and women possess the right to freedom of religion and conscience. No one should be forced to act contrary to conscience, particularly on questions of military engagement.

Peace and Mission

Mission is essential to the nature of the Church. Empowered and equipped by the Holy Spirit, the Church brings the Good News of salvation to all nations by proclaiming the Gospel of *shalom* in word and in deed to the ends of the earth (cf. *Is* 2:1-4; *Mt* 28:16-20; *Eph* 4:11f.). The Church's mission is carried out in the world through every follower of Jesus Christ, both ministers and lay people.

A significant dimension of the mission of the Church is realized in the very constitution of the Church as inter-ethnic communities of faith. The Church is one people of faith, called into being from peoples of many tongues and nations (*Gal* 3:28; *Eph* 4:4-6; *Phil* 2:11). Mission requires that Christians seek to become "one" for the sake of their witness to Jesus Christ and to the Father (*Jn* 17:20-21), and that they make "every effort to maintain the unity of the Spirit in the bond of peace" (*Eph* 4:3). It belongs to the mission of the Church to proclaim the peace of Jesus Christ to the world, and to extend the work of Christ, the *shalom* of God, to women and men of good will everywhere.

Peace and Oneness

One of the essential marks of the Church is her unity. This unity is a reflection of the very unity of the Triune God. Therefore, together with other disciples of Christ, Catholics and Mennonites take seriously the Scripture texts that call Christians to be one in Christ. Our witness to the revelation of God in Christ is weakened when we live in disunity (*Jn* 17:20-23). How can we ask the world to live in peace when we ourselves fail to heed the call to "maintain the unity of the Spirit in the bond of peace" (*Eph* 4:3)? Together we ask: What does it mean for the churches to confess "one Lord, one faith, one baptism, one God and Father of all" (*Eph* 4:5-6)? The Catholic-Mennonite dialogue report is entitled *Called Together to be Peacemakers*. This title stands as a hope-filled sign of "the unity of the Spirit."

Peace and Salvation

Catholics and Mennonites agree that the Church is a chosen sign of God's presence and promise of salvation for all creation. Catholics speak of this by affirming that the Church is "the universal sacrament of salvation at once manifesting and actualizing the mystery of God's love for humanity" (*Gaudium et spes*, 45). Mennonites express the promissory character of the Church by proclaiming that "in God's people the world's renewal has begun" (Douglas Gwyn *et al., A Declaration on Peace* [Scottdale/ Waterloo: Herald Press, 1991]), and that "the church is the new community of disciples sent into the world to proclaim the reign of God and to provide a foretaste of the church's glorious hope" (*Confession of Faith in a Mennonite Perspective*, Scottdale/ Waterloo: Herald Press, 1995, Art. 9). While the Church is still underway toward the peaceable kingdom of God, here and now the Church manifests signs of its eschatological character and thus provides a foretaste of the glory yet to come. This glory is none other than the very *shalom* of God who, as the lover of humanity, invites us "to do justice, to love kindness, and to walk humbly with our God" (cf. *Micah* 6:8).

II. PEACE AND DISCIPLESHIP

In light of the reflections just made concerning the biblical and theological foundations of peace, it is our mutual conviction that to be a disciple of Christ is to be a witness to peace. Christian discipleship is based on a spirituality which roots the disciple in the life of Christ who "is our peace" (cf. *Eph* 2:14-16), and leads to action for peace.

A. Spirituality

For Christians, spirituality consists in following the teachings and the life of Jesus, making his manner of life our own. "Christian peace witness belongs integrally to our walk as followers of Christ and to the life of the Church as 'the household of God' and 'a dwelling place of God in the Spirit' (*Eph* 2.19)" (*CTBP,* 181). As imitators of Christ, we are called to love of enemies and the practice of forgiveness (cf. *CTBP,* 180). Peace must be built up by the practice of peace. For that reason, the church must be a school of virtue where "the peaceable virtues" are valued, taught, practiced and revivified. These include: "Forgiveness, love of enemies, respect for the life and dignity of others, restraint, gentleness, mercy and the spirit of self-sacrifice" (*CTBP*, 184). We would like to call attention in particular to four virtues that contribute to peacemaking: nonviolence, forgiveness, repentance and prayerfulness.

Nonviolence

Empowered by their union with Christ, and imitating Christ as his followers, Christians are called to practice nonviolence in their efforts "to overcome evil with good" (*Rom* 12:21; cf. *Centesimus annus [CA]).* Catholics have increasingly emphasized nonviolence as central to the gospel and to their witness in the world; and Mennonites have likewise expanded their understanding of principled non-resistance to include the exercise of active nonviolence. Since Christian peacemaking is carried forward under the sign of the cross, suffering is inevitable as the price that must be paid in a sinful world for loving one's enemies in a sinful world (cf. *CTBP*, 182; *CA*, 25)

For both Mennonites and Catholics, peacemaking through nonviolence, while an individual vocation, is also a communal activity. Each of our communities understands its "responsibility to discern the signs of the times and to respond to developments and events with appropriate peace initiatives based on the life and teaching of Jesus" (*CTBP*, 181). In the Mennonite Church this discernment is exercised at both the congregational level and by larger church bodies, though sometimes too in specialized agencies like the Mennonite Central Committee. In the Catholic Church, it takes places at multiple levels and in a variety of settings: in parishes, in lay and religious communities, in diocesan and national justice and peace commissions, in synods of bishops and on the part of the hierarchy (cf. *CTBP*, 181). Inspired by the gospel, this communal discernment guides disciples in being church in a world of conflict. Through such reading of the signs of the times and the activities that result from it, the church can be salt and light to the world (*Matt* 5:11-16).

Forgiveness

In addition to nonviolence, discipleship entails forgiveness as a primary expression of the Christian life. Jesus taught us to forgive one another, and in his death gave the ultimate example of forgiveness (*Lk* 23:34). Accordingly, the church has a special role in the promotion of reconciliation. The church, especially the local church, is the place where both our communities learn forgiveness: Catholics in the sacrament of reconciliation; Mennonites, in the way the church teaches and exemplifies forgiveness and reconciliation in everyday life and practices mutual correction in the context of the Lord's Supper. We are conscious of our own duty to ask and grant forgiveness, individually and corporately. We acknowledge that in the past our churches too often failed in this regard.

We applaud the spread of public acts of forgiveness in our day and the growth of programs of reconciliation in civil and international conflicts. As Pope John Paul II wrote, there is "no peace without justice, no justice without forgiveness" (*World Day of Peace*, 2002). These initiatives represent an advance in public life at which Christians can only rejoice. At the same time, Christians ought to be a leaven for peace in the world by practicing forgiveness in their own lives and by promoting public forgiveness as a necessary element of peaceful reconciliation. By enacting forgiveness, the churches build up the culture of peace for the world.

Truthfulness

Just as peace requires justice, genuine reconciliation requires truthfulness. We learned in our own dialogue, as others have learned in their efforts at reconciliation, that the painful history of division cannot be overcome and healing cannot be effected without a purification of memories and a spirit of repentance (*CTBP*, 190–198) First, healing of memories involves readiness "to move beyond the isolation of the past and to consider concrete steps toward new relations" (*CTBP*, 191). Secondly, the purification of memory consists of allowing our consciences to be purged of all forms of resentment and violence inherited from our past and inviting the renewal of our way of acting (cf. *CTBP*, 192). Finally, the penitential spirit is manifest in the determination to resolve future differences through dialogue (cf. *CTBP*, 198). If they are to be convincing models of reconciliation in Christ to the world, Christians must repeatedly undergo this process of healing, purification and repentance.

Prayer

Finally, prayer is essential to Christian peacemaking. Down through the centuries, Christian peacemakers have drawn the inspiration and strength for their witness from their prayer, contemplation of the life of Christ and attentive openness to God's Spirit. There by God's grace they experience "the peace that exceeds all understanding" (*Phil* 4:7). So also prayerfulness is a mark of the peacemaker in our own day. Furthermore, the ecumenical witness of the churches in prayer, where divisions are overcome and we experience communion with God, is a blessing both for Christians and for the world (cf. *CTBP*, 185).

B. Action

The practice of prayer, in private life as well as in the public worship of the church, yields immeasurable fruit in peacemaking as individuals and communities participate in the church' witness for peace. Together Catholics and Mennonites share the common conviction "that reconciliation, nonviolence and active peacemaking belong to the heart of the gospel (*Matt* 5:9; *Rom* 12:14-21; *Eph* 6:15)" (*CTBP*, 179). Promoting nonviolence in the resolution of domestic and international conflicts, advancing programs of conflict resolution and conflict transformation and fostering reconciliation between adversaries, sometimes in conjunction with their secular counterparts, sometimes without, Christians find ways to realize "the gospel of peace" in today's world. Nurturing the love of enemies and the spirit of forgiveness, they also contribute to building a lasting culture of peace in our times.

We understand, however, that in the absence of justice and human rights, peace is a mirage, a mere absence of conflict. For that reason, we believe "that justice, understood as right relationships, is the inseparable companion of peace" (*CTBP*, 177). Accordingly, "the gospel's vision of peace includes active nonviolence for defense of human life and human rights, for the promotion of economic justice for the poor, and in the interest of fostering solidarity among peoples" (*CTBP*, 178). Active nonviolence plays a decisive role in transforming the unjust social conditions into a more just order reflecting the values of the kingdom of God. (cf. *CTBP*, 178–179, 184). For this reason, the education, training and deployment of Christians in the practice of active nonviolence is an essential contribution of the church and church-sponsored organizations in our time. It is the responsibility of the church to building a peaceable world in keeping with the biblical ideals of shalom and the Kingdom of God (cf. *CTBP*, 177, 184).

III. PARTICULAR CHALLENGES/ RECOMMENDATIONS/ SUGGESTIONS FOR POSSIBLE WORKSHOPS DURING THE IEPC

Besides offering the theological reflections just made, we would also suggest some particular challenges which might be subjects of specific sessions or workshops during the IEPC. They are based on the fact that the ecumenical movement, in seeking to reconcile separated Christians, is by its very nature a movement of reconciliation and peace.

(1) The ecumenical movement, for over a century, has contributed to the reconciliation of Christian communities which have been divided for centuries. Since the reconciliation of Christians is itself a contribution to peace, we recommend that the convocation provide opportunities for the participants to learn of some of the most important achievements of the ecumenical movement which have led to the breaking down of barriers of disunity, and the creation of new relationships between Christian communities which had previously been divided from one another.

(2) In the background of the centuries-long divisions among Christians there are bitter memories resulting from the conflict among Christians which led to those divisions at various times in the history of Christianity. Various ecumenical dialogue reports have addressed the question of the purification and reconciliation or healing of memories. We recommend that study be undertaken to ascertain the different approaches to the healing of memories which have been developed in the dialogues, or by specific churches, with

the goal of fostering common witness by Christians to this important factor which is necessary for peace.

(3) We affirm Jesus' teaching and example on non-violence as normative for Christians. At the same time, we recognize that Christians have adopted different perspectives and positions in the course of history, and today, in dealing with serious conflict in society. These include theories of just war, forms of active non-violence, and pacifism.

We recommend that the Convocation in 2011 work toward the goal of achieving an *ecumenical consensus* on ways Christians might advocate, together, to replace violence as a means to resolve serious conflict in society. We suggest, as a step in that direction, that the various positions which are alternatives to violence, and are currently advanced, be studied and critically evaluated together. These include, for example, (a) the right, for all men and women, of conscientious objection to participation in war; (b) the right of *selective* conscientious objection, which is the right and duty to refuse to serve in wars considered unjust, or execute orders considered unjust; (c) the position taken up recently by the WCC, described as *The Responsibility to Protect*; (d) the idea of "Just Policing" (Cf. Gerald W. Schlabach, *Just Policing, Not War: An Alternative Response to World Violence*, Liturgical Press, 2007).

(4) In recent decades, Christians have participated with members of other world religions in giving witness to peace, e.g., the meetings in Assisi (1986, 1993, 2002) at the invitation of Pope John Paul II, or the efforts of the World Conference on Religion and Peace, and others. With the understanding that cooperation among the religions of the world is vital in the search for peace today, we recommend that the convocation in 2011 organize opportunities for study of these initiatives with the hope of learning from these initiatives and building on them.

PARTICIPANTS IN THE MENNONITE-CATHOLIC CONFERENCE, 23–25 OCTOBER 2007

Mennonites
Ricardo Esquivia, Lenemarie Funck-Späth, Helmut Harder, Nancy Heisey, Henk Leegte, Larry Miller, Paulus Sugeng Widjaja

Catholics
Joan Back, Gosbert Byamungu, Drew Christiansen, SJ, Bernard Munono, James Puglisi, SA, John A. Radano, Teresa Francesca Rossi

World Council of Churches
Hansulrich Gerber, Fernando Enns

January 19, 2008

Contributors

R. Scott Appleby is Professor of History at the University of Notre Dame, where he also serves as the John M. Regan Jr. Director of the Joan B. Kroc Institute for International Peace Studies. A historian who earned his PhD from the University of Chicago (1985), Appleby studies religion in the modern period, focusing on the roles of religious actors in conflict and on the history of modern Roman Catholicism. He is the author of *The Ambivalence of the Sacred: Religion, Violence and Reconciliation* (2000) and *Strong Religion* (2003), as well as coeditor, with Martin E. Marty, of the University of Chicago Press series of five volumes on global fundamentalisms. In his capacity as a peace scholar, Appleby is coeditor of the Oxford University Press book series, Studies in Strategic Peacebuilding, and of the OUP Handbook on Religion, Conflict and Peacebuilding. As director of the Kroc Institute, he established the Catholic Peacebuilding Network, an international association of peace scholars and practitioners, and coedited its first scholarly volume, *Peacebuilding: Catholic Theology, Ethics and Praxis* (2010).

John C. Cavadini is a member of the Department of Theology at the University of Notre Dame, having served as Chair of the Department from 1997 to 2010. He received his PhD from Yale University in 1988. He is the McGrath-Cavadini Director of the Institute for Church Life. His main areas of research and teaching are in the theology of the early church, with a special focus on the theology of St. Augustine and on the biblical spirituality of the Fathers of the Church. He has published extensively in these areas, as well as in the theology of miracles, the life and work of Gregory the Great, catechetical theology, and the theology of marriage. In November 2009, he was appointed by Pope Benedict XVI to a five-year term on the International Theological Commission and was also created a member of the Equestrian Order of St. Gregory the Great, *classis civilis*, by Pope Benedict. He has served as a consultant to the US Conference of Catholic Bishops Committee on Doctrine since 2006.

Drew Christiansen, SJ, was editor-in-chief of *America*, the Jesuit weekly, from 2005 to 2012. He is currently a visiting scholar in the theology department at Boston College. Beginning in 2014, he will become Distinguished Professor of Ethics and Global Development at Georgetown University. From 2000 to 2004, he served as a member of the Catholic team of the International Mennonite-Catholic Dialogue. He was a founding staff fellow of the Kroc Institute for International Peace Studies and the University of Notre Dame. For fourteen years (1991–2004) he advised the US Catholic bishops on international affairs, and for seven years (1991–98) was director of the United States Catholic Conference Office of International Justice and Peace. In that capacity, he engaged in conflict resolution, human rights advocacy and reconciliation work in Central America and the Caribbean, the former Yugoslavia and the Middle East. He is coauthor of *Forgiveness in International Politics* and coeditor of *Michel Sabbah: Faithful Witness*. He is also a contributing editor of *The Review of Faith in International Affairs*, and his recent articles have appeared in fourteen domestic and foreign-language journals.

Mary Doak received her PhD from The University of Chicago and is currently an Associate Professor in the Department of Theology and Religious Studies at the University of San Diego. Her research focus has been on the political and practical implications of Christian faith, especially in the contemporary context of the United States. Her book *Reclaiming Narrative for Public Theology* (2004) defends a politically engaged and publicly active role for Christianity that nevertheless values and is consistent with religious freedom in a diverse society. Her articles on religious freedom, political theology, and eschatology have appeared in various collections and journals, including *Theological Studies*, *Horizons*, and *The American Journal of Theology and Philosophy*. Her current book project is an exploration of the mission of the church in the face of the challenges of the twenty-first century, especially the feminization of poverty, worldwide migration, and ecological degradation.

Thomas Finger is a Bridgefolk participant and represented the Mennonite Church USA on the Faith and Order Commission, National Council of Churches USA, for twenty-five years. He has also represented this church in dialogues with Lutherans, Pentecostals, and Orthodox. He represented Mennonite Central Committee at several assemblies of the World Council of Churches and in dialogues with Shi'a Muslims. He is now partially retired and involved in writing, teaching, and ecumenical and interfaith work, often internationally. He has authored *Christian Theology: An Eschatological Approach*

(1985 and 1989); *Self, Earth and Society* (1997); and his most comprehensive work, *A Contemporary Anabaptist Theology* (2004).

Duane K. Friesen is Edmund G. Kaufman Professor Emeritus of Bible and Religion at Bethel College (Kansas), and on the faculty of Anabaptist Mennonite Biblical Seminary, Great Plains Extension. He holds a doctorate in Christian Social Ethics from Harvard Divinity School. He has authored: *Christian Peacemaking and International Conflict: A Realist Pacifist Perspective* (1986) and *Artists, Citizens, Philosophers: Seeking the Peace of the City* (2000), and with Gerald W. Schlabach has coedited *At Peace and Unafraid: Public Order, Security, and the Wisdom of the Cross* (2005). He helped develop just peacemaking theory (*Just Peacemaking: The New Paradigm for the Ethics of Peace and War*, 3rd ed., 2008). Friesen has participated in interfaith conversation by organizing a symposium on the Middle East, as a fellow at the Ecumenical Institute for Advanced Theological Research (Jerusalem), in the Decade to Overcome Violence of the World Council of Churches, and as a member of the Mennonite Central Committee Peace Committee.

Elizabeth Groppe is associate professor of systematic theology at Xavier University in Cincinnati, Ohio. She received her doctorate from the University of Notre Dame and is the author of *Yves Congar's Theology of the Holy Spirit* (Oxford, 2004). During her years of undergraduate study at Earlham College, a Quaker school in Richmond, Indiana, she gained appreciation for the contributions of the peace church branch of the Christian tradition.

Dr. Helmut Harder (MDiv, MTh, ThD) is Emeritus Professor of Theology at Canadian Mennonite University (CMU) in Winnipeg, Manitoba. He served for three decades as Professor of Theology at Canadian Mennonite Bible College (now CMU). Areas of teaching included systematic theology and religion in modern thought. This was followed by nine years as General Secretary (CEO) of the Conference of Mennonites in Canada (now Mennonite Church Canada). During that time he helped write the *Confession of Faith in a Mennonite Perspective (1995)*. Dr. Harder has carried special assignments for Mennonite World Conference, particularly in the areas of peace theology and "faith and life." From 1998 to 2003 he cochaired the International Catholic Mennonite Dialogue. He was one of the editors of the report, *Called Together to be Peacemakers*. Since then he has lectured and written extensively on Mennonite-Catholic relations.

Abbot John Klassen, OSB, became the tenth abbot of Saint John's Abbey in Minnesota in 2000 and is Chancellor of Saint John's University. He became a Benedictine monk of the abbey in 1972 and was ordained to the priesthood in 1977. He received a doctorate in bio-organic chemistry from The Catholic University of America in Washington, DC, in 1985. He taught chemistry at Saint John's Prep School (1972–77) and Saint John's University (1983–2000), and was the director of the university's senior seminar program (1986–88), and of the Peace Studies Program (1988–90). Abbot Klassen was the director of monastic formation for the abbey from 1993 to 1999 and served as director of a Benedictine Values program for the lay faculty and staff of the university before becoming abbot. He is the Catholic cochair of Bridgefolk.

Alan Kreider recently retired as Professor of Church History and Mission at Anabaptist Mennonite Biblical Seminary, Elkhart, Indiana. He spent thirty years in England, initially doing historical research on the English Reformation and then working for the Mennonite Mission Network in various assignments: as Director of the London Mennonite Centre; as a teacher at Luther King House, Manchester; as Director of the Centre for Christianity and Culture, Regent's Park College, Oxford; and as a founder of the Anabaptist Network in the UK. In the 1980s he shifted the focus of his research to the early church. As a Mennonite who studies patristics, in 2000 he participated in the third of the Roman Catholic-Mennonite international dialogues. His recent book, *Worship and Mission After Christendom* (2011, coauthored with Eleanor Kreider) owes much to research done as a Studium Scholar at Saint Benedict's Monastery in Saint Joseph, Minnesota. He has been a regular participant in annual Bridgefolk gatherings. He is currently researching a book on mission in early Christianity.

Dr. Margaret Pfeil is an assistant professor of Moral Theology at the University of Notre Dame and a Faculty Fellow of the Kroc Institute for International Peace Studies. After obtaining a BA from Notre Dame (1987), she earned an MTS from Weston Jesuit School of Theology (1994) and a PhD from Notre Dame (2000). Her articles have appeared in *Theological Studies, Louvain Studies, Horizons, The Journal of the Society of Christian Ethics, Josephinum Journal of Theology, The Journal for Peace & Justice Studies, New Theology Review, and the Mennonite Quarterly Review*, and *America*. Her research interests include Catholic social thought, racial justice, ecological ethics, and peace studies. With Tobias Winright, she is coeditor of *Violence, Transformation, and the Sacred: They Shall Be Called Children of God* (2012); with Laurie Cassidy and Alex Mikulich she is coauthor of *The Scandal of White Complicity in U.S. Hyper-incarceration: A Nonviolent Spirituality of White Resistance* (2012). She is a founder and resident of the Saint Peter Claver Catholic Worker Community in South Bend, Indiana, and serves on the board of Bridgefolk.

John D. Roth is professor of history at Goshen College where he also serves as editor of *The Mennonite Quarterly Review* and director of the Mennonite Historical Library/Institute for the Study of Global Anabaptism. He has participated in several Bridgefolk conferences, serves on the Mennonite Church USA Interchurch Relations Church Associations Group, and was an active member in the recent bilateral dialogue between the Mennonite World Conference and the Lutheran World Federation.

Mary H. Schertz is Professor of New Testament and Director of the Institute of Mennonite Studies at the Anabaptist Mennonite Biblical Seminary (AMBS). She received her PhD from Vanderbilt University School of Religion in 1993. In the last few years, Dr. Schertz has created opportunities to spend time with pastors studying the Bible—time that is unhurried so the Scripture can form those who read it. She is working on a Luke commentary and cowrote a book on biblical-studies methodology with Professor Emeritus Perry Yoder of AMBS. As director of the Institute of Mennonite Studies, Mary helped launch the journal *Vision: A Journal for Church and Theology*, jointly published with Canadian Mennonite University. She serves on the board of Bridgefolk.

Gerald W. Schlabach is Professor of Theology and Chair of the Department of Justice and Peace Studies at the University of Saint Thomas in Minnesota. He holds a PhD in Theology and Ethics from the University of Notre Dame. During much of the 1980s, Dr. Schlabach worked with Mennonite Central Committee (MCC) in Nicaragua and Honduras on church-related peace and justice assignments. Together with Duane Friesen, he coedited *At Peace and Unafraid: Public Order, Security, and the Wisdom of the Cross* (2006). He is lead author and editor of *Just Policing, Not War: An Alternative Response to World Violence* (2007). His most recent book is *Unlearning Protestantism: Sustaining Christian Community in an Unstable Age* (2010). Schlabach is cofounder of Bridgefolk, a movement for grassroots dialogue and unity between Mennonites and Roman Catholics.

C. Arnold Snyder is retired Professor of History from Conrad Grebel University College, University of Waterloo in Ontario. He has been an enthusiastic participant in several Bridgefolk encounters. His book *Following in the Footsteps of Christ: The Anabaptist Tradition* (2004) explores and describes the Anabaptist spiritual tradition for the Orbis Books "Traditions of Christian Spirituality" series.

Bishop Gabino Zavala is a retired auxiliary bishop of the Archdiocese of Los Angeles. He earned a Licentiate in Canon Law from Catholic University in Washington, DC, was ordained a priest in 1977, and was appointed auxiliary bishop of the Archdiocese of Los Angeles in 1994. He served as the auxiliary bishop and episcopal vicar of the San Gabriel Pastoral Region until his retirement in 2012. Bishop Zavala was involved with a number of peace and justice organizations: he was the bishop president of the US section of Pax Christi, the international Catholic peace movement; was the copresident of Interfaith Worker Justice, an organization committed to educating, mobilizing, and organizing the religious community to advocate for better wages and working conditions for low-wage workers; and served as the episcopal advisor to the International Commission of Catholic Prison Pastoral Care (ICCPPC). Also, he was an adjunct professor of Canon Law and Pastoral Theology in the graduate programs of Theology and Pastoral Theology at Loyola Marymount University in Los Angeles.